The Management of Libraries and Information Centers

Volume IV:
Role Playing and Other Management Cases

by

Mildred Hawksworth Lowell, Ph.D.
Professor of Library Science
Graduate Library School, Indiana University

The Scarecrow Press, Inc.
Metuchen, N.J.   1971

Copyright 1971 by Mildred Hawksworth Lowell

ISBN 0-8108-0424-7

Library of Congress Catalog Card Number 68-12642

to

my husband

Wayne Russell Lowell

TABLE OF CONTENTS

	Page
Preface	vii
List of Cases (by case number)	xiii

Chapter

		Page
I.	Role Playing as a Teaching-Learning Process	19
II.	Personnel Cases (Cases 1-39)	99
III.	Planning Cases (Cases 40-59)	214
IV.	Organizing Cases (Cases 60-72)	263
V.	Controlling Cases (Cases 73-94)	308

Selected References on Role Playing	368
Title Index to Cases	395
Subject Index to Cases	398
Index to Chapter I	409

PREFACE

This volume, like the three which preceded it, is designed for use by those in the library profession who are concerned with the management of people at work. Growing sophistication of knowledge about organizational behavior (human relations), an increasing awareness of line supervisors' responsibilities for personnel, and the trend toward involving staff members in participative management have served to focus the attention of librarians on such topics as interpersonal and group relations, communication, counseling, and grievance handling.

Readers visualized during the writing of this volume have been those desiring to know more about human relations skills, practicing librarians interested in self-help study, training directors, workshop and seminar leaders, chairmen of programs at library meetings, and students and faculty members in library education programs. This volume should be equally useful for librarians working with children, adolescents, college students, and adults. Chapter I may also be of interest to anyone in any field, other than librarianship, who is interested in role playing as a technique or training method.

The four volumes in this set are a result of the author's belief that library education (including continuing education) can be immeasurably enriched through the utilization of various forms of simulated experience. Ideally, library school students would be best prepared for a professional career and their course work would be more meaningful for them if, as part of their curriculum, they had brief supervised experience in each kind of library and each area of library operation in teaching libraries. Such experience would be comparable to the clinical rotations in all of the medical specialties in teaching hospitals which are an essential component of medical education. Medical school students get observation and participation experience in performing laboratory techniques, in interviewing patients, in diagnosing symptoms, and in assisting physicians in care and treatment of patients. This kind of education is impossible for the preparation of librarians because no teaching libraries exist; and, if they were provided, they would be prohibitively expensive. A practical and inexpensive alternative is to provide vicarious library experience through various kinds of simulation. The focus of this set of volumes is to explore, identify, and suggest new teaching-learning simulation methods for library education at all levels.

Volume I, <u>The Case Method in Teaching Library Management</u>, described the characteristics of the case method and different types of case studies; cited uses of the method in teaching administration; identified the roles of the instructor and the student in case analysis; presented some suggestions for case research and case writing; and included five in-basket simulation exercises which could be used as tests of administrative potential.

Volume II, <u>The Process of Managing: Syllabus and Cases</u>, provided a course outline for a basic library management course, suggested readings, and case studies appropriate for each unit.

Volume III, <u>Personnel Management: Syllabus and Cases</u>, outlined all areas of library personnel management from the selection of personnel to retirement, provided a course outline and recommended readings, and included case studies involving personnel problems.

This fourth volume explores the potentials of another type of case study--role playing--to provide simulated library experience. Role playing was not included in Volume I because extensive research was required to cover the subject adequately and new techniques for writing this type of case had to be developed. This volume is designed to supplement the preceding volumes in three ways.

The first purpose is to inventory for the library profession the many uses of role playing in all relevant fields; and to point out comparable uses in libraries. The reader may be amazed at the interdisciplinary nature of the role playing technique and its myriad uses in so many fields. Many, if not most, of these uses are applicable for librarians. Excluded from this inventory are such fields as role perception, role theory, role conflict, psychological counseling, psychodramatic methods in group therapy, guidance, and psychotherapy each of which has special meaning and uses not directly applicable for library education.

The second purpose of this volume is to provide librarians with role playing cases. The writer believes these are the first ever written for librarians. Many of the cases in Volumes II and III can also be used for role playing although they are not so labeled, for example: "Central Information Desk" (4), "Baby-Sitting Service" (13), "Trouble in the Reserve Room" (15), "Problem Patrons" (82), "The Scribbler" (85), "Conflict" (143), "Spoiled Child" (144), "Jane Hale" (151), and many others. Parts of some cases in Volumes II and III, as well as those in this volume not written specifically for role playing, could effectively be role played before the whole case was discussed in small group discussions. When students go through the decision making process of analyzing the case studies in Volumes II and III, they are, in effect, role playing as they must perceive themselves in the role of the chief character in order to conceptualize alternatives and to decide on a solution. They bring to the case discussion their perceptions of the environmental setting, the problems involved, and their role as the chief character.

Third, in addition to many role playing cases, this volume contains case studies of other types which supplement those in Volumes II and III and provide new cases involving different problems. The "List of Cases" in the front of this volume identifies which cases have been written specifically for role playing. Many others, not so labeled, could also be used for this purpose. Conversely, those conceived as role playing cases would be equally useful for group discussion.

Chapter I defines role playing; gives examples or applications of role playing in classroom instruction, in training programs, in adult meetings and programs, and as a research methodology; outlines and describes the techniques and steps in the process; and offers suggestions for the preparation and writing of cases.

The structure of the rest of the book corresponds to the content of Volumes II and III. Chapter II, "Personnel Cases," will supplement the cases in Volume III. Chapters III, "Planning Cases," IV, "Organizing Cases," and V, "Controlling Cases," supplement the cases in Volume II. The list of "Selected References on Role Playing" is purposely inclusive in the hope that it will better serve the needs of those wishing to delve deeper into this area.

All of the cases are based on facts which were acquired through personal interviews, records of court cases, confidential library reports and files, correspondence, grievance hearings, and numerous printed sources. To protect the confidential nature of the data acquired, disguises of various kinds were used in writing the actual incidents and experiences into cases--such as size and type of library, age and sex of characters, and geographical location. The focus has been on the problem. The setting in a school library, for example, has no relevance to the nature of the problem because the same problem could probably occur just as well in an academic, public, or special library. For names of places, libraries, and surnames of characters, the names of colors, fabrics, trees, nuts, flowering plants, birds, rocks, and minerals were used. Given names of characters were selected at random from a list of names for boys and girls. If data about the same type of problem were acquired from several sources, the facts, incidents and characters were woven into a composite to exemplify that type of problem.

A research grant from the Council on Library Resources provided support for travel, supplies, and the services of Mrs. Mavis Siebenthal who so capably typed the final manuscript. Fellow librarians suggested libraries to visit and librarians to interview. Former students (1) provided feedback relative to the value of case study experience (obtained during my management courses) for their performance on the job after they were employed; and (2) informed me about situations and problems which they suggested I write into cases. Those library administrators deserve especial commendation who (1) envisioned the value to the profession of simulated teaching-learning materials in the area of interpersonal relations, (2) scheduled interviews with themselves and their staff members, and (3) made confidential records and files available. Some interviews are so personal and confidential that the interviewees asked to remain anonymous.

To locate all possible information about role playing, traditional eyeball searches of printed bibliographies and indexes and following up footnote citations was supplemented by a computer search of the ERIC tapes by Mr. Joseph C. Meredith and Mr. Ronald Tschudi, of the Research Center for Library and Information Science in the Graduate Library School of Indiana University.

I acknowledge, gratefully, ideas for cases which came from many practicing librarians--both those who chose to remain anonymous and the following: Rosanna P. Allen, Lucy

Ann Babcock, Lois Bailey, VaRue L. Bailey, Robert Barron, Melvin Bennett, R. Edwin Berry, Elizabeth Bradt, Clifton Brock, G. S. T. Cavanagh, Opal Carr, Christie Cathey, Evelyn G. Clement, Georgia Coffin, Sally A. Crosby, Laurence Di Pietro, Francis X. Doherty, Milda P. Drennan, Maryann Duggen, Leonard M. Eddy, Edith E. Estabrooks, Mark R. Everett, Archie R. Fields, Ralph H. Funk, Gayle Gill, David Gillespie, C. R. Graham, Cynthia Greengard, Louise M. Hall, Louise Hawkins, Paul Howard, Ruth Sheahan Howard, W. Carl Jackson, E. J. Josey, John V. Judd, John R. Kaiser, David Kaser, Melvin J. Klatt, Janet Kolrick, Maxine LaBounty, George R. Linder, David V. Loertscher, Arthur McAnally, Murray S. Martin, Dorothy Mason, Ellen Mathews, Anne Megli, Gertrude Merritt, Ursula Meyer, Vladimir Micuda, T. H. Milby, Beatrice Montgomery, Ray N. Moore, Mayrelee Newman, Jane B. Nida, Jack W. O'Bar, Donald Oehlerts, Betsy Ann Olive, Marian G. Patman, Peter Paulson, Shirley Pelley, Clyde J. Peterman, Harry N. Peterson, William S. Pierce, Mary Evelyn Potts, Benjamin E. Powell, Leon Raney, Donald A. Redmond, Fred W. Roper, Johan Ruud, M. P. Schabert, Allene Schnaitter, Don W. Schneider, Dorothy C. Smith, E. Jean Smith, Richard E. Smith, James G. Stephens, Elizabeth Stetson, Robert Stewart, Elvin E. Strowd, Cordelia Swinton, Robert Swisher, Eddy Terry, Mason Tolman, Betty Lou Townley, Robert M. Trent, Mildred L. Treworgy, Marcia Tuttle, Marion H. Vedder, John J. Voorhees, Darrel Welch, Mary Ann Wentroth, Pat Westmoreland, Tom Wilkinson, and Elaine Woodruff.

LIST OF CASES

Case Number	Case Title		Page
Case 1	Who Should Hire Librarians?	(Role Playing)	100
Case 2	Job Interview: Alvin	(Role Playing)	102
Case 3	Job Interview: Elizabeth	(Role Playing)	109
Case 4	Job Interview: Floyd	(Role Playing)	115
Case 5	An Uncertified School Librarian		120
Case 6	The Dirty Long-Johns		122
Case 7	Winter University Personnel Policies		131
Case 8	A Newspaper Room Clerk	(Role Playing)	133
Case 9	An Information Center		135
Case 10	Attempted Bribery		138
Case 11	The Immature Reference Librarian	(Role Playing)	142
Case 12	Stinky	(Role Playing)	144
Case 13	Slander and Lies	(Role Playing)	145
Case 14	Dress Policies	(Role Playing)	146
Case 15	Nepotism: Fern		151
Case 16	Nepotism: Frank		154
Case 17	The Clique	(Role Playing)	157
Case 18	Privileged Information	(Role Playing)	158

Case Number	Case Title		Page
Case 19	A Circulation Librarian		160
Case 20	Promotion	(Role Playing)	163
Case 21	Transfer	(Role Playing)	165
Case 22	Sibilance	(Role Playing)	168
Case 23	A Receptionist	(Role Playing)	169
Case 24	Music	(Role Playing)	171
Case 25	Anxiety	(Role Playing)	173
Case 26	The "Troubleshooter" in Serials		176
Case 27	Creation of a Supervisor		179
Case 28	Political Posters	(Role Playing)	184
Case 29	Marijuana		187
Case 30	Chronic Insomnia	(Role Playing)	188
Case 31	School District Unification		190
Case 32	Irrational Behavior	(Role Playing)	192
Case 33	Termination	(Role Playing)	194
Case 34	Murder		196
Case 35	Insubordination and Arrest		199
Case 36	A Leave of Absence		204
Case 37	Personality Disorder		206
Case 38	Maternity Leave	(Role Playing)	209
Case 39	I am a Librarian not a Psychiatrist	(Role Playing)	211
Case 40	A Fire		214

Case Number	Case Title		Page
Case 41	A New Junior College		217
Case 42	"Bandaid" Work		219
Case 43	On Parole	(Role Playing)	222
Case 44	Staff Concern		224
Case 45	Moonlighting	(Role Playing)	227
Case 46	"The Shelf"		228
Case 47	Homicide		230
Case 48	Steve and the "Checklist"	(Role Playing)	232
Case 49	Selection Policy	(Role Playing)	233
Case 50	Momentum	(Role Playing)	235
Case 51	Out to Lunch		237
Case 52	School Reorganization		239
Case 53	A "Bargain"		240
Case 54	Clearance	(Role Playing)	245
Case 55	Gift Appraisals		247
Case 56	Individual Recognition	(Role Playing)	250
Case 57	Mission of Research Libraries	(Role Playing)	252
Case 58	Student Periodicals	(Role Playing)	257
Case 59	Faculty Reading Lists	(Skit)	259
Case 60	A Company Union		263
Case 61	Caught in the Middle		265
Case 62	Busy, Busy, Busy		267
Case 63	Federally Subsidized Employees		272

Case Number	Case Title	Page
Case 64	Steam in the Stacks	275
Case 65	A Circulation Department	276
Case 66	Volunteers (Role Playing)	277
Case 67	An Embarrassing Policy Decision (Role Playing)	279
Case 68	A Medical School Library	281
Case 69	A Library Office Secretary	284
Case 70	Laissez Faire	287
Case 71	Hemlock High Resource Center	295
Case 72	Participative Management (Role Playing)	300
Case 73	A Sordid Scheme	309
Case 74	Community Relations	311
Case 75	The Ad Hoc Faculty Committee	319
Case 76	Conversion to a Public Library District	321
Case 77	The Unwanted Gift	324
Case 78	A Ten-Point Veteran	326
Case 79	The Tupelo Family	330
Case 80	Grant Funds	333
Case 81	Community Control	334
Case 82	Questionable Practices	335
Case 83	A Pilferage Racket	338
Case 84	The Anonymous Caller (Role Playing)	342
Case 85	Harrassment at Stonechat Branch	344

Case Number	Case Title		Page
Case 86	Access to Legal Materials		349
Case 87	An Attempted Theft		353
Case 88	Confrontation	(Role Playing)	355
Case 89	Water, Water, Everywhere		357
Case 90	A Determined Agitator		358
Case 91	Teen-Age Problems		360
Case 92	Unexpended Balances	(Role Playing)	362
Case 93	Staffing Problems		363
Case 94	Due Process and Tenure		366

Chapter I

ROLE PLAYING AS A TEACHING-LEARNING PROCESS

<u>Outline</u>

Introduction

What is Role Playing?
  Sociodrama
  Psychodrama
  Simulation
  Human Relations Learning
  Comparison with Other Types of Cases
  Research Studies of Attitude and Behavior Change

Examples or Applications of Role Playing
  Classroom Instruction
    Elementary grades
      Problem pictures and problem stories
      Underprivileged children
      Language arts
      Arithmetic
      Social studies
      Group counseling
      Intergroup education
    Secondary schools
      Business
      History
      English literature
      Economics
      Geography
      Chemistry
      Vocational education
    Higher education
      Sociology
      English composition
      Economics
      Political science
      Education
      Medicine

Training Programs
  Salesmen
  Health sciences
  Supervisors and Executives (leadership training)
  Educators
  Overseas assignments
    Peace Corps
    Air Force
  Job interviewing, screening, and training
  Religious education
  Counselors
  New careers (human service aides)
  Police
Adult Meetings and Programs
  Criminology
  Grievance procedures
As a Research Methodology
  Sociology
  Public Opinion
  Cultural Anthropology
  Communication

Techniques: Steps in the Process
  The Leader
  Physical Arrangements
  Selecting the Problem
  Preparing and Instructing the Group
  Enactment: Playing the Game
    Single group role playing
      More than one enactment
      Role reversal
      Weiringa variation
      Masks
    Multiple group role playing
  Feedback: Discussion, Analysis, and Evaluation

Case Preparation and Writing
  Format and Structure of Published Cases
  Case Research
  Focusing and Shaping the Case
  An Effective Teaching Instrument

Summary

Role Playing 21

Bibliographical Citations in This Chapter

Throughout this chapter references are made frequently to titles listed in the bibliography at the end of this book which is arranged alphabetically by surname of author. When these bibliographical entries are referred to in the text, the author's surname is enclosed in parentheses at the point of reference. If more than one title is listed for the same author, the date of publication is given as well as the author's name, like this: (Jones, 1966). If the author's name has been mentioned in the text, it is not repeated in parentheses. If the same type of information is presented in two titles, the author of each one is enclosed in parentheses, like this: (Brown) (Jones). If the publication referred to is written by two authors, their names are joined with an "and" and enclosed in one parentheses, like this: (Smith and Green).

Introduction

In recent years, it has become increasingly clear that effective interpersonal and human relations skills are essential for library staff members at all levels of responsibility. Furthermore, the current requirements of the library profession for capable supervisors and administrators put heavy responsibility upon library educators, institute and workshop directors, and in-service training personnel to utilize those teaching-learning techniques which develop interpersonal, leadership, and supervisory skills. One such technique which has great potential for library continuation programs of all kinds, for executive development institutes, for library school classes, and for interaction sessions with users is that of role playing. Role playing is not a new technique; it has been used successfully for many years in classroom instruction from elementary grades through graduate school; in training leaders, salesmen, supervisors, executives, educators, overseas personnel and others; in on-the-job training; in the health sciences, social work, and psychotherapy; in adult meetings of all kinds; in screening applicants for positions; and as a research tool in social psychology, sociology, and cultural anthropology.

Role playing has been especially valuable in management education as a vehicle for solving problems; making decisions; changing attitudes, opinions, and feelings; preparing for all kinds of interviews and face-to-face encounters;

handling grievance problems; developing sensitivity and empathy for understanding the important part feelings play in determining behavior on the job; and in revealing one's own personal faults in interacting with other individuals. Differences in educational background, experience, and general ability seem to place no restriction on participation in this technique which has been used successfully at all levels of management.

Seven major people-type problem areas confronted in everyday library work situations are: authority relations such as superior-subordinate and subordinate-superior; evaluation, appraisal, and interviewing; conducting conferences, staff, and other meetings; integration with other departments; intergroup relations; organizational design; and staff-user relations. To cope effectively with these problems requires that the supervisor know why human beings do and say the things they do; that he develop insight into the feelings of others; and that he be positive, optimistic, and friendly. Role playing can be effective through preparing staff members for their responsibilities in these problem areas.

Most library school graduates become supervisors of clerks and pages as soon as they assume their first professional position and experienced librarians have even greater administrative responsibilities. For their successful accomplishment, these positions require skills in human relations. Unfortunately, the vast majority of librarians who are promoted to administrative positions are thrust abruptly from staff member with professional expertise (bibliographer, children's librarian, reference librarian, or other) to administrator with the "survival-of-the-fittest" law of the jungle controlling the outcome.

The profession is beginning to recognize the necessity of acculturating the prospective administrator in skills necessary to function in his new role and of developing in him a set of attitudes appropriate to his new status. Such fields as medicine, dentistry, industry, educational administration, hospital administration, and public administration provide internship programs for acculturating their personnel for leadership roles. Only a very few such administrative internships exist in the library profession. The prime function of internship programs is to socialize individuals into their new role through supervised field experience in which the person directly lives the work life of the administrator. This direct contact should shape his attitudes and better fit him to play the role of administrator. Such programs are expensive and would be difficult to arrange for all prospective library administrators and supervisors. Role playing is not as effective or as thorough an acculturating device as internship programs but it does provide vicarious experience and exposure to human relations problems at little cost.

Knowledge of principles and techniques of interpersonal and human relations can be developed through lectures, reading, and discussion; but the ability to apply this knowledge comes only through actual practice which can be obtained either through learning-on-the-job or in a laboratory situation such as role playing cases provide. In order to understand and "manage" people, the supervisor must not only be able to analyze the behavior of others but must also have an insight into the way his own behavior influences others. A great majority of management problems directly involve the feelings and attitudes, hidden or overt, of the supervisors and administrators in the situation. Insights into one's own behavior can be acquired through role playing because it provides immediate feedback. Role playing can be used as a major teaching-learning technique or it can be used as an auxiliary procedure supplementing other methods; it can be used as a means of diagnosing problems or as a means of instruction; it can be used with one individual or with a group.

In library education, library training programs, and contacts with the public, role playing can serve as a social-learning method, as a basic decision-making skill, as a group problem-solving process, as one technique for guidance, as a means for conveying information or skills, and as a way of facilitating oral expression. The major purposes of library management role playing are: to understand oneself, to improve and practice skills in dealing with various human situations, to provide insights into the nature of human behavior, and to evaluate personnel.

The audience visualized during the writing of this chapter has been librarians working in all types of libraries or participating in continuing education programs, and students and faculty members in library education programs. The focus of this chapter is on practices, examples, and methodologies which seemed to offer ideas for librarians working with children, adolescents, college students, or adults; and for all types of staff interactions. The chapter does not trace the historical development of role playing. A fairly comprehensive bibliographical search located titles in many professional and subject fields; hence, this chapter is interdisciplinary in approach.

The chapter starts with a definition and description of role playing followed by some comments on human relations learning. Similarities and differences between role playing cases and other types of cases are delineated. Applications of the use of role playing in many fields are described in enough detail so that interested librarians will know which titles they need to read if they wish to use a particular method as a model for some library-related purpose or program. The process of role playing is explained step by step, including variations in methods and approach. For those librarians wishing to prepare and write their own cases, some guidelines are given for collecting data, focusing and shaping, and writing. In the back of this book is a selected list of references on role playing which have relevance for librarians. This bibliography represents about half of the total number of references examined.

What is Role Playing?

Children's imaginative games of pretending are role playing and are important rehearsal devices for the development of socialized behavior and of internalizing the attitudes emphasized by their families and by society. Student nurses and teachers accept "professional attitudes" faster by portraying the roles assigned to them in their practice work. The person who practices a speech before his family or friends in order to determine its effects on an audience as well as to perfect his own performance is role playing. Other examples: lawsuits on imaginary cases in law schools where students act as lawyers and witnesses; the war games of military groups; and mock courts or mock trials used in training law enforcement officers in presenting testimony. Many more examples are described later in this chapter.

Role playing is the flexible acting out of various types of interpersonal problems in a permissive group atmosphere; it involves action, doing, and practice. Individuals and groups can improve their effectiveness not only by talking about a problem but also by doing something about it. Two persons can role play by themselves but usually two or more individuals act out an interpersonal situation before a group and then the group discusses it. A great number of techniques have been developed to make the enactment more effective or more meaningful but the basic process of interaction between individuals is the core of the method. Since it is free of the tensions of an actual problem situation, role playing stimulates the trying out of new alternatives and solutions in life-like situations without the consequences which in reality may be punishing. In such an atmosphere the participant can safely take a chance with different kinds of behavior and thus increase his role flexibility.

Various real-life situations are created and participants have an opportunity to practice specific human relations skills in a safe laboratory environment; it is a method of human interaction which involves realistic behavior in imaginary situations. A player assumes an identity, either his own or that of another, imagines himself to be in the situation created for him, and adopts the feelings and attitudes described to him as his own. Role playing differs from acting in that it is "spontaneous," unprepared, and unrehearsed; there are no lines to memorize and no rehearsals. The actor in a play simulates reality for the purpose of entertainment; he must memorize and speak the lines written for that character and rehearse repeatedly until the play is ready for public performance. The role player is given a new name, a particular job, and certain past experiences; he is provided with either written or oral descriptions of a situation and the role he is to play; he is allowed sufficient time to plan his actions and then must act out his part spontaneously before a group; he speaks freely rather than from a script. It is a "make believe" kind of situation in which individuals act as though what they were doing is "for real." The interaction between role players should represent their own personalities as supplemented or changed by the instructions, the situation, and the feeling engendered by the interaction.

In management education, role playing is part of the decision-making process; it is not entertainment. Typical role playing situations for librarians are: a supervisor conducting an employment interview with an applicant or an exit interview with an employee who recently resigned; an employee discussing with his superior a personal problem which is affecting his work performance; and a department head discussing with his assistant such problems as morale, ethics, or behavior of employees which are affecting departmental output or efficiency.

"Role playing" is the blanket term for a wide variety of procedures in which a subject is induced to enact the behavior of another person or to assume and probably espouse a set of opinions with which he may disagree or to act out his own problems. Because it involves realistic behavior under unrealistic conditions, role playing has been called "reality practice," "experience practice," "action development," "sensitivity training," "laboratory method," "learning through doing," "situational tests," and "practice management." However, the term "role playing" is the most accepted, is more expressive and inclusive, and is used not only by itself but also to cover the terms "sociodrama" and "psychodrama." Some writers do not make discrete distinctions between the three terms and, in some cases, one finds the terms used interchangeably.

Sociodrama

Sociodrama generally indicates role playing in a nontherapeutic context where the focus is on the situation being explained. It provides a method for the analysis of social conflicts and practice in dealing with group problems. The players represent the group rather than individual personalities or represent type situations and type reactions. In this procedure, a problem is acted out in a group and has meaning for all of the members. For example, this type of role playing would be relevant for a group of librarians wishing to analyze questions of social or political action.

Psychodrama

Psychodrama is the narrowest term of the three and usually implies a technique for dealing with mental and emotional problems. The focus of psychodrama is the therapeutic treatment of individuals with deep personal problems. An individual acts out his own problem, he is the star actor and the playwright; he develops a role which merges his own private, social, cultural, and emotional elements into a synthetic experience for the purpose of his therapy. A person plays himself in various dramatic or crisis situations. Psychodrama has been used extensively in psychological counseling in a variety of settings during the past few decades. Also, it is used in psychotherapy where it has a special and clinical meaning in the changing of attitudes and behavior. Psychotherapy is based on the belief that emotional problems can be corrected if individuals act out troubling situations and analyze and practice new solutions. It should be attempted only by the trained clinician and, hence, is outside the province of library management. For this reason, it is not included in this chapter and only a few references are included in the bibliography.

Simulation

Role playing is a type of simulation and some examples cited in this chapter are labeled "simulation" by their creators although, in the behavioral sciences, the term "simulation" normally refers to a comparatively complex operating model of an actual or of a hypothetical social process or situation. Such models may be relatively simple or they may be very complicated. Most simulations involve role playing and they may also include gaming, extensive equipment, and props. Case studies, in-basket exercises, role playing, sociodrama, psychodrama, simulation, and gaming all provide simulated reality experience. They permit participants to develop insights into social processes without having to experiment with the real situations. Such experience reduces risk and usually expense while teaching participants how to function in the real setting. The objective of all these types of simulation is to create a safe and friendly atmosphere in which to practice skills where second chances are part of the process and no one is hurt through failure.

As a problem-solving procedure, all types of simulation employ all the techniques of critical evaluation and utilize a symbolic model (verbal or pictorial rather than physical or mathematical) and proceed into problem definition, delineation of alternatives for action, exploration of the consequences of these alternatives, and decision making. In addition to serving as a problem-solving procedure, the role playing activity helps the participant to understand the attitudes, perspective, feelings, and behavior of the person whose role he is playing. Hopefully, both the players and the observers will achieve a greater depth of understanding about other persons as well as about themselves.

Through simulating a given interpersonal situation, behavior can be demonstrated, observed, clarified, and evaluated; one's abilities to work with other persons and to communicate successfully in face-to-face encounters can be improved; actual interpersonal relations can be stimulated;

psychological implications of a situation and of each person's personality can be recognized; the social skills one is able to bring to a situation are involved; and practice in facing crises and dilemmas is provided. In addition, simulation can be an effective vehicle for conveying information in a more vivid way than lectures or reading, for facilitating oral expression, for developing initiative, for fostering group cooperation and teamwork, and for acting out a situation as the player sees it, thus providing actual participation in problem solution. All of those participating usually feel more of an emotional impact from having vicariously experienced reactions and emotions resulting from a problem situation than they would by hearing about it or reading an account of it. For example, acting out a specific conflict over the use of a telephone for personal use in a crowded cataloging department might be much more meaningful to library school students or to practicing librarians than merely being told that such situations create conflicts.

Librarians who work with children and are interested in using role playing will find excellent suggestions for employing the technique in elementary classrooms in the pamphlet Simulation, Role-Playing, and Sociodrama in the Social Studies by Dale M. Garvey. Appended to the pamphlet is an annotated bibliography compiled by his wife, Sancha K., who is a librarian.

Human Relations Learning

For any teaching-learning endeavor, appropriate methods and techniques must be selected. Individual learning methods might be categorized according to the basic activity involved:

(1) input (listening, viewing, and reading): lecture, conference seminar, panel, symposium, demonstration, printed materials, motion pictures, filmstrips, recordings, and programmed materials;
(2) decision making (personal involvement of learner): discussion, case study, incident process, and in-basket exercise;
(3) personal interaction (doing and feedback): role playing, laboratory, simulation, projects, understudy and internship, supervised practice, and sensitivity training.

If the chief objective of the training or educational program is to provide information of a factual nature, the first category, which is highly leader-centered, is quite satisfactory. However, if the material to be learned is subject to varied interpretation and is not precise or explicit (as are chemical formulae or mathematical equations) then a group-centered learning method (categories 2 or 3) is clearly superior. Categories 2 and 3 elicit a higher level of involvement on the part of the learner than does category 1. Retention of factual knowledge is greater in classes having a high degree of group member interaction because of the learning reinforcements which come from testing one's idea with others and from the intellectual stimulation which this generates. Furthermore, the learning of ideas is enhanced when the learners participate actively in the process; they may work on problems and exercises, they may ask and answer questions, they may explore problems and issues in depth, or they may experience vicariously the feelings or attitudes or opinions of others.

Advantages and disadvantages could be cited for each teaching method listed. Individual teachers or leaders must decide which method or combination of methods is most appropriate for achieving specific learning goals. If, in addition to imparting factual information, the purpose of the education or training is to facilitate behavioral adjustments, aid interpersonal relations, and promote self-insight, then teaching methods of categories 2 and 3 (which adopt a democratic, participative leadership style) are clearly superior to those listed in category 1. Normally, the techniques of categories 2 and 3 are used in conjunction with some of the instructional methods listed in category 1.

A set of basic assumptions about human behavior and the teaching-learning process underlie successful guidance of role playing. The central belief is that each individual has the ability to cope with his own life situations and to increase his capacity to deal with his problems intelligently. To implement this belief, the instructor or leader must permit each individual to make his own decisions and to learn from his own mistakes; he must guide enactments and discussions in such ways that participants make their own discoveries and gradually improve their levels of decision making because of their increased awareness of alternatives and consequences.

Experience in recent years with human relations

training and executive development programs has shown that
a knowledge of the principles of human behavior has little
value unless that knowledge is supplemented with skill practice.
An effective human relations learning situation should
engage a person in actual behavior. Role playing creates an
active approach to personally meaningful and significant problems,
produces a high degree of involvement in the participants,
and forces the players to use themselves as resources.
When a person acts out a problem, his ideas are complicated
by the unpredictable responses of the other role players; he
cannot control the situation but must react and respond to
the actions, emotions, and reasoning of others. This unique
element in role playing makes it a powerful learning method.

All management education courses and training programs
profit from some kind of practice which provides an
opportunity for participants to learn from their mistakes
under conditions which protect them from any actual penalty
and in situations in which they have the sympathetic help of
the teacher or leader and of group members in exploring
the consequences of their decisions or solutions. For example,
a supervisor may be able to quote the theoretical
concepts and principles on how to discipline an employee,
yet he may create additional problems even when he reprimands
an employee for a minor offense because he lacks
communication or interpersonal skills or he is unaware of
how his behavior affects others. It is difficult to acquire a
skill unless it is practiced under circumstances that give
the learner guidance in preventing errors.

Practice is required for learning any complicated
skill. For example, athletes and musicians must train and
practice under supervision for many years before their skills
are perfected. A medical student must dissect bodies in
the laboratory to develop surgical skills under conditions
approximating those he will encounter when working with
live human beings. Similarly, an inexperienced person
should not be put in a supervisory position in a library until
his skills in leadership, supervision, and interpersonal relations
have been developed through some type of reality practice.

The acquisition of self-insight is almost impossible
without receiving some outside assistance. Both skills and
insight must be developed by the person doing something because
he must know the consequences of his actions. Neither
practice in doing nor full feedback occurs in the first cate-

gory of learning methods listed above; involvement and
partial feedback are provided in the second category, but
full feedback results from the third group. The problem of
developing skills and self-insight can be partially solved
through various kinds of simulation which put the learner in
a situation somewhat similar to real life and require him
to act. The teacher or leader can control such conditions
as stimuli (to which the learner must react) and feedback,
or reinforcement, of the actions of the participants. Stimuli
and feedback cannot be controlled in on-the-job situations.

Learning resulting from role playing becomes active,
participative, practical, and useful, and provides both observation and feedback. As a result, players improve their
understanding of others; increase their conscious awareness
of their own feelings about problems and persons; identify
their own blind spots; perceive information or facts which
they ordinarily failed to see or hear; acquire insight into
the effects of their own behavior, attitudes, emotions, mannerisms, and even tone of voice on other persons; explore a
variety of possible ways to practice and develop their skills
in handling problems and persons; become more comfortable
in acting in new ways; and can observe how others handle
problems and imitate or adapt successful approaches and
methods used by others.

In their book Roleplaying in Business and Industry,
Corsini, Shaw, and Blake found that common and persistent
human relations problems in business and industry can be
effectively analyzed and studied by role playing methods.
They believe that these methods are more useful and more
dramatically effective for the inculcation of human relations
skills than any other learning or training technique. Techniques based on their experience with this method are outlined in their book.

Reinhart's research investigated the effects of role
playing upon the attitudes and discussion behavior of teacher
training students. She found that it (1) helped to bridge the
gap between precepts taught and methods practiced by instructors; (2) promoted identification with and interpretation
of the thoughts and feelings of classmates; (3) increased
perception of self, others, and society; (4) evoked class
discussions that more nearly approached a problem solving
level; and (5) promoted the acceptance of social responsibility in sharing curricular preparation.

Role playing is adapted to investigating normal, everyday problems rather than the abnormal or the atypical. It is useful, for example, in studying problems arising from an individual having only a partial view of the situation; from communication failures; from misunderstood or ignored feelings of others; or from unclear goals or policies. It has become increasingly popular as a technique for training supervisors, for developing sensitivity to interpersonal relations, and for understanding group and organizational behavior. The person who has rehearsed real problems in an artificial environment gains self-confidence, assurance, and skills almost as well as if he had encountered the experiences in real life.

Comparison With Other Types of Cases

The case method is discussed rather fully in Volume I of this set of books. The following types of cases were described: case problem or issue case; case report or appraisal case; case history; development, sequential, or series case; legal case; "armchair" case; incident process; and in-basket case or simulation exercise. The role playing case is yet another type. The in-basket exercise is a type of role playing in that the person is assuming the role of another and is making his decisions. Some of the cases in Volumes II and III can be used for role playing although they are not specifically labeled as such. To name a few: Central Information Desk (4), Baby-Sitting Service (13), Trouble in the Reserve Book Room (15), Problem Patrons (82), The Scribbler (85), and Jane Hale (151). Also, role playing can be effectively used in conjunction with other types of cases by having the participants play out a part of the case they are studying. By combining role playing with case analysis and discussion, it is possible to add depth and breadth beyond those problems involved in the interpersonal relationship of the role playing.

What are some similarities between case studies and role playing cases? The two methods are similar in a number of respects. Both methods

 (1) are project or laboratory methods providing active learning experience which involves participants both intellectually and emotionally;
 (2) stimulate participants to think purposefully and creatively in relating theory to action;

Role Playing

(3) require the participant to define and analyze the problem, to determine available alternative solutions and the possible consequences of those alternatives, and to make decisions;
(4) include discussion which affords not only opportunities to develop communication skills but also to acquire new insights through the interchange of ideas and points of view;
(5) describe actual real-life problems which are disguised to prevent embarrassment of the real persons who were involved in the situation;
(6) create a spontaneous history of common experience and dialogue which serves as a basis for initiating, maintaining, and evaluating natural inquiry;
(7) do not give solutions because there are no right and wrong "answers";
(8) develop new insights and skills in dealing with others;
(9) provide vicarious experience through projection into the case to try out new ideas without running the risks that experimenting on the job entails;
(10) illustrate how the same situation can be perceived differently by different persons and may have several solutions;
(11) offer a constructive method or frame of reference for approaching the analysis and solution of any human problem in the future; and
(12) provide a basis for repeated reinforcement of learning when participants refer back to case experiences when related situations are discussed later.

Some of the differences between role playing and other types of cases include:

(1) Subject matter. -- Management role playing cases are usually centered in the area of human and interpersonal relations; other types of case studies include all phases of the management process - planning, organizing, motivating, and controlling.
(2) Length. -- Role playing cases are normally quite short, cover a limited time span, include just one incident, and have few characters; some case studies, noticeably case reports and case histories, may be quite long, cover a period of

years, include a number of incidents, and have many characters.
(3) Participant involvement. -- In role playing cases, participants tend to be emotional because they identify with the characters and the problems and hence require insight into the needs and feelings of others; other types of cases tend to be more logical and intellectual and include more managerial principles.
(4) Content. -- Role playing cases usually emphasize the human element in everyday work situations, whereas other types of cases are likely to emphasize facts, organizational structure, plans, policies, controls, and other administrative problems.
(5) Feedback. -- Interaction between the participants in role playing provides immediate and continuous feedback during the enactment indicating the effect of one person's behavior on others. In other types of cases no feedback comes from the solution arrived at because there are no characters to react to the decision; however, participants do get feedback to their ideas from their own discussion group.
(6) Action. -- Role playing cases differ from other types of case studies in that they carry the decision into action. For example, in other types of case studies, the decision might be to dismiss an employee but the participants do not have to follow through and tell the employee. In a role playing case, the player must face the employee and inform him of the decision.

Research Studies of Attitude and Behavior Change

Much of applied role playing has been carried out without the practitioner knowing or appreciating the psychological processes involved. Experimental study of role playing as a source of attitude, opinion, and behavior change began in the 1950's. Realizing that role playing is significant not only in itself but as a means of evaluating general theories of attitude change, a number of research studies have been carried out by psychologists, sociologists, and educators. This is an exciting area of social and educational psychological research and the implications have broad importance. Nearly all of the significant research in this area which had been published prior to 1969 was reprinted and summarized in Role Playing, Reward, and Attitude Change, edited by Alan C. Elms. Librarians interested in acquiring background in this area will find this volume "must" reading. The titles reprinted there have not been included in the bibliography at the end of this book.

Other studies not reprinted in Elms, because they were published after that book came out, are summarized below. No attempt has been made to inventory all research studies in this area, so these cited are probably only indicative of the types of studies currently being reported.

Darroch compared the findings generated by role playing subjects with those produced by subjects who were actually exposed to experimental conditions. He was concerned with attitudinal reaction to forced compliance. Respondents were asked to indicate how they personally would respond to an experimental treatment. The major aim of the laboratory study was to examine the effect of manipulated variables on relationships (correlation) between self-rating and attitude change.

The evaluating process by which one activates his concepts of the role of the other in the course of guiding his own behavior from childhood and the factors which contribute to it are the focus of a study by Kerckhoff: "Early Antecedents of Role-Taking and Role-Playing Ability." The individual's ultimate behavior takes into account not only the conception of the role of others but also his conception of self. Accurately anticipating the responses of others is dependent upon the clarity and accuracy of one's conception of both self and other--this involves both sociological and anthropological meanings. These concepts evolve through time and are dependent upon the individual's experience with others.

It has been observed in several experiments that role playing, or active involvement by a subject in presenting arguments supporting a controversial position, has a uniquely effective capacity to induce the subject's acceptance of that position. Greenwald concluded, in his study "The Open-Mindedness of the Counterattitudinal Role Player," that the effectiveness of role playing in inducing opinion change may be due in part to its success in getting subjects to evaluate information opposing their own position in unbiased fashion.

Zimbardo did a research study under a grant from the

Quartermaster Research and Engineering Command of the U. S. Army entitled "The Effect of Effort and Improvisation on Self-Persuasion Produced by Role-Playing. " One of the findings pointed to the greater modification of attitudes following role playing than following passive exposure to persuasive communication. This study tested effort and dissonance as they related to attitude change.

Videotape provided the vehicle for recording and examining instructional strategies and their effects on sixth grade children in a research study by Judith Ramirez entitled <u>Teacher Behavior in Role-Playing: A Study in Interaction Analysis.</u> Her hypothesis was that role playing requires of the teacher skills that are not involved in conventional modes of teaching. Results indicated that teacher behaviors related to the specific teacher role playing functions (warm-up, discussion, enactment, and summary) are significantly different from one another. In addition, results showed that teacher-student interaction during role playing differed significantly from teacher-student interaction in conventional social studies classes.

"Role Playing as a Technique for Developing a Scientific Attitude in Elementary Teacher Trainees," by Hughes, analyzed the effectiveness of three types of attitude change techniques for changing the attitude of these trainees toward science. "Assessment of Role Induction and Role Involvement in Creative Drama," by Lazier, developed systematic scientific procedures for the study of improvisational drama with children, especially ways of assessing what the typical creative drama teacher does with children, what children do when they are acting, and what effects this might have on the rest of their educational development.

A projective role taking test was revised by Feffer with respect to procedure and scoring categories in his <u>Role-Taking Behavior in the Mentally Retarded.</u> He concluded that the revised test was both reliable and valid and provided a basis for study of the relationship between role taking ability and behavioral indices of social adequacy.

Examples or Applications of Role Playing

The role playing technique has been used successfully in a variety of ways by many different groups. In this section, examples will be described briefly in order to inform librarians of the extent of use and the techniques employed. As librarians read these examples they may get ideas for utilizing similar techniques in continuing education programs, in library science courses, or in other ways. Examples will be cited of use in classroom instruction, in training programs, in adult meetings, as a means of screening job applicants, and as a research tool. The technique is also used extensively in counseling and guidance, in social service, and in psychotherapy. These areas will not be included in this chapter because they have little relevance for library management purposes and also because librarians do not have the background or training to be clinicians in these fields.

Classroom Instruction

Elementary grades

In the elementary schools this technique is used extensively in teaching human relations (Shaftel, 1964). Role playing provides a suitable learning experience in schools which are concerned with the social development of boys and girls, with their moral and spiritual education, and with their personal-social needs. The Shaftels believe that it is easier for children to solve their own problems if they can look at them through the eyes of someone else. The method is for the teacher to read aloud to the class a carefully structured story of a typical problem of childhood. The story terminates in a dilemma and has no ending. Then, the children finish the story through role playing sessions. These enactments help children to understand themselves and others, to develop interpersonal and group skills, to learn to accept their feelings, and to think in terms of consequences. For young children, problem situations may center around such developmental problems as how to shift to the role of brother or sister when a new baby arrives in his family.

Problem pictures and stories. -- Fannie and George Shaftel believe a simple and efficient way to present such problems to children is through the use of problem pictures or brief problem stories. Their publication Words and Action, published in 1967, consists of twenty large, mounted photographs illustrating typical problems young children encounter at home, in school, and in their neighborhoods. A teacher's guide accompanying the photographs describes role playing techniques, applicable to preschool and primary grade children, which offer practice in problem solving and alternatives of behavior. People in Action, published in 1970, also contains twenty photo-problems for which teacher's guides are available. These are designed for preschool and primary grades. Values in Action, also published in 1970, consists of ten color filmstrips with coordinated records and a teacher's guide for grades four and five. Nine of the filmstrips are devoted to value clarification through role playing and discussion and one is a demonstration filmstrip showing teaching in an actual class.

The theory and methodology of role playing is presented in Part I of Shaftels' Role-Playing for Social Values, and Part II contains problem stories which simulate problem situations which a child is likely to encounter and end with a dilemma to be solved by the class. In finding solutions to a dilemma, children must choose between certain values-- for example, between a social value and personal interest, between loyalty to the group and honesty, or between winning dishonestly and losing honestly, or many other sets of values. This excellent volume is concerned with role playing in a simulated situation as a means of teaching such social science related concepts as ethical behavior, group responsibility, citizenship, and individual integrity.

Some incomplete or unfinished stories describing complex problem situations which provide the basis for group improvisation are included in Role-Playing Methods in the Classroom, by Chesler and Fox, and in Learning About Role-Playing for Children and Teachers, by Nichols and Williams. A collection of one-page unfinished stories for children in grades four through seven are available from the National Education Association and are entitled Unfinished Stories for Use in the Classroom. These focus the attention of boys and girls on ethical problems typical of those they encounter in school connected situations. By capturing their interest, children are encouraged to express themselves thoughtfully and forcefully either orally or in writing. The stories avoid both abstract theorizing and pat solutions. They are grouped in three general categories: "Responsibility for and Commitment to Others," "Personal Shortcomings," and "Shortcomings of Others." Every story title is the same with the exception of the name of a child; for example "What Should Peggy Do?", "What Should Gail Do?".

The Multimedia Division of Doubleday and Company

has produced some of the N. E. A. unfinished stories in Super 8 color sound cartridges, Super 8 magnetic sound reels, and 16 mm films. These are designed to stimulate individual expression either written, orally, or in role playing; to emphasize interpersonal relationships, particularly those between peers, parent and child, and teacher and pupil; to highlight decision making; and to point up the differences in individual reactions to similar situations. The teacher does not impose his own standards but uses nondirective language allowing accepted patterns of behavior to emerge from within the group.

Often in elementary education, cases are not written for classroom use; instead, they evolve from some phase of the instructional program and the problems and roles are worked out orally by teacher and pupils.

Underprivileged children. -- In discussing changes in educational theory and practices concerning the teaching of disadvantaged children, Frank Riessman advocated the use of role playing in three reports: "The Significance of Socially Disadvantaged Status," "It's Time For a Moon-Shot in Education," and "The Strategy of Style." He stated that educators have not paid enough attention to individual styles of learning in children. The written word may not contain the meaning for a child that the spoken word holds. His reading ability and interest in abstract learning will be much improved if he is made aware of his style and encouraged to discuss and participate in role playing activities concerning the subject matter he studies abstractly.

Fantine and Weinstein also discussed the learning style of disadvantaged children pointing out that it is inductive rather than deductive because the child's mental style is more concrete and problem-centered than abstract-centered, more physical and visual than aural, and more game and action-centered than test-oriented. One example of the inductive approach is role playing in which a child becomes physically and mentally involved in a situation. The authors claim that this teaching method draws generalizations from the child's specific frame of reference, from his action, and from his individual style of expression.

In his "Instructional Content For Depressed Urban Centers," Harry Passow presented ideas for teaching disadvantaged youth in several subject areas. Role playing is one of the techniques suggested as an experience centered activity useful in compensatory, special, and vocational education programs.

Those children who find writing difficult will often express themselves very well when acting out their own endings to unfinished stories. In teaching culturally deprived children who were antagonistic to school, teachers, and learning, Crystal found that they responded to role playing more spontaneously and enthusiastically than to any other classroom activity because it provided action which appealed to these children; also, it helped to change their attitudes toward school and learning. Another area in which role playing was effective with culturally deprived children was in introducing them to library facilities, use of the card catalog, the arrangement of books on the shelves, and the reasons for library rules (Anderson). Most of the children had never owned a book, not even a coloring book. One child at a time would play "librarian" while another played "borrower."

For eight weeks in the summer of 1964, more than two thousand Negro children went to freedom schools in Mississippi (Zinn). The teachers met no official qualifications and they taught not from books but from life, trying to link the daily headlines with man's intellectual tradition. Much use was made of role playing.

A comprehensive experimental research study in Israel demonstrated how role playing can further the intellectual development of underprivileged children. The problem, the study, and the findings are presented in Effects of Sociodramatic Play On Disadvantaged Preschool Children by Sara Smilansky. This study has much to offer educators, librarians, and social service workers in the United States who are working with underprivileged children. It will help them understand the reasons for differences in the behavior and achievements of children from different sociocultural backgrounds.

A number of diagnostic studies revealed that children of immigrants from various Middle Eastern and North African countries were not prepared to cope with the demands of the school curriculum in Israel and consequently tended to fail in school. This process of failure apparently began in the first grade and constituted an ever-widening scholastic gap between these children and those whose parents came from middle and high sociocultural backgrounds (European).

Scholastic failure had far-reaching effects on the emotional and social state of the child and resulted in marked deterioration in such traits as initiative, power of concentration, and attitude to work and study.

Observations of childrearing practices in the homes of children from different sociocultural backgrounds revealed differences in elaboration of concepts between privileged and underprivileged children which resulted from direct environmental influences. From an early age, the privileged child was taught by the adults in his environment how to collect scattered facts and weave them together into concepts and how to use these concepts in solving problems; but the underprivileged child was left alone to form his concepts accidentally and to test their relevance to his problems. The primary problem for educators seemed to be to find ways to help the underprivileged child relate and utilize his scattered experiences and isolated concepts and to convert them into new conceptual schemes so that he could more meaningfully absorb additional information and experience from his classroom, home, and environment.

The researchers were astonished to learn that children from the low sociocultural strata played very little and most of them did not participate in sociodramatic play at all. Hence, these children failed to experience the developmental sequence of play behavior through which a normal child moves from one stage to the next in keeping with his biological development. They found that role playing drew from the child's scattered experience, knowledge, and vocabulary in an imaginative way; served as a vehicle for the child to express himself in action and verbalization; engaged the child in prolonged social interaction with his peers; enriched his language; and broadened his concepts.

This project in Israel and the other projects described in this section are examples of role playing without a written case or a script.

Language arts. -- General semantics was taught to fifth grade children by employing experimentation, role playing, and active discussion of personal reactions (Lauer). The children were shown how verbal expressions could be used to reflect accuracy or distortion in what was desired to be expressed.

To develop the reading ability of slow learners during

a summer camp program, skits and role playing were among the teaching techniques employed in the spoken language program. Details of the tests used, the skill areas taught, the motivations, and teaching methods are described by Arthur Miller in his "Demonstration Program in Remedial Reading and Language Arts."

A vehicle for teaching English--reading, writing, and speaking--to culturally different and culturally disadvantaged children was devised by Trout through a unit she called "Protest Movement." For quick stimulation and interest, she asked the children to choose from a collection of pictures something they wanted to sell (motorcycle, radio, car) and to write ads. Through reading and role playing they "sold" their products to the class. After becoming aware of the power of words, the children read about race relations, Civil Rights, black power, and similar topics. The study climaxed with the children portraying representatives from black power, Black Muslims, and other groups through role playing. This unit created an atmosphere where the children could bare their fears, frustrations, prejudices, disillusions, and hopes.

The chief goal of teachers of English as a second language and English as a standard dialect is to broaden the linguistic repertoire of their students so that the latter will have greater social acceptance and mobility, broader range of occupational options, and greater ability to compete on an equal footing with other members in the mainstream of society. If the language of these children in minority groups differs from the national norm, they are apt to remain in a socially and economically disadvantaged status. For many of these children long-term goals and such middle class rewards as academic grades, teacher approval, or parental support seem ineffective motivation. As natural behavior, Lee Salisbury found that role playing could provide the bridge between classroom patterned language drill and real life in teaching Eskimo children whose native language was Tenl and Hawaiian children whose native language was Hawaiian Pidgin. He stressed that language instruction must be spontaneous in a specific situational context and must vary in style from context to context.

Another project designed to improve the teaching of English was carried out in Edinburgh, Scotland (Taylor). The experiment was planned to provide a creative learning experience for reluctant learners in improving their speak-

Role Playing

ing, reading, writing, and spelling. The children assumed the role of a Sahara Desert tribe. A chair washed up on the beach served as a focal point for the project. As tribesmen, the children were perplexed about this "thing"-- they asked each other what it was, where it came from, and what it could be used for. The teachers divided the children into small groups to write their versions of this dramatic situation. Dialogues from each group were then combined into a short drama which was cast, rehearsed, staged, and taped with appropriate background music. The author reported that although the quality of the children's writing, spelling, and use of English varied considerably from standard form, their complete attention and interest was absorbed in mime, role playing, group and individual composition, interpretative reading, memorization, and set decoration.

To provide transition from sixth grade to junior high school, Strauss and Dufour designed a unit integrating literature, social studies, art, music, and semantics for the last semester in sixth grade. Concentration in this humanities course was on role playing to explore group behavior and the dilemmas of the child as he searched for his identity and his personal values. Themes included honesty, self-acceptance, prejudice, integrity, responsibility to group and self, and revenge.

Role playing with masks was used by a speech correctionist with a group of boys who stuttered (Pollaczek). Invariably, after putting on the masks, the boys began spontaneously to act out the role suggested by the mask and their stuttering or blocking disappeared. A follow-up study showed definite improvement in speech for these boys even when not role playing and two were judged to be completely free of speech blockage.

A program to prepare non-English speaking children for entry into the first grade was developed by Louise Greenwood and others. Drills and activities for reinforcing language learning included repetition drill, conversations, short talks, role playing, and sociodrama.

Arithmetic. -- A teacher of a seventh grade class found difficulty in getting the children to comprehend percent (Pulliam). To test textbook principles, a "real-life" role playing situation was set up in the classroom. By dividing the number of floor tiles by class enrollment, "building lots" were created. "Roads" were chalked on the floor among the "lots." Each child staked a claim on one "lot" and started his own "business." The children soon found that knowledge of percent was essential to their operations and that the concepts involved were not too difficult or hard to learn.

Social studies. -- Role playing of family living situations was used as the basic technique in teaching the importance of laws and regulations for people and nations to coexist peacefully (Glogau and Krause).

To stimulate the study of medieval history, an activity project was designed for learning about the activities and social relationships of eight characters living in a French medieval manor (Williamson). The children studied background materials of this period, assumed the roles of the characters, created costumes and props, and presented a series of role playing skits which demonstrated their newfound understanding of the subject matter. The children learned about the economics, religion, and cultural aspects of the Manor and this period of history as well as the values and attitudes which characterized the era.

To help children feel more sympathy for and curiosity about another culture, five modern Japanese families were studied via role playing (Reich and Schanck). Each family was different as to father's occupation and adherence to tradition. In order to role play assigned family members, the children learned about the family structure, religion, ancestor worship, the changing economic structure, household furnishings, and some contemporary Japanese history.

Children learned about the waterways of northeastern North America and about the cities, industries, and ethnic groups which existed on or near them through tracing the route of a small wooden canoe on its way to the Atlantic Ocean (Bever and Kresse). The economics of bartering were realized through role playing transactions with the Chippewa and Huron Indians and with the French.

An innovative method for teaching environmental education to upper elementary children was conceived which involved them in the decision-making process (Asmussen) They developed a land-use alternatives model which illustrated the important dimensions of choice-making about land use while reinforcing relevant geographic concepts. The goal

Role Playing

of the project was to develop, classify, and analyze a list of possible uses for a one-mile square parcel of farm land located outside a hypothetical city. The project consisted of three components: (1) the teacher provided the class with the necessary city maps, geographical information, and other background data and information; (2) teacher led an inquiry session the purpose of which was to identify, develop, and analyze alternative land uses appropriate for the hypothetical land, and provide information necessary for subsequent role playing; and (3) role playing.

The role playing component provided experience in a decision-making process; the major emphasis was on critical thinking and social skills. The children assumed roles as members of the Citizens Committee or of the Board of Control. They had to decide from among the alternatives outlined in the second component; they assumed particular points of view and attempted to influence the city's decision-makers. Through this project the pupils experienced the process of organizing and producing a cooperative presentation much as is done in real-life situations of this kind.

Group counseling. -- Role playing was found to be an effective classroom technique for group counseling with children in the fourth, fifth, and sixth grades (Ohlsen). Counseling was defined as an accepting, trusting relationship between children and a counselor who has the ability to listen, empathize, and understand. Group counseling also provided conditions for learning because it involved treatment by the group as well as individual treatment within the group; in addition, support from parents and teachers was needed. Role playing in this context provided an organized effort to teach pupils to cope with specific problems; and an opportunity to relive a specific problem, to express feelings about it, to test ideas for coping with the problem, to obtain the group's ideas for solving the problem, and to practice solutions by interacting with the group members. After such a group counseling experience, the child usually better understood himself and the situation. An example of the kind of situation which was successfully role played in group counseling concerned one boy who was beaten up by another.

Schmidt found that group guidance was an efficient way of dealing with maladjusted children in schools and of assisting those children who showed a defeating self-concept or an inability to relate to others. The dynamics of human interaction were described. Role playing was used in helping the children adapt to the school environment and develop attitudes toward self.

A career guidance program for children aged nine to twelve which utilized role playing was reported by Helen Faust in "Room to Grow Career Guidance in Elementary School."

<u>Intergroup education.</u> -- In "Building Brotherhood," Mary Beauchamp and others recommend that children be taught to understand the basic tenets of brotherhood through reading appropriate literature and role playing. The pupils should be encouraged and good relationships between school and community should be advocated. Parents and teachers are equally responsible for giving leadership to sound intergroup education.

A report by Morton Sobel described and listed the resource materials available in intergroup relations education. Audience participation techniques such as role playing were described. In her book, <u>Intergroup Education</u>, Jean Grambs surveyed methods of presentation which included role playing and open-ended stories or scripts.

Teachers in public schools are confronted with the necessity of teaching about prejudice and discrimination as facts of life, as conditions which prevent the full development of every person, and as problems which must be solved if democracy is to function in the United States and be accepted around the world. Gertrude Noar developed a resource unit on prejudice and discrimination. One of the teaching techniques recommended was role playing. The purposes of the instruction were to encourage pupils to develop a personal code of behavior, to make new friends across racial and ethnic lines, and to challenge stereotyping.

In a nongraded elementary school where the student body was composed of black, white, and Asian children, role playing was used to provide boys and girls with an opportunity to understand discriminatory feelings and behavior which have adverse effects on interpersonal relationships (Wilson). All the children were divided into two groups as nearly alike as possible in sex, race, emotional stability, age, and academic skills. The children in one group wore blue ribbons and those in the other group wore orange ribbons. The first day of the project the blue ribbon wearers were the privileged group receiving special praise, consideration, activities, and rewards. Those wearing orange ribbons were discriminated against. The second day the orange ribbon wearers were privileged and the blue were discriminated against. At the close of each day the children were asked to respond to how they felt. Both teacher and parents believed this to be a valuable learning experience.

Secondary schools

At the secondary education level, role playing has been reported as being used successfully for teaching English language (Steed) (Allan), retarded adolescents (Arnholter) (Taylor), politics (Kariel), speech (Hamilton), nutrition (Bricker) (Kuykandall), family relationships (Westerville) (Wood), law and law enforcement (Cincinnati . . .), American foreign policy (Cecile), foreign languages (Newcomer) (Johnston) (Keitel), and social studies (Engle) (Garvey). In addition, some examples of innovative ways which have been devised for teaching business, history, English, economics, geography, and chemistry are described below.

Business. -- The value of role playing in all types of high school business courses has been discussed by Dale and by Mason; in cooperative retail training by Chapman; and in distributive education by Meyer and Haines. Scripts for two skits for use in teaching consumer education or consumer economics classes were written by Lowe: "Purple Ink," depicting some of the provisions contained in the Federal Meat Inspection Act, and "The Good Old Days," based on the Fair Packaging Act.

Observing that most office workers are discharged because they cannot get along with other persons and that skill in human relations and production standards cannot be achieved through talking about them, Kirk believed that extensive practice in handling office problems should be included in a high school secretarial course. She conducted a five-girl office simultaneously with other class activities. Each student in the class was required to apply for one of the five positions--office manager, secretary, stenographer, and two clerk-typists. Job interviews were held with each applicant who was rated on a rating form for appearance, letter of application, and performance during the interview. Students with the highest ratings were "hired" to work for the week performing jobs similar to what they would actually do on the same job in an office. Students who were not "hired" this time were required to apply again when there was an opening and keep on applying until they got a job After the week's work, they were rated on performance evaluation forms which were actually used in business and were then either promoted or fired depending upon these evaluations. Those who lost their jobs were required to apply again and start over. This competitive type of reality role playing might have possibilities for various levels of library education and training.

History. -- Two teachers reported (Dumas) (Morasky) that they found history was experienced more intimately and with greater personal meaning through role playing than through lectures, readings, and discussion. The characters and events came to life because students became more aware of the feelings and emotions of the persons who made history. By impersonating these historical characters, students gained deeper insights into the personalities and philosophies of the persons who influenced the forces operating during crucial periods. Morasky constructed a case to exemplify how this technique can be used. He pointed out that there is no formula or outline for writing cases in history nor any source for obtaining such cases so the instructor must write his own. Dumas gave some guidelines for conducting historical cases and suggested that small group decision making situations were especially successful.

As a part of a United States history course, Eastridge simulated the United Nations Security Council by having each student play the role of a delegate to the Council. Six weeks prior to the simulation date, each student researched his role by studying the background, history, religion, geographical location, military alliances, and government of the country he would represent. All the students needed, also, to study the activities and work of the Council.

A special kind of role playing technique to teach eleventh and twelfth grade students about the historical process as it manifested itself in the American Revolution, the English Revolution of the seventeenth century, American entry into World War II, and world politics following the German surrender in 1945 was developed by Gorvine. Students were not bound to make the same decisions as the actual historical figures had made; they could work out alternatives to what actually happened so long as these alternatives were consistent with the actions of the historical figures and the times in which they lived. The view of history implied in this approach was that despite the influence of impersonal forces on the flow of events, individuals do have some control over what happens and an event was not necessarily inevitable. The author believes that one reason for the success of these projects was because of the large amount and the quality of reading that the students did before the actual role playing.

English literature. -- Closely allied to the utilization in history are the ways role playing has been used in the teaching of English literature. Various methods have been reported for the student to select a character from a play or novel and to identify with that role in an enactment before a class (Barnes) (Kegan) (Mekeel). McCaleb pointed out that role playing is particularly relevant today in light of Marshall McLuhan's philosophy that the learner needs to respond to and interact with his total environment. Traditional teaching and learning methods do not lend themselves to total response but role playing does. The situations are drawn from literature itself. The writer believed that students gained lasting and profound insights into fictional characters because they felt what the characters felt. In teaching classic English novels, Magers observed that, through role playing, the student related to the characters, the setting, and the action of another age and another way of thinking and living. This experience had an impact on the student's thinking. Stieglitz approached the study of Silas Marner with his students by means of a court trial. Casey dramatized the study of poetry through role playing.

Economics. -- Basic economic principles were learned through a computerized game simulating a total environment which required the student to play a decision making role (Cybernetic . . .). The game format combined two teaching techniques--role playing and programmed instruction. The students played a series of roles such as "king" to learn how an agricultural economy worked or "manufacturer" to learn how capitalism operated.

Geography. -- When a ninth grade geography class studied a unit about Soviet Russia, each student played a role: several members acted as secret police and the rest were organized into either (1) groups representing the political bodies of the government, industry, and collective farm bosses, or (2) members of the public who were not members of the Communist Party (McCoy).

Chemistry. -- In a high school chemistry class, the chairs were arranged according to an electron configuration and were later rearranged to teach parts of an atom and other chemical concepts and processes (Plati).

Vocational guidance. -- A work-study program designed to motivate and train potential dropouts for employment was described by Charles Savitzky. Mornings were devoted to regular subject classes and afternoons to on-the-job training. Classes made use of group discussion, role playing, and field trips. The purposes of the program were to train youth in applying for jobs, to initiate proper attitudes, and to provide vocational guidance. Role playing was found valuable in developing student interest in distributive education courses (Hagenau) and in occupational guidance (Oregon).

Higher education

At the college level, published articles described the use of role playing to teach personnel relations (Grambs, 1948), psychology (Casey) (Kay), social psychology (Bowman), child and adolescent psychology (Carter), educational psychology (Coleman), nursing (Dix), anthropology (Sayres), speech (Johnson and Rau), public administration (Leemans), home economics (Westerville), and library science (Carter). In addition to these subjects, the teaching of sociology, freshman English composition, economics, political science, education, and medicine are described below.

Sociology. -- Bogardus used role playing to teach ethnic relations and social stratification. Porterfield used literature in teaching sociology with emphasis on the sociology of personality; and examined the relationship of literary social situations to role playing techniques. This study was based on the assumption that writers of drama, fiction, and poetry collectively manifest deep insight into almost every type of human feelings, behavior, and emotions in a variety of cultural settings. The author believed the student might be so submerged in his own background and culture that he would be incapable of objectively imagining there was any other way in which to view a situation and hence might react with complete lack of insight into the sources of his own motivations. The characters and situations from literature showed students how many possible perspectives there were in which to view attitudes, behavior, and emotions. He geared into the major concepts of sociology and psychology situations from more than 1,750 novels, dramas, and short stories. The evidence from these analyses suggested many situations which could be tried out in teaching sociology.

Two writers recount how they used role playing in courses dealing with marriage and the family (Gillette) (Shipman). For example, a woman student played the part of a sorority member who needed a date for a sorority party. She invited several men whom she had never dated before and each one refused (they had been instructed to do so). This illustrated negative feelings to the class.

English composition. -- A new concept in teaching freshman English composition was reported (Reform . . .). The director of the course urged students to take on various roles in their writing--one role at a time. Each role represented a personality, an attitude, or an identity. The act of writing was looked upon as play-acting with the student playing a role involving creation of self. The language used was dictated not only by subject matter and audience but also by the individual's role. This type of role playing was considered good preparation for learning to change and reverse roles so that students could see a situation from many perspectives. Also, this experience provided the basis for various writing styles of importance for a professional writer.

Economics. -- To avoid the limitation inherent in one-way communication of the traditional lecture course, Joseph tried a number of participative learning experiences for students by placing them in role playing involvements in his elementary economics and labor economics classes. Although the experiments represented a substantial investment of student time which could have been used to present additional subject matter, he felt the time spent was worthwhile because the experiences had a stronger impact on the students than any other teaching technique he had tried. He found heightened student interest, better acceptance of unfamiliar concepts, more effective student-teacher communication, and repeated reinforcement of learning as students referred back to their role play experiences.

Another type of student involvement which might be suitable for teaching international economics is the Caltech Political Military Exercise described in the next section. By introducing into that game more economic factors with a data bank and computers, additional stimulation in the teaching of economics might be achieved.

<u>Political science.</u> -- At the California Institute of Technology, a relatively unstructured game was devised for the teaching of political science, diplomacy, and leadership. In the Caltech Political Military Exercise, the players assumed roles of leaders of various countries and attempted to act as they thought these leaders would in a time of international crises. The major purposes of the exercise were (1) to provide students with an experience in crisis diplomacy and policy formation, and (2) to provide a case study of "crisis" in group dynamics. Rules for the game were flexibly designed to permit creativity on the part of the players who were assigned to roles on the basis of their leadership qualities and their knowledge of the country in which the game was played. The players reacted to such pressures as elections, personal beliefs, and commitments experienced by the person he was impersonating.

A committee, whose members were knowledgeable about the political realities which affected the area of the world in which the game action centered, was responsible for providing the framework within which the game was played. The framework involved a political crisis that determined the initial actions of the committee, a scenario which bridged the span from current time to the time of the crisis, and a complement of teams to play the game. Pregame preparation of players began after the teams were formed and the players were selected for their roles and consisted of two parts: (1) reference materials on the crisis area such as political and military strength and social and economic structure; and (2) other relevant materials for each team.

A control board, on which the success of the game depends, kept the game running smoothly and represented groups such as ambassadors, spies, and unrepresented countries. Because this board was a communication and control center, the staff included two or three persons who were very knowledgeable about the crisis, its location, and the relationship of nations; a typist for typing messages; persons concerned with the transfer of messages; the auditing of meetings, and the reporting of international and domestic news; and a filing clerk who filed one copy of every message sent to players. Periodically during each game period a news service operated by the board provided hypothetical news summaries comparable to the information that governments receive through unofficial channels.

Librarians might find a technique similar to this valuable in training sessions to prepare staff members for strategic planning before crisis situations occur such as budget hearings, legislative appropriations, bond issue elections, and community action.

Education. -- The problems regarding the teaching of low-income children and how ill-prepared teachers are for the task was discussed by Hannah. She advocated that a new system of teaching prospective teachers which would be geared to low-income children. She recommended the development of a curriculum which would include community field trips, home visits, and role playing before the teacher entered a classroom to teach. She believed that such a program would help the prospective teacher develop a teaching style which would help her have more effective rapport with these children. This same kind of preparation might profitably be included in library in-service or continuing education training programs for those who were to work in these neighborhoods.

In an urban teacher preparation program, Fantani and Weinstein discussed "Immediate Reinforcement and the Disadvantaged Learner."

Two other authors--Walters and Lansner--suggested the use of role playing in helping education students to become sensitized to and acquainted with classroom situations which they would encounter in their practice teaching experiences and, eventually, in their professional careers.

The major objective of a course, "Change in Schools," taught at the University of Pittsburgh in 1969, was to analyze several common current supervisory and curricular problems (Champagne). Students were required to create an imaginary community, devise a table of organization for the school district of that community, populate the district with a board, superintendent, and principals. They also developed mock application forms and personal history forms. Final evaluations of the course by students showed that the role playing experiences were important, meaningful, and useful.

In the teaching of art education courses, Neil found that college students were master role players so he used various dramatic situations in his courses. By asking students to identify with certain characters in the written situations he presented to them, they perceived themselves by recognizing similar actions and ideas in others. By such a "mirror analysis" they were more empathetic. The author calls this process "internalization" or "getting into another's shoes." He believed that the instructor must also experience this internalization process. If he lacks intrinsic knowledge and understanding of the students, his teaching becomes superficial and inadequate. He described one project to test the student's creativity and ability to recognize an art object. On a cold, gray, dismal day in a drizzling rain, he took a class of blindfolded art education students to the city dump where there were deserted, crumbling, half buried old buildings. He reported their learning experiences.

A guide for teachers and teachers' trainers, Adult Basic Education, was developed in three workshops sponsored by the National Association for Public School Adult Education. The manual outlined programs applicable both to trainees and to their disadvantaged clientele. Teacher training methods included role playing, demonstrations and exhibitions, field trips, films, and group discussion.

Medicine. -- At the University of Missouri School of Medicine an adaptation of role playing which has found widespread acceptance in the moot court approach in law schools was used in teaching medical students (Ramey). It is a combination of closed-circuit television, videotape recording, and role playing. This method was found successful in teaching human ecology and behavioral science which covered the role relation of the doctor and patient, cultural definition of illness, and dying and death.

Selected role players were given a written case outline sufficiently in advance of their "performance" so that they had adequate time to study it thoroughly. Also, they were given a list of related suggested readings. Prior to the class period during which the simulation was to be discussed, they assembled to tape the case and at this time were assigned to specific roles which were described in a few sentences to establish a point of view. The students were instructed to draw upon their own experience and training, their reading, and their perception of the developing situation, remembering that the purpose of the exercise was to express as many of the issues underlying the problem as possible so as to enable the viewers to understand better the dynamics of the problem. Only players actually taping were allowed in the studio so they experienced no embarrassment from performing before classmates. The videotape was shown to the class either immediately following the taping or at some later date. The class members were given the case in writing at the class session preceding the presentation. The class session began with a discussion of the issues underlying the problem, then the videotape was shown. One major advantage of this technique was the dissociation of the television image from the actual persons seated in the group. Class members could be frankly critical of the enactment without regard for personalities as they would if the classmates were performing in person.

As part of a continuing project in the analysis of the development of professional competence, the Center for the Study of Medical Education at the University of Illinois and a major specialty board collaborated on the development of new evaluative techniques (Levine and McGuire). Three of these techniques required the examiner and the candidate, or both, to role play during these three parts of the examination: The Simulated Diagnostic Interview, The Simulated Proposed Treatment Interview, and The Simulated Patient Management Conference. The Simulated Diagnostic Interview required a candidate to elicit historical information from an examiner playing the role of "patient," to obtain other diagnostic information from a second examiner, to integrate this information, and to report and explain his diagnostic impressions to the examining team. The Simulated Proposed Treatment Interview required a candidate to explain a proposed treatment to an examiner who played the role of a patient. The Simulated Patient Management Conference required five candidates to assume that they were attending a case conference at which they discussed the management of the two cases. The results indicated that these evaluative techniques provided information on aspects of competence unavailable from conventional written and oral examinations.

Training Programs

The preceding section presented examples from formal classroom environments--elementary, secondary, and higher education. Training programs are concerned with employed adults in organizations. The term "training" is commonly used in business, industry, government, and public administration. The professions usually refer to this type of program as "in-service," "continuing education," "workshop," "institute," "executive development," and possibly other titles. The aim of all such programs, regardless of title, is to improve, update, and develop individuals for better work performance. For the purposes of this chapter and in the interests of simplicity, the term "training" will be used to represent all the forms of knowledge, skill, and attitudinal development which adults need to keep up with the accelerated pace of today's work environment.

A number of different methods can be and are used in training programs. The choice depends upon the environment in which the training will occur, the purposes and requirements of the training, and the characteristics of the trainees. Because it involves both actor and spectator, role playing is among the best of the attention-getting and interest-holding devices for effective human relations training. Its controlled conditions facilitate communication by stimulating trainee activity and involvement.

From the mass of printed literature on this subject, those items which seemed most relevant and which offered the most fertile ideas for librarians have been selected. Examples are cited which librarians may be able to adapt for library purposes. The descriptions of these examples are sufficient to identify the principal features of each. Readers wishing more detail should read the sources cited. These examples have been grouped as follows: salesmen, health sciences, supervisors and executives, educators, overseas assignments, and other areas.

A sizable literature exists on the subject of role perception, role identification, and role behavior. Some of this is concerned with the indoctrination of teachers, principals, and nurses to their professional attitudes, behavior, and roles. These publications have much to offer librarians but are not germane to library management education or decision making so have not been included in this chapter.

Salesmen

Shaw made a number of suggestions for salesmen selling on television. A novel approach for training insurance salesmen was described by Alvin: a drama coach taught acting techniques which are normally taught to professional actors and theatre students. The course ran for three months, met twice a week, and each session lasted two and one-half hours. The men were taught how to use natural persuasion talents and to recognize faulty techniques. They became conscious of the need to use words which prospects could visualize. One man, who habitually used involved technical insurance terms in his conversation, developed a simpler approach by pretending to sell a seven-year-old child a policy over the telephone. The part of the child was played by the father of a seven-year-old child. By the end of the course, more than half of the men expressed the belief that some positive change had taken place in their selling habits.

Ditz found role playing an effective method of providing insurance salesmen with insight into the underlying reasons a prospect had against making a purchase even though the prospect did not realize that such reasons existed. He also used the technique as a secondary screening device for new salesmen in evaluating comprehension and ability to demonstrate basic information.

In a firm which manufactured structures for storing and processing grain and forage on farms, a technique was devised for training both experienced and newly hired salesmen which was called Total Involvement Practice Selling (TIPS) (New . . .). The purpose was to help salesmen learn about customer problems and reactions. Two salesmen at a time played the roles of "farmer" and "salesman." Before the start of the scene, the "farmer" was coached on how to play his role effectively and instructed to talk and act like a typical farmer prospect. The two salesmen walked into a room and sat on opposite sides of a table. In the center of the top of the table was a life-size unposed bust photograph of a farmer facing the "salesman" side of the table. On the back of the photograph was a complete case history of this farmer which described in detail the crops he grew, his harvests including how much he used himself and how much he sold, the acreage he owned or rented, fertility and tillability of the soil, type of livestock raised and how marketed, facts about his family, and his objections to purchasing a Harvestore unit. While the "farmer" read the case history off the back of the photograph to familiarize himself with his role, the "salesman" studied a large photograph of a long-distance view of farm buildings, fields and cattle belonging to the "farmer" in order to orient himself for the enactment. After the enactment each player filled out a copy of a questionnaire evaluating his performance and, later, they compared questionnaires to see what data each missed and discussed each other's performance in terms of that the "salesman" could have done better.

Health sciences

Role playing was one of the training methods in a continuing education program for hospital administrators (Allen); in mental hospitals to increase patient social interaction (Rosenblatt); in the training of hospital social workers (Hagan); in groups as a means of building mental health and releasing emotional tensions (Terrace); in a human relations laboratory for dietetic interns and occupational therapists (Johnson, Dale); in a simulation demonstration by a public health organization trying to detect a hypothetical epidemic and ameliorate its effects on a community (Bogdanoff); in mental health education (National Conference . . .) and also in each of the examples given below.

In the training of student nurses, the theory of psychosomatic medicine and the psychodynamics of reacting to patient illnesses and emotions was taught by means of role playing (Stein). The writer reported that a few scenes of role playing with the help of experienced auxilaries often taught the nurses more dynamics and more self-confidence than several years of graduate experience in the wards.

The growth of community psychiatry has altered service patterns and has emphasized the need for supplementing the training of public health nurses. As they could not be spared for full-time study in regular mental health programs in universities, they were trained in a series of workshops which made use of role playing (California).

Shortages of professional personnel in hospitals, county health programs, and mental health have made it necessary to train volunteers (Bartholomew) (Cooper) and indigenous nonprofessional aides (Hallowitz) (Reissman, 1964) (Reissman, 1965) (Truax) (Pine) for some of the work. Thus, with minimum professional staff, clinical service could be provided to a large number who could not be reached in more conventional ways. Increasingly, indigenous nonprofessionals have been employed to free professional personnel from routine work in community mental health services. These aides acted as friends and counselors to the clients and served as a bridge between the mental health agency and other community resources. Their activities included direct services, community action, community education, and social planning. Role playing seemed to be valuable in training the disadvantaged because it appeared to be more congenial with the low income person's style: action-oriented, problem-directed, group-centered, game-like rather than print oriented, and easy, informal tempo. Furthermore, role playing allowed the professional to reduce the role distance between himself and the disadvantaged individual when the professional learned what it is like to be in the role of the aide. Similarly, for the low-income person, it changed the setting and tone of what often appeared to him as an institutional bureaucratic, impersonal, foreign world.

To help change mental hospital aides' self-image from that of custodian to social therapist, a group was confronted with the experience of being patients in another mental health institution (Ishiyama). The goals of this in-service program were to increase the aide's consciousness of those aspects of the patient role which were crucial in the patient's progress, to develop interpersonal skills, and to raise the status and morale of the aides. Aides were hospitalized six hours without ward attendants' knowledge of their real identities; and were interviewed immediately following release and again fourteen weeks later to see what positive behavioral changes resulted from the experience.

The combination of closed-circuit television and videotape recording utilized in the teaching of medical students (which was described earlier in this chapter with examples in higher education) was recommended by the author, James W. Ramey, for training personnel in public and community health, health science interviewing, and preventive medicine. He believed this technique was especially valuable in developing insight into the manner in which a health care team functioned and the interaction of the various team members in a hospital setting.

Supervisors and executives (leadership training)

The training of leaders so that they will be more skillful in human relations has become widespread in many areas of our society. The basic purpose of most executive development programs is to train leaders. Role playing has been a popular device for discovering, selecting, and training leaders in management (Meacon); for training foremen and supervisors in safety education and accident prevention (Gardner); for teaching human relations and leadership skills (Klein, 1961) (Schwarz); for a leadership program in a naval shore activity of the U.S. Navy (Yeoman); for teaching the components of management and human relationships in U. S. Army Officer Career Courses (Hancock); for teaching the harmonious applications of human relations and regulations to the solution of day to day problems at the U. S. Naval Ordnance Plant in Macon, Georgia (Kaull); and for preparing home economics leaders for emerging programs serving disadvantaged youth and adults (Garrett).

An extensive research study of leadership training was carried out by Theresa B. Trittipoe and Clifford P. Hahn for the Personnel and Training Branch of the U. S. Office of Naval Research and published in 1961 (American Institute for Research). Although the purpose of the study was to develop and evaluate leadership training materials suitable for Petty Officers in the U. S. Navy, the methodology, the instruments developed, and the bibliography are equally pertinent and relevant in any field. The final report was in four parts. Part 1 described the methodology for developing and evaluating fifteen situational problems. The results of administering the problems in both role playing and case study format were described and discussed. Part 2 contained the fifteen situational problems; instructions for administering the problems and for the participants; general discussion guide; and evaluation forms. Part 3 described problems, results, and trends in leadership research. Part 4 was a bibliography of the leadership literature which provided the background for this study.

Supervisory employees of a medical insurance firm participated for six months in a management development program (Peskin). Three basic teaching techniques were combined: role playing, group dynamics, and a form of programmed instruction. Each person played the role of an officer in a hypothetical company. The goal of the program was to provide supervisors (1) with training experiences which would stimulate and challenge their thinking as managers and potential administrators, and (2) with the fundamental knowledge they would need in decision making. Changes in their approaches were evident not only to the hypothetical problems presented in the program but also in their attitudes and conduct on the job.

As part of the evaluation of a multi-media course for managerial personnel on problem solving discussions, a special case was developed to test trainees' application of their skills in a new setting (Ault). Each trainee played the role of a plant manager with a problem to solve; each was

Role Playing

given background information and then played the case over the telephone at an appointed hour. The telephone was used because of the geographical dispersion of the trainees. Each trainee had two subordinates available for consultation. The subordinates were supplied with carefully structured roles but were not informed as to the nature of the experiment. A total of thirty sales managers from two companies took part. Fourteen had gone through another training program three months previously and sixteen were controls. Solutions to the problem were graded on the basis of a preestablished scale. The results showed that managers with training reached better solutions and reached them faster than managers without training. The use of the telephone proved feasible thus suggesting applications in other training and research where verbal interaction is to be studied.

A complicated type of role playing, used in the training of managers, was developed in Holland by P. Hesseling which he called a "communication exercise." This exercise evolved from laboratory experiments in communication, case studies, and management games into a training device which simulated interdepartmental coordination and decision making. During an in-plant training conference which lasted one week, one day was devoted to a communication exercise. The participants were divided into teams of six which met in separate rooms. Each of five members assumed the role of a different departmental manager and the sixth member served as a chairman. The object of the exercise was to reach a decision as a team whether to accept or reject an order received by the sales manager from a customer. During the exercise only written communications could be passed between the department heads. All messages from the firm and all internal memoranda from team members went through the chairman who dated, numbered, and analyzed each item.

One corporation training director, Robert Bott, was experiencing difficulties in getting enthusiastic participation in his supervisory training sessions. So, he simulated conditions which caused participants to play real roles. An example of this was his announced meeting on "efficiency." He set up the conference room with flip charts and other visual aids to give the impression of an efficiency meeting, and hid a tape recorder in a bookcase which he started before participants arrived. After they were assembled, he handed out a change in vacation procedure, typed on official stationery, which stated "Employees will be required to take their vacations in blocks of three to five working days."

(Prior to this the plant-wise policy was for employees to take their thirteen days of vacation at one time and at a time agreed upon with their supervisors.) The director then read a letter of transmittal, supposedly, from the general manager, which stated that this change was best for employees' welfare and for increased efficiency. Some of the supervisors sat in stunned silence, others questioned and argued (both logically and illogically), or threatened; several banded together to protest the action, others ran out to phone the policy committee to voice their complaints and a few banged the table and tore up the notice. The leader tried to defend the proposed action. After the supervisors had had ample opportunity to express themselves, the leader wrote on the blackboard "Resistance to Change" and then explained the real purpose of the meeting and confessed that he had tricked them in order to get active participation. All of the different forms of resistance which they had exhibited were written on the board. Then, the tape recorder was revealed and the tape was played. Occasionally the tape was stopped to note on the board new forms of resistance. This part of the meeting was also dynamic not only for providing additional points on forms of resistance, but also many supervisors gained insight into how they had acted. The tape was erased before the close of the meeting. All reported that this technique resulted in keen interest in the subject.

  The Veterans' Administration offered a unique training experience designed to teach the principles of position management (Hitchings). A mock committee engaged in a carefully prepared bit of role playing to dramatize the complexity of the considerations involved in requests for more manpower. Management's dependency on improved organization and more skillful utilization of staff members in the absence of financial support was portrayed.

  Many derivations, combinations, and variations of role playing have been developed. One of these is management games which have recently been used frequently in executive development and management training programs. One training instrument which has been devised is a cross between role playing and management gaming and is called the "Task-Model Procedure" (Keltner). This procedure was reported to be applicable for training in communication, leadership, group processes, problem solving, and behavioral research. Construction toys, card packs, Lincoln Logs, and other construction type media were used to construct a model. The trainer hid this model behind a screen in the training

Role Playing 63

area. Trainees were assigned roles as manager, subleaders or foremen, and workers in each of two groups. Only the "manager" was permitted to see the model. He instructed two foremen how to assemble the model and they, in turn, instructed their work groups. The problem of communication became apparent almost immediately when the project began. Various suggestions for improving communication were discussed by the group and experimented with. The trainer then led the group in discussion of implications of the model problem for actual work settings.

Part of a training course for managers and supervisors in a retail store was to teach them how to improve the performance of their subordinates (Malt). A member of the training group played the role of "sales girl," showed merchandise to other members of the group "customers" but did not make a sale. Four members of the group as "supervisors," one at a time, talked to the "sales girl" suggesting ways "she" could improve her performance in order to make more sales. The rest of the group observed the enactment but the "supervisors" did not hear each other. After the enactment, the observers gave their opinions, each "supervisor" commented on his own performance, and the whole enactment was assessed and discussed.

Instructors in the Field Training Section of United Airlines developed a Letter-writing Program for training purchasing agents, claim clerks, collection correspondents, and their supervisors (Laird and Hayes). The purpose of this program was to demonstrate the importance of written interpersonal relations. Role playing took two forms (1) team teaching in which instructors read correspondence files aloud, and (2) multiple role playing by students. In the first part, the instructors made the point that feelings as well as facts are communicated through letters. They dramatized the importance of customer and interpersonal relations through letters. Instructor A read a complaint letter from a customer, then Instructor B read the reply, and Instructor A read the final letter from the customer. Discussion followed these readings. Students cooperated in constructing a check sheet embodying basic principles and techniques of good letter writing. Then, letters previously written by the participants were analyzed by the check sheet. Editorial changes were made on a transparency of each letter for overhead projection so everyone could watch. The second form of role playing involved all of the participants who were seated two to a table across from each other.

They exchanged letters each had written and each applied the basic check sheet to the other's letter. After discussion, their roles were reversed.

Barry reported experience in the training of department store buyers. A unique "group conference technique" for training supervisors was reported by Phelan. Training supervisors in human relations was discussed in an article by Stanton.

Donald Nylen and others designed a handbook for leadership training, staff development, and human relations training for use in developing nations in general and in the emerging African nations in particular. Training needs and cultural influences in English speaking African nations south of the Sahara as well as the general characteristics of individuals in groups in these nations were considered. The role and functions of trainers and the uses of such devices and activities as group experiments, paired interviews, role playing, and rating scales were evaluated. Exercises involved communication, observation, problem solving, decision making, and intergroup activities.

Educators

No one reading this needs to be reminded that confrontation of authority in all avenues of life is with us today. Confrontation and its usual result--counter confrontation-- leads to riots, chaos, disorganization, backlash, and revengeful calls for law and order. Of what help can mental health professionals be to teachers, principals, and administrators who find themselves confronted with rebelling students? Some possible solutions were described by Dr. Irving N. Berlin. Through a series of group role playing demonstrations and discussion sessions, educators were given a framework within which to understand and cope with militant student confrontation. These sessions helped to ease their tautness and actual fear and to make them think and plan ahead to avoid trouble in the future by inviting student and community involvement in planning for a meaningful education. The participants learned to distinguish between authoritative and authoritarian responses and to understand anger and react to it positively. Mental health professionals planned and supervised the sessions, interpreted both student and community needs, and helped the educators to find a more flexible and integrative way to meet these needs. The group sessions were followed up with individual consultations. Case

Role Playing

histories of successful and unsuccessful meetings and confrontations were used to evaluate what seemed to work and to analyze the data together.

In "Dissent and Disruption in Secondary Schools," Mark A. Chesler discussed the nature of student-school conflict in several crisis-torn secondary schools. Included in the paper are some role playing exercises which highlight problems.

Teachers in racially desegregated classrooms often need special instruction or retraining for the peculiar academic and social problems of their students. Role playing was reported as one of the training methods in three in-service teacher education programs which were concerned with this problem: "Teacher Training Designs for Improving Instruction in Interracial Classrooms," by Mark A. Chesler; "Teaching in Valleybrook Elementary School," by Frederick P. Venditti; and "A Plan for Improving the Education of Disadvantaged Children . . .," from Corpus Christi University. The third title focused on the education of Mexican-American children.

Nine exercises were developed by Giammatteo to develop organizational skills and personal and interpersonal insight in inner city teachers. The exercises consisted of the rationale and instructions for the user, were devoted to developing an understanding of verbal communication, and investigated such roles as the following: a teacher's helper, a white counselor and a black teacher in a conflict, and a superintendent of schools and a consultant in a race crisis. The case "Value Exploration" will serve as an example of the suggestions included for presentation and enactment. The headings are: problem, personnel, location, materials, masks (black, white, red, yellow, old lady, and old man) and procedure.

To improve teaching behavior without the threat that commonly accompanies a teacher-supervisor evaluation procedure, a group of elementary teachers, guided by a supervisor, held group sessions during a two-year in-service program (Amidon). The techniques used included Flanders' Interaction Analysis, role playing, tape recording, hypotheses development, and experimentation. This experience appeared to have a positive influence on the participants' interpersonal relationships, communications, goal-setting, and sensitivity to their verbal behavior and its effects on classroom climate and individual pupils.

To help new high school faculty members understand the problems they would face in the classroom, Kautz and Wald reported on a series of in-service meetings. Eight common classroom disturbances in high school were identified, then they were role played by a group of pupils on videotape. The tapes were played at the in-service meetings where a panel of seven teachers and a moderator reacted to the situations. The tapes were previewed by the moderator so he could better question the panel but the panel members had not seen them. Two basic questions were asked the panel for each incident: (1) what would the teacher have done in this situation? and (2) what, if any, preventive measures could have been taken to prevent the incident from occurring? After the panel members had reacted to the situation, the audience was given an opportunity to discuss the situation and the panel's reactions. The authors suggested that this technique may have some merit in preservice methods courses in education. University students in education who viewed the tapes felt that being able to see experiences in action might alleviate many of their anxieties about classroom control problems.

An exploratory experimental study of the effectiveness of situational role playing as a test of a principal's ability to deal with a variety of situations which might confront him was reported by Borg and Silvester.

Overseas assignments

Recently the concepts of human relations training have been applied to programs designed to prepare American personnel for overseas assignments. A major obstacle to effective accomplishment of both military and non-military assignments abroad is the culturally different patterns of thought, behavior, and beliefs of Americans from those of other peoples. Success in overseas operations often requires social interaction with indigenous personnel, orientation to interpersonal relations, and development of an awareness of underlying cultural assumptions and values.

An excellent evaluation of existing knowledge and experience in the area of human relations training and its relevance for training Americans to interact effectively with indigenous persons in overseas settings has been written by Foster and Danielian. They examined T-group, role playing,

Role Playing

and the case method with respect to their effectiveness and value in area training. Evidence was summarized and ways were suggested for adapting role playing methods and applications to the training of personnel for overseas assignments.

The design and development of training to increase cultural awareness was described by Edward C. Stewart in his report "Simulating Intercultural Communication Through Role-Playing." Significant aspects of intercultural interaction were simulated in a series of role playing exercises. Background material for role players was provided. Typical American values and assumptions were elicited from a trainee as he interacted with a "foreign" auxiliary who reflected a mirror image of American values and assumptions judged important to overseas performance. Possible variations in training format were suggested and some conclusions drawn for using the simulation exercises.

In his doctoral dissertation "Intercultural Training for Foreign Assistance," Charles Dove designed and tested an intercultural training program to prepare new employees for foreign assistance work. Sixty-five new Agency for International Development employees attended a week of training involving skill exercises, role playing, and simulation. Gains were noted in such areas as seeking information (as compared to giving it) and in communicating.

Peace Corps. -- The fundamental principle of Peace Corps volunteer training--total cultural immersion--is achieved through direct teaching and field experience. Trainees learn language (through intensive audiolingual methods), customs (through role playing and cross cultural studies), and attitudes (through discussion with persons who have lived in the country to be served). Working Effectively Overseas, by Spector and Preston, was prepared to help the Peace Corps Volunteers become familiar with some differences between working in the United States and working abroad, learn principles and methods of behavior that have been found effective by others who have worked overseas, and practice these principles and methods in situations typical of those likely to be encountered. The book is divided into two sections. The first discusses major overseas problems likely to be encountered by trainees, principles of effective behavior, and illustrative accounts of specific methods. The second part presents fifty typical situations for role playing solutions to the problems. The role playing was followed by class analysis, evaluation, and discussion.

Education in the Peace Corps by Jules Pagano compared Peace Corps training methods, both university-sponsored programs and in-house training by the Peace Corps, and the implications of these types of training for preparing young men and women to work with adults in the United States from foreign cultures and from disadvantaged groups. This publication included a role playing exercise and a case study for Latin America.

In order to establish tests and performance criteria for distinguishing between successes and failures in the training of Peace Corps trainees, Harvey and Kline studied the contributions of role playing to this training.

Air Force. -- Because of a need for improved interpersonal relations between U. S. Air Force military advisors overseas and the indigenous persons with whom they would work, a research program studied the relative effectiveness of two methods of training in cross-cultural skills (Eacchus and King) (Eacchus and Haines) (Haines and Eacchus) (Haines) (King). Subjects were required to play the role of an American Air Force captain who had to interact with a foreign counterpart (a player). Subjects performed a long list of distinct behaviors appropriate to the situation. Among those behaviors were actions and gestures both similar to those in American society and to those considerably different.

Using Air Force personnel in actual operational contexts, two training methods for teaching cross-cultural interaction skills were compared. The first method consisted of extensive reading of training manuals followed by three role playing sessions; the second included less reading, several role playing sessions, and self-confrontation by videotape replay after each role playing. The results showed that subjects trained under the second method learned faster and attained a higher terminal level of performance than subjects who were trained by the first method.

Job interviewing, screening, and training

Competence in interviewing and screening job applicants comes from systematic, sound training, and from actual experience in conducting interviews. Ideally, the interviewer should have background in personnel psychology, should understand the applicant's point of view, and should be perceptive and sensitive to the way his behavior affects the applicant. An interview is essentially an unrehearsed

Role Playing

play in which the two persons involved are both playwrights and actors. Hence, role playing is particularly appropriate in the training of interviewers and is usually an essential part of such training courses as it provides learning by doing. The aim is to increase the interviewer's flexibility as well as his skill and to give him experience in meeting different kinds of situations appropriately and effectively (Barron). In interviewer training sessions, each participant has opportunities to play the part of the applicant as well as that of the interviewer; hence, he experiences first hand what it means to be on the other end of the interview process. If the problems are similar to those with which he will have to cope in real life, he obtains valuable vicarious experience.

In his research report, "Analysis of Social Interaction: Actual, Roleplaying and Projective," E. F. Borgatta found that observations of role playing corresponded more closely to real life behavior than did paper and pencil projective techniques. In other words, the more similar a test is to the function itself, the better is the degree of validity of measurement. Thus a person's typewriting ability is tested on a typewriter and his swimming ability by performance in a swimming pool. Therefore, if one wants to know how a person acts in relation to others, a role playing test is more effective than interviewing him, or asking him to fill out a questionnaire, or by giving him a paper and pencil projective test.

In recent years some industrial and governmental agencies have incorporated role playing situations into their employee screening procedures. Reports from such uses indicate that the technique brings out the abilities and the weaknesses of the applicants much better than paper credentials and personal interviews. For example, in screening applicants for a secretarial position, each applicant played the role of the secretary for half an hour or longer. The personnel director played the role of visitor to the office and the man for whom she would work played himself. The applicant sat at the secretary's desk, answered phone calls from another role player, received guests (personnel director), and took care of demands from the employer.

A city police department identified applicants who were likely to succeed and eliminated those who would probably fail (Dillman). The U.S. Air Force screened officer candidates by measuring their potential military performance and effectiveness (Tupes). Paynter described an experiment in an industry where the selection interview was supplemented with a role playing situation. In this instance, role playing was considered a means of testing theory in practice and the author suggested that it should be conducted by a person experienced in interviewing techniques. A study of three job interview situations and the subjects' interpersonal behavior was reported by Weinstein.

Vocational and job counselors working with the unemployed poor have special problems. These unsophisticated clients have had little or no experience in understanding the fairly common signals which the general public uses to guide their behavior in new situations. Under the sponsorship of the Department of Labor Manpower Administration, a manual was prepared for use in employment agencies serving disadvantaged persons: Role Modeling and Role Playing in Employability Development Agencies by Jesse E. Gordon and others. The entire manual was focused on role playing for four reasons: these techniques (1) had great potential for enhancing the employability of disadvantaged persons, (2) were seldom used expertly and appropriately, (3) did not require advanced or specialized training for effective and easy use, and (4) were appropriate for a variety of settings but did not require elaborate resources. The personnel participating in creating the manual discovered that the body of role playing theory and research appeared to be unknown to those working in employment agencies; consequently these principles were included in the manual along with practical examples of application.

The manual was directed to those individuals who are trying to improve the employability of disadvantaged persons: counselors, coaches, community aides, vocational and basic education instructors, and employment agency administrators. Typical of the kinds of client needs were: learning job skills, getting along with others, using good work habits, and avoiding behavior which endangered employability. The manual included such uses for role playing as: diagnosis, rehearsal, problem-solving, modeling, attitude changes, and producing self-awareness. The term "role modeling" was defined as how to be and act in a role by imitating someone else performing that role. Throughout the manual, specific examples of role playing were given, such as: preparing job applicants for hiring interviews; "mock" interviews in which job applicants, who were being taught how to look for a job, were sent to a cooperating employer for a practice interview; reviewing an unsuccessful interview and practicing different ways of handling it; changing the attitudes of clients toward persons with whom they disagreed, disliked, or did not understand; demonstrating an ideal interview; acting out on-the-job personal problems; practicing appropriate role behavior; and one-to-one counseling.

Librarians involved in employing Puerto Ricans, Mexican-Americans, black Americans, Appalachia whites, and shy, unsophisticated and frightened poor persons would find this manual to be rewarding reading. "Some Suggestions Concerning the First Stage in the Client-Case Worker Relationship," by Frank Reissman also has some good ideas for librarians when interviewing low income persons. He points out that role playing has the potential advantage of reducing the distance between client and interviewer, of lessening negative consequences of a directive approach, and of providing an opportunity for the client to express his feelings.

In a three-month on-the-job-training program in New York City, Mobilization for Youth, Bloomingdale's Department Store, and a local union cooperated (Lorber). Twenty-nine young people aged 17 to 22 who were literate at the seventh grade level were oriented to department store work and skill training through role playing and instruction on how to act while applying for a job.

A project to find employment for three thousand disadvantaged young men and women was described in a report from the Chicago Urban League entitled Jobs Now. The primary objective was to help the clients attain employment readiness. Subjects considered in the workshop sessions were: transportation and orientation to the city, grooming and personal hygiene, money management, human relations training, and job orientation. Question-and answer-sessions, role playing, problem solving, discussions, and field trips were the instructional methods used.

A report from the Civil Service Commission described training programs conducted by federal agencies for non-college youth employed during the summer of 1966: "Youth Opportunity Campaign." The programs varied according to the mission and size of the agency and with the number and dispersion of noncollege youth employees. On-the-job-training was the educational method most extensively used but other methods such as lectures, discussions, role playing, question-and answer-sessions, films, and slide presentations were also utilized. Agencies provided individual and group counseling and a variety of skill training.

A pilot study by Charles Dailey, Project Gatekeeper, designed a program for training employers to interact with disadvantaged job applicants during job interviews and to evaluate their career potential more accurately. Training methods included videotape recordings and playback, audiotape recordings of interviews and playback, sensitivity training, role playing (simulated interviewing), and case studies.

Religious education

In his article "Using Role Playing in Christian Education," Charles Burns pointed out how religious education problems of many kinds were easier to solve through spontaneous role playing dramatizations because situations could be set forth without involving personal emotions. He defined and described several variations of role playing: problem or tension-centered, alter-ego, invisible consultants, solo role playing, and the use of puppets in roles.

Teenagers playing roles representing Protestant, Catholic, Jewish, and Negro prejudices presented problems for discussion involving open-ended conflict in intergroup relations (Crean). Techniques of presentation were described.

A study of the junior leader training programs for teenagers conducted by the Young Men's Christian Association investigated elements which affected leader growth and development (Colton). The training experience was keyed to broad YMCA purposes and stressed responsibility for oneself and others, human relations, Christian social influences, decision making, and moral values. Procedures utilized in the programs included modified sensitivity training, discussion, role playing, and demonstrations.

The Christian Education Department of the Episcopal Church held "laboratories" to help their ministers handle everyday problems of running their churches (Dramatization . . .). Such subjects as the following were role played: the emotions which parishioners may experience as they try to do church work; the problems ministers face in trying to bring order and efficiency to meetings of vestrymen, women's auxiliaries, and adolescents; and other areas of a minister's work.

Counselors. -- The "Development of Dormitory Staff

Role Playing

as Sub-Professional Counselors" was the title of a report by Ronald Jackson. Some head residents and undergraduate assistants in residence halls at the University of North Dakota were given counseling-oriented, in-service training to meet the educational and developmental needs of resident students. Sessions covered self-understanding, counseling theory and process, recognition and referral of symptoms and problems, and developmental psychology of college students. Films, lectures, role playing, and group discussions were used and readings were suggested.

A project at Monmouth, Oregon, was described by Beard and Standish which utilized a simulated counseling interview as the instructional vehicle. After training, all subjects were required to counsel a role playing client.

The pre-camp training period for camp counselors is a most essential phase of any camping program. At this time the camp director (1) becomes acquainted with his staff, (2) indoctrinates them with the camp policy and traditions, (3) assigns duties and responsibilities, (4) orients them to the camp site and its facilities and equipment, and (5) teaches inexperienced counselors new skills. In this training, role playing offered the counselors a medium for becoming more sensitive to human relations problems and more aware of the camper's feelings (Kessel).

New careers (human service aides)

A number of programs exist for training persons from disadvantaged backgrounds through on-the-job training and other methods for jobs in fields of human or public service in which a person-to-person relationship exists between the receiver and the provider of the services. Goals of new career programs are to provide meaningful entry jobs for the disadvantaged, advancement opportunities for all human service agency employees through in-service training, and development of newly skilled and professional manpower through "career ladders" from nonprofessional entry jobs to professional positions by means of formal work-study programs. Employing agencies are motivated to make changes in their structures, supervisory patterns, and attitudes to accommodate new careerists. The programs and accomplishments in these various human and public service areas should be relevant for the library profession. Many of the ideas could be implemented in libraries. Some of these new career programs in health services were described earlier in this

chapter under "Health sciences." Programs also exist in
the fields of social services, recreation, law enforcement,
corrections, rehabilitation, and education.

Role playing is an essential component of the training
methods in each of the programs described below. "Role
Play in New Careers Training," by Pantagua and Jackson,
defines the function of role playing in this context. Consideration is given to (1) the protected environment of role
play, (2) role play as an aid to group processes and increased self-knowledge, (3) implications for teaching communication and leadership skills, (4) modification of behavior
through role playing, and (5) suggested techniques and methods for the trainer in conducting role playing sessions.

Under the sponsorship of the Bureau of Work-Training
Programs of the Manpower Administration, Pointer and Fishman designed a manual which presents the fundamentals of
the new careers training model: "New Careers, Entry-Level
Training For the Human Service Aide." The manual includes
a glossary of new careers program components, basic concepts and principles of the new careers program, training
design, training methods, and program certification and accreditation.

The New Careers Development Center reported "A
Design For Large Scale Training of Subprofessionals" in
which core-skill training enabled five hundred nonprofessionals
to assume entry-level civil service positions in police, health
and welfare, inspections, and housing and relocation work.
Trainers had to be trained in knowledge of tasks to be performed by nonprofessionals, learning styles of low-income
populations, agency structure and tradition, and methodology
and training design. The program for trainees involved three
phases. During the first four-week phase, trainees learned
basic job skills through such methods as role playing and
job simulation and acquired an understanding of their change-
agent roles in the particular agencies involved. The second
phase was a four-week transitional period in which trainees
worked half a day on the job and participated in group discussion of work experiences and problems during the other
half of the day. In the third phase (which could last up to
two years depending upon the nature of the agency's work)
trainees worked on the job four days a week and received
special training on the fifth day. This fifth day might be
devoted to upgrading necessary core skills, high school equivalency work, advanced educational training, or working in a

different job in another agency.

A two-volume Training Manual For Human Service Technicians Working With Older People, by Louis Lowy, reported a Greater Boston project for training nonprofessionals to work with older adults. Volume 1 for trainers covered the qualifications and sources of training personnel, curriculum planning, training objectives, training methods and techniques (lectures, buzz sessions, discussion, workshops, role playing, and field work), and program planning and organization. Volume 2 for trainees contained curriculum materials, problems of aging and the aged in American society, resources to meet the needs of older adults in the community, and approaches to working with this age group at the individual, group, and community levels.

Gertrude Goldberg and others designed a manual for trainers of social service aides in new careers training programs. The trainer's responsibilities were defined as establishing and maintaining relationships with agency staff; getting to know the backgrounds of trainees; overcoming trainee anxieties and insecurity; orienting aides to the agency, community, and clientele; selecting materials to be covered; and preparing a kit for trainees. The manual contained an explanation of the new careers training model, a glossary of new careers terms, and training methods and techniques (lecture, observation, discussion, participation, reading, audio-visual aids, skill and process learning, demonstration, case study, and role playing). An accompanying manual for trainees contained the basic social services curriculum.

The Rutgers Labor Education Center held a ten-day residential training program in 1967 to train trade unionists and Community Action staff workers as Community Action trainers (Eiger). The purposes of the program were to understand the role of the trainer, to develop skills and knowledge in working with groups and in implementing community action training programs, to heighten self-awareness, and to investigate anti-poverty legislation. The curriculum included group discussion, films, role playing, field trips, and analysis of decision making.

Shortages in trained personnel for preschool child care and Head Start led to a pilot program at Southern Illinois University which was described by Naomi Naylor. The purposes of the program were: to develop a training model for non-professional preschool aides, to determine the value of selection criteria in trainee success, to evaluate the trainees' understanding, and to develop materials suitable for non-professionals. A four-week observation period using role playing, audio-visual aids, discussion groups, creative arts, and lecture-demonstrations was followed by a twelve-week practice teaching period.

Recommendations regarding the training of school personnel to work as teams was discussed by Bowman and Klopf in a paper, "Training for New Careers and Roles in the American School." Contents of the paper include administrative actions necessary prior to the introduction of auxiliary or paraprofessional personnel into the school, the purpose of team training, training objectives, competencies which need to be learned by all team members (administrators, supervisors, teachers, librarians, and paraprofessionals), and training techniques (which included case study and role playing).

Youth Tutoring Youth is an after school (or summer) tutorial program in which fourteen and fifteen year old underachievers who are enrolled in the in-school Neighborhood Youth Corps earn money by helping younger children (also underachievers) enjoy reading, writing, and other skills of expression. The program involves community members as supervisors. Two supervisor's manuals for these tutorial programs have been prepared by the National Commission on Resources For Youth and were published in 1968 with similar titles. They present information about goals, organization, recruiting, funding, aspects of the program, resources, remediation, role playing, and workshops.

Police

In his Ph. D. dissertation, "Role Learning For Police Recruits," John McNamara studied the recruit training program of the New York City Police Department to identify and clarify organizational and social psychological problems pertaining to the legality of police actions, prestige of police officers, interpersonal methods effective in police work, and organizational factors in the department. Data were obtained from department records, observation, role playing exercises, the critical incident technique, and questionnaires. Problems of police inactivity, organizational loyalty, and innovation were linked to problems in training.

A demonstration project designed to improve police-juvenile relations through juvenile attitude change and police understanding was carried out by the University of Cincinnati under the sponsorship of the U.S. Department of Justice. A curriculum guide was developed for social studies teachers pertaining to the law and law enforcement and for Cincinnati police trainees dealing with the nature of the early adolescent. The police training helped policemen gain an understanding of their own attitudes as well as those of juveniles.

Adult Meetings and Programs

In this section, examples will be described of role playing utilized in meetings or conferences involving individuals engaged in a variety of occupations and professions who have a diversity of educational backgrounds. These programs are not formal classroom instruction and they are not training programs; they are a means of informing the public on current or other issues. Adult study groups of various kinds, civic and service club meetings, parent-teacher association programs, and others often recreate community situations or social problems through role playing. Typical of such programs are: family life problems (Jennings), child study (Sherwin), adult leadership (Hendry), desegregation in the public schools, urban education (Hunnicutt), minority housing, juvenile delinquency, corruption in government, prejudice, political behavior, international relations, community development (Fessler), and aging and youth problems (Goldfarb and Reissman).

Criminology

In the summer of 1969 the Workshop on Crime and Correction was held for ten days on the campus of St. John's College in Annapolis, Maryland (Goldfarb) (Hammer). More than one hundred participated--twenty seasoned convicts doing time in the Maryland prison system and the rest were trial judges, police, prosecutors, probation and parole officers, legislators, psychologists, correction officials, and private citizens from Maryland. Sessions were scheduled for ten hours a day after which the convicts went back to their prisons; but informal sessions continued on into the night with most of the rest of the participants. Some of the prisoners were serving terms as short as two years, others had been sentenced to "life plus"; some had been behind bars for only one year, others for twenty years or longer. Crimes ranged from possession of narcotics to burglary, rape and murder.

The most dramatic and distinctive feature of the conference was a series of role playing episodes portraying typical prisoner's careers: being mustered into the prison "jungle," the netherworld, subculture of convict life within prisons, the parole experience, the ultimate reentry into society, and other episodes. Many role reversals were acted out--after real prisoners appeared before real parole officers, each group switched roles and played the other. The results were often devastatingly accurate. Several role playing sessions were quoted verbatim in the two references listed above.

The purpose of the conference was to get problems concerning corrections out into the open with all the relevant participants present and all being honest and frank. The various participants contradicted, pressed, ridiculed, until the problems and the lies eventually came out into the open. One day midway in the conference many of the non-convicts were processed through one of the three represented penal institutions as if they actually were arriving inmates. The officials processing them did not know that they were not convicts. The purpose was more role playing--to get the feel of the horror that lies at the end of the present correction system. They were stripped, showered, sprayed, mugged, pushed around, and locked up in dark, tiny cells and forgotten.

Would library workshops like the above be as great a shock to librarians as that conference was to its participants? For example, on a university campus, if a workshop consisting of a representative sampling of students, faculty members, university fiscal officers, and library staff members role played library service, wouldn't this probably dramatically reveal deficiencies in service and user gripes? Or, a meeting of non-users, typical users, city officials, and library staff members of a public library to discuss library programs, branch library locations, and services. Such meetings should be most effective vehicles for communication and feedback from the public.

Grievance procedures

In the settlement of tedious labor-management disputes, role playing has provided a way for each side to understand the position, feelings, interests, concerns, and behavior of the other side. A successful do-it-yourself technique for arbitrating grievances was reported by Thomas. He suggested that before discharging an employee, an in-company mock arbitration hearing be held with the foreman and the personnel manager playing the roles which they would carry out in an actual grievance procedure. The various factors which would normally come up in such a procedure should be anticipated: provocation for the grievance, the severity of the offense, the employee's service record, the firm's policies and rules, and any precedents established by similar cases in the past.

In another instance, labor relations counselors learned how to handle grievances better and to reduce their incidence during the role playing of situations (Speroff). The method permitted a trainee alternately to do, then observe, then do again; it was found to be an effective training device.

A comprehensive simulation kit for school administrators focusing on grievance procedures was constructed and presented as a special feature in the June 1969 issue of Nation's Schools (Shapiro). The purposes were to familiarize the administrators with grievance processes and procedures; and to make them aware of the need to manage conflict so that their organizations would not get torn apart by the hostility generated by conflicting interests. The hypothetical school district was faced with three separate and independent grievance situations. Each participant was assigned to play one of the twenty-two roles. The kit included background information about the school district, the community, the teachers association, the formal grievance code, and an organizational chart of the school system. For each of the three grievances, the problem was described, roles were written for each participant, and instructions for playing were outlined.

As a Research Methodology

Three articles reported the use of role playing as a research tool--in sociological surveys, in public opinion formation, in cultural anthropology, and in communication.

<u>Sociology</u>

That role playing can be used to obtain data in regular sociological surveys was demonstrated by Stanton, Back, and

Litwak. They asserted that data gathered by this method may prove better than traditional interview procedures where the inquiry is concerned with the respondent's behavior under stress or when the respondent is strongly affected by his perceptions of the reactions of others. The authors found that most respondents could role play, training interviewers was easy to administer, the results could be quickly and reliably scored, and the results were valid. The following surveys were made: parent-child relationships in foster-parent households, marital adjustment in upper-middle-class United States family households, and social-psychological factors in housing of residents of slums and housing projects in Puerto Rico.

Public opinion

The process of opinion formation was simulated by Davison through a "public opinion game." He suggested that adaptations of this game might serve as a research methodology. Players were arbitrarily assigned roles and were supplied with such information about "themselves" as home geographic area, sex, age, marital status, number of children, socio-economic status, occupation, religious affiliation, and organizational memberships. After each player had studied his role, he was "interviewed" by giving him a sheet of paper on which he checked appropriate replies to selected public issues. He was asked to react to these issues in a manner which he thought was appropriate for his role. After completion of this sheet, each player was given a second sheet on which he gave his weighted opinions on the issues he had answered on the preceding sheet. These opinions were then tabulated and the results presented to the whole group. The author stated that this procedure illustrated the way socio-economic status, personal interests, primary group affiliations, secondary group membership, and other factors entered into the formation of individual opinions on public issues. He believed this technique could also highlight the difference between private opinion and public opinion, could indicate the mechanism through which a relatively few individuals could influence the opinions of a large number of persons, and show the effects of publicity and public discussion on the opinions of a population.

Cultural anthropology

Because direct observation of drug-related behavior in the streets poses serious difficulties for the cultural anthropologist, the subculture of drug addiction was studied by using informants in a non-street simulated situation (Agar). Volunteer inmates in the Clinical Research Center of the National Institute of Mental Health at Lexington, Kentucky, were the actors who attempted to recreate real role behavior. Rather than asking about situations, informants were asked to act out situations as they would have occurred in the streets. The assumption was that this would achieve a closer approximation to the real-life situation than any other technique. The inmates acted out such situations as: obtaining drugs when withdrawal sickness had begun; robbing a drug dealer; meeting between an ex-addict and a group of friends who were still addicts; purchasing drugs from a pusher; and returning to a pusher to complain about the poor quality of drugs. Three to five role played at a time in a conference room equipped with tape recording equipment. The only observer was the anthropologist who sat at one end of the room partially hidden by the recording equipment. The group decided what they would enact. They knew the purpose of the enactment. The tape recording was played immediately following the session and any material that a patient felt was potentially harmful to himself was erased. Several checks were devised for assessing the behavior in the simulation to determine how true to life it was.

Communication

Using role playing and critique methodology, the effects on learning caused by self-confrontation via video tape replay compared with audio tape replay were investigated by Thomas Stroh. Twenty-five experienced industrial salesmen were taught listening skills, the use of open-ended and reflective questions, and related techniques. Each role played three sales interviews in private with the investigator.

Techniques: Steps in the Process

Techniques employed in role playing vary with the locale, the group (children, college students, adults) and their degree of readiness and experience with the method, the goals to be achieved, the supervisory level, the subject, the complexity of the case, and other factors. When the method is used for the first time in library school classes, in library workshops, or continuing library education programs, probably considerable preparation would be necessary to get the group ready for the experience. Role playing may take place under a variety of circumstances but its effective use depends upon the leader's knowledge of it, his assurance in using it, and his making the necessary preparation.

The Leader

The leader is responsible for creating a suitable environment, selecting the problem to be explored, choosing the actors, developing the techniques of enactment, deciding when to cut enactments, and leading the evaluation session.

The environment or "climate" should encourage frank expression of ideas and feelings. The leader is not completely non-directive but he should try to stay in the background as much as possible. He should encourage sincere, frank expression so that feelings and perceptions may be brought to the surface for exploration in an environment where it is safe to examine all facets of a problem. This position is based on the belief that the individual needs opportunity and support from the leader and from the group in facing and working through the life situations in which he must act and make a decision. Such a "climate" demands that the leader have skills in asking open-ended questions, in listening for meanings, and in asking clarifying questions, as well as in knowing what sequence the procedures should occur.

The leader must orient the group to the concept and methods of role playing so as to win their acceptance of the technique as a teaching-learning device. He must develop an understanding in the group of the principles and methods of handling others that are allied to effective human relations. He must be familiar with procedures which characterize the conduct of role playing sessions. His function is to guide, to prod, to summarize; he does not use role playing as a camouflaged vehicle for lectures. Both the development of the case and the analysis of the role playing should be participant-centered; neither should be fashioned to fit the supervisory style of the leader. The leader must be constantly alert to subtle changes in the relations between the role players; and to signs of vacillation, frustration, defensiveness, evasion, intimidation, or paternalism.

The leader should reserve the right to stop the game at any moment if necessary. Some of the reasons why a leader might wish to end the play are: if the game goes beyond its goal, if the players are rambling away from the focus of the enactment, if the action lags or resembles a charade, if players have exhausted their roles, if the emotional tension of either the players or of the observers becomes too great, if a player slips out of his role, or if the plot is being distorted.

Leaders should be warned of possible "pitfalls" in using role playing. First, in their enthusiasm for this method, some leaders have negated its value by using it too often. It should be used infrequently or it will lose the freshness which is necessary to bring out the actual feelings of the participants.

Second, avoid uncovering serious personality problems which require professional help of clinicians. When participants are uncomfortable or embarrassed, more harm than good will be accomplished if action is continued. Role playing for librarians must be kept in the area of the learning situation.

The third, and probably the major pitfall, concerns the depth of personal feeling that goes into the drama. Role playing is supposed to represent typical situations and the actors are supposed to represent typical persons. The leader must see to it that it does not focus primarily upon an individual situation in which the players are acting out their own personal problems. At this point, it is no longer action-training but rather a "psychodrama" which requires a much greater degree of skill to handle and which is beyond the scope of most librarians. The leader has to be sensitive to this and when it does develop, he should step in and shift the direction of the play.

Physical Arrangements

Role playing can take place in about any physical setting: a conference room, an office, a classroom, or an auditorium are all appropriate depending upon the size of the audience and the purposes of the session. Physical arrangements should include a private room where participants will not be disturbed and which is of suitable size and shape to accommodate the participants. Chairs should be movable so that participants can form groups of varying size with comfort and ease. The players should sit informally in the natural situation in which the action would take place. Each must be able to see the other and, if there is an audience, all the players should be visible. None or a minimum of props would be used. If enactment is staged before a large audience, the participants should be on an elevated platform with a microphone so everyone can hear.

Selecting the Problem

The leader has a number of choices to make in determining what problem should be discussed. Is the enactment to be spontaneous or unstructured; or, is it to be structured either by the leader or by utilizing a prepared case? The choice will depend upon the outcome desired or needed by the group at the time, the availability of suitable printed or prepared cases, and the skill of the leader.

Spontaneous or creative role playing is more difficult for the leader to direct because he looks for the problem to develop from the individuals in the group. The success of this type of approach depends on the leader's skill and ability to stimulate meaningful problems and upon a climate of acceptance and cooperation on the part of group members. Suggestions as to problem and players come from the group. This type has been used with school children, with training groups in individual industrial plants to improve interpersonal relations within the plant, and has potential for training programs within a library system. When using role playing for the first time, simple situations which are familiar to the participants should be used. For example, such problems as the assigning of parking spaces or time for rest breaks.

Spontaneous role playing is not unstructured from the point of view of the leader because he must always work within a rigorous, conceptual framework. However, such a framework should not inhibit his own ability to respond spontaneously to the needs and goals of the group.

The leader's preparation for directing spontaneous or creative role playing usually takes the form of writing notes beforehand about the background of the problem or situation which is to be enacted, the order in which the principal actors are to be instructed about their parts, and descriptions of each character including actions, motivations, and point of view. Reality is greatly enhanced in a human relations situation if each character gets only his side of the problem. Thus, if all the actors are out of the room and each is instructed only in as much of the total situation as he would normally be aware of, then the players can be expected to react normally to the disclosure of other aspects of the situation as the play progresses. The audience would hear all of the instructions.

For library school classes, library workshops, and executive development programs, probably the structured approach is more desirable because these groups would not have the common background of information that a staff in a library system would have. In this approach a written case with a clear, precise problem, identifiable roles and background information should be used. The case can either be assigned ahead of time or distributed and read at the beginning of the session. Whether or not the participants read the case before the session depends upon the leader, the complexity of the problem, the purposes to be achieved, and the maturity of the group in role playing techniques. In a library school class, usually the case should be on a subject about which the instructor has already lectured and the students have already read. In other words, a problem related to the subject-orientation of the portion of the course considered that day. For example, if the students have been studying motivation, the case should be some aspect of that subject.

The problem situation should have some element of challenge to the group. The design should not be highly complex because, if it is too filled with plot and counterplot, the actors and observers may become confused and the points may be missed. The situation should be specific, clear, and short. Clarity is of great importance. All concerned must understand the situation, the roles, the problem, and what they are trying to do.

Written cases may include instruction for the leader as well as for the players. For example, in their casebook Supervisory and Executive Development, Maier, Solem, and Maier introduce each case with a detailed section entitled "Focusing the Problem" which is written for the guidance of the leader. Usually this section includes (1) a description of the general class of problem illustrated by the case, (2) an indication of the primary training function, (3) the degree of skill required by the trainees, (4) the principles involved in the problem, and (5) any other information the authors think essential for utilizing the case. Shorter and less detailed "Director's Notes" introduce the problem in each case in Roleplaying in Business and Industry by Corsini, Shaw, and Blake.

Preparing and Instructing the Group

Some writers call this step "warming up." In elementary grades, teachers often start with a game of charades or pantomiming in order to give everyone practice in communicative skills before introducing the role playing problem. The purpose of preparation is to acquaint the group with the problem such as background information and how the problem fits into the fabric of the course unit considered on this particular day or how the problem is related to the purposes and goals of a workshop or continuing education program. The problem should be one that is important to the group, one with which they can immediately identify, and one which they feel a need to learn to cope with. For example, a group of library supervisors might want to consider how to handle the problem of the employee who is scheduled to be on duty at a public service desk when the library opens and who is habitually late.

The setting of the dramatization and any other items the group needs to know ahead of time should be explained. Procedures should be agreed upon so that the group knows what to expect. The session should have some kind of a timetable as guide lines: how long for warm up, how long for enactment, and how long for discussion and evaluation.

Each player must be informed about his role. Instructions should include enough detailed information about the character and his problem so that the player can assume his identity without any difficulty.

One important part of the "warming up" is the preparation of the observing group to participate actively, receptively, and intelligently. Uninstructed observers may watch passively and be bored. The observers can be given a list of questions to consider about the problem as they listen; or, they can be assigned specific tasks such as to observe one character or concentrate on consequences of actions suggested by the players.

Much of the value of role playing depends upon the discussion after enactment. If the observers have been actively listening and observing they tend to have more interest in the problem and the evaluation. The players tend to do a better job if they see the observers to be serious, attentive, and concerned.

Enactment: Playing the Game

The players assume their roles and "live" the situation, responding to one another's conversations and actions as they feel the persons in those roles would behave. No player is expected to present his role flawlessly--slips and awkward moments are taken for granted. The group should understand that the way an actor portrays a role has no reflection upon him as a person; he is simply presenting a role as he sees it. No player should be evaluated for his acting. An enactment is not a play, it is reality practice.

Single group role playing

The two most commonly used enactment procedures are single group role playing and multiple group role playing. In the single group type, one group performs while all the other members of the group participate as observers. Several variations of the single group method can be used; three of these are described below--more than one enactment, role reversal, and all participants divided into as many groups as there are roles.

More than one enactment. -- For some types of problems, more than one enactment is desirable. For example, have two or more sets of participants read the problem and the instructions and while the first set is acting, the second set is kept out of the room so they do not hear the first enactment. After completion of the first enactment, the second set of players come in to enact the same problem. This technique permits the observers to see how different individuals handle the same problem. A good example of this technique was described for a marriage education course (Shipman). Instructions for each player were typed on cards and handed to him as he came into class. One player was the "husband" whose role called for his reading the newspaper after dinner for a few minutes before leaving to play poker with some friends. A succession of girls played the role of a very fatigued wife. The instructions to the girls were to persuade the "husband" to help with the dishes. The girls came in one at a time to play the role. None of them had heard what the other "wives" had said. The class, then, could evaluate the impact on the "husband" of different personalities, persuasive techniques, and results.

Role reversal. -- Role reversal is an interesting variation of the single group method. After one enactment, the two players switch roles and each puts himself in the other's place. Usually, they not only change roles but also change chairs. Each person gets the experience of seeing things from the other's point of view. Role reversal helps to alleviate conflict by reducing self-defensiveness, by increasing one's understanding of the other's views, and by becoming aware of the positive features in the other's viewpoint and the dubious elements in one's own position. This technique can be very effective and is especially valuable for the stubborn, inflexible individual who has a narrow concept of the problem. To make role reversal more dramatic, the players can wear masks and, when they change roles and chairs, also change masks.

An interesting example of the use of role reversal was reported by Ablesser. Four adolescents met in a youth counseling office for a psychotherapy session. All of them were single ranging in age from seventeen to nineteen and had a similar difficulty: they had all stolen cars and were subsequently arrested. They did not know each other and had gotten involved at different times, dates and places. The purpose of the session was to learn the rationale of their involvement; their feelings in the vehicle immediately subsequent to their having stolen it, and what lesson, if any, they had learned as a result of their involvement. The role reversal technique was used to have them experience how they would feel if they were the respective owners of the vehicles involved. Each of the counselees had an opportunity to be the "owner."

Weiringa variation. -- An interesting variation of the single group method has been developed by C. F. Weiringa of the University Institute for Management Education, Utrecht, Netherlands. All participants were divided into as many groups as there were roles. Each group was instructed to ask themselves what the problem looked like from the point of view of their particular role. They considered alternative behavior for this player, chose one alternative, and elected one of their group to play the role before the whole class. Advantages of this procedure were: (1) the participants built up strong role identification, (2) the player felt secure in his role because he was representing his group's concept of that role, and (3) the observers were involved more directly because they had participated in identifying the role and of instructing their player. At the end of the enactment, each player exchanged experiences with his original group. Following this, the entire group evaluated and discussed the problem, the issues, and the enactment.

Masks. -- At times there are roles and situations

which seem too personal, sensitive, threatening, or controversial for any group member to take. For example, subjects involving ethics, morals, personal appearance, behavior, or political or social action. For such enactments, some leaders have found masks or puppets an excellent presentation method. The masks need not be elaborate but can simply be paper bags with faces drawn upon them. If an inanimate object is used, the player's feelings can be projected into the object. Invariably a child or an adult who dons a mask begins spontaneously to act out the role suggested by the mask and feels no inhibitions or embarrassment.

In his "America's Culturally Different Children," Donelson suggested the use of masks to help children understand cultural differences and similarities. By role playing ceremonies and feast days of ethnic groups, children can be stimulated in learning cultural traditions.

Multiple group role playing

In multiple role playing, the entire audience is formed into groups. The size of each group depends upon the number of participants required for the case to be enacted. All groups role play simultaneously. This procedure (1) places every person in a situation where it is impossible for him to escape direct oral participation, (2) dispels any feelings of shyness or selfconsciousness, (3) intensifies the discussion following enactment as all participants have been emotionally involved in the case, (4) provides an opportunity for everyone to try out his attitudes and behavior, and (5) produces a number of different solutions to the same case and thus demonstrates variations in group interaction.

A variation of multiple role playing is that utilizing dyads or pair groups. Weinstein reported having twenty pairs of college students enacting a situation simultaneously. The problem centered around criticism of one person by his close friend. The purposes were to isolate components of interpersonal behavior from individual traits and to investigate modes of resolving interpersonal stress. After completion of this enactment, the roles were reversed with the same partners re-enacting the scene. In another situation, (Zeleny) dyads were found to be especially suitable in dealing with controversial and current issues in a social studies class.

Feedback: Discussion, Analysis, and Evaluation

Typically, a role playing scene is followed by a discussion among both participants and observers which provides feedback on performance. These discussions usually cover the way in which each role was played, the manner in which the situation in the scene developed, and an examination of the insights gained from the process. Normally, after enactment, discussion begins on a high level of interest and intensity both by the actors and by the observers. Frequently discussion will bring out other alternative courses of action. The group may even decide to repeat the enactment possibly using different participants to show another way that the problem could have been handled. The leader should insist that while discussing the roles, the members use the fictitious names used in the enactment. This tends to center attention on the role playing and not on the individual player. Talking about a "role" is less personal.

Several methods of feedback can be used. The simplest and most common method is to ask the observers and participants to comment on individual performances. If the group wanders off on minor details not pertinent to the central issue, the leader may wish to interject some questions or remarks to bring them back to the issue.

Another method is to use buzz groups. The large group is broken into subgroups with instructions to discuss the enactment and to summarize ideas. The consensus of each buzz group is then reported by one member serving as a recorder for the whole group. The advantage of buzz groups is that every individual is likely to participate and, since the players cannot hear the discussion, a more honest and accurate level of reporting can be expected. After the recorders have reported, the entire group may rediscuss the various issues.

A third method (if the group is not too large) is to ask each individual in the group to make a short comment--usually a simple sentence. No interruptions are permitted until each member has spoken. The comments may be listed on a blackboard and later can serve as the basis for group discussion.

A fourth method is to record the role playing on tape, then play the tape during the analysis period (Dworkis) (Agar). This gives the actors an opportunity to hear themselves and

Role Playing   91

helps the whole group to draw principles from the case which would guide supervisors in handling this type of problem more effectively.

In a training program when a group has met for a number of role playing sessions, Corsini, Shaw, and Blake recommend the use of "observation guides." Their "Leadership Rating Sheet" and "Roleplaying Summary Sheet" are reproduced in Appendix II of their book, <u>Roleplaying in Business and Industry</u>. On the leadership sheet, trainees rated each other on stand, control, communication, attitude, emphasis, relations, structure, procedure, rate, and overall rating. Each individual was then given his own rating sheets which had been filled out by the other trainees and he tabulated them on a "Roleplaying Summary Sheet." This form contained a chart for each of the factors on which he was rated on the leadership form. By plotting his ratings on each chart, the trainee got feedback on his own performance which told him how others thought he was developing in terms of the various factors rated and shows graphically where he needed to improve.

Case Preparation and Writing

Some preparation must be made by the leader for all types of role playing cases. He must find a written case suitable for his use or construct his own. The writer is not aware of a single published role playing case in the field of library science and believes those appearing in this volume are the first. For that reason, some guide lines for preparing and writing cases seem appropriate to include in this chapter.

Even for spontaneous or creative role playing, the leader must do some preplanning and prestructuring. For instance, a librarian couldn't get up in a library meeting at which social action is being discussed and say on the inspiration of the moment "let's role play this" and expect the performance to be meaningful or effective. On the contrary, chaos would probably prevail. The leader must not only prepare some background notes but also must think through carefully and write out instructions for each player and must prepare the group for the experience. In addition, the leader must have a thorough command of the subject matter to be discussed which may require some research.

In the "classroom instruction" section of this chapter a number of examples of spontaneous role playing are cited. Although they may seem easy to do, in every case they were planned and directed by experienced teachers who were accustomed to developing learning activities. Librarians with no teaching experience might find spontaneous role playing difficult to direct until after they had acquired some experience with the technique by using prepared cases.

In classroom instruction, spontaneous role playing is consistently more effective when employed as a part of a unit of study. Prior to role playing, students need to become familiar with such information as the nature of the crisis or problem, with the various forces operating to influence the problem, and necessary background information.

Format and Structure of Published Cases

Librarians who wish to prepare their own cases will find that a study of the published cases cited in this section will provide models of the various types of cases. In addition, the section "Applications of Role Playing" in this chapter which described unique and innovative uses for role playing will also serve as models.

Written cases which the writer has read varied considerably in format and structure. The simplest of all, and probably the easiest to write, were the problem and unfinished stories for children referred to earlier in this chapter written by Chesler and Fox, the National Education Association, Nichols and Williams, and the Shaftels. The elementary school librarian or children's librarian wishing to write such stories for use in teaching library skills, should read some of these for writing style, length, and content. The writing should probably be the same as for writing any fictional short stories. The ideas for problem stories usually evolve from class or library experiences or individual problems. By observing and talking with children in the class or in a library, a leader learns their concerns and then writes each problem into an unfinished story to be enacted in class. These stories present a problem or an incident of concern to the group for whom they are written. The narrative proceeds to a point where some solutions are needed or discussion required and then stops.

An important obligation of the leader in selecting situations is to ensure the personal security and privacy of each individual involved especially when enacting real-life problems. The focus of each story should be on one issue of a general nature rather than on the failings or deficiencies of individuals. The writer of these stories should aim toward balance of relevant issues, selecting neither meaningless ones nor ones that are too threatening.

A few of the periodical articles cited in the bibliography included a case or two written for use by adolescents or adults. The format for these was quite simple and usually included the "scene" or "background" consisting of about one paragraph and "role" or "instructions" for each player. These instructions included whatever information was required for him to identify with the role such as his point of view and personal characteristics and habits.

In one of the Appendixes to their book Roleplaying in Business and Industry, Corsini, Shaw, and Blake have developed ten cases which indicate various kinds of structure, format, and focusing. In addition to background information, instructions for players, and instructions for observers, at the beginning of each case is a section entitled "Director's Notes." One case is an example of a structured interrupted skit. The skit is like a play with dialogue written out for each of the two characters. Only enough information was given in the dialogue to clarify the problem and take it to the point of decision. The players read their parts in front of the group. When the skit ended, the players continued role playing in an effort to reach a solution. The authors suggested that skits are best used for evaluation purposes to demonstrate how the players "think on their feet." Skits are also valuable in presenting sensitive and ordinarily not-discussed problems or persistent problems. Such skits are usually read for the first time before the audience, but they may be given to participants to study in advance of the enactment.

Another case in the Corsini-Shaw-Blake volume is an example of a structured case designed for multiple groups to play a problem simultaneously. The case has Director's Notes, instructions for each player, and instructions for the observer. In this type of case the observer was given definite responsibilities and his instructions listed several questions on which he was to comment at the close of the enactment. After the acting, the various observers combined their criticisms and comments during the discussion.

Maier, Solem, and Maier published, in 1957, a book of role playing cases for use in supervisory and executive training. The cases were designed to give two kinds of practice in human relations training: (1) a method (role playing) which furnishes an opportunity to practice a human relations incident in a lifelike setting, and (2) a vehicle for discussion in which to analyze crucial issues. Both of these kinds of practice approach human relation issues as problems and emphasize skills in solving and presenting problems. The volume was written as a training manual for use by inexperienced leaders, by groups of persons who wished to form a study group and had no designated trainer or leader, and by an individual to study by himself for executive self-development. Because of these purposes, the authors gave more details and more explicit instructions than any of the cases cited in this chapter. The format was also more carefully structured and varied according to (1) whether there were several groups playing the same problem at the same time or whether a single group was doing it, and (2) the demands of the case. In general, this was the format they used (the headings vary somewhat from case to case):

I. Focusing the Problem
II. Role Playing Procedure
    Preparation
    Process
    Analysis
III. Materials
    General instructions (or background material)
    Role for each character
    Instructions for observers
IV. Comments and implications

In <u>Working Effectively Overseas</u> by Paul Spector and Harley O. Preston, the format includes the following headings: background, situation, your role, other's role, possible behavior (effective), possible behavior (ineffective), topics for discussion (general behavior requirements, relevance of behavioral requirements, cultural variations).

Reading the cases in the three books mentioned above would be valuable preparation for library educators who wished to write cases for use in classrooms and for librarians in public, academic, and special libraries who wish to write cases for use in workshops, conferences, institutes, or in-service training programs.

Role Playing

Writing role playing cases is not as difficult as writing other types of cases because they involve only one incident, have few characters, and are short. In Volume I of this series, Chapter 4 discussed rather thoroughly, case research and case writing for other kinds of cases. Perhaps those librarians wishing to construct their own cases should read that chapter for background information as the writing of a role playing case is similar in many respects to writing case studies. Those portions of that chapter which are especially applicable for writing role playing cases have been utilized in writing the paragraphs which follow--to which has been added additional information pertaining only to role playing cases.

Case Research

Research consists of identifying problems involving human and interpersonal relations in everyday work experience which have relevance to the participant's current responsibilities, his likely future assignments, or his relations with other staff members. To identify such problems, the case writer must have some understanding of supervision, the psychology of administration, administrative and organizational behavior, and the reasons why people work. In addition, the case writer must know enough about the subject of the case problem so that what he writes is accurate; and he must be able to identify interaction patterns and tension situations.

If the case writer is preparing cases for use in an in-service education program within his own library, he probably will want to use current problems occurring at the time in that library. But, if he is preparing cases for library science classes or for a continuing education or training program, he may need to use some of the following sources for ideas for cases: personal interviews with librarians, grievance hearings, annual reports of librarians, data from the files of library personnel offices, news items in library periodicals, or other sources.

Case writers need to cultivate sensitivity to what lies below the surface of events which he experiences, observes, or learns about. Being aware of what does not happen or is not said is as important as observing and reporting what did happen or what was said. A writer must learn to sense when a seemingly minor event may trigger a crisis and make use of the dynamics which made the situation a problem. After he has written several cases, the writer will become attuned to listening for problems which will make good teaching, learning, and training instruments.

Focusing and Shaping the Case

Before he starts writing, the case writer should (1) study all the data he has acquired about a certain problem, (2) decide on the problem focus toward which the facts and the enactment contribute, (3) select from the data what he considers significant to the focus, (4) decide on mode of presentation (skit, single or multiple role playing, etc.) and characters (less than five) and their roles. The next step is to shape the case so that it contributes to the goals for which it is written. The writer should try to capture a truthful picture of the elements in the problem and to represent reality accurately. The written case should be a literary creation in that it presents content in as interesting and dramatic a form as possible. He will find that much of the data he has acquired regarding the case is extraneous because it does not contribute directly to the focus. In gathering data, he cannot foresee just how much data will be required because, like any creative piece of work, the case may take a shape he could not visualize until he was in the act of writing.

Case writing is fundamentally no different from other forms of writing. The mechanics of good writing and literary standards which are outlined in basic guides to writing should be adhered to. These include good English, grammar, punctuation, choice of words, and style. Guides to writing short stories and plays are especially helpful if the writer wants to construct problem stories or skits.

After the case is written, check it by asking yourself some questions such as: is it plausible and realistic; is it clear and logical; is there enough background information; has enough information been provided for each role; has the writer slanted the case by using "colored" propagandistic words; is the case too detailed or not detailed enough, are more or less characters required.

Ideally, the case should be tested on a class or a group before it is used in any teaching or learning situation. This will show up inadequacies and point to the need for modifications or rewriting.

Role Playing

Fictitious names should be used for the characters, names of libraries, and any other identifications in the case. This provides anonymity to those who furnished the data as well as to the players in the case. Disguise helps in confining case analysis to the facts without destroying the essential reality of the situation.

An Effective Teaching Instrument

A number of suggestions to aid training specialists in translating experiences in their own plants into role playing situations were offered in "Guides to Writing Role Playing Cases" by Wallace Wohlking. His recommendations seem equally applicable to writing cases for classroom instruction or in adult meetings. He identified and described five characteristics which make a case an effective instrument:

(1) it should be easily understood--hence, long complex sentences and unnecessary facts and data should be avoided;
(2) it should stimulate and motivate the trainee;
(3) it should be written in such a way that the training group readily identifies with the problems;
(4) it should describe apparent behavior but avoid moralistic comments on behavior which would result in pre-judgment or stereotyped responses;
(5) it should not include information about complicated technical problems.

According to Mr. Wohlking, cases need conflicting motivations and goals to sustain the involvement both of players and of observers. He identified six categories of conflict resulting from (1) emotions and motives within the individual, (2) allegiances emerging as a result of pressures and demands on the individual, (3) perceptual differences arising from distortion in communication or perceptions, (4) differences of goals between the individual and the organization, (5) competition for position and power, and (6) unpleasant interaction related to the organization's technology, procedures, or norms.

With the guidance of this chapter and the bibliographical sources listed, any supervisor, administrator, personnel director, library educator, or workshop leader should be able to construct a case from current problems or situations arising on the job or some problem common to a group of librarians, assign roles for players, and select an enactment style to suit the group.

Summary

In this chapter an attempt has been made to define role playing; to present it as a technique applicable in teaching human and interpersonal relations to librarians; to compare and contrast it with other types of case studies; to cite applications of the technique in classroom instruction, in training programs, in adult meetings, and as a research methodology; to give sufficient detail about the process to enable readers to visualize what happens and how to proceed; to suggest sources for anyone wishing more information; and to offer guidelines for constructing and writing cases.

Although not exhaustive, this chapter is fairly comprehensive and representative of the printed sources of information about role playing in all subject fields and in all areas of education and training which seemed relevant and have implications for librarians. Hopefully, enough detail has been given so that librarians can use this valuable technique after reading this chapter. For those wishing more background than this chapter offers, the selected bibliography at the end of the book is provided.

Chapter II

PERSONNEL CASES

The cases in this chapter cover a rather wide spectrum of personnel problems which are representative of those involved in each of the ten personnel functions:

Recruitment and selection cases include such problems as job interviewing, position classification, certification, civil service, status personnel policies, and faculty rank.

Orientation, training and development cases include promotions, transfers, professional ethics, conflict of interest, personal appearance, grooming, nepotism, bribery, disloyalty, misrepresentation, termination, "privileged" information, academic freedom, and invasion of privacy.

Behavior and motivation cases include problems of work environment, performance, group conflicts, human relations, group behavior, anxiety, and insecurity.

Leadership and supervision cases are concerned with staff morale, delegation, rights of employees, authority and power, work rules and conduct, turnover, resistance to change, and personnel codes.

Participation in decision making and communication are represented by cases which present problems in library environment and climate, and barriers to communication.

Discipline problems include drug abuse, disloyalty, tardiness, arrest, absenteeism, insubordination, incompetence, probation, disciplinary action, theft, and murder.

Health and benefit cases include physical and mental illness, retirement, fringe benefits, and working conditions.

Case 1

WHO SHOULD HIRE LIBRARIANS?

(Role playing)

Roles:
    Jeff Amber, Director of Libraries, State University Library
    Bill Chert, Head, State University Library Personnel Office
    Arthur Quartz, Vice-President for Academic Affairs, State University

(Role players should represent the two opposing points of view and should bring out the reasons why each one thinks he should be responsible for selecting professional librarians. This will involve the question of academic status.)

* * *

Employment at State University is handled in three offices: faculty members receive their appointments through the Dean of Faculty's office, students are interviewed and screened through the Student Employment Office, and all other employees are processed through the University Personnel Office.

About six weeks after Jeff Amber became director of the University Library, he received a telephone call from Bill Chert, Head of the Personnel Office; "I have just received the latest edition of <u>A Classification Plan for Staff Positions at Colleges and Universities</u> published by the College and University Personnel Association (Urbana, Illinois: 1968). The job specifications for Librarians I, II, III, and IV differ in a number of respects from those we drew up for this campus five years ago. Will you please assign one of your staff members to work with me in revising the specifications for professional librarians so that they are in line with those printed in this book?"

Mr. Amber had never heard of this publication and inquired about its purpose and content. Mr. Chert replied, "This is the basic guide for position classification in colleges and universities. The overall organization of academic institutions is sufficiently different from the typical governmental, business, or industrial organization that academic

Personnel Cases 101

personnel officers need classification materials clearly identifiable with our particular requirements. This publication provides valuable guidelines for us. My staff and I are reviewing all of the job specifications in this volume with each area represented on this campus. The volume contains not only class specifications by areas of work, but also presents underlying principles and purposes of a classification plan for academic institutions; reasons for and limitations of job evaluation; the format and administration of class specifications; suggestions for assigning positions to classes; and audit, control, and maintenance of a classification plan. Sample job descriptions are given for all service areas represented in an academic institution: architectural, automotive, buildings and grounds, crafts and trades, custodial, data processing, editorial, electronic, engineering, fiscal (accounting, auditing, purchasing), food, heat and power, housing, laboratory, library, nursing, office, personnel, printing, safety and security, and stores."

Mr. Amber had not yet had time to investigate the employment procedures for library personnel, so he was ill-prepared for this request. His own appointment as full professor had come through the Dean of Faculty's office. He asked, "Do you mean to tell me that you search for and screen professional librarians as well as our supportive staff?"

Mr. Chert assured him that his office had always been responsible for all service personnel on campus, which included all library employees except the Director. With mounting impatience, Mr. Amber replied, "In my opinion, professional librarians are not comparable in education or responsibilities with secretaries, technicians, or any of the other work areas you have mentioned. Librarians are part of the University's instructional staff rather than service staff; hence their appointments should come from the office of the Dean of Faculty. Furthermore, I intend to fight for full faculty status for my professional staff. From now on, I will handle the employment of all professional librarians and you can forget about their job descriptions. I firmly believe this is one of the functions and responsibilities of my office."

Mr. Chert could not understand Mr. Amber's point of view and in an authoritarian tone announced, "According to the administrative organization of this University, all non-faculty and non-student personnel matters must clear through my office. The job specifications for librarians need to be up-dated and I have assigned a member of my staff to do this in cooperation with a member of your staff. I will expect the same kind of cooperation and consideration from you that I am receiving from the other service departments of this University."

Angered and annoyed, not only with Mr. Chert's attitude but also with the organizational framework of the University, Mr. Amber said, "I will take this matter up with Vice-President Quartz as soon as I can get an appointment with him. I want all professional library positions removed from your jurisdiction."

This morning a conference has been scheduled with Vice-President Quartz to discuss the employment procedures for professional librarians.

Case 2

JOB INTERVIEW: ALVIN

(Role Playing)

The public library in Bluebonnet served a population of about 66,000; and consisted of a central library, two branch libraries, and various small collections placed in convalescent and general hospitals, fire stations, and parks. The collection included books (approximately 137,000 volumes), motion pictures, filmstrips, tape recordings, phonograph records, art reproductions, pictures, large print books for the visually handicapped, and talking books and tapes for the blind. The library system was organized into eight divisions under the administration of the library director, Mrs. Bittern. The divisions were: circulation, reference, serial and government publications, young adult, children's, audio-visual, technical processes, and extension. The professional staff totaled sixteen, the non-professionals thirty-one full-time, and students who worked part-time. In addition to directing and coordinating the activities of the divisions, Mrs. Bittern was responsible for personnel, finance, and public relations.

At present the position of Assistant Head of the Reference Division is vacant and she is searching for someone with the necessary qualifications. Here is the description of the position which was sent out to library schools:

Bluebonnet Public Library

Announcement of Staff Vacancy

Assistant Head, Reference Division

Duties: assist the public in locating and interpreting library resources; instruct the public in the use of the card catalog, indexes, and other reference sources; provide reader's advisory service; prepare bibliographies; recommend new resource materials for the collection; interpret library policies and procedures to the public; and be in charge of the main library in the absence of the library Director and the Head of the Reference Division.

Hours: 38 hours per week. The main library is open 75 hours per week so the Head and Assistant Head of this Division are scheduled on a shift basis so that one or the other is always on duty. This will require some evening and weekend hours.

Fringe Benefits: three weeks paid vacation, seven days sick leave per year, four holidays (January 1, July 4, Thanksgiving, and Christmas), state retirement, group insurance, medical insurance.

Salary: $9,100-$9,500 depending on applicant's qualifications.

Personal qualifications: Master's degree from an accredited library school; at least two years experience relevant to responsibilities of this position; personality and personal appearance suitable for working with the public.

Mrs. Bittern has received several applications for the position. The one which seemed most promising was from Mr. Alvin Croton who indicated special interest in and enthusiasm for this position. Although she has some questions about his qualifications, he is the best candidate so far. She has invited him to the library for an interview which is scheduled for tomorrow.

Role for Mrs. Bittern, Director, Bluebonnet Public Library

This position has been vacant for three months. Your first attempts to fill it were to try to find someone on the staff to promote. Three staff members were capable of doing the work and, for their professional development, you think should be transferred to positions of greater responsibility. But each of them was perfectly happy in the position she held and was not interested in higher salary, more responsibility, or change of status. One didn't want to work nights or weekends, another preferred her less demanding work in circulation, and the third didn't want to learn anything new.

The responses you received from library school placement officers were disappointing because they had few persons to recommend. One of them told you that your position would be hard to fill because not many qualified persons were interested in living in your community and because the salary listed was not competitive with similar positions in school, special, and academic libraries. But this is the salary specified for this position in the classification schedule and you cannot offer more salary without changing all professional salaries. Mr. Croton was the only applicant who seemed remotely qualified and genuinely interested in the position. He had his credentials sent and Mrs. Bittern has studied them. In chronological order, they present this information:

1963 - AB from small liberal arts college. Major: history. Minor: English. Accumulative grade point average on a four-point scale: 2.9. His credentials included a recommendation written by his college history professor:

> Mr. Croton has been my advisee since he entered college. His work in the field of history was excellent during his freshman and sophomore years, when a rather factual background is important. I was concerned at the time to discover that his other grades were somewhat lower. I discovered that he read history as a hobby, perhaps to the neglect of his other courses.
>
> As he began to take advanced courses in history, I discovered that he had some limitations, even in history. He reads voluminously for his term papers, but he needs a little pressure before he

turns such papers in as completed. He proved
to be of good "B" standing in writing analytical
essay examinations, but he is not of "A" caliber
in advanced courses.

Mr. Croton is very much interested in library
science. I believe that he is capable of getting
a master's degree in the subject; however, I believe that he falls slightly short of becoming a
top library executive.

The college librarian wrote this about him:

Mr. Croton worked as a student assistant in the
library this past year. He has proved to be a
faithful worker and has shown an interest in learning the various phases of library work.

He was in the library methods class which I
teach, and I found him to be an able student, but
not one I would call brilliant. It may be that he
tends to spend too much time on the subject or
project that interests him most, and as a result
will not have enough time to do that for which he
does not have an aptitude. At times he may put
off doing assignments until forced to get them in.

The one big drawback which I see in Mr. Croton
is what appears to be an immaturity and a slow
pace in working. His slowness may be due in
part to the newness of the work. He has improved somewhat as he continues to repeat a certain task. He does appear to be accurate in anything he does, but he often has to be reminded to
do certain routine tasks which are required of all
the student assistants. Along with some others,
he does not think far enough ahead to save time
and energy in doing a task.

I do not feel that I have had enough contact with
Mr. Croton in the classroom to judge whether or
not he is capable of doing research. I do feel,
though, that his natural interest in the library
field, his ability to do well in those subjects
which greatly interest him and his willingness to
do any of the tasks to which he has been assigned
in the library will be enough incentive to carry

him through library school. He will probably do
better work under supervision than being the head
of a library or a department.

The only extra-curricular activities in which I
know that he has engaged were the YMCA working
with grade school boys, and he had a few bit
parts in some of the college plays. He is a faithful and conscientious worker in his church.

1966-67 - student in library school. His academic
achievement "spotty," but he averaged 3.2 on a four-point
scale. His library science faculty members evaluated him
as follows:

> (a) He is only an average B student. His embarrassed or nervous laugh is rather annoying.
> He tries to be cooperative and helpful.
>
> (b) He has apparent good intellectual abilities
> but is immature in attitude and conduct. He
> would need supervision in his work, at least for
> a while. As my graduate assistant he was always
> willing and cooperative, but not always too accurate and at times rather slow.
>
> (c) His class work was uneven and rarely was
> performed at the level he appears intellectually
> capable of doing. His personal appearance leaves
> much to be desired--he is careless in grooming
> and dresses rather sloppily. His use of English
> is inferior. His handwriting is large and angular
> resembling that of a grade school child.

1967-69 - worked 22 months in large metropolitan
public library
circulation department - 3 months
audio-visual department - 4 months
small branch - 2 months
acquisitions - 6 months
genealogy department - 7 months

You contacted the Personnel Director of the above library for a recommendation and an evaluation of his work
and this is what she told you over the phone:

> He was initially assigned to circulation. He com-

plained that there was too much walking and too much standing and his feet hurt; he requested transfer to the audio-visual department. Here he spent too much time looking at motion pictures and filmstrips and listening to records and tapes for his own enjoyment and amusement; the head of the department requested he be transferred out of that department. Mr. Croton was interested in a branch in a middle-class neighborhood but no vacancy existed so he settled for a small branch in a run-down Mexican-American neighborhood. The Supervisor of Branches had been trying for several months to find someone fluent in Spanish, empathetic to the residents, and capable of supervising a staff composed of local indigenous nonprofessionals. Failing to find such a person, she accepted Mr. Croton although he met none of these qualifications but he was eager and enthusiastic about the position. He had studied Spanish in his undergraduate program. It soon became evident that he was not fluent in Spanish, could not communicate in any way with the staff or the patrons, and was not interested in participating in the local community activities which was expected of the librarian of that branch.

As he evidently was not successful in working with the public, he was transferred to the Acquisitions Department of the main library. He seemed quite happy with this assignment and remarked, after he had been on the job for several months, that it was "Wonderful not to have to answer silly questions from the public." However, this enthusiasm did not last and he became careless in details and his supervisor could not depend upon consistent quality in his work. When a vacancy in the Genealogy Department occurred, he applied for this position pointing out that his undergraduate major was history and he thought some sort of reference work was what he was best suited for. Again, he was enthusiastic about the new assignment and told a fellow staff member "What a relief not to have the pressure I had in Acquisitions. Here I can work at my own speed." Seven months later he resigned to take another position.

The following evaluation of his work during the twenty-two months at Metropolitan Public Library was among the credentials which the library school had sent:

> Mr. Croton has high moral standards and good intentions. He is friendly, amiable, kind, patient, considerate of others, and well-disposed. He is loyal to institutions, causes and individuals. He has a tendency to involve himself continually in new activities and new phases of his duties rather than seeing things through and honoring present commitments. He does not seem to have administrative ability or a desire to assume supervisory responsibility.

1969 - to date: Assistant Director of a small public library.

Role for Alvin Croton

You are twenty-seven years old and single. You are unhappy in the medium-sized public library in which you are now employed. You find the people in the town provincial, narrow-minded, and unfriendly. The librarian has lived all his life in this town except when he was away at school. You find him to be a domineering, inflexible, politician who resists change and has no concept of what a public library in the 1970's should be like. You want to get out of this job as fast as possible. You had not visited the town or the library before accepting the position so you had no idea what you were getting into.

You have written your library school for a list of openings in the medium-sized public libraries and have read the lists of jobs printed in Library Journal. You have applied for every public library position which sounded interesting. These positions are located in eight different states. The one at the Bluebonnet Public Library interests you more than any other and you are going to work hard to get it. You know your work record at Metropolitan isn't good and your present boss wouldn't give you a good recommendation; so, you have got to "sell" yourself to Mrs. Bittern and her staff.

Recently you became engaged to the most wonderful girl you have ever known and you want to get married as soon as you find a job you really like and feel secure in it.

Personnel Cases   109

You are motivated to make a success of your next job because you want a home and family. With the help of your fiancée, you have purchased a new suit, ties, shirts, and shoes for the interview with Mrs. Bittern and her staff. Your fiancée thinks you look "sharp." You are determined to impress Mrs. Bittern!

Case 3

JOB INTERVIEW: ELIZABETH

(Role Playing)

Some libraries are famous for their size, others for the wide range of their collections. The Raynard Library, however, has gained its world-wide reputation not for its size (at present 55,000 volumes) nor for the range of its holdings (largely American, British, and western European works), but rather for the uniqueness of its treasures: rare illuminated manuscripts, the only copies of the autographs of famous persons, first editions, and many literary and artistic rarities.

The original collection was selected piece by piece as a personal hobby by Thomas Raynard during the late nineteenth and early twentieth centuries. After his death, his son, Thomas, Jr., continued to collect individual manuscripts, art objects, and rare books. By 1920 he had succeeded in bringing together a collection of more than 19,000 volumes, 1,305 manuscripts, 1,098 prints, and numerous art objects which in quality and range made it the peer of many old well-established rare book libraries in Europe. To house this collection, he built an appropriately magnificent building which in itself was an acknowledged masterpiece of American architecture designed by a famous architect. He then turned over the building and its contents to a self-perpetuating board of trustees to administer and set aside an endowment of several million dollars to support it.

The collection was made available to the public free of charge for reference use only. No material could be removed from the building. Today the Exhibit Room is open to the public daily from 9:30 a.m. to 5 p.m. and contains a permanent exhibition of paintings, sculpture, and art objects. Occasionally special exhibits are displayed. The Reading Room is open during the same hours but is locked

at all times. The privilege of access to the Reading Room
and use of any materials is extended only upon written application made to the Director. Satisfactory written credentials
must accompany each application. Only recognized scholars
or researchers are admitted.

Like most great libraries, the Raynard Library has
been blessed with a scholarly, highly professional, brilliant,
and devoted staff. The first director's acquisition policy and
skill are revealed in the library's holdings during that period.
One staff member for many years was responsible for innumerable noteworthy monographs and was one of the nation's
distinguished art historians. The present staff works together harmoniously with no conflicts or friction. Many of
them have been on the staff for many years and their work
is their life.

Role for Dr. Grackle

You are the Director of the Raynard Library and are
at present searching for a cataloger to replace the incumbent
who will retire in two months. Her area of responsibility
is autograph letters and documents of western European and
American historical and literary personages, artists, and
others, dating from the eleventh to the twentieth centuries.

The chief requirements for the position are: (1) a
liberal arts degree which included courses in art appreciation
and art history, western European and American history, and
literature of the eleventh to the twentieth centuries in Europe
and the United States; (2) a master's degree in library science which preferably included courses in history of books
and analytical bibliography (evolution of printing techniques,
principles of bibliographical description, rare book librarianship, and the antiquarian book trade); (3) work experience in a
rare book collection; and (4) a personality which will not upset the equilibrium of the present staff nor "rock the boat"
in any way.

Although notices of the position were sent several
months ago to every library school, only one application has
been received--from Mrs. Elizabeth Beech. She will arrive
tomorrow for an interview. You are disappointed that you
have not had several applicants from which to choose. After
studying Mrs. Beech's credentials, you have a number of
questions about her personality, attitudes, and behavior. If
a new employee lacked some academic background or exper-

Personnel Cases

ience for the work he is to do, this could be corrected through in-service orientation and training. But, neither you nor any member of your staff are qualified to help an individual modify his character, attitudes, or personality. You want to be very sure the person you employ will not upset the happy work relationship which exists on your staff or cause emotional tensions.

This is what you have learned about Mrs. Beech from her credentials:

> From age 18-22: university student majoring in history, with minors in art history and English literature. Grade point average on a four-point scale - 2.7;
>
> Part-time student assistant in the Rare Books and Manuscripts Department of the university library: applied leather dressings to bindings, helped prepare and check in binding, and assisted with displays and exhibits;
>
> Age 20: married a fellow student;
>
> Age 23: full-time work in same Rare Books and Manuscripts Department assisting with brief or temporary cataloging;
>
> Age 24: library school, grade point average: 3.3 (three-point required for graduation). Courses taken included one in "History of Books and Printing" and one in "Analytical Bibliography";
>
> Age 25-26: two years full-time employment in the Special Collections Department of another university.

Recommendations written to library school for her admission:

1. (history professor) Her academic work in the history department was uneven in quality. She often became so interested in some particular aspect of a course that she was inclined to go too fast and hence overlook some basic facts or concepts involved.

2. (faculty member in art department) I have known Elizabeth since she started her freshman year. She was an

indifferent and immature student during her freshman and sophomore years but, since her marriage two years ago, she has matured from a girl with high-souled but impractical enthusiasms to a woman with high ideals who understands and accepts the world as it is.

    3. (faculty member in English department) I was her counselor in the English Department. At her best, Elizabeth is a straightforward, outgoing girl who relates easily to others her own age. However, she tends to be somewhat emotionally unstable--for example, when she becomes discouraged over a test grade or her class work, she tends to be very depressed.

    She and her husband are active as draft counselors in assisting men desiring to be classified as conscientious objectors and those who want to escape to Canada to avoid the draft. They have participated in several campus demonstrations. I think you should know this when you consider admitting her to your School. I doubt if other faculty members here who may be writing recommendations for her know about this activity.

    4. (from head of Rare Books and Manuscripts Department, University Library) Mrs. Beech was employed in this Department part-time during her four years of undergraduate work and full-time this past year. She is industrious and intelligent and has a natural talent (considerably developed this past year) for cataloging and descriptive bibliography. Her latest task here was the temporary cataloging of a collection of seventeenth century literary works, a task which included checking for duplication (including minor press corrections and illustrative variants), checking against highly involved bibliographical descriptions for variation, identification of disbound parts of unidentified volumes, and the assignment of simple subject headings. She did a competent job. Her quickness of mind and enthusiasm are qualities not often enough found.

    In reply to your question, "Do you believe the candidate will be successful in library school?", I believe she will be _if_ her interest continues. If she loses interest, she will _not_ do well. She needs considerable encouragement and motivation.

    I expect her graduate work will be somewhat uneven (depending upon her enthusiasm) but generally better than her

Personnel Cases

undergraduate work.

Here are the evaluations written by library school faculty members:

1. Mrs. Beech is capable of doing superior academic work but she appeared to be lazy in this course. She grasped some ideas readily and easily but seemed to have some sort of mental or emotional blocks to accepting other ideas. She lacks common sense. She prepared satisfactory written assignments, talked too much in class (showing off before students), and gave one excellent oral presentation. Her appearance and grooming left much to be desired.

2. Mrs. Beech is a bright, alert student who works hard. She has imagination and initiative and works well on her own. She has taken considerable interest in this cataloging course. She has a pleasant personality, and is eager, and interested in others. Occasionally she is apt to be critical before getting all the facts but I suspect this is enthusiasm more than anything else.

3. She was the most disagreeable student I have encountered during the fifteen years I have been teaching library science courses. She argued not only with me but also with her classmates; tried to dominate all class discussion; and was inconsiderate, rude, dictatorial, and irritable. She appeared to be very tense with hatreds and prejudices seething inside of her which were evidenced in outbursts of sarcasm and cruel remarks which several times brought tears to the eyes of fellow classmates. She was absent at least one-fourth of the class sessions.

4. A telephone call by Dr. Grackle to the dean of students of the library school provided this additional information: she had tried to organize a student boycott of one class in the library school during her first semester on campus but had been unsuccessful because she could not get students to cooperate. They ignored and ostracized her and this seemed to sober her and she did not attempt anything of the sort again. However, she and her husband did participate in some campus demonstrations and she got her picture in a local paper twice during the year--once carrying a peace sign in a protest march down town and a second time as a participant in a sit-in demonstration on campus.

Evaluation of her work from her supervisors in the

Special Collections Department where she has been working for the past two years since library school:

1. She is astute, efficient, intelligent, and dependable but has little patience or tolerance.

2. Professional attitude - poor
   Competence in present assignment - average
   Personality and personal appearance - average
   Administrative capacity - below average
   Initiative - below average
   Health and energy - below average
   Employee's strengths - extremely bright and ambitious
   Employee's weaknesses - abrasive, argumentative, militant, self-aggrandizing

Role for Mrs. Elizabeth Beech

You are twenty-six years old, married, no children. Your husband has just finished his Ph. D. degree and has accepted a college teaching position in the city where the Raynard Library is located. You are very eager to obtain a library position in that city. As you are especially interested in rare books and manuscripts and this is the only vacancy in this type of library in the city, you will try hard to convince Dr. Grackle that you are the right person for the position. You know that you do not have all the educational background Dr. Grackle wanted, but you are willing to work hard to acquire that background on your own time if he employs you.

Bothering with grooming has always seemed like a waste of time to you because you would rather do more interesting things. Normally your straight hair just hangs down limply over your shoulders and back; the ends are skimpy, feathered out, and ragged looking because they have never been trimmed; you rarely brush your hair so it has a perpetually disheveled look. You prefer to wear blue jeans or slacks but, in your present position, women staff members are expected to wear skirts. When your present supervisor learned you were applying for this position at the Raynard Library, he told you rather bluntly that you had better do something about your hair, grooming, and clothing. He suggested you buy new feminine-looking dress, coat, hose, and shoes. You have taken his advice and a hairdresser has shown you a hair style to get your hair out of your eyes and

Personnel Cases   115

piled on your head. You have practiced walking in your new shoes.

Case 4

JOB INTERVIEW: FLOYD

(Role Playing)

The Middle East collection in Timothy University Library was housed on a separate stack floor of the central library because of the languages involved. This collection served the curricular and research needs of the Middle Eastern Studies program which was interdepartmental and interdisciplinary and provided coverage of the Arabic and Islamic regions of North Africa and of the Near East. The Program included language study in Arabic, Hebrew, Persian, and Turkish; and area courses in comparative literature, anthropology, fine arts, geography, history, and political science. The librarian, Mr. Rice, has developed the collection over a period of years and had done all the selection, cataloging, and reference work with the assistance of part-time students who were studying in the Program. About two years ago the volume of acquisitions increased to such an extent that he needed a full-time professional assistant in addition to the part-time students. After a budget allocation for such a position was approved, the university library personnel director searched for a person with the necessary qualifications.

Job specifications for the new position required a knowledge of Arabic and of one other language, a master's degree in library science, and library experience. After months of searching, Mr. Elm finally located a young man, Mr. Floyd Birch, who was enrolled in a library school, had capability in Arabic and Turkish, and had some library experience as a student assistant in the reference department of his college library. Mr. Elm interviewed Mr. Birch at the latter's library school and brought home a packet of his placement papers to submit to Mr. Rice for his consideration.

Role for Floyd Birch

You are twenty-eight years old, single, and an American citizen. You were born in the United States. At the age of four you moved with your parents to Cairo, Egypt, and lived in various middle eastern countries until the age of fifteen when your parents sent you to the United States to attend a private secondary preparatory school. Prior to this time you were enrolled in various elementary schools in middle eastern cities which offered instruction to European and American children whose parents were stationed overseas. Your father is a geologist working for the exploration division of a large American oil company. You are as fluent in Arabic as you are in English and can read, write, and speak Turkish.

Your choices of a major (geography) and a minor (anthropology) in college reflected your background of experience in living in foreign countries and knowing about other cultures. After receiving your bachelor's degree, you accepted a position with a geographical foundation in the United States where you used the foundation library extensively and got well acquainted with the librarians who interested you in librarianship as a career. After two years with the Society, you resigned to study library science.

<u>Role for Mr. Rice, Librarian of the Middle East Collection at Timothy University Library</u>:

You have been unhappy that Mr. Elm has not found a suitable staff member for you long before this as your need for one is acute. You are quite relieved and happy that a person with the necessary qualifications has been located. You have studied Floyd's credentials and you have some doubts and questions in your mind. You note a gap when he was not in school and not employed and you are curious to know what he did during that three-year period:

Age 6-14: pupil in various Middle East elementary schools
14-18: student in a U.S. preparatory school
18-22: student in an American liberal arts college
22-25: ?
25-27: map research in an American geographic foundation
27-28: library school

The transcript of his undergraduate record was good showing a broad range of courses and an overall accumulative average of 3 (B) on a four-point scale. His credentials contained three letters to the library school recommending his admission. One was from a professor under whom he had undergraduate courses:

> Floyd Birch has been a student of mine in a variety of courses during the past four years. His work has been consistently satisfactory. At times he has shown an ability to grasp the nature of fairly complicated and intricate problems and has often supplied the necessary insight for the enlightenment of his fellow students. He has a generous nature, and that gift of good humored patience which is so advantageous to one whose work brings him into contact with students and faculty. The wide range of his information and his manifest interest in cultural matters of many kinds should prove to be valuable assets in the library career he has chosen. He is an intelligent man, original, poised, and sensible.

Two recommendations to the library school for his admission were from library staff members of his college where he was a student assistant:

> 1. The usual student duties include shelving publications, filing catalog and reference cards, and helping patrons. He has advanced in responsibility so that at present he verifies all of the shelving and much of the card filing as well as being scheduled for responsibility of the Reading Room when no staff member is present.
>
> He is very intelligent and has wide interests as well as a competency in specific areas of knowledge. He has proved to be capable in both detailed work requiring accuracy and in working with patrons in the use of the materials. I believe he is a good candidate for admission to the graduate program.
>
> 2. He learned all locations and routines extremely quickly. He does exceptionally good work, no matter what the task. He is accurate in detailed work and clever at solving reference problems. Mr. Birch has a broad knowledge of many subjects and certainly a witty and pleasant person to work with. I feel strongly that he has much to offer the library profession and I heartily recom-

mend him for library school.

Floyd started his library school program at the beginning of the summer session and carried three courses. Students were expected to make a B average in order to stay in the program--he earned one B and two B-'s. Three faculty members wrote evaluations:

> 1. He cut one-sixth of the classes in this course, appeared bored most of the time, and handed in several assignments late. His book talk centering around Egypt was outstanding and well presented. His voice is well modulated, he speaks fluently and well, held the attention of the class, and had a certain flair for it. He brought some artifacts and pictures which he had acquired to show the class. His final score in the class was 17th in a class of 38 with a grade of "B-." He could have done "A" work if he had tried. He just didn't take the course seriously.
>
> 2. A more intelligent student than grades or performance in class indicate. He responded willingly and intelligently in areas in which he had a knowledgeable background. His attendance was irregular; I know he was ill part of the time. He did not turn in any work until after the end of classes. His readings for the course were too limited as evidenced by abstracts and projects submitted. Examination grades brought final class grade to a "B-." More industry plus interest could have earned an "A."
>
> 3. He participates freely and helpfully in class discussions and does well on written work. But he is often absent and he often turns work in late. Perhaps he is in poor health of some kind.

During the fall semester, he was enrolled in five courses in which he earned 3 B's, one F, and one Incomplete. Because of his failure to earn a B average, Floyd was warned that he was on academic probation for the next semester and would have to earn some A's to bring up his average to an acceptable B. Floyd promised to attend classes more regularly and to work harder. He claimed that during the last year his doctor had discovered that he had a violent allergy to pollen and dust and had advised him to move to another climate. The faculty member whose course Floyd had failed reported:

> On the day on which the final examination was scheduled, Floyd encountered me on the campus and returned to my office with me. He opened the discussion by saying that he had stayed up practically all night to complete an assignment which he had not turned in, but that he had not yet completed the typing of the work. I responded that I was sorry that he had not communicated with me sooner, because the work was due ten days ago on the last day of classes. I reminded him that I had warned him before Thanksgiving that he should not place himself in the position of turning in any class work at the end of the course when it might prove impossible to grade because of other commitments. When he asked if I would reconsider my position, I said no.
>
> I inquired what he thought his grade for the course should be at this point. He acknowledged that he had been absent from at least 50 per cent of the classes and had turned in approximately 35 per cent of the class work for a numerical value of perhaps 35 per cent altogether.
>
> I assured him that I was personally sorry for him in the position in which he had placed himself and informed him that I regretted very much that he had placed me in the situation of having to record his failure. I also informed him that I had discussed his attendance and failure to turn in the class work with the library school faculty. He did not take the final exam.
>
> I believe he has very serious problems which are in the province of the psychiatrist or clergyman rather than of the professor.

The credentials indicate that he is currently enrolled in five courses this semester but there are no faculty evaluations of his work because these will be written after courses have been completed.

You have some serious doubts in your mind about Floyd's work habits, motivation, health, and personal attitudes. You asked Mr. Elm to invite Floyd to campus for an interview. Floyd arrives tomorrow.

Case 5

AN UNCERTIFIED SCHOOL LIBRARIAN

Larry Bishop had been teaching in the elementary grades of one of the county consolidated schools near Lawrence for several years. For the past three years he had been working toward a master's degree in library science by taking one extension course in Lawrence each semester and two or three courses in the library school at the state university during the summers. Philip Tilney, librarian at New Hampton Junior High School in Lawrence, first talked with Larry Bishop when the latter called him about a class problem he had in an extension course in library science. Tilney continued to receive telephone calls of this nature over a period of months, but he did not meet Bishop until two summers later when the former visited the University Demonstration School Library where Bishop was doing library practice work as part of his master's degree program. Bishop reported that he was "really doing well" in the situation there.

Soon after the summer session ended Bishop informed Tilney that he had been hired as an elementary school instructional materials specialist. His only audio-visual preparation had been two courses he had taken in a university extension center; the only library experience he had was the library school practice work that summer; and he had not yet completed the requirements for the master's degree in library science. He was to be responsible for setting up a Title III ESEA Social Studies program which was funded at $300,000 for a period of three years and involved all of the fourteen elementary schools in the system. Also, he was to be the librarian for one elementary school and would be on an extended contract (i.e. he would start working three weeks before school started). Because of this extended contract, he would be second highest paid school librarian in the city in spite of the fact that all of the other school librarians were well qualified for their positions, were certified, and were experienced. No other school librarian was on an extended contract.

The principal of Tilney's school had known Larry

Bishop as a teacher at another elementary school in the
county and told Tilney that Bishop was a "trouble maker, a
poor teacher, and always doing things the wrong way. I
can't understand how he convinced the superintendent that he
could handle this ESEA program."

The first two or three months of the school year
Bishop called Tilney frequently and asked questions primarily
about cataloging and classification which indicated little understanding of these activities or of the basic vocabulary of library science. He had received unit cards from Follett.
What should he do with them? For cataloging and classification, he indicated he was using the "red book" (The Elementary School Library Collection, published by Bro-Dart
Foundation), the eighth edition of Sears List of Subject Headings (because the ninth edition omitted the Dewey Decimal
Classification numbers), and the Children's Catalog. He had
no copy of the Dewey Decimal Classification and Relative
Index, although he later ordered a copy. He said that he did
not use it "because it was so incomprehensible." He continued to use the "red book" and Children's Catalog for cataloging and classification although they were designed as selection tools. Somewhere Bishop had heard about catalog card
sets issued by the Catalog Card Corporation of America,
which included classification labels which could be peeled off
and placed on book cards, book pockets, and book spines.
However, when he used the service, he placed labels on the
book pocket and spine, but typed the classification on the
book card.

The telephone calls to Tilney continued at home as
well as at school. In addition, Bishop began almost daily
visits to Tilney's school library for an hour or more each
time. He would copy cards in the card catalog and take
notes on the filing system. One day in January, when Tilney
discovered Bishop going through the shelflist in his office, he
"blew up" and told Bishop to quit phoning and to stay away
from this library. The telephone calls and visits stopped,
but other librarians in the school system reported that Bishop
had extended his range by calling them for assistance, in-
specting their card catalogs, and "borrowing" library supplies
(which he did not replace).

One day in the spring the principal of Bishop's school
revealed that Bishop could not be certified as a school librarian in the state because he had failed his library practice
course the previous summer. The principal had contacted the

faculty member at the library school responsible for the
practice course to inquire how Bishop could meet school library certification and was told that Bishop would have to
take the practice course again with a grade of "B" or higher
and would have to take one more three-hour course and pass
with a grade of "A" in order to bring his accumulative grade
point average to a "B." Bishop refused to do this and pointed
out that the federal project for which he was employed did
not require school library certification as long as he had
the "necessary training"--which he insisted that he had because he had taken certain audio-visual and library science
courses.

The state school library supervisor confirmed that
certification was not required for school librarians working
on federal projects as long as the person had the "training."
She cited a problem situation involving this same question in
a school library in a neighboring city where a public librarian (who had had some audio-visual and some library science
courses but lacked certification) was working on a federal
ESEA project.

Case 6

THE DIRTY LONG-JOHNS

Cast: Mr. Alexander, Chief Librarian of the Big City Public Library
Mr. James, Head of the Business Department of
B. C. P. L.
George Eliot, a new employee in the Business Department
Mr. Joseph, a staff member of the Business Department

The Business Department of Big City Public Library,
serving a metropolitan population of about 750,000 residents,
had serious shortages on its staff for more than a year--
everyone was overworked, yet high standards of service had
been maintained. The Chief Librarian, Mr. Alexander, had
been unable to fill an important vacancy in this department
which is the B. C. P. L.'s most dynamic service center. The
present Head of the Business Department, Mr. James, was
scheduled for promotion into the library's administrative
structure where he was badly needed. Since there was no
one on the current staff of the Business Department who could

be considered a potential department head, it became urgent that a new person be found to be trained for the job.

By what seemed to be a fortunate coincidence, Mr. Alexander received a letter of inquiry regarding any openings in the Business Department from a man in his mid-thirties, a graduate of a well-known accredited library school. The letter was somewhat ambiguous, but seemed to indicate that its writer, George Eliot, was on the staff of the Business Department of the Smith Memorial Business Library (which was considered to be the best business library in the country). So Mr. Alexander immediately sent George Eliot the library's official employment application forms and asked for copies of transcripts of his academic records. The material was returned in a remarkably short time, and after examining it briefly, Mr. Alexander invited Mr. Eliot to come to Big City for a personal interview and offered to pay his travel expenses. The information on the application forms and the college transcripts were all very impressive. Eliot had an undergraduate degree (cum laude) with a major in business and high grades from his library school courses.

Mr. Alexander had been Chief Librarian of Big City Public Library for twenty years, had a good professional reputation, and had been very active in the A. L. A. He had been administering the library the same way for twenty years and had firm convictions about library administration. His methods of recruiting personnel included visiting library schools, personal contacts with other library administrators, and--when they were forthcoming--unsolicited inquiries from persons interested in joining his staff. He never advertised vacancies in library periodicals. He had little faith in written recommendations but much confidence in his own ability to "size up" people, and based his decisions on his personal interviews with the applicants. Although he asked for help from his department heads in reviewing applicants, he made the final decisions himself and never hesitated to overrule his department heads if they did not agree with his decisions.

When Mr. Eliot arrived for his interview on a chilly winter morning, Mr. James was somewhat taken aback by the sight of the tall, bearded man who stepped off the elevator. It was not so much the beard, as the bright red vest, the spats, and umbrella--but, after all, it was a cold morning late in November. Mr. James had never actually known anyone who wore spats. (Mr. Eliot was apparently oversensitive to cold, for he also wore long-johns.) The day of the interview went very well. People were soon calling Mr. Eliot "George," for he seemed a likeable fellow, pleasant, agreeable, well-read, and articulate. "Why did George want to leave such a fine library as Smith Memorial?", one staff member asked. The reply indicated that a different type of experience was wanted at this time.

As was the custom at the B. C. P. L., Mr. Alexander talked to the applicant for ten or fifteen minutes in the morning, then sent him off on a series of scheduled interviews and tours of all departments. Each department head sized up the applicant, sent him on his way, then went to report to Mr. Alexander. Late in the afternoon, with all of the various reports in, Mr. Alexander concluded the interview-- salaries and fringe benefits were discussed, the numerous benefits of living in Big City were dwelt upon; something was learned about the applicant's hopes and dreams. It seemed that Mr. Eliot was married but had no children. He was a veteran of the Korean War, had spent a year travelling in Europe, was an amateur actor, and even played the cello. His health was fine ("Never sick a day in my life").

After George Eliot left, Mr. Alexander and Mr. James met to discuss the applicant. Both agreed he had potential and would probably make a fine addition to the staff; yet, perhaps, some caution was necessary. Mr. Alexander said that George would come to B. C. P. L. for $1,300 less than the listed salary for the position. This struck Mr. James as being rather odd, but Mr. Alexander had found out that George wanted the job very much and would come for this amount (Mr. Alexander couldn't resist the chance to save a little money). "Besides, if Eliot turns out to be a good man we can always give him a raise." Both finally agreed that Eliot would join the Business Department staff as another professional, and at first his only administrative responsibility would be to handle the pages in the department. If his work proved satisfactory at the end of the fiscal year (in seven months), he would be made assistant head of the department, given a big raise, and would start to take over some of the responsibilities of the Head so Mr. James could move up on the administrative ladder, knowing the department was in good hands.

Although at the time of the interview, Mr. Eliot indicated he should give Smith Memorial Library a month's notice, when he received the offer from B. C. P. L., he said he could report for work in one week. This seemed a bit strange to Mr. James, but since George had said that it was all right with Smith Memorial, he decided not to pursue the matter further. Mr. James knew the personnel director at Smith Memorial Library quite well and almost phoned him to make sure there would be no ill-feelings--but, it had been a hard day, and Mr. James did not make the call.

George Eliot started to work at Big City Library on the first day of December. Within four months he was in serious trouble and his future with the library was in doubt. From the point of view of Mr. James, this period fell into three clearly defined sections. During the first month, George was on the receiving end--being taught his job, given a chance to learn the "ropes," getting to know people, asking questions. The second phase, which coincided with George's second month on the job, began with George's abilities somewhat under question and, when it was over, Mr. James was convinced that George simply could not handle the job and perhaps had some serious psychological problems. The last phase, the final two months, produced turns of event which convinced Mr. James that Eliot could not even begin to handle this job, and, furthermore, had become a serious threat to the smooth functioning of the entire department. During these two months, Mr. James thought he fully understood George, his limitations and potential and was trying to find a solution to the problem of making George into a useful and constructive member of the team (by this time, any thought of George becoming the assistant had been abandoned).

George Eliot had to be fitted into a staff which included, besides Mr. James, three librarians with master's degrees, one "non-professional" (Mr. Joseph, a vigorous and ambitious young man in his mid-thirties who had never studied any library science course, but who had two degrees in business and extensive business library experience), two subprofessionals (college graduates), one secretary-clerk, and five high-school pages. The only potential problem envisioned by Mr. James was the relationship between George Eliot and Mr. Joseph. Unfortunately for all concerned, Mr. Joseph would not go to library school to get a degree, and in B. C. P. L. he could not advance into an administrative position without the degree. Yet, Mr. Joseph was a valued staff member, contributed innovative and constructive ideas, liked his work, was enthusiastic and cooperative, worked long hours, and was completely dedicated to the advancement and improvement of the Business Department. He had been with the department for five years, the period of its greatest period of growth, and knew it inside and out. He resented the fact that he was not being considered for the job of department head.

However, despite this potentially dangerous area, Mr. James knew that Mr. Joseph was reasonable, and if George Eliot could prove his own worth and demonstrate his professional librarianship, he could win Mr. Joseph's respect. The first few weeks went very well. Everyone in the department, including Mr. Joseph, did his best to help George in his new job. During these first two or three weeks, not much was asked of George because the work of the department was so vast and complicated that the staff agreed George should be broken in slowly. The veteran staff members worked with him at the reference desk, showed him the resources, and gave him time to examine things on his own. They hoped that very soon George would be able to assume a major part of the department's work, thus relieving the others who were much overworked.

The first reaction to George was good. With his beard and red vest (not to mention the spats) he was somewhat of an oddity, but at this time no one was critical. His initial nervousness seemed to linger longer than necessary and there was a certain tenseness which could perhaps be attributed to being in a new situation. It soon became evident that George was not the out-going, extrovert type, but was very quiet and introspective, seemed guarded in his relationships with other staff members, and made no close friendships. Yet, Mr. James soon became rather fond of George and wanted to know him better.

The situation began to change as soon as George was given specific tasks and responsibilities. There were a series of attempts to turn over to him some of the professional routine jobs. In each case the results were the same. The job was explained to George in minute detail; he seemed to understand, but almost immediately, when put on his own, he began to change it. For the most part his changes were such that they could only be considered irresponsible or quixotic. For example, the report and pamphlet file was set up so that one professional librarian was responsible for checking each week a large quantity of sources for non-book business material. The library served high-powered business concerns and had developed a very extensive information service which big business in the area had learned to depend upon. Mr. Joseph had been doing this work but really didn't have time to do it. The job was explained to George. The first hint of trouble came to light when Mr. Joseph, quite upset, brought Mr. James ten pamphlets on such diverse subjects as contemporary French theatre, a directory of eighteenth century Italian cello makers, and an illustrated folder about Disneyland. Mr. Eliot apparently had misunderstood the sort of material needed for the file. After a long talk with him, Mr. James was confident that all would go well now (after all George had only been on the job three weeks; but, on the other hand, he had an undergraduate degree in business and experience at Smith Memorial and should have known what should be selected for a business collection). A week later Mr. Joseph stalked into Mr. James' office, threw two pamphlets about ballet on his desk, and stalked out without a word.

Another area where George was assigned to work was the clipping file. This was a unique service with B. C. P. L. Dozens of newspapers from major U. S. cities and business periodicals were scanned for items of interest to businessmen and manufacturers: such things as new product development, new markets, new management or selling techniques, etc. The actual scanning for material was done by a professional (again Mr. Joseph) who simply checked the material and added a subject heading, then a clerk clipped the material and filed it. With remarkable patience Mr. Joseph explained this job to George and supervised his work in this area for one week, putting him on his own the second week. Mr. James, when he looked in on things to see how George was making out, was disturbed to find that George was not only missing some very important material, but was selecting some material for the clipping file which was not even remotely related to the activities of the Business Department. Furthermore, George decided on his own that it would be better if he himself clipped and filed the material, so he had been sitting at the public service desk with a pair of scissors doing his own clipping and filing. Again, the established and tested procedures were discussed and explained to George, but whenever Mr. James was not around, George still continued to do it his way. From time to time, Mr. Joseph (who still kept a sharp eye on the clipping file) pulled some "oddball" item that George had filed and left it on Mr. James' desk. These clippings were so far fetched, that Mr. James was beginning to wonder how firm a grasp George had on reality or what he had learned in his business courses.

A number of other incidents took place before the second month was out. The most serious of these involved George's relationship to the pages. Within six weeks after George took over the job of directing the work of the pages, three of them resigned without notice. One day, in Mr. James' presence, George had a violent exchange with one of the senior pages. The attitude of the page was not the upsetting factor, but the way George handled it. George lost control completely and lashed back at the page. Later, when George regained his composure, he told Mr. James that the pages did not like him, that they made fun of his beard, and that they talked about him behind his back. Mr. James did not believe this was true, but could not convince George of this.

By this time the second month of George's employment was drawing to a close. Everyone in the department had lost confidence in him and all were beginning to feel that they were having to "put up" with an incompetent librarian. Hardly a day passed that Mr. James did not have to listen to at least one disgruntled staff member complain about George. Mr. Joseph became unrelenting in his criticisms. George could do nothing right, and Mr. Joseph was getting very, very unhappy. As the busiest time of the year approached, Mr. James found that not only could his new staff member contribute nothing to the department, his influence was creating dissatisfaction and poor morale in a department that had run smoothly for many years.

Mr. James took the matter to Mr. Alexander, and it was decided that even though George's future looked pretty bleak, he was a nice guy and should be given another chance. He had until July to shape up.

One morning, Mr. James was interrupted by Mr. Joseph (the relationship between the two was already under severe strain thanks to George). "Would Mr. James care to have a look at one of the public filing cases?" "If Mr. Joseph thinks it's that important, yes." On arriving at the filing case (one of twenty-five pamphlet files placed in a public service area and consulted daily by library patrons), Mr. Joseph, with more dramatic flare than the occasion demanded, flung open a lower drawer of the file to reveal, of all things, a soiled pair of men's long-johns. Mr. James looked at Mr. Joseph; Mr. Joseph looked at Mr. James. They both looked at the long-johns. Neither said a word for both knew that this intriguing situation had something to do with George. The offending garment was taken to the department work room.

Personnel Cases 129

Later George saw it, blushed, quickly scooped it up in a newspaper and disappeared (presumably to his locker).

Thinking over his twelve years as a departmental administrator, Mr. James could find nothing in his experience to prepare him for this situation. He had never had to cope with such irrational behavior. He knew that before the morning was over, everyone in the library would know about the incident. Up to this point, Mr. James had hoped he could salvage something for George; somewhere in the organization find a place for him. But now, though the incident with the long-johns was not without humor, he knew that George had a real problem, and that George would have to shape up pretty fast or part company with the library. Also, this was the sort of incident which should not reach Mr. Alexander's ears via any medium other than Mr. James, so a hasty conference was held.

Now, as far as anyone at the B. C. P. L. knew, Mr. Alexander had never actually fired anyone; yet, one way or another, when he wanted to get rid of employees, they were gone shortly thereafter. In this case, Mr. James was instructed to explain to George that the library did not need his services any longer, and that he should start looking for a job immediately and turn in his resignation within six weeks.

So with a heavy heart, Mr. James called George into his office. In so far as was possible under the circumstances, he broke the news to George with sympathy and compassion: "You are to resign and be gone within six weeks . . . if not, you will be fired." Although Mr. James had fired people before, this one shook him up more than the others. It was the way George took it. George pleaded for a job, any kind of a job. He would even work in a branch, in the bookmobile, even catalog if he had to. Generally when Mr. James "let people go" before, the erstwhile employees had, in so many words, told Mr. James he could "go to Hell"; so, moved by George's impassioned pleas, he agreed to set up a meeting between the three of them (George, Mr. James, and Mr. Alexander) so George could plead his case with the head librarian. The meeting was scheduled for the following morning.

At the appointed hour it was a different George Eliot who reported to work at the Big City Public Library--an "unbearded" George. In the emotional scene on the previous afternoon, George had indicated that Mr. James was "letting him go" because of the beard, and no amount of protesting by Mr. James could convince George otherwise. His face looked naked, and he blushed and looked at his feet, as Mr. James could not avoid looking at the, heretofore, hidden chin. Nor was George alone, for beside him stood his wife. It was Mrs. Eliot who spoke. Would it be all right if she went to the meeting instead of George, because he was so upset? Certainly an unusual request, but a quick phone call to Mr. Alexander revealed that it would be all right.

The meeting lasted an hour and a half. Of the three people present, Mr. James, Mr. Alexander, and Mrs. Eliot, it was Mrs. Eliot who did most of the talking. Mr. James said comparatively little. Mr. Alexander was at his very best, the past master of the probing interview. For Mrs. Eliot, he had sympathy, understanding, and advice. Her husband was not his problem, not the library's problem, but her problem. With subtle skill he won her confidence. At first she spoke little and quietly; she was shy and nervous, and on the verge of breaking down. Then, as if she welcomed the chance to talk to someone about her problem, especially to this nice, friendly, fatherly Mr. Alexander, she told him everything. It gushed out almost without interruption. The sad story of George, the product of a broken home, a misfit who had serious psychological problems since the age of sixteen. After he received his undergraduate degree in business, George went to Korea, a private in the infantry. For two years he served his country under fire, but in the process old psychological scars were opened. He had a long series of jobs after Korea. First as a high school teacher (that job lasted one semester), then a variety of odd jobs; he sold encyclopedias from door to door; drove a bus; and during it all was under psychiatric treatment off and on for more than ten years. He lied more than once. Yes, he did have a job at the Smith Memorial Library, but they had fired him six months prior to his applying at B. C. P. L. , and had told him he was "untrainable. " At the time he applied to B. C. P. L. he was not employed anywhere. "How did he get into library work?" Ironically enough a psychiatrist recommended this as a suitable profession for him. So, his wife supported him while he studied in a library school and earned a master's degree. His wife reported that he was unhappy, moody, and frequently talked about suicide. He had known his work hadn't been going well but thought it was the fault of Mr. James, his beard, and numerous other imagined enemies.

The future of George Eliot in the Big City Library

system is now in Mr. Alexander's hands. What courses does he have open?

Case 7

WINTER UNIVERSITY PERSONNEL POLICIES

When the Winter University Library collection outgrew the central building in which it was located, a decision was made to build a new library for graduate and research use and to utilize the present building as an undergraduate library. After the new library was under construction, staff requirements for the undergraduate library were established and the Associate Director for Public Services, Mrs. Beech, searched for possible applicants. After interviewing several persons for the position of Coordinator of Reference Services, she offered the position to Paul Benham, who was twenty-seven years old and had five years of successful and pertinent experience as an assistant in the reference department of a large university library.

During his initial interview with Mrs. Beech, Mr. Benham learned that librarians at Winter University enjoyed academic status (i. e., librarians were appointed by the Dean of Faculty as were the faculty), but that only those who taught in the Department of Library Science, an undergraduate department, were accorded faculty rank in addition to academic status. Also, during this interview, Mr. Benham pointed out that he was interested in furthering his education beyond the master's degree in library science. He was assured that not only was this possible, but it was also encouraged by the library administration. In fact, a university regulation allowed all academic members of the university to take up to four semester hours of credit each term free of charge. In addition, the time spent on such classes was not time which had to be "made up." Salary was discussed and definite agreement was reached with regard to this. The position was offered to him but he did not accept then because he said he wanted to think it over for a few days (he had also been offered another position in another university system).

Upon returning to his home several hundred miles away, Mr. Benham weighed the merits of the two positions and decided in favor of Winter University. He wrote to Mrs. Beech at once notifying her of his acceptance of the position she had offered, which was to start on January 1. By December 15 he had received no confirming letter from Mrs. Beech, but neither had he heard anything from her to lead him to believe that the offer had been rescinded. He moved his family and furniture to Central, the city in which Winter was located. He called Mrs. Beech's office as soon as he arrived in the city and was assured by her secretary that a letter confirming his employment as of January 1 had been mailed on December 14. He then left town to visit his parents for Christmas. Upon his return, he received several letters which had been forwarded from his old address. Among them was the letter from the Director of Libraries at Winter confirming the oral agreement reached with Mrs. Beech with one exception. The letter informed him that the salary which had been promised him could not be met. Instead, a salary of four hundred dollars per year less was to be his starting salary. Since Mr. Benham had already gone to considerable expense in relocating his family in Central, he could not refuse the position and leave, but was virtually forced to accept this altered offer.

In addition to the altered offer, he soon learned that he was under no contract to Winter other than one of a verbal nature. When he inquired about this, he was informed that he was on an interim appointment and that such appointments were not contractual. It was explained that the only line item open on the budget called for the rank of Associate Librarian (equivalent to Associate Professor) and that in view of his youth and limited experience, he could not be hired on this line item. He readily understood this, but felt that it should have come out during his initial interview.

Since the position for which Mr. Benham was hired did not actually exist at the time he began work and the undergraduate library would not be operating until several months after the graduate library building was completed, he was assigned several projects. These included the selection of some 75,000 titles which would make up the core of the undergraduate book collection. These selections were made partly from second and third copies of titles already in the main library's collection. The rest, he selected and ordered from funds allocated for this purpose. In addition, he worked several hours daily on a reference desk and was assigned the responsibility of separating the Latin American material from the main library collection. This separated material was to become a separate collection which would be housed in the undergraduate library as soon as it was ready for occupancy.

Because of a number of problems in connection with these Latin American materials, Mr. Benham decided to take some relevant courses in the Latin American Studies Program. In his initial interview he had been assured that he could take up to four semester hours of credit each term free of charge, but he soon found that he was expected to enroll in only those courses which met during the first or last class hour of the day. Since none of the courses which he wanted to take were offered at these times, the opportunity for him to study in this way was virtually eliminated.

Case 8

A NEWSPAPER ROOM CLERK

(Role playing)

Roles:
    Mrs. Perry
    Mr. Grove

All clerical positions in a metropolitan public library were included in the municipal civil service commission. When a clerical vacancy occurred in the library, the personnel director of the library requested from the commission a list of persons qualifying for that particular grade classification. The person employed had to be chosen from this list. If no person seemed satisfactory, the personnel director could so notify the commission and either request additional names or wait until other persons qualified for inclusion on the roster.

When a vacancy occurred for a desk clerk to serve the public in the newspaper room, the head of the periodicals department, Mrs. Perry, chose Mr. Grove from the list of qualified persons on the roster. From his credentials, she did not believe Mr. Grove was the ideal person for the job but he did possess the necessary educational background and seemed to be the best of the individuals on the list. When she interviewed him, she noted that he was in his mid-twenties, rather handsome, well groomed, and conservatively dressed. He had had some experience in an office as a file clerk and seemed interested in the newspaper room job when she explained that his duties would consist of checking in newspapers as they arrived, preparing them for display, shelving back issues, and filling requests from patrons.

During the first two days Mr. Grove was employed in the newspaper room, Mrs. Perry worked with him to orient him to the position making sure he was informed about policies, became familiar with the procedure manual, got acquainted with the staff of the whole periodicals department, and visited all the departments of the library.

During the first two weeks he was on the job, Mrs. Perry received several complaints from patrons that he had irritated them by being rude, gruff, abrupt, and unapproachable. His supervisor reported that his work performance was unsatisfactory but hoped that it would improve with time. Mrs. Perry called Mr. Grove in, told him of the complaints and his unsatisfactory performance, and suggested more diplomatic ways of handling people. She explained that copies of the complaints and a report of this interview would be sent to the civil service commission to be placed in his personnel file. She warned him that if he did not improve, he would be discharged. His only defense was a statement about the "stupidity" of some of the requests from the public and a promise to try harder in his work performance.

A week later a pleasant-mannered, neat-appearing matronly lady came to Mrs. Perry's office to complain about the very discourteous treatment she had received from Mr. Grove and subsequent embarrassment she had experienced. The patron explained that both she and her husband were retired and were frequent visitors to the newspaper room. Due to the fact that the newspaper room was divided into two sections (a large section for men and a smaller one for women), she and her husband were seated in their respective sections and, when her husband motioned to her to come and read something in the newspaper he was reading, she walked into the men's section and started to read the article over his shoulder. At this point, Mr. Grove stormed over to her in front of all the readers in the room and in a very loud and abusive tone of voice ordered her to return to her section with the threat that if she ever attempted to do that again she would be removed from the room. This caused her a great deal of embarrassment to the extent that she felt Mrs. Perry should be told of this incident.

Later in the day, before Mrs. Perry could take action on this incident, another caller came to her and reported:

> Today in the newspaper room, I asked Mr. Grove for the New York Times which another person had

been using for almost forty-five minutes. When I approached Mr. Grove and explained that most papers are only held about fifteen minutes, he rudely grabbed my slip from me, crumpled it up in a ball and threw it on the floor saying that he did not have time to watch how long people held on to papers and that I would just have to wait.

The next day Mrs. Perry called Mr. Grove to her office to discuss these two incidents.

Case 9

AN INFORMATION CENTER[1]

The Tucker Investment Company was recently organized as an investment counselling firm located in a large city which employed about forty persons of whom half were professional investment managers holding master's degrees in business administration.

The company maintained extensive files of its correspondence, of reports from the large nationwide firms which sell investment information report services, and of internally generated reports and memos. Subscriptions were received for more than fifty business periodicals and newspapers. Each professional employee received a personal copy of the Wall Street Journal as a fringe benefit and a mark of status. Annual reports of firms and other sources of business information were collected. Internally generated memoranda, even those dealing with the most trivial matters, were kept for record; these materials made up the largest single item in the company's information collection. Naturally, the files in which these materials were kept were growing rapidly. A full-time clerk was employed to organize and file the various sources of information, but some members of the firm were dissatisfied with the rather haphazard manner in which the files had been developed.

Recently the managers of the firm called in a management consultant from a nearby university business school faculty to study the file problem. He recommended that a professional librarian be employed to take over the organiza-

---

[1]Source of Ideas: John F. Peters

tion of the company's information sources and to develop a special library and information center.

Subsequently, several library schools were contacted, applicants were interviewed, and the position was offered to a Miss A who would receive her master's degree two months later. Miss A was impressed with the Tucker Company and they with her. Without any clear definition of the demands or nature of the work, beyond the fact that it was a professional librarian that was wanted, she accepted the position at a salary much higher than the norm for library school graduates that year. She understood that she was to organize the vast amount of information at present in the files. She assumed that she was to establish an information center which would provide library services for the investment managers. She was told that she would report to Miss B, who in turn reported to Mr. C, the comptroller, who reported to the president. Miss B also supervised the custodial staff and several secretaries.

When Miss A first came to work, she met Miss D, the file clerk who had previously been working with the information sources of the firm and who expressed great relief to be rid of the filing job. Miss A was also assigned a secretary and given a desk in a large, well appointed, comfortable room which she shared with several secretaries. There was no library room as such--only a file room which contained the crowded and badly organized files and some wall shelving. Books and periodicals were kept by staff members in their offices.

After seeing the physical arrangement and the conditions under which she would work, Miss A talked with her supervisor, Miss B, about the possibility of getting space assigned specifically for an information center. Miss B thought this a good idea and suggested that Miss A prepare a memo outlining the amount of space needed, where the files should be moved, which services she would like to provide for the staff, and the size of collection she believed the company should have. The memo was prepared, Miss B approved it and sent it on up the chain of command.

After Miss A had worked for two weeks on organizing the files, she realized that they were large enough to warrant, in her opinion, a computer-prepared permuted index. Since the firm owned a computer system, she hoped to utilize this equipment. It was at this point she learned that the "library" had no funds or budget per se. Every item of library expenditure had to be requested and cleared individually by Miss B and by the comptroller, Mr. C. Miss A prepared a detailed report of the desired program for a permuted index. This was approved by Miss B, but turned down by Mr. C on the grounds that it would be too expensive.

Somewhat later, Miss A decided that since the Wall Street Journal was so important to the business world and to Tucker Company in particular, it would be valuable to have a microfilm copy of the paper. She requested a microfilm reader, the last two years of the Wall Street Journal on microfilm, and the Index of the Wall Street Journal. She intended to establish a policy of buying the current year and one back year on microfilm each year. Her request was approved by Miss B and Mr. C, but when the materials did not arrive, she investigated and found that the order had been countermanded by a member of the finance department who thought the expenditure was too great.

Soon after the microfilm order was countermanded, she got a reply to her memo requesting space for an information center: "Sorry, no space available." She soon became convinced that the members of the firm did not understand what an information center was supposed to be. So, she prepared a paper on the subject which she routed to the staff members. She also routed certain articles, clipped from Special Libraries, which applied to the investment firm's information needs. She received no response to these efforts. At the same time she continued to work on the files, and, indeed, spent the greatest part of her time filing. Although she had a secretary, there was now no file clerk. She began to feel that she was actually only a highly paid file clerk and that she would never be allowed to perform as a professional librarian in the position. She carried some of her complaints to Miss B, who was sympathetic but believed that management could eventually be convinced that they needed a real library. Miss A thought that management should not have to be convinced, and that they were not ready for a library or a professional librarian. Because she had no status or freedom of action, and could not develop a library information center as she thought it should be developed, she resigned. In her letter of resignation she pointed out that they needed only file clerks in their present operation.

Case 10

ATTEMPTED BRIBERY

Conrad Hawk was acquisition librarian for Otter State University which started as a two-year state normal school early in the twentieth century, then became a four-year teachers' college, and now is "exploding" into an "instant" university. Enrollment and faculty have increased dramatically in the last three years. Courses have proliferated. The library staff has been hard pressed to meet the ever-changing and increasing demands for materials and services-- so many things happening every day, not enough staff, and many decisions of all kinds to be made for current operations and for establishing policies for the future. It was necessary to "cut corners" just to exist and frequently the staff made operational decisions which, under normal conditions, would have been decided in other ways. There was little time for planning.

As a means of acquiring retrospective collections quickly, the acquisition department had made a number of block purchases on certain subjects; and, in one instance, had purchased the entire stock of a book store which went bankrupt.

As a result of various news articles in the press of the state which pointed out the need for a better and larger library at Otter State, the library had received, as gifts in their wills, the personal libraries of former faculty members, of prominent professional persons, and of alumni. When they arrived, these block purchases and gifts were stored in boxes in the basement of the building in which the library was located. A library building was under construction.

The contents of the boxes were systematically examined and sorted by various staff members and those titles selected for inclusion in the collection were moved to the catalog department for further checking and for cataloging. Duplicates and other titles not needed in this library but useful in an academic collection were sent to the exchange department to be used as exchanges. The remainder of the books were rejects--worn out textbooks, out-of-date and inaccurate books, books containing misinformation, and books unsuitable for an academic library (such as light loves, westerns, and detectives). These rejects had to be sold, given

Personnel Cases

away, or destroyed before the library was moved into its new building. Somewhere between six and ten thousand volumes had to be disposed of.

The staff of the acquisition department knew that possibly some of these books might be useful in research libraries which were building collections in depth or in historical collections; but there was no shelving on which to display the books nor any other way to arrange them in a logical order--hence they were all stored in boxes. As the staff went through each box they put an identifying mark on the outside of the boxes which contained discards.

To notify other libraries of their existence would have required taking the books out of each box, typing a card for each title, arranging the cards by authors, typing and reproducing lists, compiling a list of libraries to which the book lists should be sent, and mailing the lists--all of which would require much staff time. Then, no doubt, after librarians checked the lists, they would expect this staff to find, pack, and ship the books. If the existence of these books had been announced in a library periodical, librarians would have phoned and come to look at them and the staff would have had to take time to answer questions, to show visitors where the boxes were stored, and possibly lift and shift boxes. Any of these efforts would have required untold amounts of nonexistent staff time as well as prohibitive labor costs. The only reasonable solution from the point of view of this overworked acquisitions staff was to assign a maintenance man to load the boxes in a truck and transport them to the city incinerator where they were burned.

Soon after this operation started, an antiquarian book dealer from another part of the nation and a stranger to this library, called on the acquisition librarian, Conrad Hawk. Some other librarians he had called on in another institution in the city had told him about the books being burned at Otter State. The dealer, Mr. Rose, asked Mr. Hawk if he might look at the books to see if there were any titles he would like to buy. Mr. Hawk had known and done business with several antiquarian dealers and had found them to be honest. Although he did not know the reputation of this man, Mr. Hawk assumed that Mr. Rose was reputable. Here is Mr. Hawk's account of what happened:

> I told Mr. Rose he could go to the storage area and take any books he wanted and then give me a

credit memo which we could use to buy books from him. I had looked over the catalog he had given me and I saw titles listed which we could use in our collection. He spent several days in the storage area unsupervised. He did all the labor of sorting, repacking into boxes those he did not want, loading what he selected into his car, and transporting them. He was really doing us a favor because we no longer had to handle the books he took nor haul them to the incinerator.

On the last day Mr. Rose was sorting books in the storage area, he told me he had a sister living in this city and would like to take her, my wife, and me out to lunch. I thought that was going a bit 'overboard' because no salesman had ever invited my wife to lunch as well as me. But I said 'yes.' We went to a rather exclusive high-priced restaurant. He turned out to be an overly friendly, palsy-walsy, backslapper, name-dropper who tried to impress me that he knew many important librarians.

I am certain now that he took many more books than those represented on his credit memos. Several months later other acquisition librarians told me about buying old fiction titles from his catalog which had book plates from one of our large gift collections. Upon investigating, I found that in the confusion of sorting so many boxes full of books, we failed to check a group of boxes from a wealthy donor's personal library which contained beautiful editions of so-called 'standard' older fiction. He had evidently taken all of these and also had taken many more titles of all kinds which were worthless to us but were valuable to him because he could sell them for six to ten or more dollars each. Even some of the out-of-print light loves, westerns, and detectives he could sell. I had no idea of what he took or their value so I had to take his evaluation of them on his credit memo.

A few months later I received a set of golf clubs as a Christmas gift from his sister. I wrote a note on the back of the card which came with the clubs: 'I cannot accept these because I am doing business with your brother. Accepting them would constitute a conflict-of-interest.' I sent the clubs back to her. I was angry that this man thought I was so stupid that I would fall for something like this. No one likes to be taken advantage of and nobody likes other persons to think he has larceny in his heart. He probably thought I was playing the game with him and that there would be lots more discards so he was 'buttering me up' for the future. He knew what our budget situation was like and he knew from dealing with other 'instant' universities that budgets were going up rapidly and he wanted to be in on the ground floor.

The next time he came to town, about two months later, he came into my office and I asked him, 'What did you think you were doing sending me a set of gold clubs?' (His smile seemed to say, 'you dumb bunny.') 'I don't know how you evaluate me but my evaluation of you surely dropped down and I feel badly about this.' He said that I was very valuable to him because of my background and knowledge, that he had learned much from me, and the golf clubs were just a goodwill gesture.

Several weeks later I received a fifty dollar bill in an envelope (with no return address), wrapped in a plain piece of paper on which had been written one word, 'Thanks.' I knew it had come from him. I was furious to be put in this awkward situation. It disturbed me so much that someone would try to make a fool of me. I figured that if I sent it back to his office someone there would pocket it and he would never have known that I returned it. So, I put it in the collection basket at church. The next time he called at my office I told him that I knew he had sent the fifty dollar bill but he feigned innocence. 'By trying to bribe me,' I said, 'you really harmed yourself. Remember I go to library meetings and, if it came up in confidence, I would tell other acquisition librarians of my experience with you and you would lose business. I think you have services to offer but I will never again place an order with you.'

Case 11

THE IMMATURE REFERENCE LIBRARIAN

(Role playing)

Roles: Mrs. Raymond, head librarian, Springfield Community College
Mrs. Thiem, reference librarian

The Springfield Community College library served 15,000 full- or part-time students and had a rapidly growing collection of 45,000 volumes. Because of the broad scope of its operations and the long hours it was open, versatility was required of its twelve full-time employees. The seven clerks handled overdues, checked in periodicals, did minimal reference work (when they were the only persons in charge during supper periods or weekends), manned the circulation desk, and were responsible for some training of the fifty student employees when they were working side-by-side with them. The professional librarians had administrative responsibilities for cataloging, reference, processing, and circulation.

Mrs. Raymond was head librarian. Two months before she received this appointment, a new reference librarian, Mrs. Thiem, was hired by her predecessor for one academic year (until her husband completed work for a master's degree at a local university). Mrs. Thiem was twenty-two years old and had received her master's degree in library science just prior to her employment at Springfield Community College on September first.

After several months, Mrs. Raymond concluded that Mrs. Thiem was competent in her reference work but immature socially and as a supervisor. Mrs. Thiem seemed ill at ease with the other reference librarians but she was forming friendships on and off duty with a few of the clerks and the student assistants. Her relationship with them was one of a colleague rather than one of supervisor and worker. If their names came up in staff meetings, she was able to provide complete personal details.

Several of Mrs. Thiem's special friends among the clerks and student assistants proved to be poor employees.

Personnel Cases 143

They expressed dissatisfaction about library policies; talked to friends while on duty; left their posts; sulked about assigned hours; did not work when supervisors were absent; or quit without notice.

Mrs. Raymond did not know whether the students became poor workers after receiving Mrs. Thiem's attention or whether Mrs. Thiem gravitated towards the poor workers. The relationship was a source of distress to the head librarian but she did not have any proof of Mrs. Thiem's corrupting staff morale with which to confront her.

Midway through the second semester, several members of the staff discussed, in Mrs. Raymond's presence, the fact that Mrs. Thiem seemed to have a "crush" on one of the men who shelved books part-time, talked to him often, and had scheduled him to work on her night. Mrs. Raymond had no conclusive evidence of an indiscretion and did not think she would broach the subject because Mrs. Thiem was supposed to leave on August 31.

Early in June, Mrs. Thiem went out for a rest break with a female student assistant and stayed one half hour. Mrs. Raymond was angry not only because Mrs. Thiem would take such an extended break for herself, but also because she set such a poor example for a student. Mrs. Raymond discussed with Mrs. Thiem various aspects of professional ethics and attitudes, and suggested that she act like a professional person, think like a manager rather than as a part-time student assistant, and dress like a young matron instead of like a coed. Mrs. Thiem was contrite and said that she felt more secure in socializing with her inferiors than with her peers. She promised to act more like a professional.

During the spring and summer, Mrs. Thiem's husband was interviewed for several positions but the weeks passed and he did not receive a job offer. This morning (August 10) Mrs. Thiem asked Mrs. Raymond if she could work in the library for another year because her husband had decided to continue his graduate work.

Case 12

STINKY

(Role playing)

Roles: Mrs. Palm and two bookmobile librarians

How can you tell your supervisor that she stinks?

This is a problem facing ten women who work in the bookmobile division of a large regional library serving a rural population. Each of us works on a bookmobile for four days and in the headquarters office on the fifth day. Our schedules are so arranged that two of us are in the office each day sharing the small room with our supervisor, Mrs. Violet Palm, and her secretary.

Mrs. Palm is a widow of about forty with two children to support. She is a dedicated, capable librarian; runs an efficient operation; holds regular staff meetings to keep us informed; is fair and considerate in her treatment of us; and tries to let us participate in the making of decisions. In physical appearance she is repulsive: rather obese, careless about her clothing which usually has dirty spots and needs washing or dry cleaning, her hair is always messy and looks like it needs shampooing, and she always smells. To work with her in that small room is a kind of torture unless one has a head cold and can't smell anything. Behind her back we call her "Stinky."

Some individuals can smoke and non-smokers can smell tobacco smoke about the person's hair and clothing as well as "smoker's breath"; other smokers seem to radiate offensive odors (caused from smoking) from every pore in their skin in addition to the bad breath and smoky smell. Mrs. Palm was one of the latter. She smoked a small pipe almost constantly all day, keeping the room filled with smoke from the foul-smelling tobacco she used. Even the women on the staff who smoked cigarettes found her pipe tobacco offensive. Non-coffee drinkers usually find "coffee breath" disagreeable to smell--Mrs. Palm has that too. Her clothing smells as if it is impregnated with stale body oils and underarm perspiration. The combination of pipe tobacco, smoke, coffee breath, body odor, and dirty clothing is overpowering! We wish there were some way to deodorize her.

Case 13

SLANDER AND LIES

(Role playing)

Roles:
      X, Librarian, Taupe Regional Library
      Z, Assistant Librarian, Taupe Regional Library

During my twenty years of professional experience, Z is the only staff member I have ever worked with whom I couldn't trust. When I was interviewed for the position of librarian of Taupe Regional Library, I knew Z wanted the position and had tried hard to get it. He was the last one I talked to that day and he told me I would be a fool to take the position because of all the problems I would encounter in organizing a group of small independent libraries into a regional system. He pointed out that I was an outsider and would not get much cooperation from the librarians in the region (he had grown up in the area and was well known). In spite of his advice, I accepted the position; the organizational problems involved presented a real challenge to me. After I had taken over, Z was the most courteous member of the staff and he did many things for me and seemed to be loyal. Subsequently I learned that he was "knifing" me in the back all the time with the staff, the board of trustees, and with influential persons in the community. I learned about this from individuals from each of these groups who came to me and told me what he was saying and asked why I didn't do something about it.

    His position as assistant librarian involved supervision and management of many persons as well as personnel and budget. He was in a position to influence staff against me if he was so inclined. He slandered me, told lies about me, and misrepresented me in every possible way. I have compiled a list of these slanders and lies and tomorrow will confront him with them. As I see it, there will be no peace on this staff until one of us leaves, and I intend to stay. I plan to ask for his resignation.

Case 14

DRESS POLICIES

(Role playing)

Roles:
        Director of Libraries
        Head, Circulation Department
        Young professional employee (officer of Staff Association and representing that organization)

Violet University is privately endowed, has a coeducational student body of approximately 9,000 undergraduates and 1,500 graduate students, is nationally known for its schools of law, medicine, and business, and is located in a medium sized city in a state known for its conservatism. The University Library contains about two million volumes in a magnificent new main building and five departmental libraries.

Financially the operation of the University is dependent to a large extent upon endowment income and returns from the annual gifts from alumni and friends of the institution. Throughout the history of the annual campaigns, gifts have steadily increased year after year--until last year, when they dropped dramatically and disastrously. The officer in charge of the campaign has been informed by many regular and generous donors that they will no longer give to the University because it has become too "radical." These donors refer specifically to open visitation, which was introduced last year into those dormitories where the occupants had voted for it; to the participation of some students and faculty members in various demonstrations, sit-ins, and marches; and to the unconventional, unkempt appearance of some students.

Because Violet University was the first academic institution in the area to accede to student demands for open visitation, the newspapers covered it too completely, both in news reports and in editorial comments. Much of the coverage was misleading and seemed to be maliciously maligning both the University administration and the students. Although only about one percent of the student body and about half a dozen faculty members have participated in various demonstrations and marches, the newspaper publicity was such as to convince many persons of the general public that the University was composed largely of "radicals."

The reduced returns from gifts last year made it necessary to cut budgets in every area of the University this year--including the Library's. The chairman of the annual giving campaign recently reported to the Board of Trustees that returns this year are even slower in coming in, and the amounts are smaller.

A few days ago, the Director of Libraries received the following letter from an influential member of the Board of Trustees, who is president of a bank in the state's largest city, as well as an alumnus of the University's School of Business:

> I was in Violet University Library yesterday and was shocked to observe the appearance of a young man at the circulation desk whose hair came to his shoulders, and whose face was almost covered with hair. In the Reference Department, I observed a young woman, identified as a staff member by the name tag she was wearing, whose dress was extremely short. When she reached to a top shelf to get a reference book, her underwear showed beneath her dress. Both of these employees were highly visible to the public. If these two are typical of the personal appearance and dress of library employees, it is no wonder that the donors of our annual campaign are losing their enthusiasm for supporting this University. May I suggest that you screen applicants for library positions more carefully and not employ those who are unconventional in dress or appearance, and that a dress code be formulated and enforced for the staff? You might even adopt some type of uniform for your staff, such as is customary for airline stewardesses, clerks in some stores, and employees who deal with customers in some banks.
>
> Like bank employees, librarians meet the public and should have some standards and guidelines for employee dress, appearance, and grooming. In my opinion, librarians should dress as conservatively as bank employees. In a recent survey in banks, ninety two percent reported having dress policies. These policies were either tacitly

understood or were in written form and publicized; they considered what is acceptable for both men and women. All employees are advised about cleanliness, neatness, deodorants, nails, Afro hair styles, and gum chewing.

For women, policies covered such areas as mini-skirts, maxi-skirts, culottes, pants suits, textured and colored hose, boots (worn indoors), sandals and bare legs, see-through blouses, wigs, and extreme styles in makeup.

For men's business dress, the policies covered sideburns, mustaches, beards, long hair, sports jackets, bell-bottom trousers, medallions and other styles of jewelry, shirts (short sleeved, sport, deep toned), and no tie.

Recently, at my bank, we employed a fashion consultant to assist our employees in their decisions about grooming, choice of clothing, hair styles, makeup, and other matters.

Role of Director of Libraries:

"In this library we try to practice participative management. The department heads have the authority and responsibility to choose and to terminate their own staffs, both clerical and professional. Normally they consult me about major appointments, but I rarely overrule their decisions. I expect them to handle their staffs as they think best. I expect that if the appearance or dress of any staff member becomes extreme or objectionable, the department head will discuss the matter with the individual and take action if necessary. I realize that every aspect of the University is being scrutinized critically by the public, and that the University needs the financial support of donors. I will leave to the discretion of the department heads and the Staff Association officers whether or not they wish to adopt some sort of dress code for the staff. I will communicate their wishes to the trustees.

"To date, the university administration has not felt the necessity to establish an official university-wide policy for dress of employees. Because there are such diversified conditions of work, any policy which was adopted would have to be very broad and general. As a library administrator, my

Personnel Cases   149

own personal guidelines for dress which I suggest to my department heads as a base for their policies are: (1) dress should be functionally effective, (2) it should be in reasonably good taste with current styles, and (3) it must not be exceptionally distracting. These guidelines are applicable for both male and female employees. I believe my department heads in this library would probably agree with these guidelines subject to interpretation for any special departmental conditions. "

Role of Head of Circulation Department:

"The young man at the Circulation Desk, to whom the Trustee referred, has worked part-time for this department for three years. He started as a freshman and is now a first semester senior. He is one of the finest young men I have ever employed, is capable, conscientious, punctual, and loyal. He was clean shaven and had conventional short hair until he returned this fall after spending the summer in Greece as an archaeological field assistant. He said that they rarely got to a town where there was a barber so all the men let their hair grow and many also let their facial hair grow. Having grown the hair, he decided to leave it until his family and friends saw him. When he returned in the fall, he said that some of his friends thought him more handsome with longer hair, mustache, and beard. He asked me if I objected to his retaining them. I suggested that he have all hair trimmed so that he looked neater--which he did. I think before he is interviewed for jobs, he will shave off the beard and get his hair cut. His clothes are neat and clean, and he is not a 'hippy.'

"We have some others on the student assistant staff who have longer hair and are less neat, yet again these young men are good workers and valuable staff members. Most of them work as shelvers in the stacks, so are not visible to the public. Some professional staff members, both in my department and in other departments, feel that we should not employ any young man with long hair or hair on his face, and that we should release them if they grow hair after being employed. My personal feeling is that this type of appearance is common on college campuses, and as long as the man is neat and clean and gets along well with the rest of the staff, and the University accepts him as a student, I think the library staff are not in a position to say that he cannot be employed because of his appearance. Students with similar appearances are employed in other places in the University. If one of my young woman staff members wears a dress that is too short or too tight, I merely suggest to her that such a dress is not particularly suitable in a public place where she has to reach and bend often to get books off the shelves and to use the card catalog. So far, both the young men and the young women to whom I have spoken about appearance or dress have taken my comments in good stead."

Role of young professional employee (Officer of Staff Association and representing that organization):

"It has been customary for the library staff in the Medical School to wear the same long white coats that the freshmen medical students wear. I have talked to members of that staff and they are happy about that custom because they can wear any old thing under those coats, and hence don't have to spend money on clothes for work. On the other hand, they say that the coats are certainly not flattering to women, and it would be pleasant to see the form of a figure occasionally instead of the loose baggy coats. The staff get tired of white all the time, and would welcome seeing a variety of clothing styles and colors on themselves and others.

"If this issue were discussed in a Library Staff Association meeting, I fear there would be serious unfavorable reactions. As far as the staff is concerned, there is no problem about appearance or dress because the situation is being handled satisfactorily now. So far as I know, individual staff members have not resented suggestions from department heads. For example, girls take no offense when told that they should be moderate in wearing eye makeup or should wear their hair in some style so that it is not continually falling in their eyes or interfering with work. I have heard one staff member tell another that a certain costume was not appropriate. Personally, I think we express our personalities through our hair styles and dress, and I would hate to see them standardized. However, if you agree that this should be put to a vote of the Staff Association, I will be glad to see that it is done."

Case 15

NEPOTISM: FERN

Bluegrass University with a student enrollment in excess of 25,000 was located in a small city of about 23,000. The only other libraries in the city were a small public library (which employed three professionals) and three school libraries each of which had a certified school librarian in charge. The city was some seventy-five miles from a large city in which there were libraries of all kinds which required professionals with many different capabilities.

Staffing the University Library had been difficult because few librarians with the necessary qualifications were interested in working in a rural environment. Furthermore, if a man's wife wished to work, employment possibilities outside the University were limited to teaching in the public schools or working in an office, in food services, or in a store. Commuting to the big city for other kinds of employment was prohibitive because of distance and cost of transportation. Consequently, as a result of the above conditions, several married couples had been employed through the years. The Library Personnel Code had no statement about nepotism to prevent such employment practice. Hiring couples on the same staff, however, created some serious problems which are exemplified by the following example and the case following this one.

In searching for a person to fill the position of Head of Public Services, Craig Aspen, Director of Bluegrass University Library, recalled a man in his late thirties with whom he had worked in another university library in the past. He remembered Winslow Heron as an outstanding, versatile, capable, dynamic, and innovative librarian. As a person, he was outgoing, approachable, and empathetic. His experience included shelver and later stack supervisor in his college library during his undergraduate years; four years in the U. S. Army; and, after library school, academic library experience first as serials librarian, then as assistant reference librarian, and, currently as head of a large circulation department. Mr. Aspen thought the position as head of Public Services at Bluegrass would be a challenging promotion and an increase in salary for Mr. Heron. After some correspondence and a visit to the Bluegrass campus, Mr. Heron accepted the position. One condition of his acceptance was that his wife, Fern, also be employed but not in Public Services. At that time the Personnel Division of Bluegrass University had no written nepotism policy preventing the employment of a husband and wife; but it was generally understood that a husband or wife could not be employed in the same department where the spouse had access to personnel records or would supervise or make any recommendations about the other's work. Couples could work in different departments of the same division of the University.

Several years earlier, Mr. Aspen had met Fern socially and remembered her as being rather quiet and retiring. At that time she was working as an executive secretary. Mr. Heron informed Mr. Aspen that his wife would finish a master's degree in library science in two months and that she was prepared for a professional appointment. In order to secure the professional expertise of Winslow Heron on the staff, Fern was employed as a beginning cataloger.

When Mr. Aspen studied Fern's transcript from library school, he was disappointed to see that she had made only a mediocre record. She soon turned out to be a serious personnel problem. She was temperamental, incompetent, feuded with other members of the staff, and gossiped. Her immediate supervisor, Mrs. Swift, had so much respect and admiration for Fern's husband that she covered up for Fern and did not report these problems to the head of Technical Services. At first, Mrs. Swift called mistakes to Fern's attention and tried to teach her, but Fern resented criticism and pouted and sulked so much that Mrs. Swift decided it was easier to revise all her work and to correct the mistakes than to return them to Fern for correction. Three years after Fern joined the staff, Mrs. Swift retired.

Mr. Teak had been a cataloger in the department for about two years, was exceptionally capable, and cataloged about three times more than any other cataloger. He was quiet, didn't believe in socializing with co-workers, was punctual in reporting for work, and put in a full day's work every day. The head of Technical Services had observed Mr. Teak's work performance, his harmonious working relations with his typists, and his ability to make decisions; and he believed that Mr. Teak would probably be a good supervisor so made him head of the Cataloging Department although he was younger than the other catalogers.

Mr. Teak set standards of performance and production which he expected his catalogers to meet. He was outspoken, blunt, and honest. Fern's work fell far below these standards. Mr. Teak conceived of his job as being responsible for providing leadership and direction to his staff, improving methods so as to eliminate the backlog of uncataloged materials, and selecting and training new staff members. His philosophy was that the catalogers were experts who would do accurate work and would not require his close supervision. He had several sessions with Fern pointing out her errors and trying to teach her. She resented his criticism and couldn't understand why a new boss should find fault with her work when Mrs. Swift rarely found any errors (she had no idea that Mrs. Swift proofread everything she did).

Mr. Teak finally gave up trying to teach her anything and assigned a newly appointed cataloger to revise her work. Fern did not have tenure, but he knew he couldn't fire her because of her husband. He investigated the possibility of transferring her to another department. The library was organized into three divisions: Technical Services, Public Services, and Branches. The only area to which she might be transferred were the acquisitions section of Technical Services or to Branches. The head of acquisitions refused to take her because his work required a high degree of accuracy and he feared Fern did not have the capability inasmuch as her cataloging performance was so poor. Mr. Teak talked to the head of Branches about a transfer but the only vacancy was one which required working with the public and neither of them thought Fern had the personal qualifications for that.

In contrast to Fern's performance, her husband, Winslow, was most successful in his work, effective in interpersonal relations, and had become virtually indispensable to the administrative structure of the library. His salary had been increased substantially each year, he had moved up one rank in faculty status, and he would receive tenure as soon as he qualified in length of service. His wife had received no merit increases in salary, no promotions, no change in rank, and never would achieve tenure. This situation is rife with elements of unequal competition and rivalry which could cause much personal unhappiness for the couple.

A further complication which seriously concerns Mr. Aspen and other staff members is the potential hazard of each of them knowing too much. By virtue of Winslow's executive position, Fern probably gets more "inside information" about many areas of the library's operation and administration than her supervisors do. Conversely Winslow may get from his wife distorted reports of what is going on not only in Fern's department but also in other areas of the library as well as her emotional reactions to other staff members. The possibilities of this situation cause anxiety for supervisors and heads of departments who prefer to do their own reporting to Winslow.

Are the heads of Technical Services and Cataloging forever "stuck" with Fern in order to keep Winslow on the staff? Or, should she be terminated at the risk of Winslow's resigning? Are there any other alternatives? What are the nepotism policies of other libraries?

Case 16

NEPOTISM: FRANK

(For information about Bluegrass University, see Case 15)

For all of his career, a prominent citizen of the state was employed as an officer in the U. S. diplomatic service in several Central and South American countries. He collected both retrospective and current printed and manuscript materials of all kinds about the countries in Central and South America. After his death, his widow gave this vast collection to his alma mater, Bluegrass University, which had an active Latin-American studies program. This new collection more than quadrupled the library's holdings in this area.

A new staff member was urgently needed to catalog and provide service for this new collection. Qualifications for such a person included fluency in Portuguese and Spanish, background in Latin-American Studies, a master's degree in library science, and library experience. Finding a person with these qualifications proved to be very difficult. At last, after about six months of searching, Miss Maria Sorrel was "discovered" and was invited to the campus for interviews. She met all of the qualifications except that of experience.

As a child, she lived for ten years in Rio where her father was an attaché in the American Embassy and she learned to read, write, and speak Portuguese as well as English. She accompanied her parents on their frequent vis-

Personnel Cases   155

its to other South American countries. As part of her undergraduate program in Latin-American Studies in the United States, she studied Spanish and, during her junior year, studied at the University of Mexico in Mexico City. Then followed two years in the Peace Corps working with Indians in Guatemala. During this period, she and other Peace Corps volunteers traveled extensively in Central America.

When in Washington, D. C. during her initial Peace Corps indoctrination, she spent several days in the Columbus Memorial Library of the Pan American Union and in the Library of Congress. Contacts with librarians in these libraries interested her in librarianship as a career; so, after her Peace Corps tour of duty, she enrolled in a library school. At the time of her interviews at Bluegrass University in early April, she was within two months of completing her master's degree. The library staff members who met her decided she was just the right person for the position. In addition to having the necessary language and background qualifications, they found her to be gracious, outgoing, cheerful, considerate, and personally attractive. Her transcripts for both undergraduate and graduate work indicated superior scholarship and her library school faculty recommendations were excellent. She was very interested in working with this exceptionally fine collection, in the geographical location of the University, and impressed with the staff members and the organizational structure of the Library.

In discussing the details of the position with the Personnel Director, she mentioned that she and another library school student were planning to be married late in August after her fiancé, Frank, completed work for his master's degree. Her acceptance of a position would depend on his also getting a library appointment in the same community. Since the only possibility of a library position here was in the University Library, offering her an appointment meant one would have to be offered to him also. Maria accepted the offer and agreed to start work on July 1. The Personnel Director agreed to send for Frank's credentials and to offer him a position depending upon his background and qualifications and vacancies which were available as of September 1.

Frank's credentials proved to be rather disappointing--his undergraduate major was English; he had tried to earn a living at free lance creative writing for three years but had been unsuccessful, so had decided to become a librarian. His accumulative grade point average for his undergraduate work was below that required for admission to the library school to which he applied and he lacked two science courses. As a consequence, he was accepted on probation with the stipulation that he pass the science courses and earn grades of B or higher in three basic library science courses. After completing these required courses with grades of B, he was admitted to the master's program. The library school faculty recommendations were rather noncommittal and "luke warm," giving the Personnel Director the impression that he was no great "prize" but perhaps he would turn out to be a satisfactory staff member. In view of their great need for Maria's abilities and no other person had been found who met the qualifications, Frank was offered a position at the beginning professional level. Maria's salary was at the next higher professional level because of her special qualifications.

Maria found her work with the Latin-American collection exciting and intensely interesting; she fairly glowed with happiness which radiated to others working with her. She said often, "How wonderful it is to be doing what I most like to do and to be paid for doing it!" She worked longer hours than she was scheduled because she got so engrossed in what she was doing and was often seen taking materials home with her for reading there. The faculty of the Latin-American Studies Program were happy with her work, welcomed her with "open arms," and invited her to talk to classes both about bibliographical sources in her area and about countries and peoples of Latin-America. She was popular with the library staff also.

Frank was assigned to the School of Education Library as a reference librarian. Initially he made a good impression on the Personnel Director, the Librarian of the School of Education (Miss Veech) and the staff generally. He had a tall, straight figure, his hair was dark and wavy, and his voice low-pitched and pleasant, he was a good conversationalist, and was personally charming.

He started working on September 1. By mid-November Miss Veech complained to the Personnel Director:

> Frank is a glib, know-it-all smart-aleck. He won't follow instructions, pays no attention to procedures, undermines and sabotages my relations with my student assistants, misrepresents me to faculty and students, gossips constantly with

anyone and everyone, and flirts with women students. He is late repeatedly and is quite irresponsible in other ways. According to the 'grapevine,' if he is to come on duty after Maria leaves for work, she sets two alarm clocks to waken him at the right time but even they do not get him out of bed. He has never yet finished any bibliographical assignment I have given him. He gets well started and then apparently tires of the job and puts off finishing it. I have talked to him repeatedly about his unsatisfactory work performance and have tried in every way I know to make a responsible staff member out of him but he is impossible. Here is my report in writing requesting that he be terminated or transferred to another branch or department.

In the spring, the Personnel Director had received from his library school a transcript of his undergraduate work, and evaluations from the three faculty members under whom he had classes during the first semester. After receiving Miss Veech's report, she phoned the library school asking for a complete set of Frank's placement papers which would include a transcript of his library school courses and faculty evaluations for the second semester and summer session. By studying these, she thought she might learn more about him so she would be able to judge whether he had capabilities for another position in the library. She learned from these papers that Frank had incompletes from two courses in the spring semester and one course in summer session; hence, he had not received his degree in August. Faculty statements indicated that he frequently turned in assignments late and missed classes. There seemed to be no reason for this except procrastination.

Case 17

THE CLIQUE

(Role playing)

Roles:
Mr. Bill Iron, Librarian, Liberal Arts College
Miss Opal, Head, Cataloging Department, Liberal Arts College

Soon after Bill Iron became Librarian of Liberal Arts College, a vacancy in the Catalog Department occurred. The head of the department, Miss Opal, recommended Miss Pearl for the position and presented her placement papers to Mr. Iron. After studying the papers Mr. Iron agreed that she had all the necessary qualifications so offered her the position.

Only after she arrived and moved into an apartment with Miss Opal and her first assistant, Miss Ruby, did he discover that he had been tricked. He learned that when his predecessor offered Miss Opal the position as head of the department three years ago, she accepted with the condition that Miss Ruby be employed as her first assistant. Later, she tried to persuade Mr. Iron's predecessor to employ Miss Pearl but he refused because he knew that the three of them had lived and worked together while they were employed in the Cataloging Department of another college, and that there had been staff problems because of their closeness. Mr. Iron did not know these facts until after Miss Pearl had started to work.

Six professionals and fourteen clerks were employed in the Cataloging Department. When three of the six professionals spent all their time together, both on and off the job, they formed a tight little clique which created personnel, morale, and communication problems with the rest of the staff. Mr. Iron soon realized what a great mistake he had made and was angry that he had been duped. He has called Miss Opal to come to his office this morning to talk over the problem with her. He is convinced that the three of them cannot continue to work together in the same department.

Case 18

PRIVILEGED INFORMATION

(Role playing)

Roles:
    Director of Libraries   Reference Librarian
    Assistant Director   Director of Technical
    Circulation Librarian   Services

At Water University circulation records were auto-

Personnel Cases   159

mated last year. As a by-product of this new system, a
store of machine-readable transaction data increased to the
point that reliable answers can be supplied for a number of
questions. A semester-by-semester tabulation could begin
to establish profiles of student borrowing by class-year and
subject. Further sorting of data could provide "reading profiles" for individual students, groups of students, and faculty
members. Data could possibly provide some answers to such
questions as the causal relationship between academic achievement and library use, and the contributions of the library
collection to the educational process. Useful information
could be provided academic advisors as to the identity of non-
borrowers and the borrowing records for commuters, dormitory students, students in specific courses, part-time students, and married students versus unmarried students.
Runs could be made of the total accumulation of data or of
any desired sample.

After this automated circulation system had been in
operation for several months, a reporter from the student
paper interviewed the circulation librarian and wrote a feature
article about it. This created considerable interest among
some faculty members who asked for special runs for peri-
odic reports on their assigned reading lists. One faculty
member asked for a list of books circulated to a student who
was involved in a plagiarism case.

The circulation librarian, accustomed to giving borrowers maximum service, provided these faculty members
with the information they desired. But, when the following
two requests came in, he questioned the ethics involved and
referred the requests to the director of libraries for a decision.

(1) One department chairman asked for a total data
accumulation report on the reading of his faculty members
which he said he needed for making promotion decisions.

(2) The Dean of Faculties asked for a report of all
titles borrowed by twelve faculty members who were being
considered for dismissal. He thought these records might
help him (along with other evidence) to assess the quality of
these persons.

At its next meeting, the library's administrative council (Director of Libraries, Assistant Director, and department heads) considered questions relating to the librarian's

relationship to the library patron. Is anything the librarian knows of the patron through their service relationships "privileged" information comparable to the minister and his parishioner, the doctor and his patient, the lawyer and his client, and the reporter and his sources? What is the potential of automation for massive invasion of privacy? Could the information obtained from computerized circulation records be used as a weapon against academic freedom?

Case 19

A CIRCULATION LIBRARIAN

The population of Union County was approximately 118,000 of which 78,000 were in an urban area. In the county were sixty-two elementary and secondary schools, a business school, a two-year vocational school, and a liberal arts college of 6,000 students. Several major industries, two television channels, and four radio stations were located in the county.

The Union County Public Library had a headquarters library and three branch libraries within the city and two bookmobiles to serve areas outside the city limits. Annual circulation was in excess of 500,000. The staff consisted of four professionals: Miss Jones (county librarian), Mrs. Martin (assistant librarian in charge of public services), an assistant librarian in charge of technical services, and a circulation librarian. Sub-professionals were in charge of the three branches, the two bookmobiles, and assisted in reference, circulation, and technical services. A number of clerks and pages completed the staff.

Miss Jones had difficulty hiring and keeping professional and even sub-professional employees. Staff members classified as sub-professional were college graduates with an undergraduate minor (eighteen hours) in library science. Miss Jones was competing with the schools for these sub-professional librarians who, in some cases, could qualify as elementary school librarians, and, in others, were certified either to teach in their major field of study at the junior or senior high school level or to serve as junior or senior high school librarians. However, since the college had many graduates in the field of education, numerous qualified applicants for the teaching positions were available so those with a library science minor had few opportunities to teach

Personnel Cases   161

in their major field of study and only a limited number of school library positions were available annually. Hence, they accepted temporary positions in the public library until they could get into the school system either as librarians or as teachers. When interviewed for a position in the public library, the fact that the individual considered the position temporary was not expressly stated, but became apparent when she often left with very short notice to accept a school position which opened up unexpectedly, paid better, and offered shorter hours and longer vacations. In many cases sub-professionals stayed with the public library two or three years before changing positions or moving to another city or state. These employees were high-caliber and competent, but they were a young, mobile group and turnover tended to be high.

Professional librarians were even more difficult to hire and keep when the secondary schools and the college offered alternative sources of employment at higher salaries.

At a time when the position of circulation librarian had been vacant for six months, Miss Jones received an application from Mrs. Anderson, a recent widow with a master's degree in library science. Mrs. Anderson had been a teacher-librarian in a neighboring, rural county and had just retired at age fifty-five. She stated that she had never had the opportunity to use her education as a librarian to the fullest, was interested in a public library position, and wanted to live in Union City because her brother lived there. She indicated that perhaps she might be interested in working in the public library for several years, and it was within the realm of possibility that she could work there until the age of sixty-five--a period of ten years. Mrs. Anderson had the highest recommendations and was extremely well regarded in her home town.

Miss Jones referred the application to Mrs. Martin, the Assistant Librarian, in charge of all public services. The duties of the circulation librarian were to supervise clerks and pages, to be responsible for adult readers' advisory service and service to young adults, and, at scheduled times, to work at the reference desk. Occasionally, in the absence of both Miss Jones and Mrs. Martin, the circulation librarian was in charge of the entire operation of the headquarters library. Anyone in this position should understand all circulation methods, make decisions in unusual or debatable situations, establish rapport with the public, and have a wide knowledge of library resources.

During a personal interview, both Miss Jones and Mrs. Martin spent considerable time with Mrs. Anderson and, after the interview, decided that, although not an ideal applicant, Mrs. Anderson had some qualifications for the position. The position was offered to Mrs. Anderson and she accepted.

After an initial overview of the library's operations conducted by the head librarian and the assistant librarian, the acting circulation librarian (who would soon be returning to a school library position) acquainted Mrs. Anderson with the circulation procedures. This seemed to take a longer time than was usual with new personnel, but Mrs. Martin thought this was to be expected since everything was being explained in detail in an effort to give Mrs. Anderson a complete understanding of the circulation methods which were fairly complex. Annual circulation from the headquarters library was approximately 270,000.

Mrs. Anderson proved to be conscientious and was very interested in her work. However, after several months, it seemed that her grasp of the total situation was not as firm as it should be, and she was reluctant to accept responsibility in the areas where she had the authority to make decisions. While the circulation assistants made a pretense of deferring to her, it was fairly obvious that any one of them performed more efficiently than did Mrs. Anderson, although in some cases they also were new in the system. Furthermore, she had not established rapport with the public and seemed to be ineffective in the reader's advisory capacity.

As Mrs. Anderson's supervisor, Mrs. Martin talked to her often about various aspects of her job pointing out better ways of handling her subordinates, of making decisions, and of serving the public, but no improvement was ever noticeable. Mrs. Martin reported each of these conferences to Miss Jones. When Mrs. Anderson had been on the job for ten months, Mrs. Martin recommended Mrs. Anderson's employment be terminated, stating, "Mrs. Anderson is no asset to the library system and we should fire her. She has many good qualities--reliability, intelligence, punctuality, a cooperative attitude, complete honesty, and pleasantness, but she simply has not developed into a capable supervisor, does not accept responsibility, and is ineffectual in reading guidance." Miss Jones pointed out the difficulties they always had in finding professionals.

Before any action had been taken toward termination, Miss Jones was contacted by an official who was seeking a head librarian for a county library which was being organized. The proposed library would be much smaller than the Union County Public Library and would be located in a largely rural county adjacent to Mrs. Anderson's home county where she was well known and respected. The county board of commissioners was considering offering Mrs. Anderson the position but would not do so until they first consulted Miss Jones to ask if she would recommend Mrs. Anderson.

Miss Jones pondered the problem. She knew that being head librarian of a new library would require that the librarian win public support through extensive promotion and publicity, plan activities and services, develop a building program based on activities and services, organize all work to be done, select and train a staff, supervise both staff and activities, and make a multitude of decisions. From her performance as circulation librarian, Miss Jones was convinced that Mrs. Anderson did not have the necessary qualifications or abilities for this position.

When she told Mrs. Martin about the request for a recommendation, Mrs. Martin said, "Here is a chance for us to get rid of her without firing her! Why don't you recommend her for the position?"

Case 20

PROMOTION

(Role playing)

Adams is a city of a million and a half population served by an extensive public library system totaling in excess of two million volumes. The administrative staff for operation includes three coordinators (adult services, children's services, and reference services), two supervisors (branches and extension, and technical services.)

Role for Mr. Edwin Stock, Coordinator of Reference Services:

You are responsible for the following operations in the

central library: general reference, telephone reference, information desk, and subject departments (local history, science and technology, business and economics, art and music, and social sciences). Also, you coordinate the reference services in the branches. You work constantly to build morale among your staff through careful and thorough orientation for all new staff members (pages, clerks, and professionals), staff participation in decisions, in-service training programs, and encouraging staff members to take formal courses in local higher education institutions. One of your policies is to promote from within wherever possible. When a vacancy occurs, you post a notice of the vacancy on all staff bulletin boards throughout the system and invite qualified staff members to apply.

The man who is head of your business and economics reading room recently resigned to accept a job as librarian of a corporation library in the city. The vacancy has been posted and you have received several applications. This morning you are interviewing Mr. Dwight Myna for the position.

Role for Mr. Dwight Myna:

You are twenty-eight years old, single, and have been an assistant in general reference where you have been employed since you received your library science degree two years ago.

At the age of seventeen, when you were a senior in high school, you enlisted in the United States Naval Reserve program and applied for active duty immediately following high school graduation. Because you were proficient in typing and were interested in office work, you were rated as a yeoman. For the first year you were assigned to the Special Services office of a large naval base in the United States where you handled correspondence, mimeographing, filing, requisitions, reports, and invoices. The rest of your two-year tour of duty you spent on an attack cargo ship (AKA) in the Mediterranean fleet. The ship carried a battalion of Marines plus their supplies and equipment and eight MIKE boats for landing both marines and their equipment. These small boats also served as a taxi squad for the fleet when it was in a port. You were one of three yeomen working in the ship's office. Your responsibilities included processing personnel papers and leave requests; handling the paper work for the Navy Training Courses and the correspondence courses for the U. S. Armed Forces Institute; sorting, distributing, and dispatching mail; and the usual office work of mimeographing, filing and typing. The last four months of this tour of duty you served as office manager.

After your discharge, you spent four years in a liberal arts college majoring in economics and one year in library school.

The salary for the position as head of the Business and Economics Department is one thousand dollars higher than you are earning in your present position. The qualifications call for background in business and economics, experience in library reference work, an ability to communicate and cooperate well with others, adequate supervisory skills, and a willingness to accept the added responsibilities of the position.

You know that two other staff members have applied and have been interviewed for the position. Both of them have had more library, business, and supervisory experience than you have had but you don't think they have as much economics background as you have. You are going to try to convince Mr. Stock that your experience in the Navy was good business background. Also, you are willing to take some business courses in a local university if you are appointed to the position. Although your supervisory experience is limited to being office manager for four months on your ship and to directing pages in your present position, you hope he will think you have potential in that area. You think his observations of your working relations with colleagues and your service to the public in your present position will satisfy the qualification of getting along with others. You are very willing to accept the added responsibilities of the new position. You want the appointment very much for two reasons: the subject area and the additional salary. The latter would make it possible to pay off your college loans faster.

Case 21

TRANSFER

(Role playing)

Adams is a city of a million and a half population served by an extensive public library system totaling in excess of two million volumes. The administrative staff for operation includes three coordinators (adult services, children's services, and reference services), two supervisors (branch and extension), and technical services.

Role for Mrs. Emma Teal:

You are the Assistant Director of the Adams Public Library System and you are in charge of personnel. A new position has just been created--Coordinator of Service to Deprived Areas--which will be supported by federal funds. The job description has not been defined specifically because the individual appointed to the position will have to explore opportunities for cooperation and coordination with such community programs as Community Action, Head Start, basic adult education, and urban renewal; and with library activities and programs for the culturally deprived in all library departments and branches.

The Director of Libraries believes that the person appointed to this position should be someone with experience in the library system as the job will require background knowledge of the operations, policies, and personnel of the system. You have studied the background, experience, and potential of all possible persons who could be transferred to this position. Your choice is Mrs. Pearl Brant, a handsome, capable black woman who is coming in for an interview this afternoon. Mrs. Brant does not know why she has been asked to come to your office. The salary for the new position is the same as that Mrs. Brant is now receiving. This sum is stipulated in conditions of the grant and you cannot alter it. Your job will be to persuade Mrs. Brant to accept this transfer by appealing to her professional dedication and the challenging aspects of carving out a new area of service and creating a new position.

Role for Mrs. Pearl Brant:

You are a widow forty years old with three children to support: a son who is enrolled in a local college majoring in mathematics and hoping to be a junior high school teacher, and two daughters in high school. You have worked in the Adams Public Library System ever since you graduated from high school. You worked part-time to support yourself during the six undergraduate years and the two years in library school; then full-time as a professional since that time. Your experience has all been in branches. For the past nine years you have been head of a branch in a ghetto neighborhood.

You conceived the idea of creating a storefront library where the old, the poor, the defeated, and the young could find a haven surrounded with materials to read or look at or to listen to. The supervisor of branches was skeptical but you convinced her to let you try it--and it has been a great success. The Police Community Relations group, the Neighborhood Legal Assistance Foundation, social workers in the area, and others have cooperated. The residents of the neighborhood feel welcome in this dingy-looking building with its comfortable old furniture (none of which matches), its friendly atmosphere, and its two affectionate cats. Some of the fiction is old and dog-eared but, to the borrowers, this condition is a recommendation that others have read them. Answering questions is an important function--how to kill rats, what to feed a baby, how to recognize symptoms of childhood diseases, where to get eyeglasses cheap, where to buy an old refrigerator or stove without getting gypped, where to get a free bath, how to get treatment for drugs or alcoholism or veneral disease.

The worn condition of a number of filmstrip viewers is evidence of their constant use. The record and tape players equipped with headphones, also, are in use most of the hours the library is open--older persons listening to popular music of their youth in the mornings to teen agers listening to the latest in rock music in the evenings, and those interested in listening to classical music, or speeches, or bird calls, or anything else at any time of day.

All of your staff are non-professionals who live in the neighborhood and are well acquainted with the residents. During the summers, they take library materials and toys to the population in an old panel truck converted for this use and tell stories in school playgrounds, church basements, and other places. On warm summer evenings, your staff show motion pictures outside and the audience sits on the steps and porches of nearby buildings or on the curbs or on the few rickety chairs which belong to the library and are set up for this purpose.

You feel your roots are here and you are very happy in your work.

Case 22

SIBILANCE

(Role playing)

Roles:
    Mrs. Acorn
    Pearl
    Personnel Director

How can you deal with someone who performs on a "just barely" level, who will not accept criticism of her work from superiors, and whose constant talking disturbs others? Mrs. Acorn has sought answers to these questions during the four months since she became the head of the Acquisitions Department in a large university library. Her staff is composed of several bibliographical searchers, and a number of clerks and part-time students. Although the department was operating fairly well when she assumed the position, she has made a number of changes in organizational structure, physical layout, methods, and work assignments to improve efficiency and output in order to reduce the backlog of work, and to make the most efficient possible use of public funds. All of her staff, except Pearl, have accepted her suggestions for changes and have been cooperating in learning new methods and techniques. Pearl presents a dilemma.

Pearl is thirty-three, a college graduate, and highly intelligent. She is quite attractive in appearance and dresses neatly. A slight separation between her two front teeth adds to rather than detracts from her appearance. However, when she talks, this separation causes a sibilance which penetrates every corner of the large room in which the department is located. And, since she talks almost constantly, the hissing becomes well-nigh intolerable, cannot be ignored, and distracts everyone. Because she is intelligent and has done the same type of work for several years, she completes the required minimum of work each day. She has worked longer in the department than any other employee (eleven years) and considers herself not subject to minor rules and regulations. She has resented and resisted some of Mrs. Acorn's changes and does not share the concern for greater efficiency to reduce the backlog and keep up with current order requests.

Within the first few weeks after she assumed this position, Mrs. Acorn discussed with Pearl her talking and her low level of performance. Pearl asserted that her seniority in the department should give her some privileges and that the former head of the department had never found fault with her work. She pointed out she did meet the daily quota. Mrs. Acorn told Pearl that (1) she was reducing the efficiency of the whole department by her talking; (2) she was a very poor example for the newer employees; (3) she had no special privileges because of seniority; and (4) she must improve her work performance. That discussion took place one month ago. Mrs. Acorn can see no change in Pearl's talking or performance. She has a conference set up today with Pearl and the Personnel Director.

Case 23

A RECEPTIONIST

(Role playing)

Roles:
      Associate Director in charge of personnel
      Hazel, a receptionist

In a large university library, the director and two associate directors share a suite of offices which include a private office for each director, an office for two secretaries, and a reception area. Hazel, the receptionist, sits near the door of the reception area, is responsible for greeting all guests, receiving and routing all telephone calls for the occupants of the suite, and taking messages. Hazel's conduct and work attitudes were first noticed by the two secretaries. It was quite common for her to tell a person telephoning the director that "he is too busy to talk to you," and she often compounded this insult by not offering to take a message. When a caller did insist on leaving a message, she quite frequently got the name or number wrong or failed to give the message to the person who was to return the call.

Her manner of handling guests who came to see the directors was rude and inefficient. For example, one day she ignored a visitor and he was forced to ask her for assistance. Hazel acted surprised that he would disturb her and did not respond very pleasantly to his presence. Usually a caller would just stand in the reception room not knowing whether to remove his coat, to sit down, or to walk out.

Frequently, visitors would request magazines or use of the phone; Hazel's usual response would be to stare blankly at the guests and to shove the phone or magazines at them. Occasionally she was in a talkative mood and would tell the visitors in great detail about her six-months-old baby. The secretaries were quite embarrassed by Hazel's behavior and tried to cover up or smooth over for her. They often greeted visitors themselves, hanging up the guests' coats and inviting them to be seated. Hazel did not seem to notice or mind. In fact, she was away from her desk quite frequently, which left all her duties to the secretaries.

Another problem that her co-workers noticed was her intense inquisitiveness. Of particular annoyance to them was her attitude about rest breaks. All library employees were allowed two fifteen-minute breaks per day. Every time one of the secretaries left her desk, Hazel would say, "Going on your break, are you?" Or when she returned, "Gee, you have been gone a long time. Wish I could get by with that." Furthermore, she made such comments if someone were a little late for work or left a little early in the evening.

Hazel had a tendency to interrupt and become involved in the secretaries' private conversations. Her inquisitiveness even extended to persons who were visiting the library. One day she was overheard asking a stranger who was waiting to see the director, "What have you got in your package--something for us?"

The secretaries were upset by her behavior and felt that it disrupted the normal operation of the office; they finally discussed the matter with the two associate directors. Both men were aware that there was a problem because of complaints they had received from persons outside the library, but had not realized that it was as serious as it was. The secretaries emphasized that they felt Hazel could do a much better job than she was doing.

The Associate Director in charge of personnel just asked one of the secretaries to work at Hazel's desk and has asked Hazel to come into his office for a talk. Her probation period of three months will be up in four weeks. The Associate Director will evaluate her performance with her, make suggestions for improvement, and warn her that she will be discharged if she does not improve markedly in the next two weeks.

Case 24

MUSIC

(Role playing)

Two months ago the staff and collection of the Dial College Library were moved into a new building. The acquisition and cataloging departments are located in one very large area on the ground floor. The heads of the two departments have glassed-in private offices but the rest of the area has no permanent partitions. Each staff member has some privacy provided either by low partitions, card files or book shelves near his desk. Ample room has been provided for all furniture and equipment with some room provided for the addition of more staff members at some later time. Air conditioning, excellent lighting, posture chairs, and pleasing interior decorator touches make for superior physical working conditions. The combined staff of the two departments totals about twenty-seven full-time (clerks, subprofessionals, and professionals) and six part-time students.

When this area was planned, the architect persuaded the staff building committee that piped-in music would be psychologically beneficial for staff morale. He pointed out that experience in business and industry had proved the value of background music in relaxing workers and in drowning out distracting noises. So, there are speakers in the circulation, acquisition, and cataloging departments, in the administrative suite of offices, and in the staff lounge. In each area, switches provide control of the sound system for on or off, volume, and channel selection. Two channels are piped in from a commercial sound system downtown which also serves doctors' offices and other places. One channel plays background music from musicals, light opera, and semi-classical instrumental compositions; the other plays rock and roll and jazz. Also, the system can be controlled within the library for playing phonorecords or phonotapes and as a loud speaker system.

In the technical services area, the music has resulted in bitter conflict among a formerly very congenial staff. Friendships of many years have been ruptured, animosities have developed, and tempers have flared. Verbal "battles" occur frequently over which channel should be tuned in and about the volume level. At one extreme are staff members who like either type of music and at the other extreme are those who dislike any music during working hours. Still others neither like nor dislike it but have learned to tolerate or ignore it or else wear ear plugs to shut it out. Curiously, the division on which channel is preferable is not according to age as one would expect. Some younger members prefer semi-classical background music and some older members like loud rock and roll. What an individual likes, dislikes, or tolerates seems to depend more on his type of work or his cultural background rather than on age.

In general, those who do more or less mechanical types of work like the music very much--unpacking boxes of books in the receiving area, loading finished books on book trucks ready for distribution, marking books, pasting, sorting cards, filing, and typing. The ones who want no music at all are those who must do concentrated mental work and who must make decisions constantly--classifiers, catalogers, searchers, and revisers. They maintain that the music is distracting so that they cannot concentrate on what they are doing. Several times, a "desperate" staff member in this latter group has turned off the sound only to be glared at by those who want to listen and be the target for verbal abuse. Those who enjoy rock and roll want the volume turned up very loud and others complain that the vibrations hurt their ears.

Roles:

Elliott: Thirty-five years old, has worked as receiving clerk and dispatcher in acquisitions for fifteen years, sings in his church choir, plays a violin in a community orchestra, and likes to listen to quiet melodious background music while he is working.

Libby: Nineteen years old, graduated from a high school secretarial course six months ago and types cards in the catalog department. She likes jazz and rock and roll-- the louder the better. She says that typing catalog cards all day is pretty dull work and the music helps to make the job bearable and the day go faster. She frequently turns up the volume.

Kathleen: Fifty-five years old, catalogs rare books and manuscripts many of which are in Greek, Latin, or modern foreign languages. Her work is exacting, and requires meticulous, precise cataloging. She claims that any kind of music makes it virtually impossible for her to do her

Personnel Cases   173

work because she cannot concentrate and must rethink her decisions after every distraction. She has tried wearing ear plugs but they irritate the skin in her ears. She has also experimented with ear muffs but they are uncomfortable and do not shut out the sound very well. She would like to see the speakers removed from the technical services area and thinks that then peace will be restored to the two departments.

Case 25

ANXIETY

(Role playing)

At the University of Yellow, the twelve departmental librarians reported to the Associate Librarian. Tom Sparrow, Librarian of the Chemistry Library, had an appointment this morning with the Associate Librarian to discuss a personnel problem. Here is what he reported:

"Opal is upsetting the morale of my staff. She has been working as a clerk in the Chemistry Library for almost a year. Just prior to her appointment, at the end of her junior year at this University, she married an engineering student. Her purpose in giving up her academic program and in seeking a full-time position was to support her husband while he finished his bachelor's degree. At the time she was employed, she said that both of them were 'broke' and she needed the job desperately. A couple of weeks after she started working for me, she used her position as a credit reference to buy a motorcycle for her husband which is their only means of transportation. They live in a trailer along with a dog and a duck.

"As circulation clerk, she is responsible for serving users at the public desk, answering the telephone as soon as it rings, and doing any photocopying that needs doing. We discovered soon after she was employed that we had to go over the job routines and procedures repeatedly before she grasped them. Her academic record (3.8 on a 4-point scale) indicates she is smart enough to do any job in the library, but she seems to be in a 'fog' much of the time and her mind is not on what she is doing. Evidently she is either worried or not interested in the work; her chief interest is in her pay check.

"Opal not only will not assume any responsibilities in the library for anything not spelled out in her job description, but neither does she perform her prescribed duties well or conscientiously. For example, she has been instructed to answer the telephone as soon as it rings so that readers will not be disturbed. But she doesn't like to answer the phone and frequently lets it ring, hoping someone else will answer it before she gets to it. She dislikes serving the users at the circulation desk and is often surly and uncommunicative.

"Her husband is a handsome, athletic type who completely dominates her. He refuses to work at part-time jobs to contribute to their income, but expects her to support both of them. He claims that he needs all his time for studying and keeping up his physical fitness in the gym. He does most of his studying in the Chemistry Library and often hangs around the desk, monopolizing her time and preventing her from doing the tasks assigned to her. She frequently leaves her work to go over to the table where he is studying to talk with him or stroke his hair or show affection in some other way. Other staff members report to me that when I am not in my office, she and her husband go in there for huge embraces. During lunch hours they have been observed 'necking' at the water fountain. I have talked to her several times about the propriety of showing affection in public and about utilizing library time for personal conversations, but I don't seem to be able to get through to her.

"She seems afraid that she is going to lose her husband and never leaves him alone if she can avoid it. When she has medical appointments, she even wants him in the same room when the physician is examining her. This fear of losing her husband carries over into the work relationship with other staff members and causes endless conflicts. She appears to have a 'chip on her shoulder' and her attitude implies that the staff members are trying to accuse her of something. She gives the impression of feeling insecure. I have tried to give her greater responsibilities in the hope that this would develop confidence in herself, but she shows no interest in new assignments.

"She talks and gossips endlessly and asks the staff questions about sex and childbirth and other very personal matters. I have told her that such questions are indiscreet and embarrassing to the staff and that there are other and better sources to go to for such information. Several times I have told her to keep her purely personal problems to herself and that her work environment is no place to discuss them.

"She even lacks confidence in her judgment as to appropriate dress. She frequently will ask other staff members if she looks all right. For example, she experimented with false eyelashes until one staff member suggested to her that they were not appropriate in a public work environment. Another day she came in wearing a pantsuit and asked me how I liked it. I said it was a stunning outfit but that I didn't think a pantsuit was appropriate attire when she was on duty in a library. The next thing I knew she appeared without the pants and worked the rest of the day in the top of the suit. Actually the pants top was no shorter than a mini-skirt. She has no sense of propriety or behavior for a public employee.

"I have studied her folder in the personnel office to search for clues in her personal life, her social life, and her family history to understand her behavior and attitude. One of the references in her folder was from the pastor of her church who had known her and her family for years. I telephoned him to ask about her background.

"He told me that he believed her insecurity was rooted in her past. Her older sister was attractive, outgoing, and popular whereas Opal was shy and retiring, and spent most of her time doing things by herself, such as handicrafts and reading. Her parents admired her older sister and her accomplishments and constantly held her up as an example to Opal. The sister was a high school cheerleader, active in other high school activities, and dated. As an adolescent, Opal had acne, a plumpish 'dumpy' figure, and was not very well coordinated physically, so that she was not sought after as a tennis partner or even in sand-lot baseball. The height of her ambition in high school was to be a cheerleader, but she did not survive the tryouts. She had only two dates during high school. When she went to school dances, she spent most of the time sitting on the sidelines looking longingly at others who were dancing. Her husband was the only man she dated at the University and, when she was dating him, he was also dating other girls. When he proposed, she was 'on cloud nine.'

"Her anxiety over losing her husband may be well-founded. Her colleagues on the library staff fear that her husband's interest in her is almost exclusively as a means of support and that he will probably leave her soon after he gets his bachelor's degree in a few months from now and is established in a job.

"I just don't know how to cope with this problem. Can you suggest what I might do? To terminate her employment would probably increase her anxiety and her insecurity, but I am short-staffed and need maximum performance from each staff member. The library is not a social service agency but, on the other hand, I do not want to add to the girl's problems."

Roles:
  Cliff Maroon, Associate Librarian
  Tom Sparrow, Librarian, Chemistry Library

Case 26

THE "TROUBLESHOOTER" IN SERIALS

When the head of the Serials Division of a large university library (Miss Effing) announced her decision to retire, the Director of Libraries and the Personnel Director searched for a qualified person to replace her. The Director of Libraries wanted someone who had administrative ability and was capable of reorganizing the Division. Miss Effing had been employed in the library for more than thirty years and had been head of the Serials Division for the last ten years. At the time of her appointment ten years ago, her professional preparation and experience were adequate for the job; but she had not kept up with new developments in this field, had not adjusted to the growing size and complexity of the library, and seemed unable to cope with the administrative problems of a large staff. The work of the Serials Division was rather complex and specialized. The Division (1) kept the records of serial publications (including government documents) which were housed both in the main and undergraduate libraries and in forty-two branch libraries; (2) distributed serials to the libraries; (3) maintained the large serial collection in the main library; and (4) gave reference service involving serials to patrons. The records were of two types: those on Visible Record trays and those in catalog drawers.

The Division's staff consisted of fifteen persons: two professionals, four sub-professionals (who had specialized

Personnel Cases 177

background in languages), and nine clerks. The team spirit
in the Division was high in spite of the fact that the backlog
of unfinished work was frustratingly large and the staff recognized Miss Effing's shortcomings as an administrator.

For several years, the Director of Libraries had received numerous complaints from the various departments of
the university and from library staff members about the unavailability of the items in the backlog of untouched materials
in the Serials Division. He had also made some observations on his own and was convinced that the Division needed
a head who was capable of studying the situation, developing
new procedures, and working out new methods. Because
Miss Effing was so near retirement, he was reluctant to make
any changes until that time. He passed on to her the various
complaints and suggested ways of speeding up the work but
did not press her for changes.

The Director of Libraries and the Personnel Director
interviewed several applicants for the position and agreed
that the one who seemed to have the most potential was Mr.
Camp, a young man already on their staff. Mr. Camp was
twenty-eight years old, ambitious, aggressive, and intelligent.
He had worked in two other departments in the library where
he had built a reputation as a "troubleshooter." Several
times he had been commended for his creative ideas in solving problems. Recently he had completed an executive development training program offered by the university's school
of business. The Director of Libraries thought that his professional education and background plus his reputation should
have prepared Mr. Camp for supervision and for "straightening out" the Serials Division. In Camp's eyes, heading this
Division was not a prestige position but he accepted the appointment because he believed that if he were able to solve
the problems in this Division, he would make a name for
himself which would qualify him later for another administrative assignment more to his liking.

The staff of the Division had found Miss Effing to be
gentle, sympathetic, and democratic in her relations with
them; but they found Mr. Camp to be quite different--brusque,
officious, dictatorial, and self-important.

The weekend after assuming the position, he shifted
furniture without consulting any of his staff. When they
came to work Monday morning, they had to search for their
desks. He did not explain why he had made the changes and

the staff could see neither a logical pattern for the rearrangement nor an improvement in work flow.

Three weeks later he ordered his staff to rearrange the files according to a new system he had worked out which he thought would be more efficient. Most of the staff were told to suspend their normal routines and activities and work on the rearranging of files. The staff grumbled and the backlog became larger. The new system did not work (some of the clerks who had been working with the files for years could have told him this when he conceived the idea). Over loud protests from the staff, the files were rearranged twice more during the next two weeks. Complaints also came from staff members from the searching sections of the cataloging and acquisition department who had to use these files constantly. The difficult filing systems confused them.

At this university library all full-time staff members were permitted to take two ten-minute rest breaks per day. Because the Serials Division was located some distance from vending machines, the staff lounge, and the cafeteria, it was impossible for the staff of this Division to walk to and from one of these areas in ten minutes let alone eat or drink anything. Miss Effing had requested several years ago that the cafeteria come to the Division twice a day with a variety of beverages and snacks on a cart so the staff could take their breaks in the Division. But the Personnel Department vetoed this idea. Then she suggested that a small refrigerator and hot plate be made available for her Division so the staff could keep soft drinks in the refrigerator and prepare hot drinks on the hot plate. That was rejected by the Director's office, who said that he didn't want eating places set up all over the library inasmuch as they did have vending machine areas and a cafeteria.

Time clocks had not been installed in the library, so there was no way to check accurately on the time expended on breaks. Frequently the breaks extended for fifteen minutes to half an hour. The Personnel Department had always handled the situation by periodically sending around a memorandum which castigated but did not overtly threaten the employees. No one had ever been fired for overly long rest breaks. The difficulties in attracting qualified personnel and the high rate of turnover which existed made this unwise. But the memoranda frightened the staff slightly, and for a time they would return to ten-minute breaks.

Mr. Camp observed that many of his staff were taking more than ten minutes. He put the following notice on the desk of each of his staff members:

> It has been noticed that people have been spending an inordinate amount of time on their rest breaks. Unless this stops, the privilege of breaks will be suspended.

The following day the staff observed Mr. Camp noting on a chart the time when each of them left for and returned from her break. It was rumored that time clocks would be installed soon. The staff felt that Mr. Camp was being unreasonable. Morale in the Division was at an all-time low, dissatisfaction was rampant, and some threatened to look for other jobs. The backlog got larger each day.

If you were the Personnel Director, how would you handle this situation and what would you recommend to the Director of Libraries?

Case 27

CREATION OF A SUPERVISOR

When Malcolm Hawthorn planned the new library building for Balsam College, he considered the needs of the present student body of about 14,000 and the present collection as well as projected increases in enrollment, materials, and services. He knew that the library staff of eight professionals in the old building could not possibly supervise the much larger new building. Every time he discussed the building program and the plans with the President, the latter would ask, "Is this going to take more staff?" and Mr. Hawthorn would reply "Of course it will take more staff. In other academic institutions the experience has been that demands for service skyrocket when a library is moved to a new building. I expect the same increased use for our new building. Furthermore, we do not have enough staff in our present crowded quarters and they cannot possibly supervise the much larger area in the new building."

Being conservative and frugal, the President would say, "Well, we will get along with the present library staff as long as we can." As a consequence, Mr. Hawthorn planned a building that he saw no prospect of staffing with any degree of flexibility or comfort. But he optimistically believed that eventually he would acquire sufficient staff.

At the time of the move, he had four department heads: Order, Cataloging, Circulation, and Reference. Because of subject arrangement of the collection in the new building, four additional supervisors were required: humanities, social sciences, art and music, and science.

The head of each of these new divisions was to be responsible in that subject area for building the collection, for reference service, and for supervising reading room use of the collection; each would report directly to Mr. Hawthorn. Subject area books from the old Reference Room were placed in one of the four subject divisions in the new building. The new Reference collection would then consist chiefly of general bibliographies, encyclopedias, yearbooks, annuals, dictionaries, and indexes; and the rapidly expanding microform collection (all subjects). The Reference librarian would be responsible for building these collections and for supervising the Reference reading room, the microform readers and interlibrary loans.

Mr. Hawthorn had succeeded in getting beginning salaries raised so that they were competitive with salaries offered nationally and hence attracted competent, energetic, library school graduates. But salaries for the older staff members were only slightly higher than the beginning salaries and were not competitive with salaries for experienced librarians nationally. The President of the College would not approve increasing the salaries to the point where they would be comparable to those offered by other academic libraries for experienced librarians; hence, Mr. Hawthorn could not offer high enough salaries to attract applicants for supervisory positions. Capable new graduates could not take over the management of a department until they had acquired some experience. So, Mr. Hawthorn was forced to develop supervisors from those on the staff and employ inexperienced new graduates to take their places. He talked quite frankly to his staff about this. Four of the eight professionals were already supervisors and he persuaded each of the other four to assume one of the new supervisory positions although none of them appeared enthusiastic or had shown any aptitude for supervision. Mr. Hawthorn hoped that, if these four did not prove satisfactory as supervisors or were not happy in the new assignments, he could find other positions on the staff for them in which they would be happy. He intended to continue to work for higher salaries for the senior staff which would attract experienced librarians from outside when future vacancies occurred.

After about four years of experience in the documents department of a large university library, Dorcas came to Balsam College as Assistant Reference Librarian. She knew Balsam's reference collection thoroughly, was a strong collection builder and an avid book selector, and competently served the students and faculty. In addition to her master's degree in library science, she also had a master's degree in political science. Because of her background in documents and political science, as well as her five years of successful experience as Assistant Reference Librarian at Balsam, Mr. Hawthorn thought she was well qualified to take charge of the new Social Sciences Division. She had no supervisory experience except to direct the work of one clerical assistant and some student shelvers when the Reference Librarian was not on duty. Since she had done "wonders" for the Reference collection, Mr. Hawthorn confidently expected that she would do equally well in developing the new Social Sciences Division.

Dorcas was not an outgoing or warm person and rarely smiled but she was always courteous and considerate and had good professional relations with the rest of the staff. Those who worked with her admired her for her keen mind, knowledge of the collection, and willingness to spend any amount of time in ferreting out answers to difficult questions.

Over a period of about four months her staff was gradually built up one at a time: a recent library school graduate, a full-time clerk, and student assistants. Mr. Hawthorn consulted Dorcas about each appointment but she seemed most indecisive about selecting from among the applicants and left the decisions up to him, saying, "You have had experience in selecting staff members and are much better qualified than I to make the decision. I prefer that you decide which should be chosen." She acted as though she feared such experiences would be confrontations.

Mr. Hawthorn was surprised at this reaction because the other supervisors preferred to select their own staff. When each of the appointees arrived, Dorcas told Mr. Hawthorn that she was too busy to tell them what they were supposed to do and asked him to do it. He refused, saying that this was the time for a supervisor to start establishing rapport with a staff member and gaining his or her respect. Dorcas pleaded that she had never taken charge of orienting a staff member and she didn't know what to do. Mr. Hawthorn made some suggestions and then questioned her about how she planned to divide the professional responsibilities between herself and Arleen, the professional assistant, and what duties she was assigning to the clerk. Dorcas stared at him with a rather blank expression and said, "I have worked out a desk schedule to cover all the hours the library is open. Do I need to do anything else? I have so much bibliographical work to do that I don't have time to figure out what other persons should do." Mr. Hawthorn patiently explained the necessity for her as a supervisor (1) to organize the work of the Division so that each person shared the work of the Division and had certain well-defined responsibilities; (2) to work out procedures; and (3) to orient each staff member in the goals of the Division and how they contributed to the objectives of the library and the College. Dorcas felt he was criticizing her and broke into tears.

Mr. Hawthorn was so busy with all the usual problems connected with moving that he did not check carefully on the work of the individual departments and divisions during the first weeks in the new building. About three months after the move, he became acutely aware that the staff situation in the Social Science Division was explosive when he discovered that Dorcas and Arleen were not speaking to one another and service to the public consequently suffered. A few days later Arleen submitted her resignation to him and said she could not stand working with Dorcas another day. She complained that Dorcas treated her like a student assistant and gave her no opportunities to participate in the professional aspects of the work. Except for the hours she was scheduled to work at the desk, Arleen said she had no regular work delegated to her. Dorcas assigned jobs to her that could be done by the clerk or by student assistants such as filing, checking in periodicals, and typing orders for books which Dorcas had selected. Dorcas insisted on doing all the bibliographical work and tough reference requests herself and even refused to allow Arleen time on the job to study the books in the collection in order for her to acquire greater knowledge of the resources or to read reviews of new reference books. Furthermore, Arleen said of Dorcas, "She is emotional, tense, and nervous about everything. She is moody and I never know where I stand or how to approach her. If I do something incorrectly or not the way she thinks it should be done, she will 'punish' me by giving me some non-professional task like straightening books on the shelves or reading shelves or by not speaking to me for days. She never yet has told me that I did anything right or complimented me on anything I did. I have tried in every way I know to prove to her that I am capable of doing real professional work. The clerk sits idle many hours a week because she has nothing to do while I am loaded down with clerical tasks."

Mr. Hawthorn tried unsuccessfully to mediate the differences between the two but Arleen left. The next week the clerk applied to him for transfer to a typist vacancy in the Cataloging Department. When he asked why she wanted to be transferred, she said that she never knew what she was supposed to do and that Dorcas wouldn't allow her to make any decisions even about minor things. "In the jobs I have had previously, I was responsible for certain duties and procedures. I knew what I was supposed to do. But Dorcas has never told me what is involved in this job. She assigns tasks one step at a time and insists that I check back with her before going on to the next step even though I have done the same task many times before and can carry it through to completion. As a result, many tasks are unfinished because Dorcas hasn't made the decision as to what should be done next. I know that the job in the Catalog Department is well-defined and fits into a work flow pattern and I could keep busy all the time without checking constantly with a supervisor. I don't like to sit around waiting for someone to tell me what to do next."

In the course of this interview, Mr. Hawthorn was horrified to discover that Dorcas' "orientation program" for the clerk and pages consisted, among other things, of a thorough description and explanation of the Dewey Decimal Classification, cataloging filing rules, and the procedures utilized by the Order Department in acquiring library materials.

Mr. Hawthorn concluded that Dorcas was unable to discriminate between what was important for them to know and what was not important. Although she had tried to be a supervisor, it was obvious that she was incapable of planning and directing the work of others. He recognized the fact that he had made a serious mistake in appointing her as a supervisor. He hadn't realized that she had no leadership capability nor the flexibility to change her role from that of a staff member to that of a supervisor. He knew now that he should have let her continue to be the expert bibliographer, reference librarian, and collection builder that she was where she did not have to make administrative decisions or be concerned about interpersonal relationships. Her personality seemed to require that she work in a situation where she could lean on a strong leader who would provide guidelines within which she could work and would provide a pleasant, uncomplicated work environment.

Mr. Hawthorn asked himself what had he not done that he could have done? If he had been more experienced in developing executive talent in his staff, could he have utilized some techniques and motivational methods to prepare her for the new role? Or, was she basically not qualified for leadership?

Case 28

POLITICAL POSTERS

(Role playing)

This morning Barry Crane came to work half an hour early, affixed posters, pictures, and slogans on the wall near his desk, placed a propaganda pamphlet on the desk of each member in the Department, and posted announcements and slogans of various kinds on the Departmental bulletin board.

Approximately seventy persons worked in this Technical Services Department of a large public library. The social and political issues involved in the current election campaign were controversial and emotionally volatile. For several weeks, discussions among some members of the staff reflected the varying shades of public sentiment and feeling on the issues. Some members were not speaking to other members because of differences in views.

When staff members arrived at their desks this morning and saw the displays as well as the pamphlets on their desks, tempers flared and those opposed to Barry's point of view felt insulted and imposed upon. After lunch the walls and bulletin board were covered with printed materials of various kinds presenting arguments and catch phrases for the opposing side. The Department was in an uproar and emotions and conversations interfered seriously with work production.

Personnel Cases   185

Role for Barry Crane:

You are a classifier, twenty-seven years old, single, and enjoy espousing causes. During the three years on this staff, you have been active in a fund raising campaign for a little theatre, in a group working toward elimination of billboards (you personally chopped down one that was especially offensive to you and were apprehended for the act), and in pollution control. You talked to some of your fellow workers about these causes and they either listened tolerantly or were amused. But you had never before been involved in political campaigns nor circulated pamphlets or posted anything on the wall near your desk. You feel deeply involved in the issues of the current upcoming municipal election and are actively participating in the campaign.

Role for Mrs. Irene Almond, Chief, Technical Services Department:

You are fifty years old, have been in this position for about ten years, are a capable, fair, and understanding supervisor who has built an efficient Department and staff. The morale of the staff is so shattered by Barry's activities and remarks during the current campaign that you feel compelled to face the problem squarely by talking to Barry immediately. You ignored his propagandizing for other causes because they were non-political and the staff reacted with good-humored tolerance. The current situation is entirely different; not only are the emotions of the staff interfering with output but also the library's and the city employees' personnel codes do not permit such political activity on the part of a public employee.

The city personnel code states:

> City employees are neither appointed to nor retained upon the basis of their political activity.
> In return, while city employees can exercise their right of suffrage as citizens to vote as they please and express privately their political opinions, it is deemed in the best interest of the municipal government that they not engage in any unusual political party activity and that they do not participate actively in the municipal election campaigns. This rule applies whether an employee is on or off duty.

The prohibition on political activity in the municipal code warns employees that it is "illegal to assume political leadership or become prominently identified with any political movement, party, or faction, or with the success or failure of any candidate for election to public office in a partisan political campaign." The code covers such political activities as: candidacy or service as a delegate to a political convention; service as a party officer or on any political party committee; organization or conduct of political rallies; delivery of political speeches; solicitation of campaign contributions or getting out votes; publication of any statement for or against any candidate, party, or faction; organization of or leading participation in political parades or marches; distribution of political campaign literature; and partisan candidacy for public office.

The library personnel code specifies that the library's personnel officer is responsible for enforcement of the rules against political activity; but the employee's supervisor is also responsible. The latter must not only set an example, but also must take appropriate action in cases of violation, just as in the case of any other personnel rule.

* * * * * * * *

Note: Role players may wish to read about the political activities of public employees as background preparation for this case. The following titles are suggestive of the type of information available:

Dwoskin, Robert P. "Constitutional Rights of Public Librarians." Library Journal, 95: 2417-2421, July, 1970

Municipal Personnel Administration; 6th ed. Chicago: International City Managers' Association, 1960. pp. 234-236.

Stahl, O. Glenn. Public Personnel Administration; 5th ed. New York: Harper & Row, 1962. pp. 360-369.

Personnel Cases 187

Case 29

MARIJUANA

John Rayon, Director of Libraries for City Public Library, stared in disbelief at the headline on the front page of the paper when he read it at his home this morning: "Librarian Arrested." The article described how the police had discovered that Bill Silk, Librarian of Smith Branch, was growing and harvesting marijuana in the backyard of his suburban home and drying it in his basement. The yard was enclosed by a high board fence so that the "crop" had never been observed by his neighbors. According to the local legal procedures, if a person was arrested on a charge of selling the drug, he would be prosecuted under a felony statute in circuit and superior courts. A possible two to ten-year sentence could be imposed. If an individual merely possessed the drug, he would be prosecuted under a "common nuisance" charge which was a misdemeanor carrying a maximum one year penalty. According to the newspaper account "the procedure to be used in prosecuting Mr. Silk will depend upon whether he was producing the drug for his own use or was selling it."

When Mr. Rayon reached the library, he asked the Supervisor of Branches and the Personnel Director to come to his office to discuss the problem. All three were visibly shaken and upset. Both the Personnel Director and the Supervisor of Branches had already communicated with staff members who had worked with Mr. Silk or who knew him best. No one had even suspected his involvement in this activity and could furnish no additional information. One of his staff members at the Branch reported that she frequently noticed an odor like that of burning hay about his clothes and body but had thought he must have been burning trash in his yard; she realized now that that must have been marijuana. No one had observed any personality changes, impairment in verbal facility, or psychotic reaction in Mr. Silk which might result from smoking marijuana.

For several days Mr. Rayon's office received one phone call after another--from the mayor's office, members of the Board of Trustees, members of the Friends of the Library, staff members off duty, and many others.

Mr. Silk had been employed in the City Public Library ever since he graduated from library school four years ago. His first appointment was in the Young Adult Department where he was popular with readers because he related well to that age group and was knowledgeable about the collection. He was handsome, outgoing, intelligent, and conscientious in his work. When the librarian of the Smith Branch was transferred to a larger branch a year ago, Mr. Silk was offered, and accepted, appointment as librarian of Smith Branch. In the area served by that Branch were two junior high schools and one senior high school. His experience with young adults was considered valuable for this position. The Branch Supervisor was pleased with his management of the Branch during the past year and with his evident capability as a supervisor.

The staff Personnel Code contained no statement covering arrest of a staff member. The problem would have to be discussed at a meeting of the Board of Trustees. Should he be allowed to continue working at the Branch? What were the legal conditions regarding public employees who were arrested?

Case 30

CHRONIC INSOMNIA

(Role playing)

Roles:
 Miss Ramona Flannel, Head, Technical Services, Regional Library
 Mr. Jack Serge, Librarian, Regional Library

Soon after Jack Serge became librarian of a recently organized regional library, he discovered that his head of technical services, Miss Ramona Flannel, never arrived for work until 10 a.m. and frequently not until 11:30. The rest of her staff worked from 8 a.m. to 5 p.m. Monday through Friday. Miss Flannel was about forty-five years of age, intelligent and efficient, had been on the staff for twenty-one years, and had been head of technical services for ten years.

When Mr. Serge inquired about her working hours, she explained, "I have chronic insomnia and seldom get to sleep until 2 or 3 a.m. so I am too tired to get to work at 8 a.m. I put in more hours than any of the rest of my staff by working evenings, Saturdays, and Sundays."

Mr. Serge pointed out (1) that she had no business working at night alone; (2) that the rest of the staff thought she was "getting by" with something when they observed her coming in late every day and this affected morale; (3) that her subordinates needed her supervision during the hours they worked; and (4) that he needed her to be there for whatever meetings were scheduled in the morning and for any emergencies which arose.

Miss Flannel broke down in tears and said, "Your predecessors were sympathetic and considerate and allowed me to come in whenever I felt like it and to work whatever schedule I chose as long as I worked forty hours a week."

Mr. Serge replied, "I'm sorry about your insomnia but that is your personal problem to solve. In fairness to the rest of the staff and in the interests of efficient supervision of your department, I must insist that you work the same schedule as your staff. Have you consulted a physician about your problem?"

Miss Flannel stated that she had sought medical advice. She tried valiantly for a few weeks to get in earlier but gradually resumed coming in later and later.

Mr. Serge was employed to organize a number of small libraries into a regional system with his medium-sized library as the headquarters. All ordering, cataloging, and processing were to be centralized in the headquarters library, so Miss Flannel's department had to be greatly enlarged both in physical space and in staff. Many problems came up for decision when Miss Flannel was not there. In desperation Mr. Serge phoned her housemate in the hope that he could learn more about Miss Flannel's problem. The housemate said, "Several years ago, Miss Flannel's sister had a nervous breakdown and was put into a mental institution for a few months. This upset Miss Flannel, causing anxiety, worry, and depression. Her sister is now living a normal life but Miss Flannel's anxiety has not been alleviated, instead it seems to be an habitual condition now."

Mr. Serge inquired if nothing could be done for her in the way of medication and the housemate replied, "Her physician says there is no physical cause for her insomnia. He has been patient and understanding and at first gave her some medication to carry her through the period of stress caused by worry over her sister. But when she continued to complain, he refused to prescribe any more sedatives because chronic use of any sedative might lead to habituation, and some of them are potentially addictive and hence needed to be used sparingly and only during crises. He was of the opinion that Miss Flannel needed to develop some self-control over her anxieties. He believes her condition now has become psychological and has tried to persuade her to see a psychiatrist, but she has refused. My personal feeling is that she rather enjoys being a 'martyr' to insomnia, which brings her attention from her friends and a type of status and prestige."

Although this information helped Mr. Serge to understand her behavior and motivation, it did not solve his need for a head of Technical Services who could be depended upon to be on duty regularly from 8 to 5. He has scheduled a conference with her for tomorrow morning.

Case 31

SCHOOL DISTRICT UNIFICATION

In a small school district of eight elementary schools and one junior-senior high school, I was librarian of the high school and supervisory librarian of the two elementary school librarians each of whom was responsible for the library program in four schools. I had expanded the high school library collection and services and had started the elementary school libraries. I had been in this position for five years when our school district was unified with two others, one smaller than ours and the other much larger. The smaller one did not have a library program but the larger one did. I was named Coordinating Librarian of the new unified district and assigned the responsibility of developing library programs for those schools which did not have them and for improving the programs in the larger district as well as continuing the programs which I had developed in my district.

The supervising librarian in the larger district, Kelvin Cork, had applied for the position of Coordinating Librarian and was furious that I, a woman, had been appointed. He bitterly resented what he considered this affront to his prestige and reduction in his status although he remained supervisor of the same libraries he had administered for eight years. The only change was that he had to report to me and was expected to cooperate in the reorganization which the unification required.

I had met Mr. Cork at school librarians' meetings and had thought him to be cordial, polite, and professionally oriented. But I was shocked to find that the man I would have to work with was antagonistic, belligerent, rude, and most uncooperative. In talking to some of the librarians and teachers in his district, I learned that he had a medical record of emotional instability and, in fact, had been committed to a mental hospital at one time. His psychiatrist was the person who had suggested librarianship as a career for him because it was a profession free of stress! He was employed as an elementary school librarian in this school district after completing library school. His work appeared to be fairly satisfactory to the principals and superintendent. As the only male librarian in the district, the superintendent thought he was the logical person to fill the position of supervisory librarian for the district when that position became vacant two years after he had been employed. His performance as supervisory librarian left much to be desired--hence my appointment as Coordinating Librarian of the unified district.

Several weeks after the announcement of my appointment, Mr. Cork had a mild heart attack which he attributed in part to overwork and tension stemming from his devotion and dedication to his job and, in part, to harassment by the school administration in appointing me as his supervisor. He alleged that the administration disliked him and had been unfair to him.

During my first year as Coordinating Librarian, he did an infinitesimal amount of work, ignored every overture to include him in decisions involving unification, would communicate with me only through letters, refused (on grounds of health) to attend meetings or conferences, would never answer the telephone, and walked out whenever I visited his libraries. He spent all of his time and energy blocking unification of the library systems and attacking my professional performance. The administration did not want unfavorable newspaper publicity (which would inevitably follow if he were discharged and appealed to the Board of Education). He seemed very aware of this and exploited it fully. I have been given to understand that he is my problem and I simply have to put up with him.

How should I handle this situation? I need advice. I have tried to progress patiently and understandingly with him but only meet total resistance.

Case 32

IRRATIONAL BEHAVIOR

(Role playing)

Roles:
    Mr. Baker, Head Librarian
    Mr. Cress

After he graduated from library school five years ago, Mr. Cress was appointed Librarian I in a large public library system. He had grown up in this city and wished to be employed here because of family ties. He was given what was considered a typical assignment for a new professional in this library--half-time in technical services and half-time in public services.

It soon became apparent that his abilities did not lie in the public services field. Although he had an adequate knowledge of books and of reference work, his manner with the public was brusque, off-hand, and contemptuous. His supervisor in public services talked to him several times about his treatment of patrons and he would improve for a while but then would revert to his former behavior. Finally, the supervisor requested that he be transferred. As soon as a vacancy developed, he was placed full-time in cataloging. Here his work was reasonably adequate (but by no means outstanding) and he did his share of the work. However, his personality faults became more and more evident as time went on. He was truculent, alienated his fellow workers by his sneering attitude and air of superiority, and was given to irrational bursts of anger. He was moody, temperamental, morose and secretive, talkative and over-friendly, brusque and sharp-tongued, and occasionally verbally violent. For a long period he was extremely careless about his personal appearance, and remedied the situation only after repeated remonstrance of his supervisor and department head.

This library was always understaffed because salaries and fringe benefits were not competitive with those of school, academic, and special libraries in the area. Turnover of all types of employees was high but especially among professional staff. Because competent catalogers were extremely hard to recruit and hold, Mr. Cress's personality was tolerated by his supervisor and his fellow workers. The head of technical services talked with him often about his attitude and behavior and pointed out that he could not be promoted until and unless he improved markedly. Mr. Cress blamed his behavior on frustrations caused by the administration's "deliberate persecution and lack of understanding."

Before the end of his one and one-half year probation period, the head librarian, Mr. Baker, called him in and explained that he should have been dismissed during the probation period because of his behavior, his attitude toward fellow workers, and his just-adequate work performance; but, because of their dire need for catalogers, he would be kept on. The librarian informed him that he would be granted permanent status with the understanding that he would never be promoted. Mr. Cress verbally accepted this status.

Three years later, after he had been on the staff for four and one-half years, Mr. Cress took the examination for Librarian II and passed. He then petitioned the Board of Trustees for a promotion. They reviewed his case and decided that Mr. Baker's action in granting him permanent status with the understanding that he would never be promoted was not a legal action. He was promoted to Librarian II. (Librarian I's normally acceded to Librarian II after two years of service and the passing of an examination.)

A crisis occurred yesterday when Mr. Cress, in a fit of rage, physically attacked a fellow worker. The latter refused to press charges in spite of the fact that he sustained minor injuries. In this library system it is practically impossible to dismiss an employee with permanent status unless he is grossly incompetent, is convicted of a crime, or is guilty of something equally drastic.

Mr. Baker called Mr. Cress to his office this morning. Mr. Cress has just arrived.

Case 33

TERMINATION

(Role playing)

Role for Mrs. Hemlock:

You have been librarian of Redbud Public Library for fifteen years. Your staff is composed of four professionals (heads of technical services, reference, and two catalogers), eleven full-time assistants, some of whom have had two or more years of college and some library science courses; and fifteen part-time students. Through the years you have tried to develop a career program encouraging the high school students to go on to college, attempting to recruit college students to become librarians, encouraging the full-time clerks to finish college and/or study library science courses offered at extension centers and urging your professional staff to continue their education in one way or another.

Five years ago you employed Miss Madden as a full-time clerk in the Circulation Department. She was eager, alert, and intelligent and got along well with everyone on the staff. You thought she would make a good librarian and talked to her about librarianship as a career. She said she had to support herself so could not take a year off to go to library school. You then offered to adjust work loads and schedules to permit her to take a summer leave of absence without pay to attend library school. Miss Madden accepted the offer eagerly. When she returned at the end of the summer, she told you how grateful she was for this opportunity, how pleased she was with her courses, and that she hoped you would arrange schedules and grant her leaves every summer until she finished the degree. After she returned from the third summer session, the staff noticed a changed attitude; she acted as though she were quite superior to all of them and frequently "showed off" some of her new knowledge by pointing out in an obnoxious, critical way how "stupid" and "out-of-date" many procedures and practices were.

You were very disappointed in her and had several talks with her during the year about her attitude. The next year, after she received her master's degree, she was appointed head of the Reference Department. Her attitude was even more superior and condescending than it had been the year previously. You found her to be a disruptive force to

Personnel Cases

the cohesion of the whole staff. Because of her degree, her ideas and criticisms carried considerable weight with the non-professionals and the students on the staff who felt that she was probably right about what she did. After she was initiated into Altrusa Club, she became insufferable. One professional staff member remarked that she had never seen a person so changed by a graduate degree and membership in a club. Both seemed to go to her head. She broke all kinds of small rules that the staff were aware of and probably many more that on one observed. For instance, all the staff knew that they should never answer a reference question over the telephone without telling what the source was even if it was as simple as spelling a word. She did it all the time. Staff members reported that she would tell patrons that a certain question could be answered in such-and-such reference book but that this library did not own that book and she would make no attempt to substitute another source or offer to contact another library to get an answer.

You talked to her about this kind of performance but did not seem to "get through" to her and she continued to be a "law unto herself." Recently several patrons reported to you that she had supplied misinformation to them and had been very antagonistic and haughty when they returned for right information. A board member reported several complaints from the public that she would not look up information in which she was not interested or would do a sloppy job of finding an answer.

You have concluded that you must ask for her resignation. You have made an appointment with her for this afternoon.

Role for Miss Madden:

When you received your A. B. degree majoring in secondary education with a concentration in social studies five years ago, you expected to teach in junior or senior high school somewhere. However, there were practically no openings in this subject area so you were unsuccessful in obtaining a teaching position. You learned about a vacancy on the staff of your home town library (Redbud Public Library), so you applied to Mrs. Hemlock for the position and were accepted. You had never considered librarianship as a career but soon became interested after working for several months. Mrs. Hemlock urged you to study for a master's degree in library science. So you took a leave of absence each summer in order to study at a library school.

About the time you received your master's degree the position as head of reference at Redbud Public Library became vacant and Mrs. Hemlock offered it to you. You accepted and have been in this position for one year. You enjoy the status and prestige of the position but are annoyed with various rules and regulations which you consider unnecessary or downright silly. You have had several "run ins" with Mrs. Hemlock about this and she has been sharply critical of your work performance. She is just behind the times in a lot of her ideas, you believe, so you ignore her suggestions. You are a little disappointed in some staff members (whom you used to be close to) because they seem to have changed in their attitudes and friendliness. You think their loyalty to Redbud Public Library and to Mrs. Hemlock is absurd.

Case 34

MURDER[1]

Saints Church represented one of the nation's finest examples of architectural beauty and interior design. The grounds around the Church were lavishly landscaped and maintained by capable gardeners. No money had been spared in building and equipping the Church. The large library was privately endowed and contained priceless manuscripts as well as a currently useful reference and circulating collection. One full-time janitor was assigned to take care of the library and the church office to keep them as clean and polished as possible. The man who had held this post for the past twenty years died several months ago. The library and its artistic and religious treasures were the chief interests of his life and he was devoted and conscientious in keeping them beautiful and shining.

His replacement was Mr. Hemp, a strong well-built man in his thirties. Mr. Hemp was carefully instructed in how to care for the library, its floors, windows, shelves, furniture, art objects, and equipment; but he did not seem to remember what cleaning materials should be used to clean which items and he was not thorough in what he did do. The

---

[1] Fisher v. United States, 66 S. Ct. 1318 (1945)

Personnel Cases

librarian, Miss Kafir, was very unhappy with his work but tried to be patient with him in suggesting how he could improve.

The library was opened daily at 9:30 a. m. but the clerk came on duty at 9. Miss Kafir usually came in at 8 a. m. because she found she could accomplish more during this quiet, uninterrupted time than she could later in the day. One morning in March when she came into the library, she saw that the rugs had not been vacuumed and the inside glass entrance doors had not been cleaned. Both of these tasks had to be done daily before the library opened. Mr. Hemp worked from 5 a. m. to 1 p. m. Monday through Saturday. Repeatedly she had had to remind him to keep to the schedule provided him, to show him what had not been done, or to tell him to do a job over again. She realized that she could not expect the kind of performance from Mr. Hemp that she got from his predecessor but she did expect Mr. Hemp to remember what he had been told and to follow instructions. In her opinion the neglect of a regular daily chore was inexcusable.

She searched for him and found him in the church basement eating his "lunch." She asked him to come up to the library and he followed her. After entering the library, she pointed to the glass doors and the rug and asked him why they had not been cleaned today. He shuffled his feet uneasily and said, "Well, they don't look dirty." Miss Kafir scolded him severely, "You are to follow instructions and do just what you have been told to do. You are the stupidest, laziest, most irresponsible man I have ever encountered. If your work doesn't improve in the next month, I will fire you." This angered him and he impulsively slapped Miss Kafir. She screamed and he turned and ran out of the library. Her screaming unnerved him.

In a few minutes he returned to the library with the broken end of a pole in his right hand. These poles were used for carrying church banners during processionals and recessionals. She screamed for help when she saw him. He struck her on the head and she fell to the floor continuing to scream. He seized her by the throat until her body went limp; then, he dragged her to a janitor's mop closet in which there was a sink. Her diamond and emerald ring came off in his hand as he was dragging her and he put it in his pocket. After depositing her body in a corner of the closet, he wet a sponge and went back to the library to clean up the

spots of blood on the floor along the path he had dragged her.
Miss Kafir recovered sufficiently to scream again and he
hurried back to the closet to shut her up. He took a knife
out of his pocket and stuck it into her throat. She was then
silent. He locked the closet and left the church.

When the library clerk arrived at 9 a. m. she saw
Miss Kafir's coat and purse in her office and assumed that
the latter was probably in the church office. Later in the
morning a secretary from the church office came looking for
Mr. Hemp to do something about a leaky pipe but the library
clerk said, "I haven't seen him all morning and neither have
I seen Miss Kafir--is she down in your office?" The girl
replied that Miss Kafir had not been in the office that morning. They were puzzled and concerned. The secretary left
to look for a pail in the janitor's closet and discovered Miss
Kafir's body. She ran to the library to inform the clerk
about what she had seen and then called the police.

When two detectives apprehended Mr. Hemp in his
home he still had Miss Kafir's ring in his pocket. He was
very nervous and shaky; he told the detectives, "I did not
want to kill her, but her scolding and threat to fire me
bothered me. I don't know why I hit her, I just felt I had
to. When she screamed, I just tried to keep her from making any more noise."

At the trial the jury had to decide whether Mr. Hemp
was to be convicted of murder in the first degree, murder
in the second degree, or manslaughter. The psychiatrists
for the defense stated that Mr. Hemp was mentally somewhat
below the average, had psychopathic aggressive tendencies,
low emotional response, and borderline mental deficiency.
They said that he was unable, because of his deranged mental condition, to resist the impulse to kill Miss Kafir. His
whole behavior seemed that of a man of primitive emotions
reacting to the sudden stimulus of insult and proceeding from
that point without purpose or design.

The defense contended that Mr. Hemp was insane and
that there was no deliberate intent to kill. They defined insanity as a disease or defect of the mind which makes a person incapable of knowing what is wrong, of refraining from
doing the wrongful act, and of understanding the value and
quality of his act. If the jury decided he was insane, the
defense believed he should be acquitted; if they decided he
was sane and did not kill intentionally then he was guilty of

Personnel Cases   199

second degree murder or manslaughter.

    The prosecution presented evidence that Mr. Hemp was capable of understanding what he did and believed he should be indicted for murder in the first degree. They explained to the jury that murder in the first degree is the killing of a human being purposely and with deliberate and premeditated malice.

    Punishment for murder in the first degree was death by electrocution; punishment for murder in the second degree was imprisonment for life, or for not less than twenty years.

Case 35

INSUBORDINATION AND ARREST

    Wishing to receive continuous feedback from the young people of the county, the staff of the Balsa County Library established a Youth Advisory Council five years ago. The Council represented a cross-section of the private and public junior and senior high schools in the county. Two representatives were elected by the student body in each of the seven schools. The Young Adult Supervisor, Mrs. Cayne, represented the library staff and served as an advisor to the group and liaison with the various library departments.

    The Council met monthly during the school year. The meetings were held in the library auditorium except when the group visited departments in the library. The chief purpose of the Council was to serve as a two-way communication channel between the junior and senior high school students of the county and the library staff. Students were supposed to tell their Council representatives their opinions and feelings about the library: gripes, satisfactions, questions, suggestions, and problems. The library staff asked the Council's advice about what interests and subjects young people want to know about, what services and programs were desired, what hours of opening were most convenient, and many other matters. Activities of the Council during meetings included book talks, motion picture and filmstrip previewing for their recommendations as to what should be purchased, selection round table discussions to recommend book and periodical purchases, visits to every department in the library to learn about the work in each, programs presented in the library auditorium on special subjects for the general public, and a breezy news sheet written by several members of the Council and distributed to all junior and senior high school students in the county.

The library staff believed this Council affiliation to be very valuable in contributing to the fine rapport with all the young people. The use of the Young Adult Department had increased dramatically in the last three years and it became necessary to employ another staff member in the Department. Hopefully, this new member could take over the time-consuming work with the Youth Advisory Council. Mrs. Cayne was reluctant to give up this contact but she had so many other pressures and duties which no one else could do that she felt perhaps a younger staff member could carry on with the Council inasmuch as it was successful and well established.

The library director, Mrs. Fin, interviewed several applicants and chose Lois, a young woman of twenty-four who was extremely well qualified for the position. During her undergraduate years, she had worked as a camp counselor. Since she graduated from library school two years ago, she had been working in the Young Adult Department of a metropolitan public library system where she had gotten some excellent experience under an able supervisor. She said her only reason for changing positions was because her boy friend had recently been transferred to Balsa and she wanted to be near him. Her references spoke of her as intelligent and capable, arrogant and head strong, creative and innovative, industrious, energetic, and ambitious. One reference mentioned that she had participated in some student demonstrations when she was an undergraduate. Mrs. Fin phoned her present supervisor to ask about this and the latter said that she did not know of any such activity during her employment on that staff.

Lois started to work in July. Mrs. Fin informed her that she was to take orders from and report to Mrs. Cayne, the Young Adult Supervisor, who would assign duties, schedule hours of work, and supervise her work. She learned the procedures quickly, fit easily into the work patterns, got acquainted with the staff, and endeared herself to the young adult patrons because she was so knowledgeable about the collection. It was evident at once that she enjoyed working with young adults and they liked her. She seemed especially adept at helping them with reference problems and in guiding their reading. Her memory for names was phenomenal and the students were so pleased when she remembered them and addressed them by name.

When Lois was employed, no mention was made of the Council. Mrs. Cayne didn't want to commit herself to turning over that important work to someone else until she was sure the person could handle it adequately. By the middle of August, Mrs. Cayne had observed Lois enough that she felt confident to recommend to Mrs. Fin that Lois take charge of the Council. Mrs. Fin agreed with Mrs. Cayne so the latter asked Lois if she would be interested. Lois smiled broadly and said she would really enjoy that work and would be glad to take on the responsibility. Mrs. Cayne explained the purposes of the Council and gave Lois copies of the programs for the past five years. She also told her, "All meetings must be held in the library. You should work with the students in planning programs several months in advance, and you must discuss your plans for each program with me and get my approval before you commit yourself to the group."

During the second week of school the representatives were elected and the first meeting of the Council was held the following week. A few days after that meeting Lois asked for an appointment with Mrs. Fin, the library director. Lois smiled sweetly as she said, "The Council members at their first meeting this fall decided they would like to hold their October meeting in my apartment. Is that all right?" Mrs. Fin was taken aback with the seeming innocence of this request. "Didn't your supervisor, Mrs. Cayne, inform you that all meetings of the Council must be held in the library?" "Well, yes," Lois replied, "but I thought an exception could be made if you gave your permission." Mrs. Fin was angry that the newest and youngest staff member was by-passing her supervisor. She informed Lois that holding all Council meetings in the library was a policy decision of the library staff and the library board which could not be altered without the approval of both of them. Furthermore, she pointed out, "Mrs. Cayne is your supervisor and all Council plans should be discussed with her for her approval and should not be discussed with me." As she rose from her chair and started for the door, Lois said, "Well, I thought you would be more sympathetic to the wishes of the young people."

A few days later the president of the board called Mrs. Fin to report that he had received a letter from the

student officers of the Council requesting permission for
Council meetings to be held outside the library whenever
they chose to do so.   "What's all this about?" he asked.
Mrs. Fin told him about her conversation with Lois and said
that she was sure Lois had suggested the students write the
letter.   At the next board meeting, the board reaffirmed its
policy that all Council meetings be held in the library inasmuch as it was a library-sponsored organization.   The decision was communicated by letter to Mrs. Cayne, Lois, and
the students.

The October and November meetings were held in the
library but Mrs. Cayne was sure that there were extra meetings being held in Lois's apartment and perhaps in other
places because she and other staff members observed many
secretive conversations between Lois and some of the Council
members.   Also, Lois did not socialize with any members
of the library staff nor did she appear to have any adult
friends but she seemed to identify with the high school students.   Staff members frequently reported seeing her in various places about the town in the company of high school students, both those who were members of the Council and
others.

Late in November Mrs. Cayne received a telephone
call from the Supervisor of Audio Visual Services in the library reporting on the unavailability of certain films on drugs
which Lois had requested for the week between Christmas and
New Year.   Mrs. Cayne had heard nothing about any drug
program.   She called Lois to her office, told her about the
phone call, and inquired about the December program.   Lois
said the students wanted a whole week's program of films,
filmstrips, and discussion of drugs, and so she had planned
it.   Mrs. Cayne was furious and said, "You know I must approve every program or activity for the Council meetings before you make any definite plans.   Why did you go ahead
without consulting me?"   Lois replied that she felt the Council was her responsibility and she did not see why she had
to check with anyone else.   Mrs. Cayne explained to Lois
that holidays could never be used for programs because the
library was always overcrowded with normal activities.   Special programs had to be presented at times when normal library business was more or less slack.

While Lois was still in her office, Mrs. Cayne phoned
the secretary, who did the scheduling for the auditorium, and
confirmed the fact that it was booked solid for that holiday

Personnel Cases

week. Then, Lois asked to have an all-day Saturday session on drugs in January. Mrs. Cayne remembered talking recently to the director of the county Youth Commission about a drug program they were planning. She phoned him and found that such a program was to be given in a few weeks and they expected the cooperation of the library in displays, lists of materials, and other activities. Mrs. Cayne pointed out that the library staff had to work with other agencies in the community on programs so that they did not duplicate each other's efforts. She suggested that Lois convey this information to the students in the Council and urge them to work with the Youth Commission on their program. Lois was very unhappy about the whole session and sulked as she left the office.

In February, she requested a week off without pay for personal business. The request was granted. A Balsa newspaper reporter attending a convention of Students for a Democratic Society spotted her at the meeting dressed like others in the organization and not at all like she dressed when on the job. He reported this to Mrs. Fin who expressed the hope to him that he might be wrong. He insisted that he was sure of her identity and added that her longhaired, beaded, boy friend was with her. Having read about the goals of the SDS to infiltrate high schools, Mrs. Fin feared for what Lois might be doing to the high school students in Balsa through her work with the Council. An employee could not be dismissed on hearsay. Lois's probation period would expire on June 30.

Later in the spring an irate parent called Mrs. Fin berating her staff for their unwholesome influence on his daughter. After several minutes of almost inarticulate accusations, Mrs. Fin finally learned that the previous weekend Lois had taken a car full of high school students to a rock music festival where they had camped out in mud and rain for two days and nights along with several thousand others. Mrs. Fin assured the father that some disciplinary action would be taken and asked if he would be willing to give this account at the next library board meeting and he agreed.

Several days later during a "student" demonstration on a college campus in the next county, several "students" were arrested by the police. The next morning the newspapers and television programs carried pictures of the demonstration. One oversize, closeup picture was of a fighting

Lois being carried to a patrol car by four policemen--one each for each arm and one each for each leg. The caption on the newspaper picture read, "Miss Lois ----, Young Adult Librarian at Balsa County Library, arrested during SDS demonstration."

Case 36

A LEAVE OF ABSENCE

Clifford Ironwood was head of reference and bibliographical services in the undergraduate library in a university library system. He had held this position for four years and prior to that had been a reference assistant in the social sciences area of another university library. Wishing to make a career of university library administration, Mr. Ironwood decided that he needed a doctor's degree and that, at age twenty-nine, it was time to start working toward that goal. After weighing the advantages and disadvantages of a doctorate in a subject field or in library science, he decided one from a library school having a strong information science program would be most desirable. After choosing the library school he preferred, he wrote a memorandum to his immediate superior indicating his intention and made a tentative request for a leave of absence contingent upon his admission to the program of his choice.

Before requesting this leave of absence, he investigated the University regulations regarding such leaves. He specifically requested in the memorandum a clarification of his "academic status." Librarians at this university had academic status (i.e., were appointed by the Dean of Faculty as were the teaching faculty members), but did not have faculty rank, sabbatical leave, tenure, or other perquisites accorded those with faculty rank. He learned from the Faculty Handbook that "... leaves of absence ... may be granted by the President ... to regular faculty members with tenure." It was debatable whether he was "regular" faculty and he certainly did not have tenure. The reply he received to this point was somewhat general, and stated that his job would be there for him upon his return but did not spell out the precise conditions of a leave of absence for a library staff member.

All of the written correspondence, including the first memorandum which Mr. Ironwood wrote to request the tentative leave of absence, and the subsequent one confirming the fact that he had been admitted to a Ph. D. program was exchanged between Ironwood and his immediate superior, the Chairman of Reference and Bibliography.

Several months after Mr. Ironwood left the University and had started on his doctoral program, he wrote to the Business Office of the university stating that he was on a leave of absence, but that he would like to withdraw the funds which he had deposited in the state retirement system. He received a brief reply from the Business Office telling him that individuals on leaves of absence were not entitled to withdraw these funds. He then wrote to the Chairman of his department and asked her for copies of the leave transactions. He explained that he wanted to study them to see if he indeed wasn't eligible to withdraw these funds. To this request, he received the answer that the forms were not in duplicate and that an attempt had been made to Xerox them, but that this attempt had been unsuccessful.

Finally, in view of the lack of any formal statement with regard to the leave, Mr. Ironwood wrote to the Chairman of Reference and Bibliography and told her that because of the regulations of the University and the lack of any substantiation of the "leave," he was forced to accept the alternative that the only context in which his retirement funds could be discussed was one in which he had been terminated. He, therefore, wrote her a formal letter of resignation. At the same time, he wrote a letter to the Business Office stating that he had written to his supervisor announcing his resignation and that he wanted to initiate withdrawal of his retirement funds.

In response to his letter to his supervisor, he received a reply which was somewhat hostile. It said that the University had been considerate of his request and that he was conducting himself in an unprofessional manner. Mr. Ironwood is still ignorant of whatever procedure was used to effect his departure from the library, and believes that the administration was at fault for not clarifying the matter. He is also sure that the library administrators think that he has abandoned them in a highly unethical manner.

Case 37

PERSONALITY DISORDER

At the time Z came to State University to study for a master's degree in history one and one-half years ago, he was employed as a full-time stack supervisor in the University Library. The head of the Circulation Department, W, selected him from among several applicants for the position because he had four years of experience as a shelver during his undergraduate years in a college library. In her recommendation, the college librarian said: "When Z worked for me as a stack page, he was quick, accurate, and intelligent, but occasionally his behavior showed immaturity. I have no idea about his supervisory capabilities. He may be overqualified for your position."

The job description for stack supervisor called for two years of college and some experience in a library. When W asked Z why he wanted this job, Z replied that he had to support himself and needed a job. He had applied for a teaching assistantship in the history department but had not gotten one. The only other jobs for which he seemed to have a chance were to work on an assembly line in a local manufacturing plant from 4 to 11:30 p. m. six nights a week, or as a night janitor on campus. He said he preferred the stack supervisor position because he was used to that type of work, liked the academic environment, and the working schedule would be more flexible and more agreeable. Although as stack supervisor he would have to work some weekends and nights, he preferred that schedule to working a set shift every night.

The stack supervisor was responsible for supervising one full-time assistant, one full-time carrel attendant, and ten part-time student shelvers. He and his assistant staggered their hours so that one of them was always on duty during the time the stacks were open. The Assistant was a backup for the Supervisor and took his place in making decisions about special problems and emergencies, as well as directing the rest of the staff when the Supervisor was not on duty. The Supervisor trained the shelvers, assigned duties and book trucks to them, made out work schedules, and made decisions about shelf reading. The carrel attendant was responsible for checking the more than two hundred carrels daily and charging to the carrels books which he found had not already been charged. He put one charge slip in each book to indicate that it had been charged, and a Keysort card was made out to go into the circulation file indicating the carrel where the book was located. At the end of each semester, the carrel attendant either renewed books on the carrels or cleared them off for return to the stacks. Any excess time that he had after checking the carrels, he was assigned by the Supervisor to shelve books, read shelves, or some other duty. The Supervisor also made shifts in work assignments depending on the amount of work and pressures at different times during the semesters.

During his first year as stack supervisor, Z did a creditable job of directing the work flow so that books were shelved promptly, shelves were read systematically, and shelvers were assigned specific tasks and responsibilities. He seemed to get along well with those he supervised and with the rest of the Circulation Department staff, who found him congenial, agreeable, and cooperative in their contacts with him. Occasionally he was absent for a day or two or was late in reporting for work. At such times W was sympathetic and solicitously inquired whether Z had been ill and permitted Z to make up the lost time. At State University, all non-professionals were required to have time cards which were punched in on a time clock when they came on duty and when they left each day. So, there was an accurate record of Z's tardinesses and absences. All sub-professionals, clerks, and pages were paid on an hourly basis so received remuneration only for the actual hours they worked.

Gradually during the last six months, the level and quality of his work have deteriorated. He has been late repeatedly--not just a few minutes but half an hour or longer; and he has been absent at least one day a week. In fact, during the last six months, he has been absent twenty-six days or about 15 per cent of the working days. On the days he was absent, he would usually phone in after the time he was scheduled to go on duty and announce that he would not be in that day but give no excuse. This tardiness and absenteeism put a heavy burden on his Assistant. Frequently, W communicated his concern to Z and inquired about his health and whether he had any personal problems. Z's answers were always rather evasive but he gave the impression that he hadn't felt well. When this pattern of behavior continued, W pointed out that the quality of his work was not acceptable because books were not getting on the shelves fast enough, his Assistant had too much work and responsibility, shelvers needed his supervision, and the general condition of the shelves was unsatisfactory. W asked Z if something about the work, the staff, the set-up, or something else was causing difficulties. Z said that there were no problems but that he was ill. When W asked him if he had gone to the Student Health Center for medical attention, he said, "Yes, I have some blood disease which I contracted through an insect bite or a scratch, and this disease developed as a result. The prognosis is not very good and left me in a debilitated state." At another time later, he claimed to be suffering from a virus infection.

W was well acquainted with many of the physicians at the Student Health Center, so he phoned the office to learn which physician had examined Z. The head receptionist said that his record showed he had never been to the Health Center. W then went to see the psychiatrist at the Health Center who was a personal friend and told him about Z's behavior in as great detail as possible. The psychiatrist said that he recommended Z come in for both physical and psychiatric examinations. From W's account, the psychiatrist said that on the surface it appeared to him that Z was playing a psychological game with W and was not physically ill. He asked W if he had read Games People Play, by Eric Berne (N. Y.: Grove Press, 1964) which he described as a popularized account of the psychology of human relationships. "Perhaps," he said, "reading this book will give you some clues to Z's behavior. I would hazard a guess that Z is playing a childish role and is enjoying your attention and bewilderment." W had not read the book so secured a copy at once.

When W confronted Z with the fact that he had lied about going to the Student Health Center, Z laughed and said he had concocted his tales of illness as a hoax. He then contended that he was run down physically as a result of being overworked on the job and needed days off to rest. "Why didn't you discuss this with me months ago so that I could have made some changes in your workload?," W said. "I didn't feel I could talk to you about it," Z replied.

"You know I am always available any time and you surely showed no hesitancy in coming to me often about wages, special requests, and problems with your staff. I don't see why you could not talk to me honestly, seriously, and straight-forwardly about the reasons for your tardiness and absences," W said.

When Z failed to respond to this statement, W suggested to Z that he go to the Student Health Center for physical and psychiatric examinations. Z refused to go.

Case 38

MATERNITY LEAVE

(Role playing)

Gomer University Library <u>Personnel Code:</u>

<u>Leaves of Absence</u>

Leaves of absence without pay may be granted for attendance at school, maternity, illness, travel, or work experience that would be of benefit to the library. All leaves except military are permissive and must be approved by the Personnel Office, the Director, and the Board of Trustees before being granted.

Leaves of absence, except for military service or maternity, do not exceed one year. A written statement of intention to return must be filed with the Personnel Office at least sixty days before the date of expiration to leave. The absence of this request implies an automatic resignation. If it is necessary to exceed a leave, a request may be submitted to the Personnel Office, at least sixty days before the date of expiration.

Every effort will be made to fill a vacated position for the period of the leave only. If it becomes necessary to fill a vacancy with a permanent appointee, the employee on leave will be placed on a reinstatement list at the expiration of his leave and will be offered the first vacant position for which he is qualified. An employee on the reinstatement list may refuse any position except the one he vacated when he went on leave.

<u>Maternity Leave</u>

A staff member, upon becoming pregnant, should arrange for resignation or leave by notifying the

Personnel Office in writing by the end of the third month of her pregnancy.

A staff member with two years or more of satisfactory service may be granted a leave of absence, effective at least three months before and to continue generally for three months after the birth of the child, although this may vary with the individual situation. Such a leave does not exceed two years after the birth of the child.

A staff member with less than two years of satisfactory service should terminate her employment at least three months before the expected birth. After the birth she may apply for reemployment and will be given preference over new applicants when a suitable vacancy becomes available.

Role for Mr. Claude Pine, Personnel Director, Gomer University Library:

You received this interdepartmental communication this morning:

To: Mr. Claude Pine
Personnel Director
Gomer University
Library

From: Miss Sylvia
Maple
Librarian
Undergraduate
Library

March 20, 1969

I would like to apply for maternity leave. According to the Personnel Code, you should be notified in writing prior to the end of the third month of pregnancy. Therefore, I request maternity leave from June 15 until October 15. I have been employed continuously in this library since I graduated from Library School in June, 1960. As a professional staff member, I am entitled to twenty-two working days vacation plus one additional day for each of the four years I have worked after five years, or a total of twenty-six. May the first twenty-six days of my leave be considered my vacation for which I will receive my usual salary? That will reduce by that number of days the length of the leave without pay.

Personnel Cases   211

Role for Miss Sylvia Maple:

You are thirty-one years old, tall, slim and attractive. You walk with lithe and easy grace. Your hair is shiny, healthy-looking, long, wavy, and chestnut-colored. You dress in colors and styles of clothing which become you. You have been conscientious, capable, and efficient during your nine years in the Undergraduate Library. You started at the information desk and were promoted whenever there was a vacancy until you became head librarian. Both faculty members and students like you and value your gracious and willing assistance. You participate actively in staff association activities as well as in the state library association where you currently hold a committee chairmanship. You have attended several national ALA meetings.

Case 39

I AM A LIBRARIAN, NOT A PSYCHIATRIST

(Role playing)

The Kale Public Library collection totals about 250,000 volumes and the city's population is approximately 80,000. The library serves as the central reference library and processing center for a four county library system composed of thirty-nine small libraries.

Role for Mrs. Grace Bramble:

You have been head librarian of the Kale Public Library for several years. At an annual meeting of the American Library Association you sought the advice of one of your close friends about a perplexing personnel problem hoping she would have some solutions to suggest. This is what you told her:

> My most serious personnel problem was inherited from my predecessor as I did not employ either of the individuals involved. Because of its nature, this problem is difficult to deal with, flares up mildly on occasion, is upsetting at the time, and then is more or less forgotten until the next time. However, it is always there, must be dealt with continually, and requires a constant awareness and alertness.

On my staff are two overly sensitive, touchy, moody persons who are at times impossible to deal with. Their feelings are easily hurt; they are narrow minded and intolerant; they can be easily upset by the schedule, the public, the temperature, the lighting, perfumes or odors, the moving of furniture or equipment, or by some word or action of others on the staff. These individuals (one man and one woman) require 'handling' or coddling; they must be approached in just the right manner at just the right time. I have to sense their present mood each time before I approach them about anything. They may not be sick enough for a psychiatrist but neither are they well adjusted enough for a happy, satisfactory relationship with their supervisors and fellow employees. They are not without good points and certain abilities in varying degrees. They can be utterly charming and considerate some of the time, but the problem is there and I have to watch for it every moment. Both of them are mature individuals, have permanent status, and are not likely to seek employment elsewhere.

These two persons are evidently insecure in varying degrees but do not seem to realize that they have personal problems. They need bolstering and encouraging which I can give them to a degree. But I am a librarian not a psychiatrist; I do not have the necessary educational background to help them straighten out their lives. I can listen and be sympathetic to a point, which I believe does help. I am convinced that there is no completely satisfactory solution and that the staff and I must live with the problem. We do the best we can with them and ignore them when they are particularly petty. Tact, maneuvering, and sometimes, rather devious methods are required to keep things running smoothly. We try to deal with them impartially, schedule work loads as equally as possible, show no favoritism, 'coddle' them when we have to, and hope for the best.

Role for Miss Alice Juniper:

As supervisor of branches in a large public library system, you are responsible for a staff larger than Mrs.

Bramble's. You have a reputation for your skill in interpersonal relations and for your knowledge of personnel management. You have taken education and business courses in personnel guidance and continually study in this field as well as read widely in mental hygiene. You assure Mrs. Bramble that her problem is more prevalent than is generally realized, is usually glossed over by most library administrators, and remains for the most part insoluble. But you do have some suggestions for her.

Chapter III

PLANNING CASES

As a basic management function, planning involves selecting a course of action for a library as a whole and for every department and employee. All administrative and supervisory personnel should be concerned with planning. A rational approach to the selection of goals and objectives and to the determination of means for reaching them are provided through planning. Good planning considers the nature of the future in which decisions and actions are intended to operate.

Cases in this chapter exemplify such areas of planning as establishing goals and objectives; identifying mission; developing policies, procedures, rules, programs, and strategies; scheduling; and the making of decisions. Hopefully, these cases will provide some vicarious experience in understanding some of the facets of planning, the roles of staff members in the planning process, the importance of planning, and the necessity of flexibility in adapting to change.

Case 40

A FIRE

Huckleberry Branch of Metropolitan Library was located in an area designed for a store in a small neighborhood shopping center. The electric clock on the wall behind the charging desk stopped at 4:15 a. m. on Sunday morning because fire cut off electric service at that time. Before the fire reached the library, several stores on one side of the library were fully ablaze. When fire department personnel saw that the fire might spread to the library, they went into it and spread canvas over most of the stacks, the wall shelving, and the furniture to protect them as much as possible.

Firemen determined that the fire had started in a

beauty parlor and had spread to stores through a common attic. The roofs of two stores collapsed and the contents of the other two stores were completely destroyed. The library was the last area reached by the fire which was brought under control while the roof and walls were still standing.

A fireman saw a notice posted on the front door of the library: "In case of emergency, call the branch librarian, Mrs. Janet Hickory, phone number _____; or, the main library information desk, phone number _____." He knew the information desk would not be open at 4 a. m. on Sunday, so he called Mrs. Hickory. By the time she arrived at the scene, the fire was under control and all she could see was smoke in the library. After the firemen removed their hoses and the smoke cleared, she had an opportunity to move in closer and inspect the remains. At first glance it appeared that the entire collection of about 25,000 books (minus those in circulation) had been lost. A closer look showed that most of the juvenile books, practically all of the reference collection, and many other books on the lower shelves suffered little or no damage. The greatest fire damage had occurred to the books on the upper shelves of stacks and wall shelving. Many books had charred spines and would have to be rebound; others had been damaged by water. Some had fallen off the upper shelves and were both burned and damaged by water on the floor. The action taken by the fire crews in protecting the books with canvas, and also in cleaning the water out of the building promptly, had undoubtedly helped to minimize losses. Fortunately, the contents of the circulation and registration files, the card catalog, and the shelf list were not damaged. The cases were burned and charred and would require extensive refinishing or might have to be discarded; but the cards inside were undamaged.

Mrs. Hickory's first thought was the necessity of keeping the general public away from the remains to prevent stealing. She phoned the director of libraries to report the fire and to request his advice about personnel to sort the collection, to pack what could be salvaged, and to transport what was left of the collection, the furniture, and the files.

The director asked the city police to station several men at Huckleberry Branch until the salvageable contents could be moved. He phoned the head of maintenance and the supervisor of shelvers, asking them to round up a crew to come to the site as quickly as possible. The man in charge of all library vehicles phoned the director offering the services of several trucks and drivers--he had heard the news over radio and television. Also, staff members came from all over the city to offer their services when they heard of the fire through the news media.

Mrs. Hickory stayed at the site to supervise operations. By the end of the day everything that could possibly be salvaged had been packed in the trucks and the trucks driven to the library garage.

The next day (Monday) the Supervisor of Branches phoned the head of the city real estate management office to request new space for the Huckleberry Branch in the same neighborhood. Later in the day the real estate manager located and rented a recently vacated market building about five blocks from the fire location. The trucks unloaded their contents at this new location on Tuesday.

What a dismal sight Mrs. Hickory and her staff faced! The store building had not been cleaned or redecorated after the last occupants moved out. It needed to be renovated for library use, a partition or two put in, all walls and ceiling painted, and light fixtures installed which would give enough light for reading. Water soaked books which needed immediate attention were packed helter skelter in boxes--even mixed with charred books. Smoke damaged volumes would all have to be cleaned before they were shelved. Books with charred bindings would have to be sent to the bindery. Shelving was lying on the floor as it had been dismantled from the other building. Some of it was warped from the fire and would have to be examined by experts to determine whether it could be repaired and utilized. All of it was dirty from smoke and would have to be washed before any books could be shelved on it--also the units would have to be put together and placed in some logical order on the floor. The furniture and card file cases were a dreary lot. Some water damage, some charred fire damage, and everything covered with smoke residue. One of the first priorities would be an inventory to determine losses in order to file an insurance claim.

Put yourself in Mrs. Hickory's position. Determine priorities of planning, types of plans, staffing requirements, service to the public, physical facilities, and other problems.

Planning Cases 217

Case 41

A NEW JUNIOR COLLEGE

A new state-supported junior college will open two years from now in Obsidian, a city of 40,000 located at an elevation of about 2,500 feet with mountain ranges on two sides. The nearest college (a teacher-training institution) is located about 150 miles away across a range of mountains.

For years the residents of this area of the state have clamored for a state-supported junior college. Three years ago the Obsidian Chamber of Commerce sponsored a study of the area to ascertain the personnel needs of business, industry, schools, hospitals, agriculture, labor, and the professions. The results of this survey were submitted to the Board of Directors of the State System of Higher Education. The Board decided that the need for a junior college did indeed exist in Obsidian. To ascertain types of programs and curricula which should be offered, the Board asked the School of Education of the State University to study the area.

A survey of students presently enrolled in junior and senior high schools of the area was made to determine (1) how many might be interested in attending this junior college if it were built, and (2) what courses of study they thought they might wish to pursue (terminal or preparation for transfer to a four-year academic institution).

On the basis of the two surveys, the State Board purchased one hundred acres on the edge of the city for a campus, appointed a president and instructed him to plan the campus (with the assistance of an architect), to decide on curricula, and to choose a faculty according to the needs of the curricula. The President to date has selected the following to work with him: a dean of instruction who is to work on curricula, a comptroller in charge of all business functions and physical plant, a dean of students to plan residence halls, and you as librarian to plan the library. The State Board has engaged the services of an architect to work with the five of you on planning the campus and the buildings to be erected thereon.

By the time you accepted your appointment, the following decisions had been made:

> estimated student body when college opens two years hence--about seven hundred

dormitory accommodations for one-fourth of
the student body (it is estimated that three-
fourths will live at home)

terminal programs (two-year) leading to Associate of Arts degree in secretarial and office methods, accounting, computer technicians, vocational
agriculture, printing trades, auto mechanics, and
restaurant management

pre-professional curricula (students will transfer
after two years to one of the state's four-year
institutions): teaching, nursing, agriculture, engineering, and business administration

general liberal arts: social sciences, humanities,
communications, biological sciences and physical
sciences

You have two years to get ready for the students, faculty, and curricula. You are responsible for planning the building, the library staff, the collection, the services, and the organization of the collection. For the purposes of this case, do not be concerned about cost but incorporate what you consider to be ideal. Assume that you will be allotted a reasonable amount of money to build a functional and prac- tical building, to employ an adequate staff, to acquire a col- lection suitable for the curricula, and to provide necessary services. In a state supported institution, you must be prac- tical and economical in spending the taxpayers' money.

What will be your priorities for planning? What do you do first, second, and so on? What decisions must be made for short- and long-range planning? Who should you consult and work with in the planning? What should be in- cluded in a building program? What standards and criteria would be useful in establishing space needs for staff, users, and the collection? How do you decide how many and what kinds of staff should be employed and when and in what order they should be employed? What decisions must be made con- cerning collection building--will it be print-oriented or multi- media? How will you decide about methods of cataloging and classification--traditional or innovative; card catalog, com- puter print out, film cartridge, or other?

Case 42

"BANDAID" WORK

For several years the Superintendent of Schools in the city of Wilson had been under considerable pressure from the public and from teachers for establishing libraries in the 128 elementary schools. As a first step toward meeting this demand, I was employed six months ago as Supervisor of Elementary School Libraries. The position of Supervisor of Secondary School Libraries had existed for many years and each of the junior and senior high schools have excellent instructional materials centers. Both of us report to the Assistant Superintendent who is responsible for instruction.

When I was offered the position I was told that I would be responsible for supervising the centralized Learning Resources Center which served all of the elementary schools, for studying the needs of the schools for instructional materials, and for devising both long-range and short-range plans for establishing a library in every school. I was chosen for the position because of my experience as a classroom teacher, elementary school librarian, and supervisor of school media centers in a small city. I knew when I accepted this position that it would be a tough challenge for me.

The Learning Resources Center provided all types of materials for teachers and children in the elementary schools: books, vertical file (clippings, pamphlets, flat pictures), periodicals, slides, transparencies, phonotapes, phonorecords, filmstrips, motion pictures, maps, and a professional education collection. In addition, there were collections of objects such as rocks and shells; large display boards showing samples of petroleum products, wheat, coffee, and other geological, agricultural, and botanical items; examples of arts and crafts from other cultures and other peoples; and many other similar teaching materials.

Teachers phoned in their requests and deliveries and pickups were made daily by trucks. For example, if a teacher was planning a unit on fish, she would receive all of the teaching materials on the subject regardless of format unless she specified some she did not want.

Classroom collections of fifty books were available for one month loans but renewable if requested. Each collection for fourth grade, for instance, would contain different titles so that if a teacher returned collection number one and requested the next collection (number two) the latter would have titles unique to that collection. These collections were housed in especially built boxes which could be stood on end and converted into bookshelves in the classroom after the top was taken off the box. These collections were checked over and weeded every summer. Worn volumes were rebound or discarded, dirty covers were cleaned, and books with outdated contents were replaced with newer up-to-date books.

When I assumed the position, I found three full-time persons working with the collection at the Center (one cataloger and two clerks who filled requests from the teachers for materials), several typists, and part-time high school student shelvers.

Officially there were no elementary school libraries, but some collections were known to exist. One of the first things I did was to send out a form letter to each elementary school principal asking whether there was a library collection in the school, how it was housed and organized, who was in charge, and a brief description of the collection. I was surprised to learn that approximately two-thirds of the schools had some sort of collection which had been accumulated without any help from the staff of the Learning Resources Center. At several schools, the nucleus of the collection had been purchased from Goodwill Industries for five cents per volume. Many of these volumes were discards from public libraries and family homes. New books in the collections were either donations from teachers and parents or had been purchased by the school's PTA. All of the collections were supervised by volunteers: mothers, teachers, or members of the Junior League.

My next step was to visit each of these so-called "libraries." I was very depressed after seeing the miserable rooms in which most of them were housed, the poor quality of the titles, and the volunteer service. The volunteers were dedicated, enthusiastic women but they only spent a few hours a week in the "library" and no one was responsible for supervising or coordinating their work. They were not there long enough to get acquainted with the needs of the children or the curriculum and only a very few of them had any background in children's materials, and those who did had limited background. None of these libraries could ever be effective until each one was supervised by a certified elementary school librarian. In my opinion, most of the contents in each of the collections should be promptly burned and replaced with attractive, readable books suitable for today's children. I would like to see extensive use of paperbacks.

Where many cities had used federal funds to develop individual school libraries, all of the funds for this school system had gone into the centralized collection. I have been told that special funds will be available next year under the Economic Opportunity Act for establishing seven elementary school libraries in inner-city schools. I have not had time to explore this possibility. No new city funds have been allocated for establishing libraries in individual schools. If I can work out a program of development which is approved by the Superintendent of Schools and the school board, some money for the program will be available; but probably a bond issue will be required to fund the establishment and staffing of really effective libraries.

Since the persons working with the elementary "libraries" have heard of my appointment, I receive many calls to help them. All of them plead for more books and are ignorant of the usual library supplies, so I am now offering library supplies as one of the services of the Center. To give them some books immediately, I have inaugurated a weeding program at the Center. In the past, it has been customary to order forty or more copies of basic titles for which the Center staff believed there would be a demand. Some of these are outdated and need to be discarded, others are still suitable for use by elementary children. When I looked at the book cards for these multiple copies, I discovered many of them had not circulated for a long time. I now have a clerk systematically checking multiple copies on all the shelves and have given her guidelines as to what to do, depending upon how up-to-date the books are and how often they have circulated. She is to leave only about three copies on our shelves and the rest are to be distributed one copy to a "library" as far as they will go.

This is all that I have accomplished in the first six months on the job. My ultimate goal is a real library in every elementary school with a professional librarian supervising each one--probably only one day a week for a few years. If each librarian had five schools, I would need twenty-five librarians!

What I am doing now with the "libraries" is what I

consider "bandaid" work--providing temporary emergency expedients to give token help (advice, supplies, and distribution of surplus copies) until professional expertise and suitable collections can be furnished through a systematic development program.

* * * *

To the reader: If you were in this role, what short- and long-range planning would you do? What would you include in a planning program? How would you "sell" your program to the Superintendent of Schools and to the school board? What would be the next step? If a bond issue is necessary to obtain enough money for your program, what strategies and public relations would be required?

Case 43

ON PAROLE

(Role playing)

Roles:
    Miss Count, Personnel Director
    Monty Okemah, applicant for library clerk position

Wright County Library serves a population of about 500,000, has a collection of about 750,000 volumes, and offers services from a main library, six bookmobiles, and seven branches. All positions in the library are classified by grades. The occupation title for the beginning level in the clerical classification is "Library Clerk." This can be the first step in a professional library career if the individual continues to prepare himself educationally for advancement. Employees in the clerical grades are encouraged to study for bachelor's degrees and then to go on for master's degrees in library science. Because of this emphasis on career goals, persons employed for these beginning positions are more carefully selected than they would be if the position was merely filled to get certain work done at the lowest labor cost.

The job description for Library Clerk is as follows:

Planning Cases 223

Library Clerk

Essential Functions: Under direction, performs routine clerical duties associated with various library functions required to order, catalog, and circulate library materials.

Representative Duties: Under direction of staff personnel, performs routine clerical duties including typing, filing, charging and discharging library materials, recording statistics, processing reserves and overdues, registering borrowers, driving a bookmobile and assisting the librarian, and assisting in the clerical work connected with ordering, cataloging, processing, and binding.

Qualifications: Graduation from high school plus one year of library experience or two years of general office experience. Completion of one year of college may be substituted for the experience required. Ability to type from clear copy at the rate of forty words per minute; do responsible clerical work with speed and accuracy; learn and apply specific rules, regulations, procedures, and methods; interpret library regulations and policies to the public; establish and maintain cooperative working relationships with others; and display judgment and tact when dealing with the public. Bookmobile drivers must have a valid state motor vehicle operator's license.

At present, Miss Count has four openings in the Library Clerk classification to fill. She has received an application for bookmobile driver, supported with good references, from Monty Okemah who meets the job requirements as to education and experience: he is a high school graduate, has worked two years in a library, can type at the rate of more than forty words per minute, and has a valid driver's license.

Mr. Okemah is an American Indian, twenty-five years old, neat, well groomed, and clean shaven; has a tall, straight, well-built body, and appears to be strong and healthy. He is married and has one son. He spent the last two years in the state penitentiary and is now on probation. He was released long before his sentence expired because of exemplary conduct. While in the penitentiary, he worked in the library and became interested in librarianship as a career. The prison librarian has written a letter recommending that he be employed in the Wright County Library and that he be encouraged to enroll in the local university to study for a bachelor's degree with a master's degree in library science the ultimate goal. A reference letter from his high school principal attests to his good character and to his mental ability to pursue college work. Miss Count phoned his reservation for a reference check on him and talked to an older member of his tribe who claimed that Mr. Okemah was "framed" by two men in his conviction for theft and vouches for his honesty and integrity. Mr. Okemah says in his application that he wants to prepare himself to develop libraries to meet the needs of his people.

Mr. Okemah is waiting in Miss Count's outer office to be interviewed by her.

Case 44

STAFF CONCERN

State University Library dated back to the middle of the last century. At the time of this problem situation, the library system consisted of nine branches which served departments or professional schools and a large central library built in the last ten years. The total staff numbered more than three hundred of whom about one hundred had academic appointments. The senior staff consisted of heads and assistant heads of departments in the central library and heads of branches. Some of these staff members were concerned about the overall administration of the library; this group represented all ages from the late twenties to the early sixties. Their length of service on this library staff ranged from three to twenty-five years with the median length of service ten years. All were seriously interested in the overall development of the library; none were considered cranks, revolutionaries, or had ulterior motives. Their concern had been building up over several years and had reached a point where they believed this should be communicated to the library administrative staff. When they met with the administrators to present their concerns, the administrators expressed a desire to learn more about the conditions and to try to find solutions. They asked that the concerns be written into a position paper and presented to them formally. The following memorandum resulted:

To the administrative staff of State University Library:

We, the undersigned senior staff members, wish to convey to you our deep concern about the overall administration of this library system. Although we have not conducted a survey of all senior staff members, we believe this paper represents a consensus of their opinions as well as ours. This knowledge has come from two sources: (1) the informal flow of information gained in day-to-day operations, and (2) opinions expressed during several meetings of a few senior staff members.

We wish to emphasize that we are acting in good faith from a sincere dedication to professional service of the highest caliber. We have no interest in blaming any individual or individuals but are concerned about some aspects of the overall administration of the libraries which we believe, if not corrected, will lead to the deterioration of staff morale and library service.

Because you do not provide us with the necessary direction and leadership, we feel handicapped in fulfilling our prime professional obligations which are to provide library materials and bibliographical services. Specifically, we cite the following deficiencies in your administration:

1. You have not communicated to the staff clearly defined objectives, priorities, and policies; in fact, these appear to shift from day to day and situation to situation. Many of your decisions seem to be made to take immediate care of crises instead of being based on overall system-wide goals and policies.

2. You do not appear to take time to give serious operating problems sufficient study. Are you spreading your interests and energies too widely? Or, should you make more use of delegation?

3. You frequently fail to look at the effects of a decision on the whole system. The management technique utilized seems to resolve isolated small problems without relating them to the total system and without looking for causes. Cross-depart-

ment study is almost non-existent. For example, a decision affecting technical services may not envision the serious consequences upon public services; or, conversely, decisions which result in poor public service may nullify the work of the most capable acquisition and cataloging personnel.

4. Problems brought to you through the usual channels are frequently ignored or you appear to reject any responsibility for facing them.

5. There seem to be conflicts in the delegation of authority and responsibility. We suggest that you study the overall organization, structure, and chain of command.

6. Job applicants should be screened more carefully. Frequently persons are appointed who are not fully qualified for the vacancies. Is this the result of failure on your part to recognize the need for certain professional skills in given positions or insufficient knowledge about how and where to search for qualified personnel? For example, a recent appointment in the rare books department had neither the necessary language background nor any understanding of the materials she was to work with.

7. We earnestly request the provision of a continuing education program. We cite especially the need for training understudies in supervisory positions so that if the incumbent supervisor is ill or resigns, informed continuity will be insured.

8. We believe many of your responsibilities could be delegated to staff committees which would give you more time for overall thinking and planning and would put more decision-making at lower levels of the organization. For example, a search and screening committee responsible for recommending persons to fill vacancies; a promotions and tenure committee; a grievance committee; a committee to revise the personnel code; and others.

Signed:
———
———

Case 45

MOONLIGHTING

(Role playing)

Roles:
  Director of Libraries
  Two moonlighting staff members

The personnel code of Metropolitan Public Library did not prohibit staff members from holding other jobs in addition to their full-time library positions. For example, it was fairly well known that one man in the circulation department had a franchise on a gas station and worked there most of his waking hours when not on duty in the library. An attractive young woman in the catalog department had worked during her undergraduate and library school years as a waitress in a Playboy Club. She accepted a position in the catalog department so that her working day there would be over at 4:30 p. m. and she could continue to work the dinner hours at the Club. She wanted to take a trip around the world and her savings mounted faster with two jobs. It was rumored, but not confirmed, that one of the children's librarians substituted as a topless waitress on weekends.

Several staff members worked ten or more hours a week compiling bibliographies for local societies or industries. One of the children's librarians put on a regularly scheduled series of puppet shows for a local television station. One of the assistant librarians operated a financially substantial business as a library building consultant for other libraries. Some of his colleagues asserted that he spent more time and more creative energy on the consulting than he did on his work for Metropolitan Public Library and that his consultant earnings exceeded his library salary. Another staff member was editor of the state library association journal. No doubt there were many other examples of moonlighting.

The Director of Libraries and the library board were forced to face the problem of moonlighting and to devise tighter regulations as a result of a threatened conflict-of-interest case involving a staff member. For several years, this man had received a regular retainer fee from a library supply house for installing equipment, shelving, and furniture in Metropolitan Public Library's branch libraries. Even though he had no responsibilities for purchasing, a rival library equipment firm threatened to sue the library.

The library board announced a policy which stated that henceforth no person on the staff could receive compensation for work done for any company with which the library did business. In addition, the board took over control of any library-related employment of staff members including consultant work, editing, and compiling bibliographies. Any such outside employment would have to be cleared with the Director of Libraries.

Soon after this policy statement was released by the board, a delegation of staff members called on the Director of Libraries to protest this decision. The delegation was composed of those staff members affected by this new policy. They contended that they were being discriminated against because their moonlighting was library-related. Why, they asked, didn't this policy apply equally to all the rest of the moonlighters?

Case 46

"THE SHELF"

Southmore High School served a suburb with a population of some 25,000 mostly in the middle socio-economic level. A survey of the community revealed that 85 per cent of the students upon graduating from high school attended college. It was upon these facts that a curriculum and, of course, the library were planned.

From its beginning, the library was considered to be one of the more important and functional departments in the school. The staff consisted of three professionals and two clerks which served a student body of 2,000. Mr. Smith, a man of fifty, was head librarian. Because he was particularly interested in the technical services area, he did the ordering, cataloging, and processing of materials. Miss Green and Mrs. Young, the other two professional librarians, spent most of their time working with the students and faculty.

The librarians encouraged all faculty members to make recommendations for the purchase of materials. The individual teacher would make an order card, give it to the head of his department for approval and the head of the department then sent the order card to the library. Only the minimum information was requested. On the order card it was not necessary to indicate the source of the review or the reasons for requesting the book. The head librarian very rarely rejected any of the material requested. If he did reject an order, the cards were simply "misplaced." No selection policy for library materials had ever been officially adopted. There was one on paper if anyone asked but it was not official.

During the third week in November, Mr. Lucky, a first year teacher in the English Department, filled out an order card for _____. The request was signed by the head of the English Department, who sent it to the library. The book was ordered. When the book arrived, Mr. Smith began to catalog it. As he was examining the book, he began to read it carefully. He decided that the book was not suitable for the library. He placed it on "The Shelf" in the work room. There were approximately twenty other books on "The Shelf" which had been ordered and then not placed on the open shelves.

In the middle of January, Mr. Lucky came to the library to check on the status of the book he had ordered. Mr. Smith told Mr. Lucky the book had been received and that after he had carefully read the book he felt it was not suitable for the library. He then showed Mr. Lucky "The Shelf." Mr. Lucky was furious that Mr. Smith would question his recommendation of a book. After several harsh words to Mr. Smith, Mr. Lucky left the library.

At Southmore High an Advisory Council consulted with and advised the superintendent on practices in or operation of the school affecting students, staff members, or public relations. Members of this Advisory Council also interpreted to those members of the professional staff to whom they were responsible the actions and decisions of the superintendent and the school board.

The Council had been set up and organized on the following basis:

Each faculty member had one preparation period per day. All faculty members who had the same preparation period (e.g. first hour) elected one of their group to serve. There were seven faculty members--six elected through periods plus one elected by the librarians and the counselors--

and the Superintendent. The Superintendent acted as chairman at the meeting. The secretary was selected from among those elected to the Council.

The Council met one evening per month. All faculty members could suggest items for the agenda. Minutes of the meeting were published the following day in the Faculty Bulletin. The recommendations made by the Advisory Council could be accepted or rejected by the Superintendent and the Board. The Board had accepted about one-third of the recommendations made by the Advisory Council.

The regular meeting of the Advisory Council was scheduled for the evening following Mr. Lucky's encounter with Mr. Smith. Mr. Lucky was a member of the Advisory Council. Even though the matter was not listed on the agenda, Mr. Lucky presented his version of the episode with Mr. Smith. He was still angry when he told the group about "The Shelf" and suggested they go down to the library and see it. All members then trooped down to the library and viewed "The Shelf." No member of the library staff was present when the Council visited the library.

After the discussion of the matter, the Council (with tentative approval by the Superintendent) wrote a recommendation that appeared in the Faculty Bulletin the next day. The recommendation stated that all orders for library materials originated by faculty members and approved by their department head must be ordered by the head librarian, cataloged, and placed on the open shelves for use by the students.

Case 47

HOMICIDE

A woman student came running out of the stacks of Gray State University Library and breathlessly announced to the attendant at the charge-out desk, "A girl has fainted down in the stacks in the sub-basement area where the yellow ribbon ends." The attendant phoned his supervisor, head of the Circulation Department, who hurried down to the location in the stacks which the student had indicated. An attractive young woman was lying in a curled up position on her left side in a stack aisle and was indeed unconscious. As there were no phones or any other communication equipment in this oldest portion of the stacks, he climbed three flights of stairs to the Circulation desk and phoned the campus security officers. In about fifteen minutes, an ambulance and two officers arrived at the library loading dock.

They carried a stretcher to the striken student. When they lifted her on the stretcher, they observed blood under her torso and, when they put her on her back on the stretcher, they saw a small spot of blood on her blouse over her heart. With great difficulty they carried the stretcher up the narrow stack staircases and out to the ambulance and drove to the Student Health Center. The examining physician found that she was dead and that she had been stabbed with a sharp instrument which had made a small incision but had pierced a major artery.

The young woman's notebook contained her name and address: she was a graduate student working on a master's degree in history and had evidently been reading old newspapers which were housed in the sub-basement where she was found. This sub-basement was under the original library building which had been built in 1909. At several later dates, more stacks were built around this original building so this portion of the stacks at present constituted a complicated maze. The original stone foundation walls were bearing walls so could not be cut through to connect with the newer stack areas. Six different colored ribbons guided users to these six difficult-to-find areas of the stacks.

After the security officers had removed the unconscious young woman from the library, a page cleaned the blood off the stack aisle. The examining physician notified the state police of the death and the latter took charge of the case and proceeded to investigate. They informed the library staff that the body should not have been touched until after the police had investigated. The Circulation librarian defended his action by saying that he had not seen the blood and thought the girl had fainted. Hence, he decided that she should be rushed to the Health Center for treatment as quickly as possible. "Had I realized that she was dead, I would have known that she should not be touched until the proper officials had made thorough examinations," he said.

The state police interviewed every employee in the library to obtain clues. No one had heard any commotion, the murder instrument was never found, and the murderer was never identified or apprehended.

The day following the murder, the director of libraries called the heads of departments together to consider what should be done to prepare the entire staff for any such emergency in the future, what procedures should be set up, and who should be responsible for decisions and for initiating action.

What staff orientation, rules and regulations, and procedures do you recommend? What campus offices should be contacted for information? What channels of communication should be recommended?

Case 48

STEVE AND THE "CHECKLIST"

(Role playing)

Roles:
    Steve
    Mr. Nogle

Steve Goodson, a senior at George Smith College, had not paid his library bill of $10.50 for a book that he had lost during the winter quarter. On the first of April, a list of names of students who were not to be given library service for the remainder of the school year was posted in the library.

Early in May, Steve tried to check out three periodicals at the Serials desk. However, Jean Graves, the clerk on duty, noted that Steve's name was on the "checklist" and refused to circulate the periodicals to him. A few minutes after Steve had left the desk, his fiancee, Debbie Duke, came to the desk and asked to check out the same periodicals which Steve had requested earlier.

Jean Graves then went to Mr. Nogle, the Head Circulation Librarian, who was on duty that night, and told him what had happened. Mr. Nogle went into the Serials room and asked Debbie if she were checking out the periodicals for her own use or for Steve's use. Debbie said, "For me, naturally!" Mr. Nogle then told Jean Graves to check out the periodicals to Debbie, who left the library promptly.

The next morning, Steve came to the library and ac-

Planning Cases 233

cused Mr. Nogle of embarrassing his fiancee, and demanded that he apologize to Debbie. Mr. Nogle denied that he had embarrassed Debbie and explained the library's policy on the matter of an unclear record. He reminded Steve that if he wanted library service, he should pay the fine. He would then be able to have service at any of the library's desks for the remainder of the year. Steve then opened his briefcase and plunked down a bag containing $10.50 in pennies.

Case 49

SELECTION POLICY

(Role playing)

Roles:
    Mr. Hatson, Librarian, Dale Public Library
    Henry Atkins, new member of the Library Board

Whenever an unsolicited gift subscription to a periodical started arriving in the Dale Public Library, the clerk who checked in periodicals routed the issue to the head librarian, Mr. Hatson. He would examine the issue and decide on its disposition in accordance with the library's selection policies.

When an issue of Church and State appeared on his desk, he examined it and found that it was a monthly published by Americans United for the Separation of Church and State, a non-profit, tax-exempt organization. Prior to 1968 this organization was called Protestants and Other Americans United for the Separation of Church and State. Never having heard of this organization, Mr. Hatson looked it up and found that its purposes were (1) to reeducate the public as to the importance of separating church and state for religious freedom; (2) to appreciate the First Amendment to the U.S. Constitution; (3) to study legislation and court decisions regarding church and state; (4) to take remedial actions in the courts when actual violations of church-state separation occurred which could not be eliminated by negotiation; and (5) to resist efforts to join church and state by tax support.

Mr. Hatson found that the periodical editorially opposed use of public funds for sectarian purposes and presented accounts of litigation and other actions involving Americans United and city and state governments. He learned that

Dale had its own local chapter of Americans United and found newspaper accounts of recent highly controversial episodes involving some large city chapters.

Because of the general negative and highly biased nature of the publication, Mr. Hatson returned the issue to the periodicals clerk with instructions to put it on closed shelves, retain it for one year, and then discard. He based his decision on the library's selection policy. The section concerning religious publications stated that only those periodicals listed in periodical indexes would be offered to the public on open shelves. Six leading religious periodicals were thus displayed on open shelves. In addition, some thirty other religious publications, representing many denominations, were housed on closed shelves but were equally available to the public. Only a limited number of periodicals could be displayed on open shelves because of space limitations. All unsolicited periodicals were kept for a limited time and then discarded. Church and State thus was treated the same as the other thirty-odd periodicals on closed shelves.

Henry Atkins, a Dale school teacher, had recently been appointed to the library board. At the board meeting in June, Atkins charged Hatson with censorship for failing to place Church and State on the library's open shelves. He asserted that Hatson had exercised undue influence over the display of library materials by refusing to put out this periodical which was based on "sound factual authority." Hatson replied that Church and State failed this very criterion in that it presented no positive program, but merely attacked and often inaccurately attempted to tear down views to which it was opposed. As far as factual authority was concerned, countered Atkins, no suit had ever been filed attacking the veracity of Church and State. Hatson defended his decision by referring to the board's policy regarding the selection of religious publications for open shelf display from Reader's Guide to Periodical Literature, and that those outside this limitation were to be evaluated at the discretion of the librarian.

In the course of the discussion, Atkins revealed that he was president of the Dale chapter of Americans United.

Case 50

MOMENTUM

(Role playing)

The staff of the Taro Public Library frequently put on ambitious programs for the public and cooperated actively in various community endeavors. For example, each year during National Library Week special programs, exhibits, and events were always carried out. Recently, in cooperation with the League of Women Voters, three luncheons were sponsored at the library on the subject of how to develop a sense of civic responsibility. The luncheons were catered and served in the library. This meant a lot of work for the staff as they were responsible not only for the speakers and the programs but also for carrying in tables, chairs, and dishes because the library had no kitchen or dining facilities. The luncheons were well attended and considered a big success.

Role for Mrs. Dock:

You are the librarian of the Taro Public Library. Your staff consists of fourteen full-time employees, four part-time adults, and sixteen part-time college students. Your staff works together harmoniously, cooperatively, and efficiently. You have observed that the week following every "big push" like those described above, there is always a loss of momentum: little groups talking, long-time goals lost sight of, and only routine essential jobs done. You are not a "slave driver" or a shrew but your staff is never large enough to permit slacking off at any time. The staff seemed to work best and most efficiently when engaged in planning a special event. After the event, they did not appear to be physically or nervously tired. The "let down" appeared to be merely reaction to the relaxation of pressure or to a change of tempo.

You define "tempo" as the pace at which the staff in an organization gets things done, the speed with which problems and opportunities are identified, the attitudes and alertness to seeing new service opportunities or to improving procedures, the origination of new ideas and the putting of these ideas into operation, and the reaction to change. During the preparation for a special event, the staff saw many things which needed doing and had many ideas for improvement or change; but, you observed that after the event they are not thinking so keenly or so productively.

You have regular monthly staff meetings of the entire staff except the pages. You have decided to present this problem at the next meeting but, before you do, you want to talk it over with your two department heads to get their suggestions. That meeting with them is scheduled for this afternoon. You believe that it is possible to get the staff into the swing of things faster by planning ahead for this period after an event and hence prevent loss of tempo. Possibly have the staff write down, during periods of preparation for events, their ideas for more efficient procedures or operations, the problems which developed, suggestions for innovation or change or new services. Then, after the event, check this list to get new inspiration to avoid a period of "let down."

Role for Mr. Kudzu:

You are twenty-nine years old and have been head of public services in this library for three years. Prior to that you worked as a reference assistant in a large public library. You are open-minded and receptive to innovation and change. You try to operate circulation and reference efficiently and to serve the needs of the community. You are always watching for new ways to serve groups in the community. For example, when you were a member of the expectant parent class at the local hospital, you observed the need for a brochure listing suitable reading materials and sources of information for this group. You and your staff prepared such a brochure for that class and it has been distributed to every class since as well as at the library. Another example, which has been popular with the public, was a reading list for brides which is sent out to every prospective bride as soon as the engagement is announced in the local paper. These lists are also distributed to the dress shops and department stores which have bridal consultants.

During the preparation for every special program, your entire staff is involved and many non-routine activities are necessarily neglected. You, too, are concerned with this "sag" in productive work after each program and would like to plan to avoid it the next time.

Role for Mrs. Guar:

You have been head of technical services in this library for fifteen years and before that you were a cataloger in a small college library. You are forty-five years old. Although your staff is involved only on the periphery of public programs, the attitudes and change of tempo and the sort of "holiday" atmosphere in the public service areas affect the work environment of your staff also. To keep the work in your department moving at an even pace you, too, would like to avoid such let down periods in the future.

Case 51

OUT TO LUNCH

Jay Fig recently assumed the position as Head of the Order Department of a metropolitan public library in which he was responsible for spending about a million dollars per year. Prior to this position, he had worked on the staff of two other large libraries. In these latter positions, he had been aware that acquisition librarians were "courted" by vendors but he had no idea of the magnitude of this attention until he assumed his new position.

This library's personnel code had a clearly well-defined policy as to gifts:

Gifts:

The library's services are equally available to all. Members of the staff may not accept valuable gifts or money from patrons or from firms doing business with the library. Staff members are permitted to accept food products and other inexpensive items, usually worth less than $5.00.

Industries made extensive use of the reference department, especially the science desk. Quite often these firms would send a small gift to each member of the reference department staff at Christmas--pen and pencil sets, boxes of candy, gift cartons or baskets of fruit, fruit cakes, maple syrup, calendars, plants or bouquets, and other items most of which were expendable. These were gestures of good will to show appreciation for services rendered. Occasionally patrons would go out of their way to tell the staff members how pleased they were with the service and offer cash tips. One gentleman recently offered ten dollars to a reference staff member who had supplied information on a very difficult

problem which had saved the man months of work. The
staff member thanked him and explained that she was a city
employee and this was what she was paid to do. He was
very impressed that the staff provided such superior service
to everyone.

Once a local candy company asked the entire library
staff to suggest names for a new type of candy which they
were beginning to make and offered a cash prize to the staff
member who suggested the name they selected. This offer
was approved by the chief librarian before it was announced.
The company was very pleased with the responses and with
the names suggested. In addition to awarding the cash prize
to the person whose name was chosen by the company, the
company sent a box of this new candy to each full-time staff
member throughout the system.

Mr. Fig wondered if these good will gifts influenced
the recipients in any way. But he felt that much of the attention he received from equipment vendors, book jobbers,
publishers' representatives, and others was intended to influence him in the placement of orders. He was offered
tickets to athletic events, plays, and musical events; was invited to cocktail parties, lunches, and dinners; and he had
numerous opportunities to play golf, to go on fishing expeditions, and to ski.

He wrestled with his conscience about where to draw
the line. He did not want to be indebted to any person or
any firms with whom or with which he did business. Should
he refuse all invitations? Or, if he accepted some, what
ethical criteria could be applied in differentiating between
those he accepted and those he rejected? He felt a responsibility to set standards for his staff as well as for himself.
Normally, he was the only person in his department to receive offers and invitations; but in case order department
staff members were approached, he thought a firm policy
should be established.

He finally decided to accept only luncheon invitations--
nothing else. He felt this could be justified on the basis that
business would be discussed during lunch, that he had to take
time to eat anyway, and that he could do two things at once--
eat and learn something about the dealer. He enjoyed talking
to these representatives because he could "pick their brains"
in some particular areas. In many cases the publishers'
representatives and the jobbers knew more about books than

most librarians. He believed it was part of his continuing education to find out what these representatives did and what changes were taking place in the publishing industry. Also, Mr. Fig had the opportunity of informing bookmen about gaps in certain subject fields in which publications should be written. Normally, if such conversations took place in the office, Mr. Fig was harassed with telephone calls, questions from his staff, and other interruptions. At lunch, such interruptions did not occur. He realized that he always had to be aware of the fact that he was usually getting a sales pitch along with lunch and might be influenced one way or another. However, impressions could be negative as well as positive. For example, Mr. Fig remembered one man who represented a nationally known jobber. He didn't know books at all--he could have been peddling soap. Mr. Fig was adversely influenced in this case--he reasoned that if the representative wasn't interested enough in what he was selling to be knowledgeable about the products then perhaps his bosses thought this way too and they were interested only in profit, and he preferred to do business with persons who understood books and the book trade and who were selling service as well as books.

Case 52

SCHOOL REORGANIZATION

The Board of Education of the Andra School System approved an administrative reorganization plan to eliminate the three junior high schools, change the number of grades in the elementary and high schools, and create some middle schools. The system would then include:

Level	Grades	Number
High School	Grades 9-12	2
Middle School	Grades 6-8	7
Elementary School	Grades K-5	14

The Superintendent of Schools believed that this was the time to bring all of the libraries and audio-visual services under the supervision of one person to provide supervision, coordination, cooperation, and better services. Prior to this time, the libraries and the audio-visual services had developed more or less independently in the various schools.

You have just accepted the position of Supervisor of Libraries and Audio-Visual services. Your responsibility is to develop adequate educational media centers in each of the schools. Each of the present elementary schools has a small book collection; the junior high school and the high school have fairly good collections. There are some audio-visual materials in each of the elementary schools but none in the junior and senior high school libraries. The librarian in each of the twenty-three schools will report to you. One of the two high schools is currently under construction and will be ready for use when schools open next September at the same time as the reorganization plan goes into effect. You are to assume your position on February 1.

Assume that you have adequate funds for any reasonable program you wish to develop. Outline your objectives and goals. What long- and short-range planning must you do? What types of plans will be involved? Are there any premises and constraints to be considered? How can you involve the library staff in planning? What kind of organizational structure will you plan? How many and what types of personnel must be employed?

Case 53

A "BARGAIN"

Little space for expansion was available in the stacks of the Linden College Library. The arrival of newly bound periodicals from the bindery usually necessitated extensive shifting to make room for them on the shelves. An addition to the library was included in a campus building program but the present financial status of the college gave the library staff no hope that the addition would be built for many years. Temporary storage space for little used materials was provided in the basement of a classroom building several years ago but was quickly filled to capacity.

This liberal arts college library was founded by a protestant denomination during the third quarter of the nineteenth century. In addition to support from the church, an endowment supplied additional funds. Compared to other academic libraries during the years, the Linden library budget had been more than adequate to build up an above average college library collection which was especially strong in periodicals and serials. Continuous runs of many titles dated

Planning Cases

back to the latter part of the eighteenth and early nineteenth centuries.

Inflation, decreased yields from endowment investments, increased costs of labor and equipment, and less support from the church resulted in drastically smaller annual budgets--hence no immediate prospects of any new buildings. The library staff had to "make do" with the present facilities.

The staff had discussed having some of the early serials and periodicals microfilmed and offering the physical volumes for sale or exchange to other libraries; but cost estimates were too high even to consider. When the chief librarian, Dorothy Chat, received the following letter, it appeared to be a happy solution to their problems of space and cost:

Palm City Microfilms, Inc.

Dear Librarian:

We are happy to announce our new exchange program whereby you can exchange, without charge, your bound or unbound serials and periodicals for microfilm. The program offers you three alternatives:

(1) Volume for volume exchange. That is, for each physical volume you wish to exchange, we will give you the same volume in microfilm.

(2) Incomplete sets. In many instances, we will offer you the complete unbroken file on microfilm for your incomplete set.

(3) New titles for your collection. If you have hard to find back files of serials and periodicals which are in demand by other libraries, we will exchange at a ratio of as much as one to four; that is, for each of your physical volumes we will supply microfilm copies of four volumes of any serial or periodical which we have in stock.

This exchange offer represents no money outlay from your library budget. You will not even have to pay any transportation costs because our trucks will pick up your physical volumes and deliver the microfilm reels.

In addition to our exchange program, we have in stock microfilm copies of several hundred titles which are for sale at prices 25 per cent to 40 per cent less than any other microfilm publishers. These items are available within thirty days from receipt of your letter.

We are also in the market to purchase complete sets, partial files, or odd numbers of certain serials and periodicals in all fields and languages. We do not handle popular newsstand materials or trade journals. We will gladly send you our current buying list.

Enclosed are two lists: (1) our current buying list of periodicals and serials which we will consider for exchange, and (2) titles available for sale on microfilm.

If you are interested in any of our offers, we will be happy to send one of our experienced consultants, without charge, to come to your library, evaluate your needs, and recommend a program to fit your needs. Please write me the dates which will be most convenient for you and I will try to schedule a visit by one of our consultants at one of these times.

Sincerely,

Neal Shrike
President

To Dorothy Chat, this offer seemed like a happy solution to the Linden College Library space problem. Scanning the list of periodicals desired for exchange, she recognized many titles of which Linden Library possessed long runs. Also, in the list of microfilms for sale, she saw a number of titles which her staff would like to add to the collection and for which they would be willing to exchange some seldom-used volumes.

Somehow, though, the offer sounded too good to be true. She wanted to investigate the legality and feasibility of such an exchange, to learn something about the firm and its reputation, and to find out whether any other librarians of her acquaintance had experience with this firm.

At Linden College, any transaction involving college-owned property had to be approved by the president's office and the transaction had to be handled through the office of the treasurer. Any new library policies involving off-campus relationships had to be approved by the faculty library committee. For instance, a number of years ago when exchange relationships between Linden College Library and other libraries were established for exchanging college publications and duplicates, the faculty library committee approved the general policy for exchanges. But this policy would not cover the type of exchange program offered by Palm City Microfilms, Inc. Hence, before the library staff could consider this program, Miss Chat would have to talk to the college treasurer about legality and procedure and to the faculty library committee about policies.

Miss Chat circulated Xerox copies of Mr. Shrike's letter to the professional members of her staff for their comments and mailed copies to other librarians asking if they had had any experience with this company. As a further check, she sent a copy of the offer to a member of the college's board of trustees who was a prominent banker in the state's capital city, asking whether he could obtain any information about the firm's financial status. Here are the replies she received:

A member of the Linden Library staff commented, "Mr. Shrike does not indicate prices he will charge for the microfilm he has for sale or prices he will pay for physical volumes he wants to buy. This information is basic to any discussion of the offer."

Two librarians reported that they had had no experience with Mr. Shrike or his company and had never heard of them. The acquisitions librarians of two university libraries stated that they had done some business with Mr. Shrike in both exchange and cash operations and had no complaints.

The librarian of a liberal arts college in an adjoining state said, "Mr. Shrike's exchange offer sounded like such a bargain that I accepted his offer to send one of his consultants to our campus. Mr. Shrike came himself driving a panel truck. He talked to our professional staff to learn our needs, checked our holdings of some titles, and made us an offer. He proposed to supply us with complete runs on microfilm of certain periodicals in exchange for our broken runs of the same titles. He pushed us to agree to the proposal at once so that he could take with him that afternoon the volumes listed in his proposal to us. We were so dazzled by his generous offer that we agreed to his removing the volumes. That was six months ago and to date we have received only a fraction of the microfilms he agreed to send and those were not of standard quality. Repeated letters and remonstrances to him have brought no results.

"My advice to you is to ignore his offer or, if you do decide to do business with him, to obtain payment or microfilms prior to giving up your materials."

The librarian of a large public library wrote: "We have not done business with Mr. Shrike and suggest that you be very careful about any agreements with him on the basis of unsatisfactory dealings that other librarians have had with him. One library received a bad check from him, others report that he is a crook and a liar and will cheat you sooner or later. Mr. Shrike specializes in small isolated college libraries. I know of one such library which was almost denuded through its gullible librarian."

The acquisitions librarian of a large college library advised, "Those librarians who tell you that their dealings with Palm City Microfilms have been favorable have probably already been 'hoodwinked' by Mr. Shrike and the librarians do not want to admit their mistake. I suspect that Mr. Shrike is disposing of the materials, which he gets from libraries on 'exchange', to legitimate book dealers for cash and that librarians could do business with these same book dealers at a considerable advantage to themselves rather than letting Mr. Shrike make a profit on the materials.

"In a recent meeting of acquisitions librarians, I learned that at least sixty libraries have been victimized by Mr. Shrike. The libraries so victimized were evidently blinded by the 'bargain' and thus allowed him to take the original copy before they ever received materials in payment and, in many cases, never did receive the microfilm. If you do business with this firm, I suggest that you insist upon receiving the microfilm to collate them to ascertain their quality before you give up your own volumes."

Planning Cases 245

The banker member of the Linden College Board of Trustees acquired this information: "Through several sources of information available to bankers, I have received detailed reports on Palm City Microfilms and its president, Mr. Shrike. The company has been doing business at the same address for three years in an old rented brick building in a commercial district. Mr. Shrike has been unwilling to furnish financial details relative to his business for banking and trade reference. The company supposedly has an inventory of several thousand dollars in used books and periodicals with fixed assets estimated in low four figures.

"Mr. Shrike, the reported owner of Palm City Microfilms, Inc., filed for bankruptcy three different times in the past twelve years, was indicted seven years ago on charges of embezzlement and forgery and served a prison sentence, and frequently changes the name and address of his company to avoid other legal action against him."

Case 54

CLEARANCE

(Role playing)

The personnel code of the Metropolitan Public Library system is in the process of being revised. The revision is a project sponsored jointly by the staff association, the Personnel Officer, and the Executive Council (the top administrative officers). Representatives from each of these three groups constitute an ad hoc Personnel Code Revision Committee. One section after another of the Code is being studied by the Committee. Today the following regulation is to be reviewed:

Clearance Policy

(1) Articles, letters to the editor, or other forms of writing prepared for publication by a staff member and signed by him as a member of the Metropolitan Public Library staff must be cleared by his Division Chief or Coordinator and the Deputy Director or Director before being submitted to an editor or publisher.

(2) Outlines of speeches or written scripts must

also be submitted sufficiently ahead of delivery to permit clearance by the same individuals.

Role for librarian representing professional members of the Staff Association:

You and several of your colleagues believe this rule is a form of censorship as well as an invasion of your rights as responsible members of a profession. Why should you not be allowed to express your expertise or opinions without the intimidation and humiliation of clearance? You believe that librarians should participate actively in professional organizations and contribute often to professional journals; but this policy inhibits the desire to do either one. You want this rule deleted from the revised Personnel Code.

Role for Deputy Director:

As members of the municipal civil service system, the library staff is subject to all the rules and regulations for municipal employees. These rules are incorporated in the appropriate places in the library Personnel Code. This rule is one that was copied from the municipal employees' code; it is part of a broader regulation which enjoins all employees from political activity even to folding papers and stuffing envelopes. Employees can contribute their efforts to non-partisan community activities such as mental health centers, local control of schools, and intergroup relations. The purpose of these rules is to prevent "crackpots" from sounding off either in writing or in speeches and possibly causing problems for the city administration; they were not intended to discourage professional activities of librarians. In fact, when the rules were written, the library staff was probably never even thought of.

Clearance approval by library officers is practically automatic. None of the officers can recall ever disapproving but they have made what they considered constructive criticism to improve content or style. They believe it would be unwise to challenge or delete this rule from the library code unless or until it is deleted from the municipal code.

Planning Cases

Case 55

GIFT APPRAISALS

As curator of the rare book collection of Greenbrier University, Ernest Midway was frequently called upon to place a value on a letter, an autograph, a manuscript, a rare book, or a collection of such items which were given to the University Library. Always, the donor asked for this appraisal in writing so it could be used to claim a deduction on his income taxes as gifts to a tax-exempt institution. On occasion, he was asked by a donor to prepare a special type of document to satisfy Internal Revenue Service examiners.

Until about seven years ago, Mr. Midway would try to place a true, current, acceptable value on items of minor value. This figure represented the price at which the object could be sold at the time of the appraisal or at the time of the gift. He never attempted to arrive at an appraisal figure for any gift in excess of five hundred dollars but suggested to the donor that this was his responsibility.

An increasing number of requests for appraisals and a very unpleasant experience when Mr. Midway had to prove in court his competence as an expert in appraising rare books, precipitated the adoption of a firm library policy regarding appraisals:

Gift Appraisals

(1) Members of the staff of Greenbrier University Library do not appraise gifts to the library; they may suggest to donors the desirability of appraisals and may refer donors to such sources as auction records, <u>Book Prices Current</u>, dealers' catalogs, and commercial experts. In addition, they may suggest that the donor should consult a capable tax attorney or accountant.

(2) The appraising for tax purposes of a gift to Greenbrier University Library is the responsibility of the donor since he requires the appraisal. The donor must bear all appraisal costs.

(3) The acceptance of a gift by the Library, which has been appraised by a disinterested party, does not imply an endorsement of the appraisal by

this Library's staff or any member of the staff.

Since the adoption of the above policy, donors had accepted it without question. Recently, a problem has arisen with one donor, Mr. Hugh Litchi, one of the state's most powerful politicians who has been a staunch supporter of Greenbrier University for many years and has been influential in obtaining favorable legislation and appropriations for the University in the state legislature.

After his wife's recent death, he decided that at his age (late sixties) it was wise to move from his large home to an apartment. Subsequently, he sorted all of the possessions which he and his wife had accumulated during their more than forty years of marriage. He offered to the Board of Trustees of his alma mater, Greenbrier University, his collection of papers, books, manuscripts, paintings, and sculpture. This "valuable" gift was accepted gratefully by the Board and was publicized widely in the news media of the state.

The gift was received in the University Library two months ago. When the crates were unpacked, all items were listed, books were routed to the Acquisitions Department, and the rest of the items came to the Rare Books Department for disposition. The staff of the Acquisitions Department checked the books with library records to determine whether they were duplicates and to decide which titles should be added to the collection and which should be discarded. According to the library's gift policy, all donors were informed that gifts were accepted with the understanding that the library staff was not obligated to add all gift titles to the library collection but had the right to dispose of any items not retained for the collection. Many of Mr. Litchi's books were old editions, or for some other reason, undesirable for the university's collection, so would be discarded or sold.

Midway in his career, Mr. Litchi served as U. S. Ambassador to an obscure African country. His "papers" consisted chiefly of correspondence relating to his personal political career (which would have some value for future historians to throw light on the state's politics during this period) and carbon copies of letters relating to his less-than-earthshaking months as ambassador. The theme of many of the latter was "Please get me out of this place quickly." The collection of paintings and sculpture were all from this African country and would probably be turned over

Planning Cases

to the Fine Arts Department. Greenbrier University had no African studies program.

The Director of Greenbrier's Library has just received a memo from the President's office asking for an appraisal of Mr. Litchi's gift which the latter needs for his federal and state income tax returns. The Director called the President and cited the Library's gift appraisal policy. The President would not accept this as an answer to Mr. Litchi and has demanded a list of all items in the gift and an appraisal of the value of each item. He said, "It would be an insult to Mr. Litchi, after having given us this valuable gift, to ask him to hire a tax attorney and a commercial appraiser to evaluate his gift. You are all experts and should be fully qualified to do the appraising."

The Director replied, "An appraiser must show that a market exists for the material and must be able to cite instances where similar material has been sold recently for comparable prices. Many of the books are simply old and out-of-date and have no current market value. Neither does a market exist for Mr. Litchi's correspondence, paintings or sculpture. Our only method of appraisal would be to seek for the sale of similar material from some individual who may be accepted by the state tax division and the Internal Revenue Service as comparable in status and prestige to Mr. Litchi and use that figure as a basis. I fear we will not find any such comparable case."

The President still insisted that the library staff come up with an appraisal figure which would be "fair to Mr. Litchi."

The Director telephoned this information to the Acquisitions Librarian and to Mr. Midway. He asked them to think about the problem and to come to his office for a conference tomorrow. He told them that he had gotten the impression from the President that a true, current, market value would not be acceptable inasmuch as the total collection has little value to the University and such a figure would be very low. The Director does not want to be a party to fraud or deception nor does he want to involve his staff. He knows full well that any staff member who makes or assists in making an appraisal must be prepared to defend his appraisal in court or to the Internal Revenue Service. This is a delicate political situation as well as a problem of professional ethics.

Case 56

INDIVIDUAL RECOGNITION

(Role playing)

At Eucalyptus University Library, it was customary policy for staff members to receive no individual recognition for bibliographies compiled, for news articles or student handbooks written, or for orientation courses developed. The only identification on productions of this sort was the name and address of the library and the name of the director. Through the years, various staff members have occasionally remonstrated against this policy when they were personally involved, but it never became a real issue. Recently, two staff members worked for almost three years on a library orientation moving picture to be shown continuously during freshman week each year. This picture replaced the time consuming library tours previously conducted. The film showed each of the departments of the central library and each of the branch libraries, gave simple directions about how to check out books and how to use the catalog, and introduced fundamentals of shelf arrangement and classification of books. When the film was completed, the list of credits at the beginning of the film identified the audio visual personnel who manned the cameras, who did the graphics, and who edited the final result. But no mention was made anywhere in the film of the two librarians who had conceptualized the content, interviewed and selected the student actors, made complicated arrangements in the various departments and branches for filming, and wrote the script. The only credits in the film for the library staff stated "Produced with the cooperation of the Director of Libraries, Dr. William Locust, and his staff."

This film served as a catalyzing agent for the staff to bring the issue of individual recognition into the open. The issue was brought up at the last staff meeting and an ad hoc committee was appointed to study the problem. The committee has gathered data and has scheduled a conference with the Director to request a policy change.

Role for Dr. William Locust, Director of Libraries:

You believe that the long-established policy of staff anonymity for any library-sponsored projects is sound because staff members are being paid from the library budget

Planning Cases

to do these projects which are part of their responsibilities. By having only your name on the bibliography, handbook, or other item produced, any feedback comes through your office which you believe is good, sound administration utilizing the chain of command. You can then pass on whatever comments (whether praise or censure) to the appropriate department heads for transmission to the staff members involved. If individuals were identified, feedback would no doubt come to them and your office might never be informed. How could individual recognition be given to the professional staff in acquisitions, cataloging, and circulation for their contributions to the total library operation?

<u>Role for Mrs. Elsie Ash, chairman of the ad hoc committee:</u>

You have been head of reference services in this library for a number of years. You firmly believe that individuals who produce creative projects should be personally identified for at least three reasons:

(1) To make it possible for users to communicate directly with the responsible person or persons for clarification and for suggestions as to omissions or additions.

(2) To encourage high professional standards for whatever is produced. If the person responsible is not identified, he might do a "sloppy" job inasmuch as any criticism would not come to him personally.

(3) To boost staff morale and pride in undertaking demanding creative assignments. Although, theoretically, done during working hours, actually many personal off-duty hours are devoted to such projects as preparation of a new personnel code or staff manual, the writing of a new student or faculty handbook, the creation of an effective display, and the production of the freshman orientation film.

You are representing the sentiments and opinions of the staff association in requesting that Dr. Locust change the policy regarding individual recognition.

Management of Libraries

Case 57

MISSION OF RESEARCH LIBRARIES

(Role playing)

Because of its reputation as an outstanding collection of American historical materials, mail requests for information came to the Mallard Historical Society Library from all segments of the population from grade school children to senior research scholars. The quantity of mail was so great that a junior professional, Miss Irma Indigo, and a typist were assigned full-time to sorting and handling the mail. Requests for access to study certain documents or portions of the collection were answered by sending them formal application blanks to be filled out and returned with the names of references.

Many general, "blanket" requests sounded as if they came from grade school children, from high school or college students, or from adults writing speeches. This type of request was usually phrased something like this: "Please send me all the information you have about . . . " In reply to these letters, Miss Indigo sent one of several form letters explaining that inasmuch as the Library had no circulating collection, no publications could be mailed out. If the writer asked for a few specific facts indicating that he had done considerable work on the subject and just needed a little information which only this collection could provide, Miss Indigo would photocopy up to five pages which contained the information.

If the writer was a grade or high school student, the reply suggested that the sender talk to his school librarian or visit his local public library. If the writer appeared to be an adult, the form letter listed the names and addresses of historical collections in the writer's state, the state's academic institutions, the state library, and large public libraries and suggested the writer contact them.

Many letters asked something like this: "I am a descendant of _____ who was a signer of the Declaration of Independence. Will you please compile a genealogy for me. I was born in _____ on _____, the names of my parents are _____ and their birth dates and place of birth are _____." In reply to such requests, a form letter stated that the staff of the Mallard Society Library was too small

Planning Cases

and the library budget too limited to do genealogical research but that "a number of persons throughout the nation earn their living doing this work. Normally their charges are from _____ to _____ per hour. Enclosed is a list of the genealogical collections in your state and region. We suggest you write the curators of these collections for the names and addresses of genealogical searchers in the area."

Requests for information which came from serious research scholars, editors, or publishers were referred to one of the senior librarians or curators of special collections for reply.

Many requests were from graduate students writing term papers, masters theses, or doctoral dissertations. If the request displayed a lack of basic knowledge of the subject which could be obtained from standard historical works or indexes, the librarian to whom the request was referred would send a tactfully worded reply suggesting that this information was probably available in his academic library or in other large libraries in his state or region. The reply stated: "After your local library resources have been exhausted, you might wish to come to the Mallard Library to search for specific details which you lack. An application blank requesting access to materials in this collection is enclosed." Typical of this type of letter from graduate students was the following:

> I am doing research on _____. (I am not sure of the spelling of his first name nor of his middle initial.) He was born about 1815 in Pennsylvania or Connecticut and emigrated to Indiana about 1845 to teach in a newly established seminary. I believe your library may have information about his parents, where he was born, schooling he had, what led to his western migration, and any other facts you may be able to give me. I am specifically interested in the impact of his views on the educational development of the state of Indiana.

Some of these requests asked for "original" material which meant something in handwritten form. In many instances, the librarian included in her reply a mimeographed sheet explaining and defining primary source materials. The nature of some requests sounded like the writer expected the Mallard staff to do most of his research for him and send

him by return mail what would seem to be a full draft of
something which he could retype and hand in.

More specific and intelligent requests from senior
scholars were answered as fully as possible by a senior librarian or curator. If the writer asked what materials were
available on a certain subject, he was referred to or sent one
of many printed bibliographies produced by the Mallard staff.
If the writer asked for facts which would take many hours to
locate, the reply suggested a trip to the Mallard Library to
do his own searching. But if the writer needed an isolated
fact which could be readily located only in some rare pamphlet or document owned by the Mallard Library, the staff
would go "all out" to find it for him.

The Mallard staff believed they were doing a conscientious job of answering requests and making the materials
available to those who came to the library. But recently the
President of the Mallard Historical Society received several
very caustic criticisms of the library's access policies. He
has asked the library director to come to his office for a
conference to discuss the mission of the library as understood and interpreted by the library staff.

Role for the President, Mallard Historical Society:

In your position, you are understandably sensitive to
public opinion and criticism. The charges made in those
letters are serious and you need more background to answer
them. Copies of some of the letters were sent by the writers to newspapers, historical journals, and library periodicals where they were published. The Mallard Historical Society is supported privately through memberships and endowments and supplemented by some research grant funds. This
adverse publicity may discourage future donors as well as
affect future membership campaigns and also membership
renewals. The criticisms can be summarized as follows:

A college faculty member who was writing a book on
one period of American history charged that he had traveled
a long distance to study certain documents in the Mallard Library which were essential to a section of his book. He had
asked to see "all" documents pertaining to this period. He
asserted that he was given access to seven and learned later
that there were fifteen others he should have studied. He
did not know of the existence of these fifteen until another
book was published which referred to them. He charged that

Planning Cases

the library staff applied institutional censorship in permitting one historian access to the fifteen documents and not bringing them out for him to study.

Several scholars claim that over the past ten years access to various archival materials in the Mallard Library were denied or withheld from them by the library staff and consequently seriously affected their work; and, in one instance, prevented the compilation and publication of a volume. The staff member responsible for withholding the documents in both of the foregoing examples claimed that the papers in question were not available at the time due to restrictions imposed by the donor.

A doctoral candidate working on his dissertation, in an irate letter, reported that he was denied access to certain papers because they were "reserved" for a cooperative research project sponsored by a famous national institution. Another doctoral student was told he could not see certain papers because they had not been unpacked from the cartons in which they had been received from the donor and, according to library policy, a staff member must examine, sort, list, and file all incoming material before it can be made available for use by the public.

Role for Director, Mallard Historical Society Library:

You have investigated each of the charges cited above. You insist that materials are available to bona fide research scholars impartially and that your staff do not discriminate between them. The contention that materials have been arbitrarily denied or withheld has no basis in fact. In every instance cited, the staff member involved had acted within his authority and any denial of access was in accordance with library policies approved by the Society's board of trustees.

You and your staff believe the mission of a specialized research library is to be a repository of rare and unique resources which contain the materials for new contributions to knowledge. An important function is physical care of the collection and preservation not only for this generation but also for future generations. Accessibility must be regulated within a framework which inhibits destruction or damage from carelessness or loss through theft. A function of this library is not to be a source of reference for casual or general inquiries.

This library is also a researching library where many members of the staff, as part of their professional responsibilities, undertake the writing, publishing, or editing of books, reports, catalogs, bibliographies, and journals. Whenever their labors are interrupted to spend time answering casual or frivolous user requests, some future researcher will be impeded in his significant work because the Mallard staff didn't produce the necessary bibliography or list or failed to sort and file newly acquired archival material.

The researcher who does not know that certain materials exist or cannot describe his needs in perfect detail has no right to expect staff members to spend untold amounts of time doing the necessary research to identify whether or not they exist.

You and your staff see your mission as supplementing the functions of other libraries. You believe that scholars should exhaust the facilities of local libraries first and that Mallard Library should be one of the last resorts. You believe the function of public, tax-supported libraries is to serve a geographical area as a circulating collection and reference center. The staffs of such libraries are obligated to provide information on any or all subjects and the only limitations on service are normally in terms of policies regarding subjects (for example, legal or medical advice, or crossword puzzle words) or the length of time which can be spent on one search.

You believe the academic library exists to serve its educational complex; again, any legitimate request for reference or research service should be provided. Normally its resources are available also to the general public and all qualified scholars and researchers. But the academic library is not obligated by function or purpose to serve as a source of reference for casual inquiries.

No librarian in any library should be asked or expected to do more than is reasonable or to do research which the user should do for himself. The librarian can assist in the use of various indexes, bibliographies, and catalogs to locate suitable materials and can find and locate the materials for the user but the user must "dig out" what he needs for whatever purpose he wants the information.

Planning Cases   257

Case 58

STUDENT PERIODICALS

(Role playing)

Ever since the student newspaper and the annual yearbooks were started at Fuchsia University, they have been systematically acquired, bound, and indexed in the University Library. The student staffs have always maintained active exchange agreements with student newspapers and yearbooks of other academic institutions. These exchange publications were made available to students of Fuchsia University in the student government offices or in lounges in the student union, but were never kept permanently nor were they ever checked into the library.

In recent years, as student political periodicals became more and more common, some faculty members suggested that a sampling of these periodicals should be acquired and retained by the library for the sake of the history of the period--just as posters and broadsides of an earlier era were collected and retained.

A Serials Selection Committee of the staff studied the problem and made recommendations as to policy. After this policy was announced, several members of the library staff and of the history department argued for a broader policy. A meeting has been arranged to mediate the differences of opinions.

Role for Chairman, Serials Selection Committee:

In view of the heavy demand of the faculty for serials, careful consideration must be given to approval of any additions because of budget limitations. The addition of a serial title represents a continuing annual allocation of funds to acquire the title. Once added, getting faculty or library staff approval to delete serial titles is difficult to obtain. Hence, this committee must exercise great care in approving the addition of any new title. The committee has adopted the following policy on retention of student political periodicals:

> Titles will be individually selected under the normal serials selection procedure. Subscriptions will be placed for those titles on good quality paper and in a format suitable for binding. Titles

not meeting these physical standards will be retained on a current basis only. If commercial microfilm of back files becomes available for student political periodicals, purchase will be considered at that time.

Role for Mr. Kestrel, library bibliographer for Social Sciences:

You have read the "Policy on Retention of Student Periodicals" and you believe it is too narrow and short sighted. You believe that all titles of student political periodicals should be accepted as they become available regardless of normal serials selection criteria because these titles are mostly ephemeral. In regard to the statement that "subscriptions will be placed for those titles on good quality paper and in a format suitable for binding," some titles of great historical value will never meet the physical standards normally set by reference libraries but will nevertheless become important documents of contemporary intellectual history. You believe that often the passions of the moment tend to influence judgment concerning the relevant value of contemporary political periodicals, the most unprepossessing of which could turn out to be a key element in documenting the development of contemporary student political activity.

You suggest that this statement be added to the committee policy: "In addition to acquiring all student political periodicals as they come to the attention of the library staff, (1) all local political periodicals be actively searched for, no matter what the quality of printing stock or the format, and (2) back files of these be microfilmed and made commercially available to any library or institution wishing to acquire them."

You believe that this type of publication is so hard to acquire that the committee should not be diffident about their value as documentaries.

Planning Cases   259

Case 59

FACULTY READING LISTS

(Skit)

Characters:
  Mr. Mimosa, Research Director of Gannet, Inc.
  Mrs. Phoebe, Librarian, School of Business, Toucan University

   Mr. M: Hello, this is Bill Mimosa--I am research director for Gannet, Inc., a management consulting firm in your neighboring state. We have just undertaken a project which involves our consulting partners in a survey of a municipal hospital. This is an entirely new field for our firm and our partners have to do considerable study on the general subject of municipal hospitals in particular and of hospital administration and organization in general. You have been recommended to me as the nearest librarian who is competent in this field. Please mail me a list of the best sources on the subject.

   Mrs. P: Are you requesting a bibliography which will cover the entire field of hospital administration? If so, I can readily say there is not one.

   Mr. M: Our interests are not quite so broad. We want material related directly to these aspects of hospital administration, with emphasis on municipally owned hospitals:

   organization   community surveys
   financing (bond issues, etc.) services to the community
   purchasing   civil service
   capital budgets and operating personnel administration
      budgets

First of all, what is the textbook (or textbooks) in the general area?

   Mrs. P: To the best of my knowledge there is no good, comprehensive textbook. An old one is by MacEachern. However, it is not presently used. The last edition is probably ten years old. The readings given to students in this school come largely from journals. Without checking further I cannot give you any general text which would be geared to your needs.

Mr. M: I realized that this would require some checking. Would you kindly send us a list of readings used in your relevant courses and also a bibliography which would cover the areas I have indicated? The bibliography should be to the point. You need not cover everything on the subject, just the best.

Mrs. P: We do not distribute the reading lists of our faculty members without permission from them. If you wish I will give your request to the appropriate faculty members.

Mr. M: Don't you have the lists in the library?

Mrs. P: Yes.

Mr. M: Well, just photocopy what you have and send them on. We are in a great hurry. Time is of the essence. You know how consultants are. They need everything yesterday.

Mrs. P: You did not understand my previous statement. We do not distribute lists. To do so would be a violation of our established policies not to betray professional confidences. The lists are the work of the faculty members and distributed only according to their wishes. We will give your request to appropriate faculty members if you wish.

Mr. M: Well, O. K., if that is the only way. But it will probably take them some time to answer and we are in a rush. Will you be able to get your part of the information off today? A handwritten letter will be all right, just so we get it immediately.

Mrs. P: I am sorry. I do not have time to work on bibliographies for outside organizations except that occasionally I do work on a consulting basis or work on a publication. For the most part my time is completely committed to serving the Toucan community.

Mr. M: We usually find librarians quite helpful and willing to give us the information we need. Our company is one of the oldest and best management consulting firms in the country. This is for a hospital and would serve a great many people. It is for a very worthwhile purpose.

Mrs. P: I am well acquainted with the reputation of your firm and can only say that I am sure they are not providing their services free of charge. There is no reason that Toucan University should support a profit-making company with such a service as the one you request. Regardless of all this, I would still say that I cannot undertake your work. It would take, probably, two or three days' time. I do not have that much free time and neither do my staff. Would you like to have your call transferred to a faculty office? Some of them may have consulting time available.

<u>Mr. M</u>: How much do they charge per day?

<u>Mrs. P</u>: You would have to ask them. I should imagine an amount equal to, or more than that charged by the consultants in your firm.

<u>Mr. M</u>: How much do you charge?

<u>Mrs. P</u>: To profit making organizations, $150 per day. To others $100, or less, depending upon the organization.

<u>Mr. M</u>: I shall see what we can do. I do not think the firm will pay a librarian $150. You would not do it for less?

<u>Mrs. P</u>: You misunderstand me. I will not do it at all. My free time is wholly committed for several months.

<u>Mr. M</u>: There is nothing you can do to help us?

<u>Mrs. P</u>: I can do as I suggested before: I can request the faculty members who teach hospital administration to send you a copy of each of their reading lists. Previous experience leads me to believe that one faculty member will refuse but I do not know what reaction you will get from others. I can send you a guide to information sources which I distribute to hospital administration students.

<u>Mr. M</u>: Well, I guess I'll leave it at that. I thought you would be more cooperative. It will take us a long time to do this bibliographic work ourselves because we do not have the sources that you have.

<u>Mrs. P</u>: I suggest that you refer your problem to the Industrial Information Center at Zee University. They offer a research and information service to corporations on a unit-fee basis. They have a most competent staff and will

do a very thorough job for you. The Center is self-supporting and charges for service are based on the actual cost of each search. I recommend that you phone the director, Miss Cardinal, and ask her how soon her staff could do this work for you and what she estimates the cost of such a search would be. I will send you a folder describing their services to industry.

Chapter IV

ORGANIZING CASES

A foundation for organizing is provided by planning. To accomplish goals, to carry out plans, and to structure the task framework in which people perform, activities must be grouped logically and authority granted. Through the process of organizing, human and other resources are brought together in an orderly manner. Organization consists of the grouping of activities, the assignment of these activities to appropriate departments and persons, and the provision of authority delegation and coordination.

Cases in this chapter involve problems of authority relationships, delegation, organizational channels, line and staff, and physical space utilization.

Case 60

A COMPANY UNION

Prior to 1955 the Terloo University Library Staff Association had a loose kind of organization with a chairman and committees elected annually by the staff. The most active committees were Social and Welfare. The Social Committee was responsible for planning and carrying out all social affairs such as picnics, parties, and a daily tea hour for the entire staff. As the staff grew in size and the staff time necessary to devote to preparation for and cleaning up after the daily tea hour infringed on work schedules, a woman was hired by the administration to take over these responsibilities.

The Welfare Committee sent notes and flowers to those who were ill, congratulations to parents of new babies, and condolences to those bereaved by death. For new staff members, this Committee helped in orienting them to the campus and town and assisted in locating housing.

By 1955 staff needs had developed to the point that a new kind of organization was required which would offer a means of communication between the administration and the staff, between the various libraries and departments and their staffs, and between members. A Staff Association was established, a constitution was drawn up, membership qualifications included every member of the library staff, and standing committees were decided upon.

The former Social Committee became one of the standing committees with added responsibilities including a bridge club, a bowling league, and a record listening club. A new Publication Committee assumed responsibility for a mimeographed staff paper which was published regularly. The purpose of the publication was to acquaint the staff with the library system and special collections, library associations (state and national), staff activities and changes, and other news. One committee studied performance evaluations and presented a detailed report of their findings. Another committee was responsible for orienting new staff members.

The purposes of the Staff Association were to provide a means for better understanding between the staff and the administration, between professional and non-professional, and to provide a forum in which any differences could be frankly discussed, different viewpoints examined, and misconceptions clarified.

Recently the state passed a fair labor practices law. The intent of the law was to make it difficult to discourage labor organization or to impede the right of labor to organize. This law provided that an agency or an employer could not participate in, or sponsor, an organization like the Terloo University Library Staff Association which had its own administrative structure, carried on certain semi-union activities, and included in its membership both supervisors and those supervised. According to the law, such an organization took on the appearance of a company union, the sanction of which might be construed as an unfair labor practice.

The Director of Libraries reluctantly announced the provisions of this law to department heads and to the Executive Board of the Staff Association. He explained that the library administration ran the risk of being charged with violating the law prohibiting company unions. Consequently, the library administration was forced to withdraw both library and university support of the Staff Association. The Staff Association members could no longer be given time for Association activities, meeting space, support for its publications (even in terms of supplies or machine time), or even space on library bulletin boards for Association announcements.

Withdrawal of support by the library administration did not constitute abolishment. The Association could be disbanded only by its own membership. But if the Association continued to exist, meetings would have to be held after work hours in space outside the library system and could no longer be subsidized from the library budget.

Complying with this law meant a complete reorganization of all of the Staff Association activities. Should the work of committees be carried on as part of the administrative structure of the library? How should the staff publication be carried on and financed? If the Association continued to exist, what changes in membership qualifications need to be made? What implications does this law in this state have for library staff associations in other states?

Case 61

CAUGHT IN THE MIDDLE

Alma Shallot was the first librarian in a small school district of five schools. Her immediate supervisor was the Curriculum Coordinator who was responsible for all educational services in the district. The latter reported to the Superintendent of Schools who did all the hiring and firing of employees. Miss Shallot started school library service in the five schools and selected and trained a staff of clerks. She saw as her primary objective the education of the district's administrators to an understanding of a good library program.

The work proved too heavy for one person, so Miss Shallot convinced the Curriculum Coordinator that another librarian was essential to the development of the library service. Doris Sycamore, a certified school librarian, was employed and Miss Shallot was named Library Supervisor with responsibility to plan, direct, and organize the library program. Miss Sycamore was told that she would report to and take orders from Miss Shallot. The latter retained the two largest schools and assigned Miss Sycamore the three smallest schools. Each principal considered the librarian assigned to him as part of his staff.

Miss Shallot was a conscientious supervisor who painstakingly oriented Doris into the work, introduced her to school personnel with whom she would be working, furnished her with a well written job description, delegated certain responsibilities to her, gave her definite assignments, and set up a schedule for reports and conferences. From Miss Shallot's point of view, Doris Sycamore proved to be a most unsatisfactory employee who practiced every "trick" to evade responsibility. Miss Shallot was soon carrying four-fifths of the work load of the library program. This was Miss Shallot's evaluation of Doris:

> Doris tried to 'sell' herself as an 'eager beaver' but she was lazy, charming, and delightful. She came to work late, left early, used up all of her sick and personal leave time early in the year and then asked for more time off, complained continually of being tired, and claimed she was unable to attend meetings because of class assignments and schedules connected with work on a second master's degree. Her warm, outgoing personality made a 'hit' with teachers and children. Principals, unsophisticated in library work, judged her solely on her personality to the point of telling the Curriculum Coordinator, the Superintendent, and me that this was all they cared about in a librarian. They fought to keep her, maintaining they did not care if clerks were not supervised or trained, stories poorly prepared, book orders not turned in, book knowledge not updated.
>
> I counseled with her and tried to motivate her to improve her work performance and her sense of responsibility. She was very verbal, and her replies to my criticisms were subtly written praising me for my sterling qualities as a librarian but indicating that I failed as a supervisor to give her the help, support, and training that she needed. She contended that I needlessly harassed her about aspects of her job which she felt were no part of her responsibilities.
>
> Behind my back, she maligned me to the Curriculum Coordinator and to the principals using the

force of her charming personality to persuade
them that my position as Library Supervisor
should be abolished so that both librarians would
be equal and both report to the Curriculum Coordinator. After I learned about this through
friends in the 'grapevine', I talked to the Curriculum Coordinator about this crisis. She suggested
that since I was the only person dissatisfied with
Doris' work that the solution was to remove me
from any responsibility for her work but to continue the division of work basically as it was.
The Superintendent agreed with her recommendation. There I was caught in the middle between
a conniving, disloyal, deceitful, lazy subordinate
and my supervisor.

I informed the Superintendent of my willingness to
a reassignment, but that the work load had to be
equalized. He and I had several long conferences
in which we covered every aspect of the problem
with the following decisions reached: I was to
remain Library Supervisor but would report to
the Superintendent instead of to the Curriculum
Coordinator. We clarified in writing and adopted
as district policy, the areas of responsibility for
the Library Supervisor and the principals. We
agreed on job descriptions for each position in the
library program and my position was greatly
strengthened. Also we developed an evaluation
instrument for librarians.

Doris remains a serious personnel problem. What
should I do about her? How should I inform her of the above
official changes? Can she be motivated to improve her performance?

Case 62

BUSY, BUSY, BUSY

During his four years of undergraduate work, Silas
Locust worked half-time in a medium-sized city public library. Starting out as a circulation reviser and shelver, he
later was promoted to other positions as vacancies occurred
and his competence increased: borrower registration clerk,
circulation desk attendant, searcher in acquisitions, catalog

filing clerk, and, finally, the last summer as substitute for branch librarians on vacation. Following graduation from library school, he worked as assistant librarian in a college library for two years before accepting the position as librarian of Eastern Lincoln State Normal School in 1930 at the age of 25. The College had been established by the state legislature to serve an area where no college existed. One building was erected, a faculty (including Silas Locust) was employed as of July 1, 1930, to plan for the first classes which started the following September.

No librarian had been consulted in planning the large room across one end of the building which was labeled "Library." Immovable wooden shelves around all walls, an enormous semi-circular charging desk, a carpenter's version of newspaper and periodical racks, and massive tables and chairs for readers were not ideal but this was the physical setting in which Mr. Locust started to develop a library collection and plan for library service. For several years, he had only part-time student help. When the demonstration school was erected, he carefully planned the school library quarters and employed a certified school librarian to take charge. During the Depression, his staff consisted only of women employed on WPA (none of whom had gone beyond eighth grade) and NYA student help. Eventually, as the student body and faculty increased, he gradually added clerks, subprofessionals, and professionals to the staff. But always the library was more or less a "one-man show" as Mr. Locust had originated every procedure, every service, every physical arrangement and he closely controlled everything.

The original two-year teacher-training curriculum was gradually expanded to include two years of terminal and college preparatory junior college courses, then to a three-year teacher-training program, and then a four-year teacher-training institution. With the change in curricula came changes in name from Normal School to Teachers College to State College. In 1970 the institution was known as Eastern Lincoln State College; had a student body of about 12,000 enrolled in baccalaureate, master and specialist programs; and occupied many buildings on an attractive campus.

In the 1950's Mr. Locust took a leave of absence to study for an Ed. D. degree specializing in audio-visual materials and services. His title was changed to Director of Libraries to indicate his changed status and the fact that he supervised a main library, library science classes, residence center libraries, two demonstration school libraries, and a multi-media learning resources center. In 1970, the main library collection of about 300,000 volumes and the learning resources center occupied a recently completed building which was a monument to Dr. Locust's admirable planning: attractive, hospitable, well-furnished, functionally efficient, logically arranged, and economical to supervise. The learning resources center had more than fifty carrels wired for dial access, closed circuit television, a studio laboratory where recording could be done, many tape recorders, filmstrip readers, record players, and motion picture projectors.

According to the retirement regulations of the College, all administrators must retire from administrative duties at 65. Hence, Dr. Locust will give up his responsibilities as Director of Libraries and will teach library science courses.

* * * * * * * *

You, the reader, have been appointed as Director of Libraries to succeed Dr. Locust. Will you assume all of the responsibilities and duties which Dr. Locust performed? Or, do you suggest some changes? Will you take on other responsibilities? Here is what you have learned about his activities either from him, or from your observations during your visit to the library when you were interviewed, or from his staff:

Fine Money: All fine money is kept in a locked vault in Dr. Locust's office and he personally supervised all details including counting what went to the circulation desk, what was collected and put in the vault, what was sent to the Treasurer's office, and the locking and unlocking of the vault.

Staff Meetings: No staff meetings have ever been held, either total staff or department heads.

Organization Chart: No organization chart has ever been drawn up but the following head positions exist: acquisition, cataloging, circulation, reference, media center, and two demonstration school libraries. However, any staff member with a problem didn't necessarily work through his department head but went directly to Dr. Locust because any decision would be made by him and not by the department head.

Shelf List: From her glassed-in office, the head of the Cataloging Department can see only part of her department because of the position of the shelf list which blocks the view. She has requested permission from Dr. Locust to move it to another location, but he has refused because the present location is where he planned for it to be when the floor plans were drawn. "He is very possessive about his library," she said.

Periodicals Department: Believing that anyone could check in periodicals, Dr. Locust employed about a year ago a housewife who had a B. S. degree in home economics to take charge of the periodicals section which is part of the reference department. The reference librarian objected strenuously to the appointment and tried to make him realize how complicated that work had become and that it was even difficult for a professional. Dr. Locust said, "Oh, I think she can carry on all right after I show her what she should do." The home economist hadn't the vaguest understanding of library materials and refused to take advice from the reference librarian. She never did understand the intricacies of the job and finally he discharged her. Then, he spent the summer in that section "cleaning up the mess" and weeding the collection. One department head who had some serious problems which she needed to talk over with him said of those months: "I would ask if I could talk with him and he would just stand with a pile of periodicals in his arms and ask about the problem--never even suggest we go to his office and sit down to discuss it. He acted as though he were in another world and didn't want to be bothered with any other problems. So, I didn't even tell him what was on my mind and he went on with his sorting."

Card Catalog: Dr. Locust has always been most particular about the card catalog and specified how the cards should be reproduced and typed and the physical appearance of each one. His interference made more work for the Cataloging Department because the cards could be reproduced faster and cheaper by other methods. An example of his concern about the appearance of the catalog was cited by the head cataloger: "One day recently he came down to the Catalog Department and was absolutely irate. When checking the filing, he found two cards tied together with a granny knot instead of a square knot. He threw the cards on my desk and suggested that I reprimand the girls who had done this and see that it never happened again." Except for the two years he was on leave to work on his Ed. D. degree, he has always revised all filing in the card catalog. He won't trust this responsibility to anyone else even though he doesn't have the time to do this. Cards were filed daily by clerks from the Catalog Department but Dr. Locust was not consistent in the time when he would revise the filing so the cards just accumulated in the drawers above the rod. Patrons would pick up the loose cards and put them back any place or the cards would drop on the floor. Consequently some cards were probably lost and the filers got no feedback on their filing. If the Catalog Department got behind on filing, he would have a "filing bee" and have the entire staff of acquisitions and cataloging filing in the catalog at the same time.

Marking Books: Dr. Locust personally trains the students who put the call numbers on the spines of books. He wants the lettering done with an electric stylus which gets very hot and produces blisters on the marker's fingers. He stipulates that the call number must be at a precise distance from the lower edge of the spine. Several months ago after one marker left and he had not had the time to train another, the books awaiting marking were lined up on the floor across the whole end of the Cataloging Department. He does not approve of typed white labels affixed to the spine.

Ordering Supplies: Orders for supplies were placed only once a year because it was supervised personally by Dr. Locust. He would ask each department head to submit a list for his department. Then, if he thought the request too extravagant or too large, he cut it. As a result many supplies would be exhausted long before the end of the year. For example, recently, the Cataloging Department ran out of paste for the pasting machine and book plates; this held up new books until these supplies were replenished. Another problem with once a year ordering was that when the supplies arrived, the bulk was so great that it was difficult to find storage space for them.

Paper-saver: As a result of his experiences during the Depression when nothing was thrown away which could possibly be used, he was a paper saver. The staff had memos from him about saving typing size paper which had one good side for use as scratch paper. The memos were specific about types of paper to save. Wrapping paper from interlibrary loan packages was to be neatly folded and reused if the paper was not too rumpled or worn.

Dress Code: The college was located in a very conservative community and students were expected to be dressed in conventional styles of clothing. A dress code for the library was formulated several years ago. One item of the code stipulated that no woman could come in who wore pants or trousers. The intent was to avoid sloppy, ragged, blue jeans and was adopted before the dressy pantsuits and slacks became the vogue. Every person entering or leaving the library had to pass by the entrance guard and he was responsible for enforcing the dress code. The reference librarian told this: "One day a young woman came in wearing trousers and the entrance guard quoted the dress code. He suggested that she put on a skirt and then he could admit her. She explained that she commuted to campus from her home forty-five miles away, she couldn't take the time to go back home, she had no place to go for other apparel except her home, and she desperately needed to use library materials for an oral report in class the next day. The entrance guard expressed his sympathy with her plight but told her he was expected to enforce the regulation. So, she proceeded to remove the trousers, rolled them up, stuffed them in her brief case, and proceeded to go about her work. The dress code had nothing to say about a girl being admitted who wore only underwear partially covered by shirt tails so the guard let her pass."

Case 63

FEDERALLY SUBSIDIZED EMPLOYEES

Early in 1966, the mayor and City Council of Delfor decided to accept federal funds provided through Title I-B of the Economic Opportunity Act of 1964 for Work Training Programs.* The Act was established to provide useful work experience for young men and women from 16 to 22 which would increase their employability or enable them to continue or resume their education and at the same time would provide public service. The funds were available to public agencies and private non-profit organizations (other than po-

---

*Economic Opportunity Act of 1964, U. S. Statutes at Large, vol. 78 pp. 508-534, Public Law 88-452, Aug. 20, 1964. Title I-B Work Training Programs, p. 512-513.

litical parties) to enable them to carry out programs which would permit or contribute to an undertaking or service in the public interest.

The Act recommended that employment priority be given to youth who, in addition to being members of low-income families, had social or emotional problems, poor academic achievement, poor attitudes toward work, cultural deprivation, or physical or mental handicaps. Federal assistance would supply ninety per cent of the wages while the agency employing the youth would contribute ten per cent.

In Delfor, this work-training program was under the supervision of the head of the Community Action Program, Mr. Lane. He was responsible for selecting, placing, supervising, and paying the work-training employees. He contacted all of the local public agencies and institutions eligible for such assistance including the public library.

The Delfor Public Library served a population of about 200,000 and had a collection of 50,000 volumes of which approximately one-fourth were fiction. The staff was composed of two professionals, three full-time clerks, and part-time high school students who assisted in the children's room and in adult circulation.

Although no law required a public agency to accept a work-training worker, Mr. Lane managed to convince Miss Keefton, the head librarian, that she must accept one. Whether Mr. Lane actually stated that Miss Keefton was legally obligated to accept a worker cannot be ascertained. Miss Keefton, however, was convinced that he had so stated and that she, therefore, could not refuse.

The morning before the worker reported, Miss Keefton was overheard to comment, "I don't know what we'll do with her. We don't have enough staff for the professional work as it is, our other non-professionals do the clerical work, and our part-time college girls take care of the other duties. Sometimes there's not enough for them to do. Who's going to supervise her? I only hope she can type."

When Ann appeared, Miss Keefton asked if she had any clerical skills. Ann did not. So Miss Keefton took her to the work room where a staff member showed Ann how to mend and clean books. Ann learned quickly and performed her duties well the first three weeks. Then one day she

didn't come to work. The next day when she came to work,
Miss Keefton asked her why she had been absent. Ann replied, "I'm just working to get some money for clothes. I
had enough to go shopping after school, so I did." She then
continued to work well for another week until she once again
failed to report to work. When Miss Keefton tried to counsel
her, Ann stated, "You don't pay me and you're not my boss.
Mr. Lane is." So Miss Keefton called Mr. Lane to come
over and talk to Ann. When he came, Ann said she did not
want to work in a library and left.

      Miss Keefton asked Mr. Lane not to send another girl
but he assured her he had just the right girl and would send
her over the next day. Linda arrived on schedule. She also
had no clerical skills, so she was taught book mending.
Linda learned slowly but once she caught on she did well.
The only trouble, according to her supervisor, was that she
was so slow. "She'll hold the scissors in the air and look
at the tape for a full two minutes before starting to cut. And
then all her actions are in slow motion. It's eerie!"

      Linda became friendly with the janitor. He loved to
tell stories about Old Clint, the ghost who haunted the library and lived in the unfinished cellar adjacent to the work
room. One afternoon a staff member (unknown) turned off
the lights in the work room and imitated ghost noises. Linda
refused to enter the room again. She was then transferred
to dusting shelves. Two weeks after her transfer she reported that she had quit school and taken a job in a candy
factory and would not be returning to the library.

      When Mr. Lane contacted Miss Keefton about a third
girl, she again requested that no one be assigned. Once
again he assured her that he had just the girl for her. Sue
appeared the next day. She could not type but wanted to try
it anyway. After three days, her supervisor reported, "She's
hopeless! She's wasted more cards in three days than we
use in three months. I simply cannot use her." So Sue was
taught how to mend books. Two weeks later her supervisor
reported, "It's no use. She can't learn and she doesn't want
to learn." Miss Keefton assigned her to dusting shelves.
Sue seemed to like this. She said, "I feel I'm getting something done. They look so nice when I'm done." Five weeks
later her aunt sent her a plane ticket to come visit her. Sue
left without telling Miss Keefton or Mr. Lane she was going.
The day before she left, she had happened to tell one of the
college girls. The next day, when she learned that no one

else knew what had become of Sue, the college student explained what Sue had told her.

When she heard this, Miss Keefton stated, "I know I have to have those girls but there must be some way out. I don't know how I'm going to do it, but I must find some way out. I refuse to have another one of those girls in this library. It is too expensive in staff time to be continually training and is most undesirable sharing authority over them with Mr. Lane."

Case 64

STEAM IN THE STACKS[1]

The public utility company in Carob provided steam as well as gas and electricity for its customers. When the Carob Public Library was built twenty-six years ago, the library board signed a contract for steam instead of installing a furnace in the building. Through the years the service had been most satisfactory and there had never been a leak in the pipes or any accident.

During the winter months, the night custodian would turn the thermostat down five degrees at 9 p.m. when the library closed; then, the day custodian would turn it up five degrees when he came to work at 7 a.m. This morning when the day custodian turned up the thermostat, he heard a roar of escaping steam in the basement. He rushed downstairs and discovered one of the elbows had come apart. He tried to reach the turn-off valve at the meter which regulated or disconnected the supply of steam. No one but an employee of the utility company was supposed to touch this valve except in cases of emergency. The custodian was unable to get to the valve because of the collected steam. He immediately phoned the utility company, reported the break in the pipe, and asked that a service man be sent out at once to close the main valve located in a manhole in the street. The air in the basement reached 100 per cent humidity in eleven minutes.

---

[1] City of Oakland v. Pacific Gas and Electric Company, et. al. 118 P. 2d 328 (1941)

At least twenty minutes elapsed before the utility company's night service man arrived. He refused to touch the valve in the street because this was not his responsibility but was that of a steam service employee. He said he would get into trouble both with his union and the steam service employees' union if he shut it off. Instead of phoning headquarters from the library, he drove back before reporting. Someone at the company office called a steam service employee who walked from his home five blocks from the library. He neglected to bring a suitable tool with him to shut off the steam so the custodian found a wrench which could be used. After the steam had cleared in the basement, the valve at the meter was also shut off.

The stacks in the basement contained many unbound files of periodicals and newspapers and more than 7,000 bound books. The collection was exposed to the steam for more than an hour, and was damaged extensively. Some book bindings and newspapers near the steam break disintegrated. Approximately 2500 volumes of books had to be rebound, most of the rest had to be dried out or repaired in some way. The unbound items were badly soaked and some ripped all to pieces when staff members picked them up. Paint peeled off of the walls, some plaster was so soaked that chunks fell off the ceiling, and the surface of the stacks was damaged. The library board sued the utility company for damages charging negligence on the part of the utility employees.

If you were in charge of this cleanup operation, how would you handle the situation? How would you select and organize staff? What priorities would you assign to the jobs to be done? What equipment would you need to acquire? What space allocations would you need?

Case 65

A CIRCULATION DEPARTMENT

When you assumed the position as head of the Circulation Department of Sycamore University Library, the staff was composed of the following:

one professional in charge of fines and overdues (full-time)

eight subprofessionals (full-time)

circulation desk day supervisor
circulation desk night supervisor
stack supervisor
carrel attendant--in charge of some 450 carrels
tracer (searched for missing books)
filer and sorter
two check out desk attendants

forty part-time students

All eight of the full-time staff report directly to the head of the department. The library is open 92 hours a week but the two circulation desk supervisors work a total of 80 hours so for at least twelve hours a week only student assistants are at the desk. Actually only student assistants are at the desk for more than twelve hours because they have to cover rest breaks and any other times the supervisors are not at the desk (staff meetings, illness, and absences). The former head of the department was scheduled for desk duties on weekends, one evening, and emergencies.

Reorganize the department to (1) reduce the span of authority; (2) provide backup for each key position; (3) give more responsibility to the professional member of the staff; (4) clarify the chain of command so that each person reports to someone; and (5) relieve the head of the department of any scheduled desk duty. You can add two full-time subprofessionals. Draw an organization chart.

Case 66

VOLUNTEERS

(Role playing)

In the central library of a large city-county library system, an information desk was located on the main floor near the entrance. When assigned to this desk for the first time, each staff member was put through a thorough orientation by the floor supervisor. The person at this desk represented the library to the public and, consequently, was expected to be well groomed, polite, courteous, cheerful, patient, and well informed. In addition, the person had to know the layout of the building, the location of departments and collections, library rules and regulations, extension services offered by the library, and who was employed in the system. Many telephone calls were also handled at this desk.

One morning the personnel officer for the system, Mr. Wren, approached the desk and introduced a fashionably dressed young woman to the staff member on duty, Miss Enid Alder. Mr. Wren said, "This is Mrs. Jones who will be working at this desk for the next two hours. Each member of the Junior League has volunteered to spend four hours working in the library. These women will be assigned to this desk at various times during the next three weeks and thus release the regularly assigned staff members for other work. They will talk to patrons when they come to the desk and will answer the telephone. We are very grateful to these Junior League members for this volunteer service." As he spoke, Mr. Wren beamed approval at Mrs. Jones.

For Enid, this was a most frustrating and annoying two hours. Inasmuch as she was responsible for the desk, she could not leave without permission of the floor supervisor. Being very conscientious, she did not feel she could leave the desk in the hands of a stranger even long enough to go to her supervisor and ask for advice. Mrs. Jones had received no instructions, no orientation, no idea of what she was supposed to do, yet here she was seated at the desk as though she were the staff member in charge. Enid stood around awkwardly. Mrs. Jones proved at once that she could not man the desk by herself--she would listen to a patron request and then turn helplessly to Enid for the answer. To top it off, she started smoking a cigarette. Enid promptly told her to put it out and informed her that no library employee could smoke when on duty in a public area. Mrs. Jones refused and said she had been told by Mr. Wren that it would be all right to smoke. Enid was concerned about the impression her smoking would make on the patrons because most of them knew the staff rules about smoking on duty as well as did the staff. There was no ash tray at the desk so Mrs. Jones used the waste basket for her ashes.

As soon as Enid was relieved at the desk by the next librarian scheduled to work there, she reported the conversation with Mr. Wren and the presence of the Junior League volunteer to her floor supervisor, Mrs. Belle Vireo.

Role for Mrs. Belle Vireo:

You had not been informed about the request of the

Junior League to do volunteer work in the library nor had you been consulted about their being assigned to the information desk. Enid's report is the first you had heard of the project and you are wondering who in the administration made this decision. You are angry that Mr. Wren ignored the chain of command in placing someone to work on your floor without your approval or consent. You are a line officer responsible for all personnel and operations on this floor whereas Mr. Wren is in an advisory staff position where he should provide service to the line officers but he should never interfere in line operations.

You are going right up to Mr. Wren's office to confront him with this overstepping of his authority. You consider the information desk a crucial post which cannot be turned over to anyone not especially trained for the work.

Role for Mr. Wren:

You have no idea of what really goes on at the information desk. Since only attractive, personable, outgoing staff members are scheduled there, you have assumed that the person plays hostess to greet patrons as they come in. It seemed the ideal place to put these attractive Junior League women because they were gracious and charming and would make beautiful hostesses. You believe the only qualification for the person at the desk is to have a pleasant voice and manner, a pleasing personality, and an ability to communicate--and surely these women had these qualifications.

You thought Mrs. Vireo would be delighted to have all this free help to relieve her staff for more important duties. You knew that she was always complaining about not having enough staff. In your enthusiasm for pleasing the Junior League members, you sort of forgot about the organizational chain of command.

Case 67

AN EMBARRASSING POLICY DECISION

(Role playing)

At Pine Valley State University, the library was located at one end of a tree-lined grass mall. The Technical Services department was located on the ground floor and the windows on one side overlooked the mall. Whenever there was any unrest on the campus, activity occurred on this mall. Shouting, music, and other noises brought the crisis into the large technical services room where some forty-five persons worked.

One morning the student newspaper announced that there would be a two-hour demonstration on the mall that afternoon to protest a recent administration decision. Several sub-professional searchers were in sympathy with the issues involved. During the morning break, one of them, Mrs. Olive, went to the office of the Director of Libraries and asked him if they could have time off to participate in the demonstration. He said, "If you feel you must go, then go but you must make up the time." When she got back to the Technical Services Department, she reported this to her interested colleagues.

After lunch, Mrs. Olive appeared at the office of the head of Technical Services, Mrs. Butternut, and announced that the staff members listed on a card were leaving for the demonstration. This was the first Mrs. Butternut had known that any of her staff were interested in the demonstration let alone wished to participate. She stared at the young woman in disbelief. At last she said, "You have placed me in a most embarrassing position because I must either go to the Director for an official policy statement to transmit to my staff or tell my staff that you went over my head to my superior for a policy decision."

Role for Mrs. Olive:

You are twenty-four years old, have a bachelor's degree in archaeology, are married to a graduate student in English, and must work to support both of you until he finishes his program. The only employment you could find in this community (except a waitress or clerk in a store) was that of searcher in the University Library. Your husband is a political activist and he encouraged you to participate in this demonstration and to try to get the whole Technical Services Department to close down and take part. You had succeeded in interesting some fellow searchers in the issues but you had been kept too busy to talk to any others. You are ignorant about line and staff relationships and chain of command. You knew that whenever a change was made in personnel policy, the decision came from the Director's office so you thought he was the person to see about this mat-

Organizing Cases   281

ter rather than Mrs. Butternut.

Role for Mrs. Butternut:

    You have been head of this department for about six years and have a most efficient operation. The motto of the department is "The sun does not set on any unfilled orders." You believe in participative management and try to involve your staff in developing improved methods and procedures and in decision-making. You are fair, impartial, considerate, and reasonable in handling personnel problems. Staff members know you are always available whenever they want to talk with you and that you are an empathetic listener. You are knowledgeable about all aspects of management and you are very upset about this incident for two reasons. First, Mrs. Olive should have brought the request to you for action and should not have gone "over your head" to the Director. And, secondly, you are concerned that the Director used such poor judgment in issuing an oral policy decision to one staff member when any decision of this sort should have been announced to the entire staff through a written memo. Furthermore, the Director should have phoned you as soon as Mrs. Olive left his office to report the incident to you or should have asked you to come to the office while he was talking to Mrs. Olive.

Case 68

A MEDICAL SCHOOL LIBRARY

    Manzanita University, a privately controlled institution, had a medical school of three hundred students. Although part of the university library system, the medical school library was autonomous and the librarian reported to the Dean of the school. The library budget was part of the school's budget and the Dean approved all personnel appointments.

    Miss Furze had been the librarian for thirty-five years. When she assumed the position she was twenty-two years of age and had just received a bachelor's degree in library science from one of the nation's leading library schools. Prior to that she had earned a bachelor's degree in biology. She had had experience as a student assistant in a biological sciences library during her undergraduate years. One year she had a leave of absence to study for and earned a master's degree in library science. At present she is fifty-seven years old, has the rank of associate professor, and is on tenure.

Under the able direction of Miss Furze, the library has grown from 10,000 volumes to the present 80,000 volumes. The collection is considered to be well selected and supports the curriculum and limited faculty research. The student body has grown from 140 to the present 300. Except for three years, her staff has been composed of clerks and part-time student assistants all of whom she trained. Thirteen years ago a professional assistant was added to the staff. The assistant was a refugee from eastern Europe who had a medical degree from a university in his native country but was not qualified to practice in the United States. So, he completed a master's degree in library science in preparation for working in a medical library. Miss Furze assigned acquisitions and cataloging to him and she did reference, supervised circulation, and worked with the faculty.

Because of his medical knowledge, he could have contributed immeasurably in serving faculty and students. But Miss Furze treated him as though he were another clerk. She supervised his work so closely that he had no opportunity even to meet faculty members or students unless they came to his workroom or he met them outside the library. He did, however, get to know the professional staff members in the rest of the university system, participated actively in the staff association, and enjoyed various social contacts with them. The Director of Libraries believed he had much more potential than he had any opportunity of demonstrating in his present position. After he had worked in the Medical Library for three years, the librarian of the Biology Library retired and the Director offered it to him. The salary was higher than he was receiving and the work would be more varied and challenging; he would have faculty rank in the Biology Department; would teach a course to graduate students in biological bibliography; and would have a chance to work with people. He accepted eagerly. When he requested permission for the transfer, Miss Furze refused to give it. The Director could have ignored her decision, but, if he did, he was afraid that Miss Furze might retaliate by stirring up trouble for the assistant. Knowing that in this library system he would have no opportunity for advancement, the assistant resigned and accepted an administrative position in a pharmaceutical company library.

The personal relations between the Dean, the Director, and Miss Furze had deteriorated during the years; and, since this episode, neither the Dean nor the Director had been in the Medical Library or had conversed with Miss Furze unless necessary.

The Dean urged Miss Furze to employ another professional assistant at once. She didn't even search for anyone but employed two more full-time clerks instead. She told the Dean that it was easier to train clerks in the established routines and procedures than it was to adjust to another professional who might have "a lot of new fangled ideas that would upset everybody." Because of her constant close supervision, her cold and impersonal attitude, and the repetitious nature of the tasks assigned, the clerks did not stay very long. As a consequence, the personnel office was constantly searching for replacements and Miss Furze was continually training new staff.

Current developments make it mandatory that several professional librarians be employed. First, the Dean has approved a TWX hookup with several other medical, hospital, and health-related libraries in the area to furnish information to all of the doctors and dentists in the state. Second, to meet the public clamor for more physicians, the medical school will be expanded in the next four years so as to double the enrollment. Beginning next year each freshman class will be double what it is this year so that the enrollment will be greater each year for four years. Third, the school has received several large research grants which include large sums for the purchase of supporting library materials. And, fourth, faculty research interests require materials in subject areas which at present are not represented adequately in the collection.

A faculty planning committee has estimated that the library collection should double its size within the next five years, that the serial record should be available in computer printouts, and that the professional library staff should be expanded to meet the Medical Library Association standards.

The recommendations of the faculty planning committee were presented to the Dean and Miss Furze eight months ago. The Dean explained to Miss Furze that funds were available at that time for employing the additional staff and urged her to work out a new organization for the library staff, decide how the work should be divided, search for persons qualified for each position, and plan for additional space. To date, she has not listed one position in any library periodical nor contacted any library school. Several days ago the Dean asked to see her new organization chart, her physical layout for work stations and office space, and the applications she had received. She was rather evasive and said she had been "too busy" to think about any of these things.

Both the Dean and the Faculty Planning Committee are convinced she is "dragging her feet" and are of the opinion that she is quietly and stubbornly resisting the employment of any professionals in "her" library.

Retirement at Manzanita is compulsory for all faculty members at 70 and is optional (with reduced benefits) between 65-69. Those faculty members in administrative positions must give up administrative responsibilities at 65 but can continue to teach until 70.

Case 69

A LIBRARY OFFICE SECRETARY

When Mr. Fletcher assumed the position of Associate Director of Gallup University four years ago, he found one secretary, Mrs. Bruce, in the library office who had held that position for seven years. Several months after Mr. Fletcher's arrival, a stenographer, Mrs. Willis, was added to the office because the work load had become too heavy for one person. According to the organization chart, the library office reported directly to the Director of Libraries despite the fact that, in the everyday practical working situation, Mr. Fletcher was responsible for the performance of the office staff.

A few weeks after Mrs. Willis's employment, Mr. Fletcher became acutely aware of the fact that, though subordinate in rank to Mrs. Bruce, Mrs. Willis was clearly the more efficient employee. Not only were the quality and quantity of Mrs. Bruce's work output inferior to that of Mrs. Willis, but Mrs. Bruce had an abrasive personality which irritated virtually everyone with whom she had any prolonged contact. Another vexing facet of Mrs. Bruce's personality was her absolute inability ever to admit she had made a mistake. It mattered not how obvious the situation might be she would simply deny that she had done it or occasionally attempt to shift the blame to Mrs. Willis. Because of the organizational structure, Mr. Fletcher had no real authority

Organizing Cases

to make any direct changes in operational office procedures or to discipline Mrs. Bruce. He could and did suggest certain changes to the Director of Libraries and some of them were effected. But the Director was a busy man and could not devote much thought or energy to the office problem.

Finally, after Mr. Fletcher had been in his position two years, the Director made Mr. Fletcher officially responsible for the library office. At the same time he assumed that responsibility, the addition of a position of administrative assistant was authorized. In the university's non-academic classification schedule, an administrative assistant ranked above a secretary. Quite obviously, the creation of such a position should have meant a promotional opportunity for Mrs. Bruce. For the past nine years, when she had reported to the Director of Libraries, she received uniformly standard performance ratings and hence had received every merit increase. During the past two years Mr. Fletcher had repeatedly had lengthy conversations with her pointing out the deficiencies of her performance and suggesting how she could improve. But she ignored his suggestions reminding him that the Director was her boss. At no time did Mr. Fletcher consider promoting Mrs. Bruce to administrative assistant for, in his opinion, she was not even performing her secretarial duties in a satisfactory manner. She let work pile up, frequently had large filing backlogs, and the library's financial accounts were inaccurate.

After interviewing several well qualified persons, Mr. Fletcher chose Mrs. Garth who had for the past eleven years been the principal clerk in the university's accounting department. She was given complete responsibility for supervising the work of Mrs. Bruce and Mrs. Willis and for all financial accounts of the library. Her rank was that of senior non-academic employee in the library. This meant that a good part of Mrs. Bruce's former tasks were switched to Mrs. Garth. In turn, Mrs. Bruce was assigned to do the secretarial work of the Director, Mr. Fletcher, and the two assistant librarians who were soon to be appointed. Also, she was to continue maintaining the personnel records of the library staff. Mrs. Willis assisted with the secretarial work.

At the outset, Mrs. Bruce did not accept gracefully this change of duties. She was obviously resentful of the fact that she had not been promoted and felt that she had been discriminated against. She maintained that she was the senior person in service in the library office and that she should have the promotion. After a period of some six months had passed, during which she had observed the kind of work that Mrs. Garth was carrying out and the efficiency with which Mrs. Garth was performing her tasks, Mrs. Bruce volunteered to Mr. Fletcher the information that she was quite happy she had not been promoted for she would not want the responsibilities and increasing pressures that Mrs. Garth had.

A senior typist-clerk was next added to the library office--Miss Miles. Her responsibilities were to do whatever Mrs. Garth assigned to her. She proved to be very efficient and fast as well as having a pleasant disposition and a cheerful attitude. Mrs. Bruce took a dislike to her probably because Miss Miles turned out so much more work than Mrs. Bruce had ever done. Mrs. Bruce became more and more irritable and a steadily increasing air of tension developed among the women in the library office. This tension culminated when Miss Miles asked to be transferred to another unit within the library. She frankly stated that the primary reason for such a transfer was the desire to escape the unpleasant atmosphere created by Mrs. Bruce. Neither Mr. Fletcher nor Mrs. Garth wanted to lose Miss Miles. Mrs. Garth reported that Mrs. Bruce was becoming increasingly headstrong in her refusal to follow accepted office procedures, or to cooperate with the others in the office and to take orders. The only solution which Mrs. Garth could see was to discharge Mrs. Bruce. But, Mr. Fletcher pointed out, Mrs. Bruce's only unsatisfactory performance appraisal was one he had turned in recently. He said it would be very difficult to terminate Mrs. Bruce's employment since her performance reports prior to this year had always been at least standard. In effect, it would appear as if, after almost ten years of satisfactory performance, she was suddenly being discharged. Since the avenue for terminating her employment did not seem a very likely one and transfer to another library department impossible (no one would have her), Mr. Fletcher suggested they make some changes in assignment.

Mr. Fletcher and Mrs. Garth worked out a reassignment of duties within the office: Mrs. Bruce and Mrs. Willis were to continue to do the secretarial work for the Director, Mr. Fletcher, and the two assistant librarians. In addition, they were to handle miscellaneous typing jobs which Mrs. Garth would assign. Mrs. Bruce was no longer to have responsibility for personnel records. He pointed out to Mrs. Garth that there would be less long-range damage done by an inadequately typed letter than there was in including inaccurate information in the personnel files or talking about personnel matters to other staff members. After reviewing the proposed changes with the Director of Libraries, Mrs. Garth notified each of the women in the office of her new assignments. Miss Miles was assigned the personnel work and her desk and files were moved to another area of the office away from Mrs. Bruce. Miss Miles was happy with the change in duties as well as location, maintained the personnel records accurately, and kept the information confidential and up to date.

Mrs. Bruce indicated that she preferred to retain the personnel work and asked why she was being removed from the personnel assignment. She was told, again, that the quality of her performance had not been satisfactory and despite many conversations about it with both Mrs. Garth and Mr. Fletcher, she had done nothing to improve it. Mrs. Garth reminded Mrs. Bruce (1) that her new duties were definitely secretarial in nature; (2) that her reassignment involved neither a reduction in pay nor in classification; and (3) that as an institution got progressively larger and more complex it was frequently necessary to reassign tasks. The explanation did not mollify Mrs. Bruce and she was resentful of the action taken. Her resentment was manifested primarily by being moody and by not associating or communicating with other members of the office staff.

Evaluate Mr. Fletcher's handling of Mrs. Bruce.

Case 70

LAISSEZ FAIRE

Dr. _____
Professor of Library Science
Elderberry Library School

Dear Dr. _____ :

Little did I think when I left Elderberry two months ago that I would need to put into practice so soon what I learned in your management and personnel courses! Reluctantly, I have accepted the position as head of the cataloging department

at Holly College! I desperately need to talk with
you! Mr. Larch, Director of Libraries, has offered to pay my expenses to travel to the campus
to discuss my problems with you and my ideas
for reorganization of the department. Can you
take time to criticize my plans and advise me?
If you can, please phone me so we can arrange
a time that is most convenient for you. I am
enclosing an account of the situation here which
will give you some background about the present
state of affairs. When I see you, I will bring a
floor plan, the budget, some work flow charts I
am working on, details about each staff member,
and any other information which seems pertinent.

                              Sincerely,

                              Mary Heath

    You will remember, during my last semester in li-
brary school, I decided I wanted a position as cataloger in
an academic library and preferred to live on the coast near
the ocean and near mountains. Both the position of assistant
cataloger in Holly College and the geographic location seemed
to be just what I was looking for so I applied. I didn't have
enough money for travel to apply in person and the librarian
did not come to campus to interview students so all negoti-
ations were made by mail.

    The college is privately supported, non-sectarian, and
coeducational, with a liberal arts curriculum which includes
teacher education. The undergraduate student body totals
about 10,000. In just less than two hours driving time from
the campus, I can reach either the mountains or the ocean.

    I reported to the Director's office on the date agreed
upon for me to start work. Mr. Larch, the Director, told
me that the library was print-oriented although there was a
small phonorecord and phonotape collection to support music
appreciation and literature courses. The collection totals
about 105,000 volumes and the library staff about forty full-
time persons. He explained the organizational structure of
the library and then took me to the catalog department where
I met the head of the department, Mr. Bill Partridge. He
was thin, slightly built, clean shaven, and dressed in a
rumpled white shirt and nondescript tie. He was drinking a
cup of coffee and smoking a cigarette. He stared at us with

a bewildered look on his face and nervously straightened some of the piles of catalog cards on his desk.

"Bill, this is Miss Heath who received her master's degree from the Elderberry Library School two weeks ago. She will be your assistant cataloger and will start working today." After this brief introduction, Mr. Larch walked out leaving me standing near Mr. Partridge's desk. The latter looked startled and confused and I was embarrassed and ill at ease. I broke the silence, "Didn't Mr. Larch tell you I was supposed to report for duty today?" "He didn't tell me I was going to have an assistant let alone that he had hired anyone," he stammered.

After another awkward pause, he suggested that he show me around the department and introduce me to the staff. Then I was aware that the whole staff was watching us and listening to all that had been said. The department consisted of one large room and a glassed-in head cataloger's office which he explained was used by the cataloger of rare books who needed privacy to do the exacting work of her position. I asked, "Don't you have any private place where you can have conferences?" He replied that there was a conference room on the second floor which could be used if no one else were using it. The catalog department room was cluttered with desks, heavily loaded book trucks, and shelves around the sides of the room which were completely filled with books. There seemed to be no organized work flow. Each person could see what everyone around her was doing as there were no partitions around desks for privacy--not even low bookshelves. The staff consisted of twelve full-time clerks and two part-time students--all women. When we got back to Mr. Partridge's desk near the door, he found a chair for me to sit in next to his desk and suggested that he would clear off one side of his desk so I could work there until a desk or table could be found for me.

After the initial shock of my arrival wore off, Mr. Partridge became talkative, gave me some background about the department and staff, and confided some of his problems. We started talking at his desk but were constantly interrupted by his staff asking questions about details of their work. From his answers, I concluded he knew little about cataloging. He finally suggested we go to a nearby coffee shop to talk. The Student Union was next to the library, but he explained the only food service there was from machines and the room was very noisy because it was used so heavily by students. So, we walked across campus to a street which bounded the campus on one side and had a number of eating and drinking places and stores. I learned that one of the clerks had been in the department for fifteen years, another one for eleven years, and the rest from three months to seven years. The head cataloger retired two years ago. The position was vacant for about two months and then Mr. Larch promoted a young man who had been working part-time in the department for about a year while taking courses for a library science master's degree. After two weeks, the young man told Mr. Larch, "This department is such an incredible mess, I want nothing to do with it. Please transfer me to the vacancy in reference." And he was transferred. (Mr. Partridge told me that the cataloging department had the lowest status of all departments in the library and staff members got out of it and into other departments as fast as they could.) The position was again vacant for a month or two, then a girl was hired from a firm which specialized in placing temporary office employees. Mr. Larch reasoned that although the girl knew nothing about cataloging and library work, she should be able to do clerical work. That appointment was a sad mistake and she lasted only three days. Again the position was vacant.

Mr. Partridge related how he had been appointed ten months ago: "I had been teaching in this city for several years. When I learned about a year ago that some experimental teaching techniques were to be introduced this academic year, I wanted none of it. Teaching was hard enough for me anyway and having to learn a lot of new-fangled methods would have been much worse. I have always enjoyed books more than people, so I applied to Mr. Larch and he employed me for this position. He said that even though I had had no library science courses, I was intelligent and had a broad educational background. I didn't know what I was getting into and this job has been very hard for me. I didn't know anything about cataloging, classification, or how to supervise the staff. Furthermore, the staff had always done pretty much what they wanted to do and I didn't know how to handle them. I guess that is why Mr. Larch decided that I needed a professional assistant and employed you."

At noon, he took me to a restaurant for lunch. He seemed very tense, nervous and high strung and consumed two manhattans before lunch arrived. I didn't know whether his nervousness and uneasiness was due to my sudden appearance on the scene which perhaps seemed a threat to him or whether this was characteristic of him all the time. I learned later that the latter was the case.

After lunch, he asked if I would like to see the rest of the library and I replied affirmatively. He found a floor plan of the building in a desk drawer and studied it, remarking, "No one ever took me on a tour of the building so I have never been in some departments." As we walked through, he introduced me to a few persons. Later, he told me that he hadn't introduced me to all the staff members we encountered because he had never met them. Incredulous, I asked, "Don't you have staff meetings and department head meetings?" "No meetings of any kind," he said. "How do you coordinate the work of the cataloging department with other departments if you don't communicate?", I inquired. "There's not much coordination or communication," he replied.

When we got back to the department, he handed me one of the many piles of cards stacked on his desk and asked me to check them with the books on one of the five double loaded book trucks surrounding the desk. After this process the books left the department and the various slips and cards were routed to the proper places. This seemed to me to be a subprofessional job and not one for the head of the department.

His desk was completely covered with cards, papers, large ash trays full of old butts, and two dirty coffee cups. One of the clerks saw that the little space he had cleared for me to use was quite inadequate so she found an old typing table on wheels, with hinged sides which folded down, and rolled it over to the side of his desk for me. Although it was too low for back comfort, it did give me some work surface.

Evidently he found me an empathetic listener because during the rest break that afternoon, he talked continuously about himself and his problems. He apologized repeatedly for the state of the department telling me how difficult it was for him here in this new job because people didn't seem to respond and didn't really understand the work. He seemed reluctant to return to the office, but finally, after an hour's break, he said, "Well, I guess it's time to go back but I just hate to face that desk." I felt sorry for him because he didn't understand what was going on in the department and apparently hadn't tried to learn.

Mr. Larch had told me that employees in the cataloging department worked forty hours a week: 8 a.m. - 12, and 1 - 5 p.m. Monday through Friday. So, the next morning, I was on the job before 8 a.m. I was surprised to see that I was the only staff member there on time--all the others straggled in at various times but all were on duty by 8:45 except Mr. Partridge who did not arrive until 9:30. Rest breaks were supposed to be fifteen minutes in mid-morning and mid-afternoon but Mr. Partridge was gone for at least forty minutes each time and the rest of the staff all took more than fifteen minutes. He left for home about 4:15 that day claiming he had a headache. I noticed that the rest of the staff soon started leaving too.

On the morning of my third day, Mr. Partridge called in and said he had a tooth extracted and that he was very uncomfortable and wouldn't be in that day. One of the staff snickered and said, "Well, that's funny because he has false teeth!" That was the last we heard from Mr. Partridge--he never again reported for work. I didn't know what was going on or why he didn't show up. The staff didn't seem to be concerned about his absence but each went on in her own independent way doing, apparently, whatever she was in the mood to do. I continued to do the final checking on the books loaded on the book trucks which kept piling up around his desk.

About a week later a friend of his called Mr. Larch to announce that Mr. Partridge had left town that morning with his belongings and would not be back. He could furnish no forwarding address. This news reached the catalog department via the "grapevine." Gradually I was getting acquainted with the members of the staff in the department as well as in the rest of the library and through them learned more about Mr. Partridge. He was thirty-five years old, unmarried, and had lived in a shabby apartment by himself, except for his cats. He was quiet, unassuming, reserved and shy. He was afraid of responsibility because he didn't want to take the blame for mistakes. He leaned on others to make decisions and let each staff member go her own way. He rarely worked every day in a week and never put in a full eight hours on the days he was there. In the ten months he had been employed, he had used up all his sick and vacation time for about three years.

After learning that Mr. Partridge had left town, I assumed that Mr. Larch would inform me about who was to

Organizing Cases

be in charge of the department and would orient my to my responsibilities. But he did not come near the department, so about a week later I asked for an appointment with him. I told him I had no orientation from Mr. Partridge and asked if he would tell me what I was supposed to be doing and what I was responsible for. His response was "Just do what Mr. Partridge did." I pointed out that the staff, including me, needed leadership and the whole department required organization. I expressed the hope that a new department head would be appointed soon. And, then, he asked if I would be the head! I was very surprised and taken aback. After all, I had only just graduated from library school, had been on the job here less than two weeks, and my only library experience was as a filer in a university library. I had no experience as a supervisor. He suggested I think it over during the weekend and give him my answer the following Monday.

I was prepared to refuse the offer when I saw him Monday morning because I felt that I needed to work under an experienced cataloger rather than be thrust into administration so soon. I explained this to him when I saw him but he wouldn't accept my refusal because he said he felt I was qualified to handle the department. He called in his secretary and dictated a memo to the entire staff announcing my appointment. (I learned later that one of the clerks in the cataloging department had applied for the position immediately after Mr. Partridge's departure and that her application was strongly backed by a member of the board of trustees. Her only qualification was seniority among the clerks in the department.)

That evening I got out the notes, books, and syllabi for my management and personnel courses and started reviewing! The next morning I cleaned out Mr. Partridge's desk so I would have a work station of my own. I hoped to find a procedure manual, a library personnel code, list of staff, some reports, and other documents which would orient me to the organization and operation of the department, but I found none. I did find two books of statistics which had been kept by the former retired librarian--how many books cataloged by Dewey category, how many periodicals, reference books, cards typed, etc. But no entries had been made since she retired.

On top of the desk were many stacks of cards which represented cataloging problems such as disagreements over

classification, or two books with the same call number, or
mismarked books, or inconsistencies in subject headings.
Evidently Mr. Partridge planned eventually to take care of
them. During the next week, I had a personal conference
with each member of the staff to learn what her responsibilities and problems were.   Here is some of the information I acquired:

There were no job descriptions, no position classification plan, no procedure manuals, no salary scale.   Each
person was hired on an individual bargaining basis.   If one
person would accept a lower salary than another person then
the former was employed.   When I saw the list of salaries,
I was shocked at the inequities.   For example, one twenty-
five year old typist who had worked in the department two
years received an annual salary within one thousand dollars
of Mr. Partridge's listed salary.   The typist who had been
in the department fifteen years and seemed fairly competent
was earning less salary than the twenty-five year old.

None of the staff had been given any real orientation
to their jobs or supervision of their work.   They helped each
other when anyone had a problem but it was sort of like the
blind helping the blind because they were all uninformed about cataloging rules, filing rules, and classification.   They
were sharply divided between those who had been here for
several years and were interested in their jobs and the young
girls who were frivolous, were working only for the pay, and
weren't planning on staying here if they could find better jobs.
This caused quite a bit of friction between the two groups
and I feel I am sort of in the middle because I am the only
professionally educated person in the department except the
part-time rare book cataloger.   I hope I can develop morale
in the group and teach each one of them what she is to do
and how her work fits into the total departmental responsibility and contributes to the library's service goals.

Two filers were expected to spend eight hours a day
filing, the girls who sorted cards did that all day, and the
girl who marked the books was expected to do that full time.
A part-time student did all the pasting.   All of them were
bored with their jobs and I was told the turnover in these
jobs was very high.   I have already introduced some changes
here after talking with the five girls involved.   I made a list
of jobs that needed to be done in priority order.   I told them
that two hours at a time on any one of these jobs was long
enough and then to change to another job.   Now all five of

them work as a team and rotate on sorting and arranging cards, filing, pasting, and marking book spines. I delegated these jobs to them to do in whatever order they wished and made them responsible for seeing that the work got done. They seem much happier. I am trying to motivate them by setting up production goals which they should reach and giving them a chance to exercise their own decision making. I hope soon to enlarge their responsibilities by assigning to them this final checking that I am doing.

One large storeroom is full of uncataloged books. No one knows how many there are but there must be thousands.

My problems cover most of those involved in planning, organizing, motivating, and controlling: space, backlog, working privacy, communication, supervision, delegation, job classification, division of work, work flow, and others.

* * * * * * *

To the reader: List in order of priority what you would do to reorganize this department if you were Miss Heath.

Case 71

HEMLOCK HIGH RESOURCE CENTER

The community of Hemlock is located just off a major interstate highway and is about an hour's drive from a large city. Farming in the area has declined in importance, a few small industries employ about one hundred persons, and the city provides employment for many more. Two elements make up the population: an older, conservative group who have lived in the area or community many years including many retired farmers; and a growing number of younger families (young executives on the way up) with children of pre-school and elementary school age. The population has grown slowly through the years but many persons believe that residential housing projects could "mushroom" at any time and consequently increase the population substantially. With little industry and few wealthy families, the tax burden rests squarely on the home owners. The people of the community are proud of their school system but are not willing to increase taxes in order to further improve the schools.

The school system is considered progressive in leadership and programs. For more than ten years, homogeneous or ability grouping, foreign language through all grades, and trades and industries in the high school have been a part of the system's program. In the past five years a number of innovations have been introduced into the schools: team teaching, special education, modular scheduling, advanced and enriched summer studies, programmed instruction, and learning phases. The system is divided into four schools: a primary school (kindergarten through third), an intermediate school (4th through 6th), a junior high (7th and 8th), and high school (9th through 12th).

The high school has a four-track program: general college preparatory, commercial, and vocational. Forty-nine per cent of the graduates go to college. Besides the usual high school courses, the school provides courses in trades and industries, advanced math, four years of Spanish, psychology, sociology, and college English. Enrollment is about 1,700 and the faculty numbers 65.

The high school is located in a rural setting and the site has ample room for expansion and development. The building was built five years ago on an austerity budget which required many compromises and omissions. One of the neglected areas was the Resource Center. Because no librarian was consulted in the planning, the Center is too small, poorly arranged, and quite inadequate to serve the needs of the curriculum, the students, and the faculty. The Center has approximately 8,500 volumes of books (of which about 1,700 are fiction in very bad condition), 45 periodical subscriptions, 60 phonorecords, 40 phonotapes, a large number of filmstrips, mounted pictures, pamphlets, clippings, and slides. Seating space is provided for 60 students. Equipment includes a microfilm reader, "wet" and "dry" carrels, filmstrip viewers, record turntables, tape decks, and several types of projectors (motion picture, opaque, and overhead). All motion pictures used in the school are rented.

On page 297 appears a floor plan for the Center.

The hall outside the entrance doors is wide enough, according to fire regulations, for display cases and a library bulletin board, but there are none. Priorities on the limited budget have not permitted the purchase of these items and evidently no one has thought of having them built in the shop

Organizing Cases

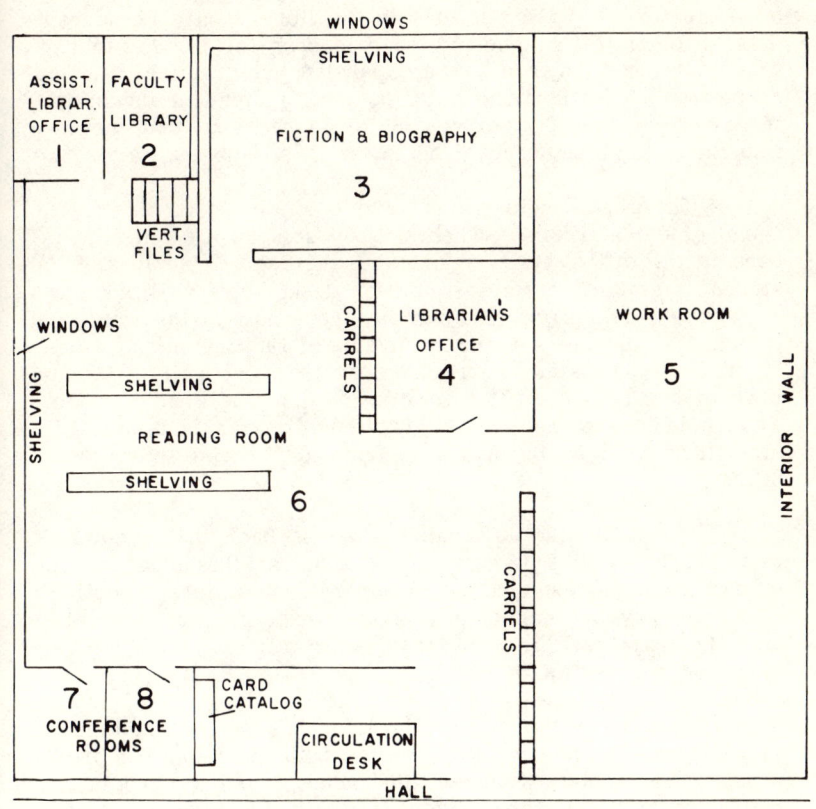

HEMLOCK HIGH RESOURCE CENTER

classes. The Resource Center is reached through a cheerful double-doored entrance of light oak. The windows on the north and west outside walls are high enough to allow for shelving (forty-two inches high) below them which somehow creates a top-heavy effect. Wherever there are no shelves, light blue ceramic tile covers the walls for sixty inches above the floor. Some visitors to the library have compared these tiled walls to a hospital corridor or the London tube. The floors are covered by an expensive but practical tan carpeting. The librarian believes that, instead of investing in carpet, it would have been better to have put that money into the collection because the latter is so sub-standard.

The glass-enclosed librarian's office (4) is directly ahead of the entrance. Theoretically some work could be done in the office while supervising the reading room and student assistants at the circulation desk; but, the librarian keeps the curtains drawn over the upper half of the west wall to shut out the glare from the overhead lighting in the reading room. The study carrels, along the west wall of the librarian's office, block the lower view into the reading room. The students and faculty feel that the librarian is isolating himself from them by operating from a removed and quiet office.

The assistant librarian's office is back in the northwest corner (1). Evidently, the reason for this location was so that each professional could supervise a different portion of the library. Unfortunately, they cannot properly supervise the main reading room from their offices, let alone carry on a program of service.

Until now, the second librarian has seemed content to do minor clerical work connected with the technical processes. Her typist, however, is housed in the workroom (5). The hidden corner office along with the lack of a definite time when she is scheduled to be on the floor assisting patrons encourages the disassociation of the second librarian from all professional library activities. The students who staff the circulation desk are the only persons visible for library service in the main reading room. The students are responsible for the current periodicals which are housed behind the circulation desk.

The fiction and biography room is primarily used by teachers who bring in entire classes to do library-connected work. The student who simply wants to come in and browse finds little room or encouragement. The shelves are crowded and provide no room for desperately needed additions to bring the collection up-to-date.

The faculty library (2) contains a reasonable stock of up-to-date professional education materials and has a pleasant view of the grounds. To prevent losses the door is kept locked; a teacher must find one of the librarians to unlock the door to gain access to the collection. Needless to say, it is not used very much.

Two small conference rooms (7, 8) west of the circulation desk, open off of the reading room. Because the doors are solid, there is no means of supervising activities within these rooms, so the doors are kept locked. Only students with written passes from faculty members may use them; a staff member must take time to check the passes and to unlock the rooms.

The workroom (5) is very crowded and is used for processing new materials, for housing back issues of periodicals, for typing, and for storing all the different types of projectors used in the school.

The present building design prevents the Center from being open evenings and Saturdays. The lack of an outside entrance directly into the library is partially overcome by the fact that the main library entrance opens from the main entrance foyer. However, there is no way to block off the hallways to prevent access to other parts of the building. Extended hours seem almost a necessity since the facilities, services, and resources of the public library are very poor.

The space situation is desperate. This so-called "resource center" was not large enough to be a book-oriented library under the old 1960 <u>Standards for School Library Programs</u> of the American Association of School Libraries. It is even less adequate in meeting the 1968 <u>Standards for School Media Programs</u>.

The area was not functionally planned with any understanding of the services and needs of a true resource center. The main reading room and the fiction and biography room are so crowded with tables and chairs in order to meet the regional accrediting association's seating requirements that it is difficult to move easily through the rooms. Unfortunately, the financial situation is such that extensive remodeling is out of the question, and the classroom situation is such that no nearby room is available.

You have just accepted the position as head librarian of this Resource Center. What reorganization, rearrangements, and changes would you make to improve utilization of space and staff and to provide better service? Draw a floor plan showing changes. Assume that you have a modest budget for some remodeling.

Case 72

PARTICIPATIVE MANAGEMENT

(Role playing)

Members of the Forest Board of Education were active, alert, and community-conscious; they believed the schools should serve the needs of the city as thoroughly and completely as possible. Through the years they had funded the addition of various vocational curricula to increase the employability of high school graduates in the city's offices and industries.

A recent employment survey conducted by the Chamber of Commerce revealed the availability of jobs in a number of areas which require post-high-school training. The length of training required for the different areas ranged from two months to two years, depending upon the nature of the job and the type of skills to be acquired. The areas identified in the surveys as needing a continuous supply of new trainees were: electronics and data processing technicians, architectural draftsmen, teacher and hospital aides, pattern drafting and draping (apparel industry), medical records, dental assistant, fire protection technology, culinary arts, police science, and food service management.

In addition to the evident need for post-high-school training programs, the Board was receiving increasing pressures to provide academic college courses (1) for those high school graduates who were inadmissable to the established colleges and universities of the state because they did not meet entrance requirements, (2) for those from low income families who could not afford to attend the established academic institutions, and (3) for those who were employed full time and wanted to work toward degrees by studying at night.

Besides training and academic courses, there was also a need in the community for basic adult education courses in reading, writing, and speaking for non-English speaking and illiterate residents.

The Board conceived the idea of developing a community college system to serve the needs as outlined above and to supplement the city's two academic programs offered in an extension center of the state university and in a church-related liberal arts college.

At the suggestion of the Board, a local newspaper publicized the community college idea and provided a blank for readers to fill out and send in if they were interested in any of the programs described. Local radio and television stations also carried spot announcements asking for expressions of interest. The tabulated results indicated a potential student body large enough for establishing community colleges at three different population concentrations in this city of about 700,000. The Board decided to start one as soon as possible; then, depending upon enrollment, interest of the residents, and success of the curricula, start a second one in about four years and a third several years after that.

Inasmuch as the student body would probably consist of students from low-income families who were dependent upon public buses for transportation, the Board decided to establish the first college in the downtown area as near as possible to a point where all city bus routes converged. They found and purchased a large empty building in this location and employed an architectural firm to renovate it. Next, they searched for and employed a president who was knowledgeable about the learning requirements of the type of students and curricula envisioned for this new college. They found such a man in Dr. Ira Crane.

Dr. Crane believed that a majority of the students would lack communication skills in reading, writing, and speaking and hence would respond better to a multi-media approach to learning rather than one that was verbally oriented. Hence, he searched for a librarian who had experience in selecting, organizing, and utilizing all communication media. He believed a high school librarian would probably have better background in all media than an academic librarian, so searched for a school librarian who had both the necessary academic preparation as well as work experience and also had an interest in cooperating in the development of an innovative learning program.

He employed Mrs. Sarah Willow, a childless widow of about forty who was head librarian in a unified school district media center where she supervised two librarians, an audio-visual technician, and a number of clerks and pages. Her school library program had included a number of audio-visual courses and she had tried to keep up-to-date in this area through summer workshops.

No job description of her position had been written as Dr. Crane expected her to evolve an innovative instructional learning resources center and he felt incapable of defining the parameters of such a position. He described to her the Board's proposed plans for developing two more community colleges, and his goals for this college. He delegated to her full authority (1) to work with the architect in planning, adapting, and renovating the floor assigned to the library; (2) to plan for and choose the furniture; (3) to search for and employ the library staff; (4) to develop policies for collection building; (5) to supervise all operations; and (6) to work with the faculty in coordinating library services and collections with the curriculum and the instructional program.

Mrs. Willow was employed in July and instruction was to start fourteen months later. Her first concern was to employ a professional staff capable of creating an instructional learning resources center. She decided that initially she needed three persons who would represent competencies to supplement hers: an academic librarian, a special librarian, and a media specialist. Although the collection in the high school media center, which she had developed, was in many respects essentially a liberal arts collection, she thought a person with academic library experience would bring to this staff a perspective, a point of view, and a knowledge of printed materials suitable for a collect collection, especially reference books, serials, and government publications. A special librarian with experience in abstracting, in providing information services to his clientele, and in justifying continuously the existence of a special library should bring to the staff the expertise to "market" and "sell" the multi-media approach to faculty, students, and Board of Education. To select, service, and repair all the audio-visual equipment, the background and experience of a media specialist were necessary.

After much searching and many interviews, Mrs.

Organizing Cases 303

Willow employed the following who reported for work on October 1: Mr. Earl Falcon (academic librarian), Miss Shirley Veery (special librarian), and Mr. Howard Fulmar (media specialist).

Role for Mrs. Sarah Willow, chief librarian:

You see your role in this community college library as a planner, a policy maker, and a coordinator. Your abilities are more suited to innovation and conceptualization than to implementation. You are impatient with detail and unconcerned about operations. You are vigorous, aggressive, emotional, and strong willed. You are media-oriented and dedicated to the total learning resources concept. You are determined to have all media thoroughly integrated into one total operation. You expect the catalog to be an index to all media so that users have only one place to look for all material in whatever form on the same subject.

You are a staunch advocate of participative management and look on this new position as an opportunity to experiment fully with this managerial philosophy. When you assumed your most recent position as librarian of a high school media center, it was an on-going, well organized, smoothly running operation in which each staff member had clearly defined responsibilities delegated to her. You introduced more participation in decision making but could not make changes in the basic organizational structure. In this new community college library, you would like full staff participation in all decisions. To this end, you have written no job descriptions nor thought through staff organization or division of responsibilities. You have a vague notion that your three professional staff members can work democratically with you to make decisions on all problems as they arise. You expect your professional staff to respect each other's competencies which complement each other, to share abilities, to cross fertilize ideas, and to coordinate and cooperate activities.

When you interviewed Mr. Falcon, Miss Veery, and Mr. Fulmar, you spoke of each being your assistant. You were thinking in terms of participative management with all four professionals sharing in administrative decisions. Several recent comments and occurrences have led you to believe that each of them thought you meant he or she was to be <u>the</u> assistant director.

You did not think a cataloger or an acquisitions librarian were necessary because you envisioned purchasing pre-cataloged and pre-processed books from a jobber and depending upon the media specialist to catalog all non-print media. However, this has proved unrealistic as some cataloging and processing has already had to be done on the premises. You have employed a full-time typist to do all the typing for the four staff members as well as to type requisitions.

You have found Mr. Falcon, Miss Veery, and Mr. Fulmar very capable, efficient, and dedicated to creating the best possible instructional learning resources center. Each of them has had to change his traditional frame of reference and professional orientation because this situation is so different from his previous library experiences. The effect of this reorientation has, at times, resulted in their all going in different directions with little coordination or communication in sharing resources and expertise. They have requested a conference with you tomorrow morning--it is now March and you have all been working together for five months.

Role for Mr. Earl Falcon:

You are thirty years old, are print-oriented, and have had eight years experience in academic libraries: two years in the acquisitions department of a large university library; three years in the cataloging department of a well-organized, old, traditional, liberal arts college library; and, the past three years as head of the reference department in the same liberal arts college library. Your ultimate goal, when you graduated from library school, was academic library administration. You believed that you needed experience in all areas of academic librarianship before you became an administrator--hence your choice of positions included both technical and public services.

When you were interviewed for the present position, Mrs. Willow implied that you would be assistant director which would qualify you to be considered for head librarian in one of the other community colleges in Forest when they came into being. She said that the Board believed experience in helping to develop and administer this learning resource center would be the right background for developing a similar one in one of the other community colleges.

You are concerned about your status in this library administrative structure. You have learned that both Miss

Veery and Mr. Fulmar think they are the assistant director. Their belief is based on impressions and implications received during their interviews with Mrs. Willow.

In addition to clarification of your personal status, you would like clear definition of work areas so that each professional has authority and responsibility in a specific area. You and Miss Veery have discussed this and have agreed that both of you should work on building the collection (materials in all media) and that you take charge of acquisitions and cataloging of all materials regardless of their format and she take charge of all circulation, reference, information retrieval, and dissemination of information (utilizing all media).

You have discovered that Mr. Fulmar is an expert in evaluating, selecting, operating, and repairing audio-visual equipment but his idea of descriptive cataloging of non-print materials leaves much to be desired. Whether the final form of the catalog will be film cartridge, computer print out, card file, or something else has not yet been determined. But, regardless of form, the descriptive cataloging input will be the same and must be uniform and thorough. You would like the responsibility for cataloging all materials which the jobber does not or cannot do. The jobber can provide current, popular print materials but those represent only a small fraction of the items which must be acquired for this collection. These include all types of audio and visual materials, programmed learning kits, sets of workbooks and basic education readers, government publications, maps, retrospective printed books, microfiche, microfilm, and technical reports. You believe only a librarian experienced in cataloging can produce a satisfactory integrated catalog of all these diverse forms and types of materials. Furthermore, you are convinced that ordering these requires the skill of a librarian with experience in acquisitions who knows sources of supply. Expecting a typist to do this is unreasonable, unfair, and ineffective.

You are a bit skeptical about how all media can be integrated into the curricula to serve non-verbally oriented students but you are willing to try.

Role for Miss Veery:

You are thirty-two years old, ambitious, hard working and have creative ideas for service to the faculty and students. Your experience includes four years in U. S. Army libraries overseas, three years in a naval electronics facility, and three years in a federal aviation agency. Although you thoroughly enjoyed the work in federal libraries, you welcomed this opportunity to work in an academic setting and to improve the employability of young men and women from low-income families. In other words, the social service aspects of this position appealed strongly to you as well as the opportunity to get administrative experience in preparation for eventually becoming head librarian of another similar community college. You thought you were to be assistant librarian here and were disconcerted to learn that Mr. Falcon and Mr. Fulmar also think that each of them is assistant director. You want this matter cleared up for the sake of everyone concerned.

You like to work with people, all of your experience has been in public services and you would like to be responsible for this area in this library. As an academic librarian, Mr. Falcon's orientation and interest is more towards collection building and the provision of learning resources than it is to the dissemination of information.

You believe that the responsibilities of the person in charge of public services should include (1) scheduling carrels and rooms for cooperative study, listening, or viewing audio-visual materials; (2) circulating all learning resources whether on paper, film, tape, or disc; (3) the housing and shelving of all materials; (4) the supervising of all microfiche, microcard, and microfilm readers and printers; and (5) planning and directing all reference service including retrieval and dissemination of information. You are especially interested in the concept of information transfer whether the information is on IBM cards, magnetic tape, or print. You hope this library can participate in whatever networks of knowledge are available in this area.

Because of your experience in special libraries, you have a grasp of service which brings a unique approach to academic problems. You brought vigor and insight to this position which are valuable assets in the integrative approach to learning.

Role for Mr. Howard Fulmar:

You are twenty-eight years old and have academic background as a media specialist. You have had very thorough training in the operation, care, upkeep, and repair of all types of AV equipment as well as the production of slides, transparencies, and graphic teaching materials. You have worked as assistant media specialist in this city's public schools. You have never worked in a library. You are ambitious and accepted this position because of the opportunity to develop a domain of your own.

In this library you believe there should be a sharp separation between print and non-print including separate housing and control. You would like to see the floor assigned to the library divided physically into a media area and a book-periodical area. Since microfiche and microfilm are film, you think that these and the readers and printers should be in your area as well as all AV materials.

You think librarians are much too fussy about cataloging, scheduling and circulating procedures; you want to take charge of these for everything except printed materials. And, of course, you expect to supervise all use and care of the machines as well as train and supervise the projectionists and technicians.

You are much less concerned with the organization and control of materials than librarians are. You don't think it is important to know where each item is located at all times. You think the idea of listing all learning resources together in one catalog is the height of silliness. You want to generate and produce a separate title list for motion pictures, for slides, for tape recordings, and so on.

Your conception of your position is to produce all kinds of teaching aids to support the curricula: transparencies for opaque projectors, slides, graphics, tape recordings of lectures, and many others. Also, you visualize the position as offering whatever services your staff will be capable of performing such as setting up films and projectors, splicing and repairing film, photographing, instructing faculty members and students in the use of audio-visual equipment, and promoting innovative instructional uses for all AF resources.

Chapter V

CONTROLLING CASES

　　　Librarians and libraries are subject to four types of control: direct, external or indirect, financial, and internal. Direct control is imposed through laws and legislation, charters, articles of incorporation, boards of trustees, and library committees. External or indirect controls include standards, certification, accreditation, civil service, unions, political interference, conditions of gifts or grants, state aid, and economic factors. Financial controls involve budgets, accounting, audits, cost studies, contracts, and bond issues. The library staff can do little to alter or change these three types of control; but they can do something about the fourth, or internal, type.

　　　Internal controls include communication, feedback, records and reports, public relations and publicity, patrons, inventory, circulation, surveys, security measures, and performance standards. Internal control is closely related to planning and is necessary to measure what is being accomplished, to compare performance with norms or standards, to identify activities or operations which are not contributing to the attainment of goals, to locate reasons for poor achievement by persons or by units of the library, and to take remedial action. Adequate control may mean making minor changes in direction to adjust to altered conditions, setting new goals, formulating new plans, changing methods or procedures, or reassigning staff.

　　　Cases in this chapter exemplify resistance to change, effects of laws and legislation, pressure groups, public relations, indirect controls, budget allocations and limitations, political interference, funding, patron control, security, vandalism, thefts, and governing board control.

Case 73

A SORDID SCHEME

His classmates in library school considered Carl Bunting to be charming, clever, sincere, aggressive but not "pushy," and personable. He had a variety of interests, was a good conversationalist, and was an amateur musician. Some faculty members thought that his public relations type personality would not only be valuable to him as a library administrator but also would help to improve the public image of the typical librarian. Both classmates and faculty members predicted he would enjoy a brilliant career as a librarian. His wife was ambitious for him and capable of assuming the social responsibilities of a library administrator's wife.

No one who knew him was surprised to learn, three years after he received his master's degree in library science, that he had become the director of a fairly large public library. A couple of years later, at the state library association meeting, he was driving a high-priced car, had ample money to spend in bars, was wearing expensive suits, and had become a rather "splashy" person. His wife was resplendent in luxurious furs, clothing, and jewels. Several persons, who had known him well in the past and who knew his approximate salary, remarked that his salary was not sufficient to support the style in which he was living. A few months later, the source of his extra money was revealed in front page newspaper stories.

During his second year as librarian of Curlew Public Library, Mr. Bunting entered into an agreement with a book dealer, Mr. Leslie Carob, by which library holdings of certain periodicals, books, and government publications would be exchanged for microfilm copies of these and other titles. During the next eighteen months or longer, they executed details of their agreement by which many thousands of volumes were taken from the library by Carob and his employees with Bunting's all too willing connivance. Mr. Bunting told his staff that Mr. Carob and his employees would be in the library frequently to remove from the shelves of the main library and the branches those materials not needed or seldom used, and, in addition, would take some bound periodicals for microfilming. Books and maps were removed from the Reference Room when the Reference Librarian was not on duty, and bound periodicals were loaded into trucks at night.

No record was made of the volumes taken and, consequently, they did not go through the established discard processing procedure. The head cataloger asked repeatedly for a list of removed items so that this information could be noted on the shelf list and catalog cards; but she was never supplied with any list.

The removed titles were taken to Carob's warehouse for storage until sold to other libraries or book dealers. To authenticate the disposal of volumes plainly marked with the mark of ownership of the Curlew Public Library, Carob used the Curlew Public Library letterhead stationery and order forms in his sale transactions. Payment was made personally to Bunting either in cash or in checks made out to him. Occasionally, when Bunting was out of town, hundred dollar bills would be sealed in unmarked envelopes and given to Bunting's secretary to be deposited in his bank account.

Items taken included manuscripts, some rare books, old volumes of the Congressional Record, and some complete runs of periodicals from the 1880's to the present. Periodicals represented most subject fields as well as long runs of such popular titles as Reader's Digest, Life, Saturday Evening Post, and Popular Science. The total value was estimated to be in excess of $30,000.

After the thefts had been going on for several months, and no microfilm copies had been received, several concerned members of the staff reported the activities of Bunting and Carob to the library's board of trustees. A special meeting of the board was called to investigate the incident. Bunting was asked why he had entered into such an "exchange" agreement without prior approval of the board. His excuse was that he believed such transactions were within his province of authority. He promised that things would be "straightened out" soon and the microfilm would be received. However, nothing was ever microfilmed. The government publications had been received on a depository basis and, according to federal law, could not be disposed of without written authorization from the Superintendent of Documents. At the board hearing, staff members said such permission had not ever been requested let alone granted.

For several months the board of trustees attempted to

Controlling Cases

handle the situation without police participation but finally called in both the city police and the Federal Bureau of Investigation. In addition to his connivance in removal of the volumes from the Curlew Public Library, the police discovered that Bunting located for Carob rare books and documents in other libraries and museums. Carob would pay Bunting a "finder's fee" for this work. The board discharged Bunting.

Several months later Bunting and Carob were tried in a federal court and sentenced to two years in prison.

* * * * * * *

Should a public library board have built into its authority structure some checks and balances to protect the library from unscrupulous librarians?

Does the librarian of a public library have the right to sell any library materials?

Case 74

COMMUNITY RELATIONS

Metropolitan Public Library system includes the downtown Central Library, nineteen branches, and two bookmobiles. The Central Library contains in excess of 2,000,000 volumes. Twelve of the branches have been constructed since 1953 and each one contains from 17,000 to 25,000 square feet with book capacities ranging from 49,000 to 90,000 volumes. The remaining seven branches are older and smaller and were built prior to the adoption of a branch library building program in the 1940's. The philosophy of this program is (1) to locate branches near supermarkets or other business locations where people are likely to go every day, and (2) to build only large well-equipped branches with sufficient resources to meet the demands of the area served. The board of trustees and the administrative staff do not support the concept of store front libraries with limited resources and inferior equipment.

Furthermore, the Director of Libraries, Guy Hector, and his administrative staff believe that the goals, objectives, policies, programs, activities, staffing, and services of each branch should be reevaluated periodically. If a certain activity or program does not fit the goals of that particular branch or the needs of the community it serves, then that activity should be eliminated. If a mistake was made in the past in locating a branch, or conditions have changed in the community so that the branch is no longer needed, then they believe it should be closed and service provided by bookmobile or by another branch.

As part of a continuing branch development program, the staff workloads, space utilization, and circulation in all branches were studied and compared two years ago. Operation charts were prepared for each branch for the same month for each of three years. These charts presented a record of man hours employed in each branch agency, circulation, and costs of circulating a book. The cost of circulating a book in eighteen branches ranged from 21 cents to 26 cents with a median of 24 cents. In the remaining branch (Alder), the cost was 41 cents per book. Obviously Alder was overstaffed in comparison with the other branches. The Supervisor of Branches pointed out that when the cost of circulating a book in a branch was so far above the median cost, it should be subject to scrutiny and something should be done to reduce this cost as it was not an economical operation.

Mr. Hector believed that the cost of circulating a book was not an ideal measuring device because it did not show advisory and reference services, but it could be used as a rough measure for estimating costs of service, for distributing book funds, and for assigning staff. Coordinators for juvenile and adult services provided safeguards in the system to prevent branch librarians from buying popular titles just to increase their circulation at the expense of buying reference tools and serious non-fiction.

In addition to costs, the operation charts showed serious understaffing in other branches and the personnel officer knew that the cataloging and preparation departments in the Central Library were desperately in need of more staff.

Alder Branch was located in a low income-low education community. The staff were involved in some social service work in addition to their library-related responsibilities. Before the Branch was opened in 1941 a committee of eight librarians and eight representative persons engaged in public or parochial school work and in settlement work in the community worked together to select the book

Controlling Cases

stock. The native language of about 20 per cent of the population was Spanish (Puerto Ricans and Mexican-Americans). About 60 per cent were black Americans, and the remaining 20 per cent were either white Americans or recent European immigrants.

Alder Branch had two floors--adult service on the first floor included a general reading room and a reference room; the second floor was devoted to children's services. The Director of Libraries, the Personnel Officer, and the Supervisor of Branches discussed the problem of high operating cost with the librarian of Alder Branch and her staff. They all agreed (1) to put the adult reference room and the adult reading room together in one wing of the first floor; (2) to move the children's department from the second floor to the vacated room on the first floor; and (3) to convert the second floor into a meeting room which was needed in that community. They envisioned the meeting room being used for a number of library-sponsored activities such as children's story hours, discussion groups, staff meetings, library programs, and showing of motion pictures. Also, the room would serve as a place for various community, educational, cultural, and local government groups to meet. Such utilization of space would require little staff time, and could be provided inexpensively.

Before implementing this decision, the proposed changes and their implications were reviewed with the budget officer and with the library trustees. By consolidating the services on one floor, five full-time staff positions could be eliminated and these persons transferred to branches which were seriously understaffed. None of the staff or board members involved in these discussions could find any arguments against the changes. In fact, they believed the provision of a meeting room would greatly improve service to this particular community. And so, the changes were made.

The consolidation of adult and children's departments was explained to the public in the local community weekly newspaper and also in letters mailed to each registered borrower of Alder Branch. Copies of this letter were also available on desks in the Branch. No mention was made about converting the second floor into a meeting room because there was no allocation for this item in the current budget. The librarian of Alder Branch did not want any publicity about the proposed meeting room until the room was ready for use and could be scheduled. The Supervisor of Branches estimated it would take ten months or longer to get a budget allocation, let bids for renovation, and purchase the necessary furniture.

About four months after the changes in space allocation and staff transfers had been made, Mr. Hector and members of the Board received copies of the following letter:

Alder Citizens' Association
_____, 19___

Mr. Guy Hector
Director of Libraries
Metropolitan Public Library

Dear Mr. Hector:

At the last meeting of the Alder Citizens' Association the following resolution was adopted to be transmitted to the trustees of the Public Library:

Resolved: That the Alder Citizens' Association be on record as objecting to the curtailment of library facilities at the Alder Branch Library due to the closing of the second floor and the crowding together of all services on the first floor. In the making of this resolution the following points were brought out:

1. It is apparent that the crowded condition of the first floor makes use of the library an unpleasant experience and deters the public from browsing.

2. Students have complained that the reference section is no longer available for general study because it has been placed in the center of the general adult department. The trustees must be aware that because of the peculiar economic situation in this community the library is the only study space available for many people who are anxious to advance and improve themselves. Many of our homes are without proper lighting and lack the type of heating that would make study there feasible.

3. In order to improve the economic condition of

the people of this community the schools in the area have been urging ambitious boys and girls to use the library as a study room so that their school progress will enable them to advance themselves. This lack of a quiet study room is a severe blow to them.

4. The fact that children's and adult's services are on one floor makes for confusion. This results in neither group getting full benefit from the services.

5. The Alder Branch Library was built a number of years ago as part of a planned community project. Along with the health clinic and the recreation and school programs, the library was expected to help uplift the community. The health center, the recreation center, and the school are still working with the object of future betterment of the community in mind and so are increasing their services while the library has curtailed its services. We feel that this is a very short-sighted policy and not at all in keeping with the type of community planning and service that the city has expected of the library.

6. It appears to us that Mr. Hector is prejudiced against this community and made these changes without logic, reason, or planning with the community.

We feel sure that when the trustees understand what we are striving to do for the betterment of our future citizens they will rectify this mistake of closing part of the library space.

                            Sincerely yours,

                            Opal Canna
                            Corresponding Secretary

* * * * * * *

Metropolitan Public Library
_____, 19___

Mrs. Opal Canna
Corresponding Secretary
Alder Citizens' Association

Dear Mrs. Canna:

At the last regular monthly meeting of the Board of Library Trustees, the members reviewed the resolution of the Alder Citizens' Association objecting to the arrangement of library facilities at the Alder Branch. The trustees instructed me to send you this acknowledgment.

The decision to consolidate services at Alder Branch was not a personal whim of mine but was based on detailed comparative studies of all branches in the system. These studies were carried out by the Library's administrative staff in cooperation with the Supervisor of Branches and the Branch librarians. The results of the studies showed that the cost of circulating books in the Alder Branch was the most expensive operation in the city and the children's department was overstaffed. The circulation of books for home reading at the Alder Branch has been decreasing every year for the past ten years. During the last fiscal year the Alder Branch ranked lowest in circulation not only among comparable two-floor branches but also among the smaller one-floor branches. When compared with the two branches most nearly comparable in size, Alder circulated only about half as many books as the other two. A third branch with approximately the same maintenance cost as Alder circulated 82 per cent more books than Alder and its registration was 126 per cent higher than Alder.

To reduce the operating costs at the Alder Branch to the average cost of operating all of the other eighteen branches, it was necessary to adjust the staff to the workload. By consolidating the services on one floor, the staff could be reduced by five members who were transferred to branches which were understaffed. These changes at Alder were part of a system-wide workload study in all branches. As a result of the study, we have reassigned the personnel so that we get more effective production and a fairer distribution of personnel throughout the system. A total of thirty positions were involved in the system-wide personnel changes as a result of this study.

While the trustees regret the necessity for consolidating services, they do not feel that the conditions have changed since that action was taken and believe that one floor is adequate for present demands.

It is not unusual for libraries to offer both juvenile and adult services on one floor. Many libraries throughout the nation function on this basis and in our own system five agencies which are operating on one floor handle a greater volume of reference and circulation work than the Alder Branch. In those five branches the one-floor plan has not deterred use of the agency, nor has it resulted in confusion which prevented either adults or juveniles from getting full benefit from the services. After receiving your letter, I asked the librarian of Alder Branch to study circulation statistics for the four months since consolidation as compared with circulation for the same months during the past five years. She discovered that the circulation during the last four months is greater than comparable months last year. This indicates that the consolidation has not discouraged patron use.

It is difficult to understand why the branch should be considered overcrowded. Alder Branch has considerably less use than other comparable agencies. Furthermore, it is the only one-floor branch where the children's service is in a separate room. At the other one-floor branches there are no walls (only bookshelves) separating the adult and juvenile departments. Staff members at Alder report that the branch has never been crowded during the last four months except on one or two occasions and then only for brief periods which are normal to any active library. As the entrance lobby and the charging desk have

been used by both adults and children since the
opening of the branch many years ago, there
should be no added confusion there. On the contrary,
one member of the Alder staff points out
that the situation is greatly improved over the
old days when children ran down the steps and
shrieked on their way to the front door. Another
says that the present children's room is actually
so much easier to supervise than the large room
upstairs that the confusion has been reduced in
that department.

Your statement that the "reference section is no
longer available" is not true. The reference
tools were previously in the adult reference department
and have merely been moved from one
wing to the other side of the building. The transfer
does not make the materials less available to
students. And inasmuch as the branch is open
the same hours and no books have been taken
away, the trustees do not consider that service
has been curtailed.

The board is sympathetic to the social and educational
needs of Alder and appreciate what the
Alder Citizens' Association is doing for the betterment
of the people in the community. At the
same time, the trustees are of the opinion that
it is their responsibility to serve the entire city
and for that reason they must consider requirements
in relation to those in other parts of the
city. They feel that in the interest of good business
management and efficient operation they have
no choice but to continue the present arrangement
in the Alder Branch. They point out that the
consolidation of service on the first floor results
in a savings in operation cost at no loss in service.
However, when the use of the Alder Branch
develops sufficiently to justify a reconsideration
of the present plan, the second floor of the branch
will be reopened. They hope that the people in
the community will make greater use of the branch
facilities than they have in recent years.

When the facts in this letter are made known to
your members, I feel sure you and your associates
in the Alder Citizens' Association and all oth-

er taxpayers who are interested in reducing the cost of government operations will approve what is being done in the administration of your public library service.

Sincerely yours,

Guy Hector
Director of Libraries

Case 75

THE AD HOC FACULTY COMMITTEE

Since its inception five years ago, Eastern Campus Library of Northern State University had been an administrative unit of Eastern's business office. Both funds and personnel were handled by the dean's assistant for financial matters, and library policy and administration were dictated by an Ad Hoc Committee of interested faculty members. During these years the "librarian," Miss Gilden, performed chiefly "housekeeping" chores and implemented decisions made by the faculty committee. Although she recommended some titles to be purchased, the library committee had selected most of the collection (13,000 volumes). Miss Gilden was a middle-aged woman who had had successful office experience before she was employed in this position. She was not a college graduate and had had neither library science courses nor previous library experience. She conscientiously did her best to serve both faculty and students as she conceived what these needs were.

The enrollment at Eastern last year was about 2,500 students, all of whom were enrolled in freshman or sophomore level courses. Those students interested in obtaining a bachelor's degree transferred to NSU or some other four-year college for the junior and senior years. No terminal courses were offered. The curriculum consisted chiefly of general education courses in the humanities, social sciences, and a few beginning laboratory sciences.

The students at Eastern as well as residents of the city in which the campus was located, had been clamoring for four-year degree granting programs which would include B. S. degrees in Education and Business. A survey made by a team of educators from outside the state last year studied

Eastern's facilities and resources to determine their adequacy for degree granting programs. The library collection was found to be inadequate to support even the present courses being offered. The strongest areas in the collection were in history, English, and psychology, but even they were not sufficient for junior and senior courses for majors in these subjects. The survey team recommended that the library be substantially improved before any additional courses be added or consideration be given to offering four-year programs. They suggested that an experienced professionally educated librarian be employed who would be responsible for building the collection, and the library be affiliated with the main library at NSU so that the librarian could receive some guidance, assistance, and supervision.

Three months ago, Mr. Jones, a young but experienced college librarian, was employed. He was told that the Dean at Eastern was responsible for employing the professional library staff and for local policy decisions. The library administrator at NSU was responsible for budget requests; administrative supervision; centralized ordering, cataloging, and processing; and whatever other professional advice and guidance Mr. Jones required or desired. Hence, Mr. Jones reported both to the Dean of Eastern and to one of the assistant librarians in the NSU library. Both the Dean and the assistant librarian impressed upon him that his first priority should be the upgrading of the collection in preparation for an expanded four-year curriculum in a few years.

From the above briefings, he assumed that he would be responsible for building the collection and would control all book funds, but would cooperate fully with faculty members in getting their recommendations for purchase. The assistant librarian to whom he reported at NSU also believed this. Mr. Jones proceeded to check the collection with various standard lists, to weed out old and unsuitable titles, to analyze the holdings by subject as compared to courses offered, and to work out procedures for ordering with the NSU Order Department, and for cataloging with the NSU Catalog Department.

In all the briefing he had received from the Dean and from the assistant librarian at NSU, no one had mentioned Eastern's Ad Hoc Library Committee. So, he was amazed when a faculty member came in one day, announced that he was the chairman of the Ad Hoc Committee, handed him a long typed list of books, and told him to order them. Mr.

Jones then learned that this Committee expected to continue selecting all the books for the library and to control the library budget; but would consider his recommendations.

The next day Mr. Jones had a conference with the Dean to discuss the functions and responsibilities of the Ad Hoc Committee; he suggested the Committee be abolished and that, in its place, an advisory library committee be appointed to represent all subject areas in the curriculum. Mr. Jones pointed out that the spending of the entire budget should be his responsibility with advice and recommendations from the faculty. This concept of an advisory library committee was a new idea to the Dean. He suggested that Mr. Jones meet with the Ad Hoc Committee and make these suggestions to them--which he did about a week later.

Not wishing to give an answer at that meeting, the members of the Committee asked for time to think about the idea. Two days later the Dean called Mr. Jones to his office and said that he personally agreed that an advisory library committee would be more representative of the faculty and that Mr. Jones was more capable of building the collection in all subject fields than was the Ad Hoc Committee, but it would be unwise to rush into such changes. "This is a faculty-oriented institution, Mr. Jones. We in the administration try to work with the faculty. This Ad Hoc Committee is interested in the library and helped build the library collection we now have; it wouldn't be fair to forget their role in the library's development, now would it?" he said.

Case 76

CONVERSION TO A PUBLIC LIBRARY DISTRICT[1]

In order to provide more and better library services and resources for all people of the state, legal provisions were made by the state legislature several years ago for the establishment of library districts. The size of such districts was not specified by law but was left up to the local library boards to decide how many towns, townships, or counties to

---

[1] Milo vs. Kutschke, 247 N. E. 2d 423 (1969)

include.

The village of Justin had been served for many years by a tax-supported public library which had been created originally by a referendum vote and was governed by an elected board of library directors. Justin was located in a county in which there were no other libraries. The library staff and the board of Justin wished to extend service to include a surrounding township by creating a public library district.

The state's Public Library District Act permitted a board of directors of a public library established within any county, city, village, incorporated town, or township to convert the existing library to a public library district in the following way:

1. The board was required to publish notices not less than twenty or more than thirty days prior to the date of the meeting at which a board of library directors intended to consider adoption of a resolution to petition for conversion.

2. The resolution to petition for conversion had to be adopted by a two-thirds vote of all members of the board.

3. The directors then were required to file with the circuit court a petition to convert. The petition had to include such facts as the history of the library, the tax rate ceiling, the geographical area involved, and any other pertinent facts.

4. Next, a court order fixing a hearing date had to be secured.

5. A notice of the time of the court hearing had to be both published and posted. Ten notices had to be posted at conspicuous widely separated places within the district at least twenty days before the hearing. Furthermore, the hearing notice had to be posted conspicuously in the library.

6. Copies of all notices and petitions for the proposed district had to be filed by the secretary of the board with the chief village officers and with the supervisors of all townships lying wholly or partially within the pro-

posed district.

7. If a petition for a referendum vote were signed by one hundred or more voters in the proposed district and was filed with the court prior to the hearing, the question of conversion would have to be submitted to the voters at the next election.

The librarian and the board members of the Justin Public Library thought that they had faithfully carried out the above provisions of the law. No petition from the voters requesting a referendum vote was received by the court prior to the hearing. So, at the hearing, the court approved the conversion of the Justin Public Library to a public library district. In the Public Library District Act, the state's General Assembly had provided this method of conversion whereby the traditional prior referendum vote would be eliminated unless petitioned for by one hundred or more voters during the conversion proceedings.

After receiving the court's approval, the Justin library staff and board proceeded to develop plans for extending service and to work out necessary arrangements with the townships involved. But the plans came to an ubrupt halt a few weeks later when a county taxpayers league challenged the proceedings leading to the conversion. They claimed that the Justin Board of Directors had failed to comply with the second half of number 6 above which required notifying the supervisors of all townships lying wholly or partially within the proposed public library district. The Secretary of the Board had filed notices of the petitions for the proposed districts with the chief village officers, but had overlooked the last half of this legal requirement to notify the supervisors.

The case went to the state Supreme Court. During these proceedings, the purpose of the law in requiring that the supervisors of townships be notified was pointed out. In establishing a procedure whereby a substantial change in the nature and governing structure of a tax-supported library could be accomplished without the necessity of a referendum vote, the General Assembly deemed it desirable that in addition to the published and posted notice, the chief executives of involved townships, cities, and villages should receive notice. The purpose of the conversion proceedings was to create a new and autonomous body with substantially enlarged authority but taxing powers continued to be vested in the corporate authorities of the villages. Boards of library directors such as these had no powers to issue bonds, purchase real estate, build, remodel or repair, mortgage property or purchase certain equipment and materials without prior approval of the corporate authorities of their respective villages. To the extent that future development plans and expenditures of the newly created district would no longer be subject to the scrutiny and prior approval of the corporate authorities of the villages, the protection to and advancement of the interests of the taxpayers and residents of the villages might be diminished. And while the conversion procedure afforded an opportunity to convert without a referendum vote, referenda would have been necessary in areas not served by an existing tax-supported library.

The decision of the Supreme Court was that failure to file copies of the notices and petitions with the supervisors of the respective townships invalidated the conversion procedure.

Case 77

THE UNWANTED GIFT

Morgana Consolidated High School served a farming and middle class residential town of 10,000 and the surrounding county; 795 students were enrolled in a general curriculum that included both terminal and college preparation but few advanced level courses in any discipline. The principal, Mr. Thomas Trimbull, was young, dedicated, well liked by his staff, and believed in delegating much of the administrative and curricular responsibility to them.

The library was a learning resources center containing nearly 6,000 items; the emphasis was on science and literature, but the social studies collection was rapidly growing, due to the interest of the teachers of this department in the library. There was a legacy of old and not very suitable volumes from the library of a small county school recently consolidated with the central system, which had not yet been sorted.

Under the leadership of the librarian, Miss Grady, the library was heavily used. She provided excellent service to teachers and students, carefully selected each item purchased, urged teachers to recommend learning materials for their courses, and had good rapport with both students and faculty.

An industrial lawyer retired about thirty years ago and returned to his home town of Morgana to live in seclusion. The recluse recently died, leaving an old house, its furnishings, and a library to his only relative, a nephew.

When the old house was put up for sale, Karl Grey, a social studies teacher at the high school, looked at it and saw the library which contained about 500 volumes. All of the titles had been published before 1930 and many were printed between 1900-1920. The books were predominantly in the subject areas of economics, business, engineering, and civil law, but included a few novels.

Grey decided that they could be a valuable addition to the Morgana High School Library and contacted the heir to learn about the disposition of the collection. The heir was anxious to settle the estate, lived a long distance from Morgana, and had no interest whatever in the old books. He said he would be glad to give the collection to the high school library if someone would pack and transport the books.

Grey next told Mr. Trimbull what he had done and portrayed in the strongest terms the value he could get as a teacher out of the collection. (Miss Grady as yet did not know of the book collection's existence or of the plans for it.) Because of his philosophy of delegating to his faculty authority for curriculum matters, Trimbull accepted Grey's appraisal of the collection and arranged for the packing and moving of the gift. A news story applauding the gift appeared in the local paper and the next morning twenty-six boxes of books were delivered to the high school library, to the surprise of Miss Grady. She called Mr. Trimbull to ask what they contained and where they came from.

When she learned that Mr. Grey was responsible for the gift, she sought him out to learn more. Grey gave her the impression that he believed the books were valuable just because they were old. When Miss Grady questioned this, and their value in relation to the type and level of education that her library served, Grey became insistent that they would be valuable; he called them "rare" books and said that they probably had great monetary value and could additionally become important teaching aids for the social studies department. Miss Grady pointed out that, in this day of rapid change, any book in the social sciences and sciences was normally out of date within ten years; and any books in these fields published prior to 1930 were of no value to today's high school students. Furthermore, she could see no possible use of this student body or faculty for old books in business, engineering, and civil law. The only economics course taught at Morgana was a one semester beginning course so students would have no use for outdated economics books, either.

That day every time she looked at those twenty-six boxes cluttering the hall outside the library, she became angrier. After classes had ended for the day and the busses had gone, Miss Grady had a conference with Mr. Trimbull and asked why she was not consulted about this gift. After all, she told him, she had the responsibility for developing the learning resources center and the decision to accept or reject gifts should be hers.

Trimbull apologized for not consulting her and defended Grey's action as enthusiasm for his teaching. He told her that the giving of the gift had been so well publicized that they would have to keep it now. Miss Grady then pointed out that 500 books could not be shelved in the small library workroom for cataloging and processing and asked where they could be housed temporarily. He offered some space in a janitorial storage area in the basement. Furthermore, as the only librarian serving 795 students as well as the faculty, she had more work than she could do.

Students carried the boxes to the storage area the next day, unpacked them, and put them on shelves. Over the weekend, Miss Grady sorted the collection and found only a few books of poetry, essays, and novels which might be useful in the learning center. Even these were unattractive editions which she was reluctant to add to the library. The rest of the collection was "junk"--outdated books on many subjects of no value to present day high school students. She found no "rare" books. She reported this information to Mr. Trimbull.

Case 78

A TEN-POINT VETERAN

Louis Everett, a black veteran in his early thirties, applied for a library clerical position in a federal departmental library. The papers supplied by the Civil Service Commission for him listed his educational background as a bachelor's degree in economics and some work at Columbia University towards a master's degree in economics. His academic record was excellent. After four years of service in the U. S. Army and an honorable discharge, he filed an application with the Civil Service Commission for any type of position for which his economics background would qualify him. Included in the papers was a statement that he had received psychiatric treatment while he was in the army which was considered a service-connected disability. According to the Veterans Preference Act of 1944, a veteran with a service-connected disability was entitled to ten points added to his earned Civil Service rating. The Civil Service Commission had not been able to place him in any economics-related position so had suggested he apply for this library opening because it might be a career ladder through which he might eventually use his educational background.

The librarian, Mr. Ian Quince, and the man who supervised the position, Mr. Charles Maize, studied Mr. Everett's credentials and interviewed him. Mr. Maize explained, during the interview, that the person employed for this position would start out by shelving books and then would be advanced to other types of work as he qualified for advancement and as openings in the staff occurred. He pointed out that Mr. Everett was overqualified for the position and feared he might be bored with the work.

Mr. Everett said that he had always enjoyed reading and, as a child, preferred reading to athletics or other activities. He reported that he had spent much time using libraries when he was in college and university and was interested in working in this library even though the salary was low and the status only that of a clerk. He indicated that he would be willing to start as a shelver and would try to qualify for better positions.

Mr. Quince and Mr. Maize agreed to employ Mr. Everett and he started to work on July 1. Mr. Maize was noted for the thoroughness and efficiency with which he oriented new employees under his supervision. After three weeks of trying to teach Mr. Everett to shelve books, Mr. Maize decided it was hopeless. Mr. Maize was a faithful, conscientious, capable black man who had been on the library staff for many years. He was very race conscious and took the position that all blacks in the library should perform better than the whites. And here this fellow was wrecking his program--his first failure. Mr. Quince assured Mr. Maize that he should not take the blame personally. Mr. Maize said that he had never supervised anyone like Everett and had not been able to figure out how to motivate him. He reported that Everett was sort of a "lone wolf" and would not associate with his fellow workers during rest breaks or at lunch. Most of the time he was sulky, antagonistic, disgruntled, and disagreeable.

Mr. Maize made some staff reassignments in order to create a place for Mr. Everett at the mail desk so as to try him out in that position. The person in this position sorted all incoming and outgoing mail, delivered mail to the various areas and persons in the library, and opened all periodicals, serials, and packages and delivered them to the right places. Everett's work was never efficient is spite of Mr. Maize's patient and helpful supervision. Everett simply could not follow instructions or established procedures and was uncooperative. Never before had there been a mail clerk in this library who could not keep up with the volume of mail--but Everett couldn't. This caused friction with staff members and, also, his inefficiency and low level of performance created a staff morale problem.

Everett frequently had periods of depression when he believed he was being persecuted by other staff members. At those times he would have to go to a Veterans Administration Hospital for medication. It seemed that every time the volume of mail was greatest, he would get sick and someone would have to take his place for a few days. Because the library was short-staffed, other work had to suffer when another staff member had to do his work.

Mr. Everett was single and the only relative he ever mentioned was his mother who lived in South Carolina. He visited her every two or three months. These visits always upset him and he would complain to anyone who would listen that he should have a much better paying job because of his academic background. He seemed to feel that he was a failure and he had lost his self respect. His fellow workers surmised that his mother must have raised questions about his job and salary.

Finally, in the spring, Mr. Maize reported to Mr. Quince that Mr. Everett would have to be dismissed before the end of his one-year probationary period. This information was passed on to the Department's Personnel Office. Subsequently Mr. Quince learned that Everett's probationary period was already up because he had worked as a messenger in the Department for three months prior to his employment in the library on July 1. This information had not been given in Everett's credentials nor furnished by the Personnel Office. To dismiss an employee after the expiration of the one-year probationary period required filing charges. A ten-point veteran had maximum retention rights in any government position; it was virtually impossible to fire him. The Personnel Department would take no action whatever so the library was "stuck" with him.

Mr. Quince was told by the Personnel Office that in about one year it might be possible to retire Mr. Everett on disability as he would have enough years of service by then. So, Mr. Quince agreed to keep him until that year expired. It was at this time that Mr. Quince learned the psychiatrist's diagnosis of Everett's condition--a paranoid with schizophrenic tendencies. This information was not furnished in his Civil Service credentials because the Army psychiatrists thought he had been "cured." Evidently his condition had deteriorated since his employment in the library.

Soon after this Mr. Everett had to enter a Veterans Administration Hospital for about six months of treatment. Mr. Quince tried unsuccessfully to get a medical certificate which would make it possible to dismiss Everett. When he was discharged from the hospital his doctors said it would be better for him to engage in normal activities and to return to his position in the library. Mr. Quince pointed out (1) that a library was not a rehabilitation center; (2) that the library was so short-staffed that every position was critical; and (3) that, although to an outsider the job of sorting, opening, and routing mail might not seem like an important position, in a library it must be performed efficiently to keep an even flow of work. These arguments did not change the decision of the hospital authorities.

During the next two years Mr. Everett's condition got steadily worse. He was in the Veterans Hospital three more times for several months each time and would return to his job in the library after being discharged. At these times, as soon as he had used up his sick leave, he would be on leave of absence without pay. Another person could not be hired in his place because he occupied a personnel slot in the budget. The money saved from his salary could be used to hire college students in the summer; but this was for just three months and did not provide staff the rest of the year.

Soon after Everett entered the hospital for the fifth time Mr. Quince received a letter from him saying that he thought he would be better the next time he returned because he would soon have a brain tumor operation. Quince took this letter to the Personnel Office and asked them to check with the hospital about this operation. There was no record of it. During the four years Mr. Everett had been on the library payroll, Mr. Maize had kept a detailed record of Mr. Everett's actions, absences, and symptoms. This record together with a copy of the letter from Everett and the report from the Personnel Office were all sent to the Public Health Service. Mr. Quince pointed out that Everett was now completely divorced from reality and it was dangerous for him to be working in the library and he could not possibly do the job. Mr. Quince requested that he be retired on disability. The Public Health Service accepted this report and Everett was finally retired.

Case 79

THE TUPELO FAMILY

For two generations the Tupelo family had been active in politics in the city of Laurel. The present head of the family was the city prosecuting attorney. His wife was very active in the Democratic party and was chairman of the county organization for many years. During her chairmanship she was influential in securing the election of the present mayor seven years ago. One of her "rewards" for this effort was appointment to the county library board as the mayor's personal representative. She liked to "run" various county activities and had been trying to get an appointment to the library board for a number of years.

The board of the Laurel County Library was composed of eleven members--the chairman of the Board of County Commissioners and four members appointed by that Board, the Mayor of Laurel, four members appointed by the City Council, and the county Superintendent of Schools. The chief librarian, of course, was an ex-officio member and secretary of the board.

The Tupelo's only son Lex was a secondary school

teacher certified to teach English and public speaking. He had been teaching in the Laurel schools for five years at the time his mother was appointed to the library board. His father had wanted him to be a lawyer, but one semester in law school convinced Lex that he was not interested in that profession; so, he returned to teaching. He did not dislike teaching but neither was he enthusiastic about it. Opportunities for promotion were infrequent in the public school system. Lex was ambitious and wanted to move ahead faster. His parents were also ambitious for him.

Three months after Mrs. Tupelo was appointed to the library board, the librarian in charge of public relations and publicity resigned to accept another position. Mrs. Tupelo told Lex about it. The salary was higher than Lex was earning and he thought the job had more prestige and status than that of a teacher. The job specification called for a master's degree in library science, a minimum of three years of library experience, and an ability to speak in public and to write news stories. Mrs. Tupelo talked to the chief librarian, Mr. Corbin, about the job description suggesting that a teacher of public speaking and English would be qualified to fill this position. Mr. Corbin explained the responsibilities and duties of the position and stated that it must be filled by a librarian. Mrs. Tupelo next went to the Mayor and other politically influential persons in Laurel and asked for their assistance in securing this position for her son. A few days later the chairman of the library board called on Mr. Corbin and told him that if he appointed Lex Tupelo to the vacant library position, the Mayor could assure Mr. Corbin that the county commissioners would transfer to the library budget about $40,000 of uncommitted funds. Mr. Corbin protested that Lex did not have the necessary qualifications for the position. The chairman said, "I thought you would be happy that I was able to get this money for the building renovations you have been requesting for several years. Surely being overly particular about one position is not worth losing all this money." Mr. Corbin was furiously mad to be put in such a situation but he held his tongue. He did point out though that appointing a relative of a board member constituted nepotism. The chairman said it did not and quoted the following excerpt from the staff personnel manual on nepotism:

> Nepotism: Relatives of library employees cannot be appointed to any position on the staff. This rule applies to all levels--custodial, secretarial,

clerical, professional, and specialists.

The chairman claimed that the rule involved relatives of <u>library staff members</u> and did not include relatives of board members. Mr. Corbin replied that even though board members were not specifically mentioned, appointing Lex would constitute bestowal of patronage by reason of relationship rather than of merit because Lex did not meet the job specifications.

At the next library board meeting, the appointment of Lex Tupelo to the position of "Adult Education Specialist" was approved. During the next six years Lex proceeded to build an "empire" of his own within the library. He started discussion groups for every age level from junior high school to senior citizens; one for high school students about how to select a college; a great books series for adults; one for inmates of a boys' reformatory which was located in the county; play reading for senior citizens; and many others. He started speed reading classes and film programs in the main library and all the branches. He co-sponsored programs of all kinds with the Chamber of Commerce, the Better Business Bureau, the county medical society, the American Cancer Society, and others. Arts and crafts classes were held in the main library and the products of these classes were exhibited frequently. These burgeoning activities encroached on the space of other departments in the main library and also took over activities which normally belonged in branch libraries or in such departments as Young Adult, Fine Arts, and Audio-Visual. Although Mr. Corbin refused to increase the budget for the Adult Education Department, Lex managed to find money from outside sources. His colleagues charged that he was too independent and cockey, and "a law unto himself"; they found him to be "an uncooperative prima donna" and hard to work with.

Lex had been in this position for six years. Two months ago Mr. Corbin announced he would retire at the end of this fiscal year. Lex applied for the position.

A search and screening committee of the board was appointed to find a replacement for Mr. Corbin. Mrs. Tupelo was a member of this committee. Their first action was to draw up a list of qualifications for the position:

> The chief librarian of the Laurel Public Library must have a bachelor's degree, have five years'

experience as head, assistant head, or business manager of a large library system or as the manager or executive officer of a large organization engaged in public or community service. The examination of the candidate will consist of an evaluation of his personal and professional qualifications, and an interview which would deal with administrative problems. If an applicant is not a librarian, he should, prior to the interview, familiarize himself with some problems concerning library administration and management.

When the library's professional staff learned of this job specification they speculated that the position was going to be someone's political reward or had been written to fit Lex's qualifications. In a letter to the board, signed by every professional librarian on the staff, the staff protested these qualifications; they demanded that the head librarian have a master's degree in library science and at least five years of administrative library experience. Furthermore, they requested that two library staff members be appointed to the Search and Screening Committee who would represent the interests of the staff. Copies of the protest and the request were supplied to all of the local newspapers and to the radio and television stations.

Case 80

GRANT FUNDS

During World War II the federal government began to subsidize scientific research projects by university faculty members as a means of obtaining needed information without setting up new federal offices or bureaus. Most of these grants at State University contained some money for the researcher to buy books, journals, technical reports, and other research materials. These were purchased directly through the University's Purchasing Department and not through the University Library's Acquisitions Department. Faculty researchers ordered whatever they pleased and considered that these belonged to them personally. Since these were bought outside the library system, they were not listed in the Library's union catalog nor in the departmental library catalogs. Hence, they were not available to students or other faculty members for use.

At first, when few grants were involved, this was not a serious problem because the amounts of money were small. The University has received more and more grants through the years, so that at present large quantities of research materials are coming to the campus outside the library system. Furthermore, the problem is no longer confined to the sciences but permeates all departments because of the diversity of grants and research funds in all subject areas. The annual published list of university research support for the last several years was impressively long involving millions of dollars. These grants came from such sources as the U. S. Public Health Service, the National Science Foundation, the Ford Foundation, the American Chemical Society, the U. S. Air Force, National Endowment for the Humanities, Atomic Energy Commission, Federal Highway Administration, U. S. Office of Education, Urban Transportation Administration, Rockefeller Foundation, American Cancer Society, NASA, Carnegie Corporation, Agency for International Development, Office of Economic Opportunity, U. S. Children's Bureau, and many others.

The faculty at State University continually complain bitterly of the inadequacy of the library's collections to sustain their research. If all of the technical reports, microfiche, microfilm, data tapes, books and journals purchased through grant funds were channeled through the library's Acquisition and Cataloging Departments, the library collections would be immeasurably enriched, the whole academic community would have access to these materials, and unnecessary duplication of titles could be eliminated. Moreover, since researchers depend heavily on the library's staff and resources for their research, the Director of Libraries believes that each research proposal should include a stipulated percentage of the grant as a direct subsidy to the library to be spent at the discretion of the library staff in acquiring needed research materials and in employing additional staff.

Case 81

COMMUNITY CONTROL

The Southeast Community Organization in Big City is a coalition organization composed of representatives of some seventy community groups. Last year the SCO achieved some control over the public schools in the community. Several months ago the Library Committee of the SCO conducted a library card and reading drive which registered more than three thousand children who had never owned library cards and branch library circulation in the area doubled. Now the SCO wants to control the two branch libraries in the area. The Director of Libraries for Big City Public Library has received a library statement approved at a recent meeting of the SCO.

The statement charged that (1) other sections of the city have better facilities than the Southeast Community; (2) there is at present no agent to stimulate cooperation between the public library administration and other community agencies; (3) there is no structure to allow local community involvement; and (4) Big City Public Library administration has not led in experimental projects of community involvement.

They requested that Big City Public Library set up a pilot project involving a locally-elected SCO Library Board for the two branch libraries in the community area to be responsible for preparation and presentation of budgets, selection of employees, handling employee grievances, and setting local library policies.

Case 82

QUESTIONABLE PRACTICES

Six acquisition librarians from as many academic libraries were seated around a circular table eating dinner during an ALA annual conference. As usual at such gatherings, they were talking about their experiences and comparing notes. Alan Flam brought up the problem of buying reprints of out-of-print books and voiced his dissatisfaction with one reprint publisher whom he accused of unethical practices:

> The You Reprint Company announces in its catalog expensive sets costing from $5,000 to $12,000 with statements 'to be printed . . .' with a date about a year later than the date of the catalog. I sent in a prepayment order for a set costing $9,000 and two years later had not yet received it. In another instance, he held a prepaid order for three years before notifying me that the title would not be published and refunding what I had

paid. I have learned that in announcing titles like this with a future date he is 'fishing for bait' and has no intention of reprinting the title unless he gets thirty to fifty orders from librarians. Unless he can get that number of orders he cannot justify the expense of reprinting. I do not believe it is ethical to tie up library funds in this manner. I suppose he has all these prepayments out at interest. But the more important point is that the money isn't being spent for the material we need and the faculty are hounding me about why it hasn't arrived. If a set is unavailable, I need to use the money for other priorities. This type of thing makes for poor public relations with the faculty who need the title. I am blamed for tying up departmental funds and for carrying over this encumbrance each year. If a title is listed in the You Reprint catalog for two years and he still doesn't have enough orders, he isn't going to get any more.

Another acquisition librarian at the table remarked, "I agree that this is unethical and I am so fed up with that company that I refuse to send them a prepaid order. If a title has already been reprinted and is in stock, then I will order but I won't order anything 'to be reprinted . . .'. I think the Vee Reprint Company handles the situation much better. He sends a list asking if you would be interested in buying this title if it is reprinted. In this way he finds out whether it would be profitable to reprint and notifies all respondents whether or not the title will be reprinted. It seems to me the honest thing for the You Reprint Company to do would be to say 'intend to reprint if enough orders warrant the reprinting' but not ask for prepaid orders."

Alan Flam interrupted, "Another thing that makes me provoked with You Reprint is that after waiting a year or more, I cancel the order and he customarily sends me a credit memo instead of refunding the money. This means that funds are tied up indefinitely unless there is another item in his catalog which we need."

A third acquisition librarian pointed out, "These reprint publishers are doing us a real service by reprinting these books but often they don't have the money to reprint so they need cash in hand to finance their operations. It is the only way for librarians to get the books because it is not a mass market and we are financing the operation on a pay-as-you-go basis. We have to hope that the firm will not fold up before we get our materials."

More discussion followed with candid revelations of names, titles, and instances. Later the conversation turned to the problems of importing books from Asia and from Eastern Europe.

Acquisition librarian number four told how he had gotten "burned" by one of these dealers.

> In the United States there are only about six dealers handling books from Croslavia in Eastern Europe. In our university we are developing a major Croslavia area so I have the responsibility of searching for and buying many retrospective titles in this area. I have to acquire them from these dealers. One dealer, who has connections with the government of Croslavia, receives all of his stock by mail. Twice a year he puts out a catalog and gives prices for all items listed. His prices are more than double what he paid for each title. Acquisition librarians normally check his catalogs as soon as they come out so that by the time the catalog is two months old he has received all or most of the orders he will receive for the titles listed. If he gets ten orders for one title, he considers this a demand and ups the price--not five or ten per cent, but 300-400 per cent.
>
> Our Croslavia Department desperately needed a several volume set of political speeches and my staff had been watching dealers' catalogs for it for several years. When this set was published in Croslavia several years ago they cost fifty cents (in U.S. currency) per volume. When we spotted it in this man's catalog for twenty-nine dollars we sent in an order for it at once. He wrote back that the set was out of print and the price had gone up to three hundred dollars. I reported to our Croslavia Department and told them this was a most unreasonable price and recommended that we cancel the order and wait for the title to appear in another dealer's catalog. The chairman of the department said they needed

the set 'as of yesterday' so go ahead and order it since my staff had not found it listed in any other dealer's catalog. So, I ordered the set and the very day the volumes came in another dealer of Croslavia books called on me. He operated from his home and he acquired his stock by making frequent trips to Croslavia and bringing back with him those volumes which he thought he could sell. He would also buy parts of sets or partially completed sets but would not offer them for sale until he had actually completed a set.

He saw this recently acquired set on a book truck on his way to my office. He asked me where we had gotten these as they were fairly scarce in the U. S. and I told him this was the only set available. He was a bit abrupt in his reply and said there must be at least twenty sets for sale in the U. S. and that he had two in his home. I accused him of kidding me but he said he wasn't and that you had to know where to get them. He inquired how much we had paid for the set and when I told him three hundred dollars, he wanted to know why we had paid so much. He said he was asking forty-five dollars a set for the two sets he had in stock. I was really 'burned up' that I had been gypped by the first dealer. I could not return the set because we had already put our mark of ownership in them.

The other acquisition librarians laughed as they exchanged knowing glances and admitted they too had made some unwise purchases from this same dealer. The suggestion was made that they ought to communicate more often with each other to keep informed about various dealers and their practices.

Case 83

A PILFERAGE RACKET

The Dunn Historical Collection of Metropolitan Public Library contained many rare documents, books, and letters. Recently, when the curator, Albert Crow, was preparing an exhibit of rare books and archival materials to display during the city's 175th anniversary celebration, he spotted an inter-

Controlling Cases 339

esting volume appropriately clothed in a dusty, old black binding. It proved to contain British political and religious pamphlets written between 1648 and 1651. Close investigation revealed an inscription in gold on the binding "Gift of G. III" and a British Museum stamp inside the book. He wrote the British Museum about the book and learned that it was part of a collection of bound volumes of pamphlets and newspapers given to the Museum by King George III. Upon checking the collection after receipt of Mr. Crow's letter, it was discovered that nineteen volumes were missing.

Metropolitan Library records showed that the volume had been given to the Dunn Collection six months ago by a local resident who was an avid rare book collector. A phone call to the donor revealed that he had obtained the volume from a book dealer in New York City who, in turn, had purchased it from an "English" couple. Before returning the volume to the British Museum, Mr. Crow notified the FBI of the theft. The FBI had quite a file on the activities of this couple who were wanted in seven states and nine cities for thefts of rare items from various public, university, and governmental libraries. Descriptions of the couple and their mode of operation were supplied Mr. Crow by the FBI. No photographs of the couple had ever been obtained. So far, they had eluded every trap set for them. The FBI agents said that the pair were members of a highly organized and profitable national pilferage operation. Historical documents and rare books were stolen from libraries throughout the nation and then sold to rare book and autograph dealers, private collectors, and libraries. Mr. Crow distributed photocopies of this information to all members of the library staff as well as to Metropolitan City's dealers and collectors --just in case the couple should show up in that city.

A few weeks later, a well dressed, attractive woman came to Mr. Crow's office offering to sell four letters which she claimed she inherited with other family papers. All of the letters had been written by prominent American statesmen in the early 1800's.

Mr. Crow asked the usual routine questions about the letters and examined them for authenticity. The woman said she was offering them for sale because she needed the money. Mr. Crow was interested in acquiring the letters for the collection but the price she was asking was high and he would need the approval of the library director to purchase them. He suggested that she return the following day.

Later in the day Mr. Crow's assistant reported, "Yesterday a spectacled man with a scholar's stoop came to the reading room and asked to see some pamphlets on early history of the state. I took him to the stacks and showed him the boxes in which pamphlets on this subject were kept. He selected some of them and spent several hours in the reading room industriously taking notes before returning them to the desk. This morning, he came back, chose more boxes of pamphlets, and again took more notes. When I returned from lunch, I found he had left. I checked the boxes to see whether the pamphlets had been filed in correct order in the boxes and discovered all of ours were missing and had been replaced with others resembling ours but not on the same subject." Mr. Crow examined them and found them to be worthless.

The appearance of the woman selling rare letters and the thefts on the same day made Mr. Crow and his assistant wonder if this might be the couple wanted by the FBI because they answered the general description furnished them. They reported the incident and their suspicions to the director of the library who, in turn, called the FBI. An agent came at once to the library and instructed Mr. Crow to meet Mrs. Towhee as scheduled the following day. The man arrived early the next morning in the director's office and demanded he be allowed to use restricted areas of the library "for research." These areas had been denied to him the previous day by the staff of the Historical Collection. The director granted the permission. An FBI agent and a library staff member observed him all the time he was in the restricted areas. They saw him hide in his clothing: an eighteenth century diary, a journal of an 1835-36 expedition to the Rocky Mountains, and a rare 1776 treatise on wagons. The FBI agents searched and arrested him as he left the library. Another agent followed Mrs. Towhee to her apartment when she left the library and arrested her after a search of the apartment. In the apartment, agents found seven suitcases full of historical papers, and priceless documents stolen from various libraries. They also found about one hundred forged documents among the legitimate papers. The approximate value of all documents was estimated at $500,000. The two were arraigned on a charge of transporting stolen documents across state lines and on three mail fraud warrants. They were convicted in Federal Court and each was sentenced to ten years in Federal prison. They also faced separate indictments from seven states on charges of theft from libraries.

Controlling Cases 341

The arrest and trial of Mr. and Mrs. Towhee led the FBI to the master mind of the pilferage operation--a rare book dealer, Mr. Gadwall, in New York City, and another one of his traveling thieves, Mr. Ibis. Mr. Gadwall knew the rare book market; he would spot valuable items in libraries, plan itineraries for Mr. Ibis and the Towhees and tell them which items to steal from which libraries. He also taught them tricks of thievery; he provided the men with capacious top coats which had large inside pockets in which stolen books and manuscripts could be concealed. He taught Mrs. Towhee how to walk normally even though she was holding stolen volumes between her legs and how to conceal single sheets and pamphlets in her clothing. Also, she was taught approaches to sell items and supplied with names and addresses of rare book collectors and librarians.

Mr. Gadwall paid the three thieves on the basis of the value of what they stole; then he sold the items for whatever higher price the market would bear. He removed all embossing stamps by heating a large spoon and using a bowl as a flat iron to smooth out the embossing. Frequently he sent Mr. Ibis to London with quantities of valuable stolen items disguised between commonplace bindings. Some of these he sold to certain book dealers. Others, which contained library stamps of ownership, were taken to a skillful binder who removed the stamped portions of pages, matched the paper with old paper from his stock (either exactly or by imitating aging of the paper with chemicals and heat). Then he wove the paper into the mutilated page replacing the sections removed. If printing had been on the removed section, it was replaced from old types, imprinted by hand with ink mixed to match the old ink. Mr. Ibis would then return to the United States with the "restored" volumes for Mr. Gadwall to sell.

This experience with the Towhees and the information about the operation of the theft ring made the staff of Metropolitan Public Library keenly aware of the vulnerability of the total collection to organized theft. The question of security was on the agenda for the next meeting of the administrative council which was composed of the heads of all departments and divisions. The chief of public services reported "staggering" book losses in recent years. For example, during the last two years, the Metropolitan Library System had lost the equivalent of the entire book stock of five branch libraries. Book losses, through non-return, theft, and mutilation had cost the library about $500,000 per year for the past two years, or 7.1 per cent of the total library budget. The last inventory taken of non-fiction books showed a loss of 48,000 volumes per year. In addition, messengers were sent after another 71,000 volumes which were never returned.

To combat this loss problem, the council came up with three recommendations: (1) that the staff increase their vigilance; (2) that the staff observe and study the problem in order to identify when losses were heaviest in the various library agencies; and (3) that a Security Unit be established which would be staffed by retired investigators and former members of the city's Police Department.

Can you, the reader, suggest other security measures?

Case 84

THE ANONYMOUS CALLER

(Role playing)

Mrs. Warbler was an attractive widow with a healthy looking complexion, sparkling expressive eyes, a springy step to her walk, a slim figure, and auburn hair streaked with gray. She worked at the circulation desk of a medium-sized public library located in a city of about 40,000 population. She was tactful and empathetic with the public and, through the years, had built up a rapport with them. Many patrons asked for her by name, if she was not at the desk, and others came to the library only when she was on duty to help them.

At her home one evening she received a telephone call from a man who called her by name and evidently knew her by sight. He did not seem to want anything in particular--just to talk. This went on for about twenty minutes.
A week later at the same time, he called again and this time asked her for a date. She refused, giving as an excuse that she couldn't leave her family. These weekly telephone calls pleading for a date continued for several weeks. The caller never identified himself nor the reason he always called on the same night at the same time each week. She always refused to meet him and asked him not to keep calling her because the calls upset her ailing, invalid mother who worried about them.

Controlling Cases 343

One evening he threatened to "get" some of the young women working in the library if she would not meet him. This threat worried her to such an extent that she took the problem to the telephone company which attached an electronic device to her telephone. After he hung up she would leave the receiver off the hook, go to a neighbor's home, and call the telephone company to trace the call. In this way the telephone from which the call was made could be identified even though he had hung up. She learned that he called from a different pay station each time. This weekly calling and the threats went on for four months and then suddenly stopped.

The day after he had threatened to "get" some young women on the staff, Mrs. Warbler reported these calls to the head librarian, Mr. Brier. He was sufficiently concerned that he brought up the problem at the next staff meeting.

Role for Mr. Brier:

As head librarian you are always concerned about security measures both for the collection and for the safety of the staff. This library has had its share of "peeping toms" in the stacks and of males of all ages trying to date staff members. This man might be mentally ill enough to carry out his threat. At any rate, you believe the staff should be alerted to the possible danger and tighter security measures should be taken. You want specific suggestions from your staff.

Role for Miss Millet:

You are in your early twenties, are single, very attractive, and work at the circulation desk. You and Mrs. Warbler are close friends and she confided in you several weeks ago her problem with this caller. Since the threat, you have been thinking about what might possibly be done to help protect the staff. You have these ideas:

(1) install more lights so there are no dark areas at night.

(2) reactivate a buzzer system which had been abandoned several years ago after an intercom system was installed. If a code of signals were developed for this buzzer system and the buzzer buttons were located in several inconspicuous places in the library (under desks, for example)

they could be pushed without the public knowing they had been touched.

(3) have an off-duty policeman on duty in the evenings.

(4) install mirrors and cameras like those in supermarkets.

<u>Other roles</u> could be assigned, if more players were desired.

Case 85

HARASSMENT AT STONECHAT BRANCH

The whole summer of 1969 had been one of harassment and tension for the staff of the Stonechat Branch of a large city public library. The staff consisted of Mrs. Floyd (librarian), Mrs. Julian (children's librarian), Miss Elder (part-time circulation assistant), and high school pages. Here are a few examples of incidents which occurred.

From two to twelve black boys and girls would come in for water at the drinking fountain and then saunter around the library disturbing and annoying both staff and readers by turning over chairs, running around and flipping periodicals onto the floor, and noisily opening and closing catalog drawers.

Saturday afternoons were usually very quiet during the summer so only one staff member and a page were normally scheduled to work. On one of these afternoons, Mrs. Floyd was busy helping some patrons at the desk and an inexperienced page was shelving books some distance away. About ten teenagers (who were clearly not patrons) came in and dispersed throughout the library. Several gathered around the desk and monopolized Mrs. Floyd by asking many questions. Others went into the children's area and knocked over a shelf of books--which drew Mrs. Floyd away from the desk. While she was thus engaged, one boy quickly and silently went behind the desk and emptied the cash drawer while another searched the workroom and found both Mrs. Floyd's and the page's purses and took all the money in each. The gang then ran out of the library shouting triumphantly. Mrs. Floyd reported this incident to the Director of Libraries Monday morning.

The following Wednesday evening a group of teenage youths came in. Mrs. Floyd recognized them as the same group who had caused the disturbance Saturday afternoon. She asked them either to sit down quietly and read or leave. They became verbally abusive. She called the police from the desk while the boys were milling around. Mrs. Floyd went to the workroom to lock it and found one young man ransacking the desks and files. By this time she was very angry and tried to stop him hoping to hold him until the police came. He pulled away, pushed her back so that she fell on the floor, and ran out of the library. By the time the police arrived, none of the boys was in sight.

Several nights later, Mrs. Julian, the children's librarian, Miss Elder, and a page were working. Six boys came in and walked among the reading tables talking to students who were studying. Mrs. Julian asked the boys to leave unless they wished to read. The leader was offended and began feint slaps at her face. When she did not flinch, he tapped her on the cheek. She went to the desk to call the police and he disconnected the phone. Then he picked up a large periodical and threw it at her hitting her on the shoulder. Then, they all made a hasty exit laughing as they went.

A favorite maneuver, repeated many times, was for a group to come just before closing time (9 p.m.), sit at tables near the circulation desk, mumble and stare, and refuse to budge when closing time was announced.

Despite all the scuffling, whistling, horseplay, thefts, and other harassment, the staff managed to keep a semblance of order during the summer and patrons continued to use the collection about as much as they had in previous years. On several occasions it had been necessary to call the police but only one time did they see the offenders. Because the police had been so slow in answering the calls, the staff had decided to try to manage the discipline themselves if at all possible. They were reasonably successful until early September when two incidents convinced the branch staff as well as the administrative staff of the library system that some drastic changes would have to be made.

The supervisor of branches, Mrs. Maru, came to Stonechat Branch one day early in September for one of her regularly scheduled routine visits. When she left (about 5 p.m.), she walked out the back door to the parking lot carrying her purse loosely on her left arm and Mrs. Floyd was on her right walking out to the car with her as a gesture of courtesy. They noticed three boys who appeared to be about fourteen or fifteen years old loitering near the building but did not pay much attention to them. Suddenly the women were accosted--one boy forced his way between the two women and pushed them apart, another grabbed Mrs. Floyd's right arm and pulled her farther to the right, and the third boy slid his right arm under Mrs. Maru's left arm and wrenched the purse off her arm and, in the process, she lost her balance and fell to her knees on the pavement. Then all three boys ran as fast as they could. The two women screamed and a patron just getting out of his car saw what happened and pursued the boys. When he was about to overtake them, they dropped the purse, he retrieved it, picked up the contents which had been strewn along the path of flight, and returned the purse to Mrs. Maru. The latter was examining her bruised and bleeding knees and torn hose, and was shaking all over from shock. At Mrs. Floyd's insistence, she went into the library, administered first aid to her knees, and lay on a cot for a while before going back out to her car.

By the time she reached her home, her knees were very painful; and, during the night, she experienced increasing pain in her left shoulder, arm, and hand; and one finger was swollen to twice its normal size. The next morning she consulted a physician who found the muscles in her arm and shoulder had been badly wrenched and told her they would be painful for several days but no permanent damage had been done. The swollen finger had been dislocated about a year previously and the yanking of the purse handle from her hand had aggravated the old injury.

The second incident which made evident the necessity for some drastic changes in handling harassment occurred two days later. Several times during the afternoon a gang of local teen-aged youths drifted in and out of the library making as much noise as possible under pretense of looking at magazines. The staff could not recall that any of the gang had ever checked out any library material; they ignored these deliberate bids for attention and continued with their normal work routines. When Mrs. Floyd heard the small chairs in the children's area being bumped about, she investigated. The gang leader, a stocky black youth, and some of his friends were sitting on the table and were in the process of turning the chairs around so they could put their feet on them.

With restraint, Mrs. Floyd said, "Aren't you fellows a little large to be in the children's area?" One of them replied quickly, "We're helping this little girl get her lessons," and they all laughed tauntingly. Others of the gang drifted in and stood around.

Mrs. Floyd watched and listened for a few minutes and again reminded them that they did not belong on that side of the library. She also told them that the library staff were glad to have teenagers use the library but sitting on the tables with feet in chairs was not proper use. That brought out an hilarious hoot from one and mutters back and forth from the others. Mrs. Floyd stood there quietly and those standing drifted toward the door. The leader tried to get the child to leave but she would not, so he brought up the rear of the supposed retreat.

By this time Mrs. Floyd had returned to the desk. As the youth passed her she said quietly, but angrily, "I don't want you to come back in here again." At his impudent question of "Why?", she told him that he had been in dozens of times causing disturbances. This brought on a tirade of vile, abusive, threatening language and the announcement that he would come in whenever he chose. He came behind the desk, pushed his forefinger repeatedly to within an inch of her nose and dared her to call the police. Between intelligible sentences he continued to spit out filthy names at her. She finally said defiantly, "Just why don't you hit me if that's the way you feel?" However, he just kept up the name calling. Since some of the gang had gone outside, she decided that she would try to lock them out and him in and call the police. She went to get the key.

When she came back out of the office he followed her. At the door he grabbed her arms and slung her away from the door. Before she knew what she was doing, she slapped him--hard. Of course that gave him the excuse he wanted. He punched her chest and arms with his fists while his gang looked on with obvious enjoyment. She did not fall to the floor, but fell against a radiator. She turned to his friends and asked if they were not going to stop him. They thought that was hilarious and answered, "You hit him first." She took the blows without a whimper, but was so stupified at all the filthy talk and general savage behavior that she could only shake her head in pity. This increased the angry output from him. A white teenager came to see what was going on and she persuaded him and the page to stand back, because she knew the gang wanted to cause a riot. The leader kept daring her to call the police, but she thought they would mob anyone who did, so she just "took it." Finally a younger boy on the steps persuaded the leader to leave.

Mrs. Floyd went back to the office, took some aspirin, and started to write a report of the incident to send to the Director of Libraries. About twenty minutes later Mrs. Elder came in to tell Mrs. Floyd that a woman wanted to talk to her. A crowd of about fifteen persons were standing there--six to ten of the gang, some other large young men, and some women and children.

The leader's aunt accused Mrs. Floyd of mistreating a child (he was supposed to be only sixteen years of age, but he had the physique of a man). He had also told her that Mrs. Floyd had said, "Niggers don't have no sense." Mrs. Floyd asked who heard her say it and two youths volunteered that they had. She saw that he could get "proof" of anything he chose to report, so she decided to depend on any sense of fairness which the woman had. The woman listened resentfully, for she did not want to believe that the staff had been fair to black children. She closed the session by turning angrily to him and saying, "If you're not in here, they can't do anything to you, so you just stay away!" They left with mutterings of "show them" and curses. Mrs. Floyd was relieved and pleased that the woman had enforced the order which Mrs. Floyd had earlier not succeeded in enforcing.

The next morning Mrs. Floyd called the Director of Libraries to report the incident and asked for police protection for the library until the gang of boys were apprehended. He inquired about the injuries and insisted that she see a physician. Although her body ached all over, her chest and arms were black and blue and her shoulder was swollen and bruised, the physician could find no permanent damage nor could he locate any blood clots.

A special meeting of the Board of Trustees was called for the purpose of considering what action should be taken concerning the incidents at Stonechat Branch involving the safety of the staff there. The Board decided the two most important factors involved were maintenance of public service and the safety of the library's employees. In order to provide for both, the trustees curtailed hours at the branch so that the full staff could be on duty when the library was open.

Controlling Cases 349

The Director informed the city's Urban League, the Human Relations Commission, and the Community Action Commission of the harassment during the summer. The Urban League offered to conduct an investigation. The head of the Human Relations Commission suggested that he organize some Black Unity Groups to try to change the attitudes of these groups of young people, and the Community Action Commission promised cooperation in handling discipline in the library.

Evaluate the handling of these incidents and the decisions of the trustees.

Case 86

ACCESS TO LEGAL MATERIALS[1]

The purposes of Public Law 89-511, Library Services and Construction Act, Title IV-A, passed in July 1966, were to provide library materials and library services to inmates, patients, or residents of penal institutions, reformatories, residential training schools, and hospitals supported by the state. After the passage of this Act, the governor of Sumac asked the Librarian of the State Library to appoint a committee to visit the penal institutions and the state hospitals and to report on their libraries. The team for the penal institutions consisted of one representative from each of the following types of libraries: State (chairman), school, public, academic, special, and a library school faculty member. The state's Supervisor of Correctional Institutions set up a schedule, made appointments with various staff members in each institution, and accompanied the team on each visit. The team members were dismayed at the inadequacy or lack of "library" facilities in the institutions. All of them were staffed with inmate volunteers, none of whom had had any library experience or training.

The Supervisor of Correctional Institutions had recently been appointed by the governor and was charged with developing better treatment and rehabilitation programs. Although

---

[1] Gilmore v. Lynch 400 F 2d 228 (1968)
Hatfield v. Bailleaux 290 F 2d 632 (1961)

the needs of the institutions were great and the budget was far from adequate, he had budgeted some money for libraries. The LSCA funds would contribute greatly to his plans for better library services. He believed that libraries should be an integral part of rehabilitation and that a multimedia collection would contribute to the educational, vocational, recreational, and cultural programs of the prisons.

During the visits of the team, he was much impressed with the young man representing the school librarians of the state, Gus Mark. Mr. Mark was the head librarian for a large high school multi-media learning resources center and was knowledgeable about all types of learning materials and equipment and their uses. The Supervisor believed this was the type of librarian needed for the state penitentiary who would be capable of selecting materials which were geared to the special needs and abilities of the inmates. Mr. Mark accepted the position as librarian of Sumac State Penitentiary because he saw it as a challenge to his professional capabilities.

Mr. Mark found the "library" consisted chiefly of books which had been discarded from public and academic libraries or from private homes. Most of them were old, ragged, unattractive, and dirty. The room was drab, dingy, and depressing; the furniture was old, dark-colored, and scarred from use. This "library" had been kept open a few hours a day by volunteer inmates. He had a budget to renovate the library, buy new furniture and equipment, and acquire materials.

After only a few days on the job, Mr. Mark learned that the most serious complaint of the inmates was their access to legal materials. The law collection consisted solely of two volumes of the United States Constitution Annotated, the Sumac Revised Statutes, and some Advance Sheets of the Supreme Court of Sumac. Preparation of legal documents by those who were a part of the general prison population was confined to a small room in the prison library where the law books were housed. During the thirty hours a week when the library was open, four prisoners, by appointments obtained in advance, were permitted to work there on legal matters. Each individual library appointment was for approximately three hours. Occasionally delays of from three to seventeen days occurred between the time an inmate sought an appointment to use the facilities and the time he actually used them.

Controlling Cases 351

In talking over the problem with the Warden, Mr. Mark learned that the question of the extent of a prisoner's rights to have access to legal materials recurs frequently in state and federal penitentiaries. The Warden provided him with a new regulation relating to the contents of prison libraries which specified that a penitentiary library should have a standard set of basic codes and references including: (1) the state codes for Penal, Welfare and Institutions, Vehicles, and Health and Safety; (2) the U. S. and Sumac Constitutions; (3) a recognized law dictionary; (4) a book on criminal procedures; (5) the state's Rules of Court; and (6) Rules of the U. S. Court of Appeals and of the U. S. Supreme Court. Mr. Mark ordered as many copies of these titles as he thought would provide reasonable access.

Also, Mr. Mark did some reorganizing within the library to create a legal section with a capacity for eleven persons at one time. He also extended the total number of hours the library was open to fifty-six (eight hours a day for seven days). Inmates then rarely had to wait more than one day for access.

The Warden supplied Mr. Mark with the rules and regulations in this institution regarding legal materials which had been prepared under his supervision and had been approved by the State Board of Control:

> 1. The prison library. Inmates may have access to the legal collection once a week. No law books may be removed from the prison library. Preparation of legal documents by those who are a part of the general prison population is confined to the prison library.
>
> 2. In cells. During the approximately fourteen hours each day when the general prison population is confined in their cells, they are permitted to keep a specified quantity of the following: books, magazines, courses of study (including correspondence courses), and personal papers. Inmates are not allowed to engage in the study of law, to prepare legal documents or to keep legal materials in their cells. All materials of a legal nature found outside the prison library will be confiscated by prison officials as contraband. Inmates are permitted to prepare non-legal documents, to write letters (including letters to courts,

judges, and attorneys), and to retain correspondence from courts, judges and attorneys providing such correspondence does not contain written citations or legal authority.

3. Isolation ward. Confinement in isolation is imposed only for violation of prison rules and regulations. Inmates confined to the isolation ward cannot have access to legal documents or papers.

4. Segregation ward. Inmates confined in the segregation ward do not have access to the prison library. They are, however, permitted to engage in legal research or the preparation of legal documents in their cells from approximately 8:30 a. m. to 3:30 p. m. seven days a week. Only during these periods are they permitted to have legal documents or papers in their cells. The setting of specific hours when this may be done is to enable the same guards to distribute and pick up the items.

5. Purchasing legal materials. Inmates are not permitted to purchase, acquire, or receive bound books of any kind at any time. However, they can receive or purchase a single copy of an opinion or decision in their own case.

The Warden explained to Mr. Mark that these regulations and practices were for the purpose of discouraging the informal practice of law by what were termed "cell-house lawyers." If permitted to engage in such practice, aggressive inmates of superior intelligence would exploit and dominate weaker prisoners of less intelligence. The practice also tended to develop a group of inmate leaders, which is discouraged in all institutions.

Some inmates contended that these regulations violated the due process and equal protection clauses of the Fourteenth Amendment in that they seriously infringed upon their rights of access to the courts and discriminated between indigent and affluent prisoners because the latter could obtain outside counsel for legal research, thus gaining effective access to the courts.

The inmates kept pressuring Mr. Mark for more legal

materials and more liberal regulations on access. Because all of his experience had been in school libraries, he was accustomed to listening sympathetically to patron demands and to fulfilling them if at all possible. The philosophy of service which he had acquired both in library school and in his experience was not in agreement with the prison regulations concerning access. He explained to the inmates (1) that state law clearly listed and limited the legal titles which could be provided in a penitentiary library and that these were available; and (2) that the prison regulations as to access had to be observed.

Mr. Mark talked to the Warden about this. The Warden said:

> State authorities have no obligation under the federal constitution to provide library facilities and an opportunity for their use to enable an inmate to search for legal loopholes in judgment and sentence under which he is held or to perform services of a lawyer, and a state prisoner has no due process rights to spend his prison time or utilize prison facilities in an effort to discover a ground for overturning a presumptively valid judgment.
>
> In determining whether a state prisoner is afforded reasonable access to courts, the fact must not be overlooked that inmates of a penitentiary are undergoing punishment, and that lawful incarceration brings about necessary withdrawal or limitation of many privileges and rights, a retraction justified by the considerations underlying our penal system.

Case 87

AN ATTEMPTED THEFT

The rare book library of Henna University was built about ten years ago. The shape of the building was in the form of a hollow square which created an interior light-court open to the sky. The courtyard below was beautifully landscaped and provided a pleasant view when one looked out of the windows around the courtyard. These windows were double--one pane of plate glass parallel with the exterior of the limestone building and one pane of plate glass parallel with the inside wall. The walls of the building were twelve inches thick so the two panes of glass were about ten inches apart and both were cemented in and could not be opened. The walls on the exterior of the hollow square building contained no windows. Only two doors provided access into the building--a loading dock at the rear of the building and a front entrance through which all staff and visitors entered. Both doors were strongly reinforced. The architect believed the building was impregnable.

About midnight one evening the janitor heard the sounds of moaning. He found an unconscious young man, severely injured, lying on the floor of the courtyard. Beside him was a knapsack in which were some tools (a ball-peen hammer, a screwdriver, a pinch bar) a roll of masking tape, and the library's rarest manuscript.

The janitor called the campus police who took the intruder to a hospital under armed guard. The knapsack with its contents were locked in the librarian's office. Upon searching around, the police discovered a heavy manila rope knotted at short intervals hanging from the roof down to a window which had been broken out. Pieces of glass on the courtyard floor were covered with masking tape on one side. The police surmised that the thief had let himself down from the roof on the rope, had covered the outer window glass with masking tape, had broken out the pane with the hammer, had reached through and broken out the second pane in the same manner, and then had crawled through the two window frames into the small exhibition room where the manuscript was displayed. The room was locked securely at all times when there was no one in attendance.

The manuscript was displayed in a specially built case. The manufacturer of the display case and the library staff believed the case was thief-proof. The base and frame were made of heavy metal upon which rested a box made of thick plate glass cemented together. The frame and glass box had to be raised with a crank by means of a gear mechanism to permit insertion of a book or manuscript. When lowered by the crank, the top was locked more securely than it would have been if a lock and key had been used. The crank was kept in the desk of the librarian in charge of exhibits. Inside this case the manuscript was covered by a second box made of plexiglass.

The intruder broke the glass top of the case, removed the end of the plexiglass inner case, took out the manuscript, and placed it in his knapsack with the tools. Evidently he planned to climb the rope to the roof, relocate the rope, and descend by means of the rope on the outside of the building to reach the ground. But, instead, he apparently lost his hold on the rope and fell about forty feet into the courtyard.

The building was open to visitors from 10 a. m. to 4 p. m. and the front door was locked when the building was closed. The door of the loading dock was opened only during the infrequent occasions when deliveries were being made.

The campus police believed the only possible way he could have gotten to the roof was to have entered the library with other visitors during the preceding day, hidden somewhere inside the library, then, after closing hours, climbed the narrow stairs to the roof where the air conditioning unit was located. The intruder must have known the floor plan of the building well. His motives were unknown, he had no apparent connection with the library or staff, and the attempt did not appear to be a prank. The manuscript was too well known for anyone to buy it. Was he mentally deranged? The intruder died without regaining consciousness.

Special attention must now be devoted by the library staff to greater security measures.

Case 88

CONFRONTATION

(Role playing)

Roles:
Librarian
Man studying for civil service exam
Second man

The Mulberry Branch Library was located in a neighborhood with affluent high rise apartments on one side and ghettos on the other side. Because of the two extremes in the economic status of the patrons, problems sometimes arose in the library because of differences in attitudes as to how a library should be administered. The Children's Department was open from 2 to 8 p. m., Monday through Thursday, to provide ample time for children to do their home work in the library in the evenings. On Friday and Sunday, it was open from 2 to 6 p. m. and on Saturday from 9 a. m. to 6 p. m. This schedule was based on a record of use. Normally few children came to the library after 6 p. m. on Friday, Saturday or Sunday. Those who had school work to do on these evenings were allowed to study in the adult reading and reference room. Children were always cautioned that they must not disturb the adults who were reading or studying.

To keep the children off the streets, the library staff provided games, puzzles, recordings, and filmstrips in addition to an excellent collection of books and periodicals. The staff felt very strongly a social service responsibility for the children to keep them interested and occupied in the library as many hours as possible. As a result, the Children's Department was a very busy place during most of the opening hours.

One Saturday evening several children were given permission to do their school work in the adult department. They studied quietly for an hour or so and then became noisy. Many adults were reading or browsing, so a staff member spoke to the children and told them they were distracting the adults. The children quieted down for a while and then again became very noisy.

One of the adult readers stormed up to the librarian in charge and demanded in an angry voice that the children be sent out of the library. He explained that he was studying for a civil service exam he was to take on Monday morning and that he had no quiet place in his apartment to study because he, his wife, and four children shared a two-bedroom apartment. Before he had finished talking, another adult man came over, glared at the first man and belligerently announced to the man and to the librarian, "If you send those children out, I will report this to the local community citizens association, to the authorities in the neighborhood, to the press, and to the library board. These children belong here as long as they want to stay because they have no place to go except the street. They should be allowed to stay."

Case 89

WATER, WATER, EVERYWHERE

Five months before the two and one-half million dollar Wing County Library was completed, workmen had to test a roof for waterproofing because it was to be planted as a garden terrace. To make sure that no water would leak through to the room below, they pulled a garden hose up to the roof and flooded it with water. This had to be repeated several times so each night they left the hose coiled up on the ground next to the building. One morning when they came to work at 7 a. m. they found the hose had been placed in front of the large door into the main floor and turned on full force. The water flowed through the weather stripping into the building. Water covered the main floor several inches deep and it also had dripped through the porous cement floor and through heat deflectors into the lower level where water stood one-half inch deep. Using wide brooms, workmen started at once to sweep out the water. By 3 p. m. all the water had been swept from both floors but water was still dripping through the porous concrete floor onto the lower floor. Workmen were sweeping up the last of the puddles by quitting time at 4:30 p. m. and several dehumidifiers were in operation. Extensive damage was done to wooden partitions, new furniture and equipment stored in part of the main floor, and shelving still in crates. Some of the tile on the lower floor had to be taken up and recemented.

Since the library opened six weeks ago, various additional acts of vandalism have occurred. Brass flanges covering electric outlets in floor carpeting were removed, small containers of ketchup (such as those in restaurants serving food to go out) have been thrown on the carpeting and trampled, exhibits have been knocked down, walls in both children's and adult's restrooms have been written on, toilet tissue has been strung in the restroom and wadded on the floor, bicycles were ridden up and down the bookmobile ramp entranceway and rammed against the fiberglass garage door, and leaves (raked into piles by the evening custodian for trash pickup after 6 p. m.) were thrown over the entrance steps.

No provision was made in the library budget for security guards. A custodian worked evenings but his job was to clean closed areas rather than patrol areas open to the public. The librarian suspected the vandalism was being done by a few junior high school age persons.

If you were the librarian, how would you handle this situation?

Case 90

A DETERMINED AGITATOR

What can happen to a public library staff and board of trustees and to their public image, relations, and support when a "dedicated" agitator devotes his total energy to the task of destroying them is exemplified by the experiences in one city. This bizarre case has been well documented in print.[1] Readers should read these titles for details. Briefly, here are some illustrative incidents of his activities. He is an avowed and ardent member of the John Birch Society who was elected in May 1967 to a five-year term on the library's Board of Trustees.

Removed a copy of the Paris Review from the periodical display shelves of a branch library because he complained it was "obscene."

Repeatedly attacked the library staff as "purveyors of smut, promoters of subversive literature, and wasters of taxpayers' money."

Continually harassed the staff by accusing them of lying and questioning their loyalty and competence because of membership in religious and minority groups.

Demanded direct access to all library files at any time of the day or night.

---

[1] Dow, Orrin B. "When Birches Last in the Dooryard Swung." ALA Bulletin, 63:1237-1239, October, 1969.

Gorton v. Dow, 282 N.Y.S. 2d 841 (1967)

"A Dime-Store Paul Revere," Library Journal, 92:3380-3384, October 1, 1967.

Controlling Cases   359

Searched library garbage cans at night for evidence to use against staff and trustees.

Physically assaulted the children's librarian who tried to prevent him from interrupting a children's program for slow readers.

Recruited persons unfriendly to the library to attend trustee meetings.

Criticized, in the news media, the inclusion of publications by the Council on Foreign Relations, the American Foreign Policy Association, the American Civil Liberties Union, the United Nations, UNICEF, and others.

Distributed flyers, pamphlets, and bumper stickers attacking the library's budget and staff.

Financed ads in local newspapers attacking library operations and other trustees.

Encouraged other "cranks" in the community to surface including minute-men death threats to the Library Director and library supporters.

Harassed and intimidated library employees with visits, telephone calls, and tape recordings of conversations with patrons and library programs.

Referred often in speeches and letters to other trustees as a "small, arrogant clique."

* * * * * * *

How can librarians prepare for and control such attacks on their tenure, equity, and professional career?

What are the implications of such activities for library service, staff morale, and intellectual freedom in other communities?

Case 91

TEEN-AGE PROBLEMS

Students created a serious discipline problem in the evenings in the Calla Public Library which served a population of about forty thousand. The library was open every evening until 9:20 p.m. The worst time of the week was Monday evening. Soon after 6 p.m. junior and senior high school students, a few junior college students, and some elementary school children would fill all available chairs in the reading room provided for them. One reading room was reserved for adults who wanted absolute quiet. Students, who seriously wanted to study in a quiet atmosphere, resented not being allowed to enter the adult room.

Some students were so noisy, rude, and generally troublesome that adult patrons complained to the head librarian and to the library board. The three staff members who were regularly on duty that evening admitted that they could not handle the students and asked that an additional staff member be assigned to work--preferably someone used to working with teenagers. The three on duty Monday nights were Betty, Cecil and Margaret. One or more male student pages were also on duty then.

Betty was twenty-one years old and had flunked out of junior college in her freshman year. She was responsible for charging and discharging books and for various jobs assigned to her by Margaret. She resisted and evaded all authority yet sought authority for herself. Her work performance was below average and she never did anything that she could get out of or persuade someone else to do. Many of her characteristics were similar to those of the adolescents with whom she was so harsh.

Cecil was a young man of twenty-five who was responsible for the reference desk. He had been on this library staff since completion of his library school courses three years ago. He was single and had had no experience with teenagers. His philosophy was expressed to another staff member: "I believe it is easier to influence the behavior of wild animals than it is to control the behavior of teenagers in a group. Even individually they are not easily influenced. From what I hear from teachers in the high school, students run wild in the study halls. My own feeling is that the library should not be open at night or that only adults should be allowed to use it."

    Margaret was a hard-driving mother of two well-behaved children aged eight and ten. She worked half-time at the circulation desk during hours when her children were in school and this one night a week. She had a bachelor's degree and hoped some day to take some library science courses. She was efficient, capable, and intelligent in carrying out procedures, methods, and regulations but less effective in the area of human relations. She believed that this discipline situation should be solved by phoning the school principals and the parents to report the behavior of the specific students who were problems.

    All three of these staff members resented having the library turned into a study hall or recreation center. Their technique for handling discipline was to rush up to those who were misbehaving and warn them that they would be thrown out if they were not quiet, sometimes even shouting at them. Then, a few minutes later, to throw them out. This seemed only to aggravate the discipline problem.

    One group of girls particularly irritated the staff. Even seeing them come in was enough to cause acute apprehension. A parent reported this incident to the head librarian of the Calla Public Library: "One night when it was especially busy, this group of girls were extremely giggly and noisy and were flirting with a group of boys near them. Margaret talked to them and they agreed to quiet down. However, they again became noisy and were annoying others so Betty approached them in a rage and screamed at them as though they were criminals and threatened to call the police. The girls went, protesting, humiliated, reluctant, angry." The parent questioned whether Betty had the authority to take such action.

    The Librarian of the Calla Public Library has assigned you to work in the library Monday evening and to supervise the staff as well as to control the discipline. The Librarian asked you to take charge of this potentially explosive situation because you have had considerable experience working with teenagers and with supervising staff. How would you handle the patrons and the staff? Your philosophy is that boys and girls are better off in the library than they would be out in the streets even if this makes work more difficult for the staff. You believe the young people are a responsibility of the community and the library is part of the community it serves. Also, these young people will be voting adults in the community before long.

Case 92

UNEXPENDED BALANCES

(Role playing)

Roles:
    John Oak, Acquisition Librarian
    Tom Cedar, Librarian

Until three years ago Creek University was a state teachers' college and now is emerging into an "instant" university. During the past academic year, the Creek University received several additional grants for library books but with no increase in the staff of the Acquisitions Department. John Oak, Acquisition Librarian, is faced with the colossal task of spending more than $50,000 in the next two months before the end of the fiscal year. According to state law, all unexpended balances at the end of each biennium in all state-supported agencies must revert to the state's general fund. John Oak knew that the Creek University Library collection was very inadequate in many areas and he would be sharply criticized if he let some $50,000 revert. But he and his staff simply could not generate enough orders to spend this amount in a few weeks. He took his problem to the chief librarian, Tom Cedar, who had never faced this problem before. He agreed with Mr. Oak that they needed these funds for building up the collection but he had no suggestions as to how to encumber the funds. He suggested that Mr. Oak phone the acquisition librarians at the other state-supported institutions to see if they had any suggestions.

The next day Mr. Oak reported to Mr. Cedar some ways in which the other acquisition librarians managed to carry over funds. One way was to send out phony orders knowing that they would be cancelled. For instance, one man said he would pick out a jobber or wholesaler which his department had been using and which handled only recently published popular titles. He would talk to the representative of this firm whom he knew and would tell him that he was going to send him an order for expensive sets of out-of-print and rare books. These titles could be taken from the catalogs of reprint or antiquarian dealers. The bibliographic citations would be accurate but he knew that the dealer couldn't furnish them. This order would encumber the funds and, after the end of the fiscal year, the jobber would send a credit memo for the entire order which would successfully carry the funds over to the next fiscal year.

A second person said he would buy one or more block purchases of entire collections at a stated total price if any such collections were on the market.

A third person said he often placed orders with antiquarian dealers for expensive retrospective sets if they were needed for the collection.

Mr. Oak said that the first method did not appear to him to be ethical. As to the second suggestion, he knew of no collections currently on the market which were needed in Creek's collection. Neither did Creek need any sets currently listed in antiquarian dealer catalogs because few faculty members were engaged in research.

Faculty members at Creek needed current materials to support their courses and had "deluged" the Acquisitions Department with requests. In Mr. Oak's opinion, these requests had top priority but they required many weeks of typing to get them out.

Case 93

STAFFING PROBLEMS

March 19___

Dr. Mary Holstein
Dean of Students
Library School
Morgan University

Dear Dr. Holstein:

I need your advice! When I was a library school student last year, you recommended that we stay in our first professional position for at least two years because a shorter length of time would not look good on one's record of experience.

I have been reference librarian here at Bennett Community College for six months and I do not think I can stick it out for two years. In view of the circumstances, which I will describe, would you recommend that I look for another position?

You will remember how I studied all the announcements of vacancies in your office last year. I was hoping to find a reference position in a small academic library where I would get a breadth of experience. The position of reference librarian at Bennett Community College seemed to be just what I was looking for. The college was part of the city school system and had been established two years earlier in a rented building but was to move to its own campus during the summer. The student body totaled about 2,000.

After some correspondence with the librarian, Mrs. Arocet, I paid my own expenses to go for an interview in April. Mrs. Arocet was not overly friendly but she was cordial and polite. I learned that she and a cataloger were the professional staff members and had started the library. The planned move to larger quarters in a new building made it necessary to add a reference librarian to the staff the following fall.

I asked for the job description of the position but found none had been written. Mrs. Arocet was very vague about the responsibilities of the reference librarian, saying only that the person employed would define her position and relationship to the rest of the staff. I was introduced to several clerks and student assistants and was curious to see an organization chart which would indicate division of work. Mrs. Arocet gave me a rather blank stare as though I were inquiring about a very personal matter.

The library occupied a small space and was cramped and crowded for readers, staff, and collection. I was told that two floors in one of the new buildings were assigned to the library and that there would be more than enough space there.

The position was offered to me and I accepted although I had serious misgivings about the organizational structure and Mrs. Arocet's capabilities as a planner, organizer, and supervisor. But the opportunity to step into a newly created position and to develop new services and a new collection challenged me. I reported for work on September 1.

My desk was located near the entrance to the reference area but had no telephone. The only telephones in the library were at the circulation desk and in Mrs. Arocet's office. So, any telephone reference requests had to be relayed to me from one place or the other--which was most inconvenient. I had expected that Mrs. Arocet would give me some orientation to my responsibilities but I received no instructions except that I was told to clip local papers for articles about the college and mount them in a scrapbook. Several empty vertical file cases stood in the reference area and I asked if I could be responsible for developing and maintaining a pamphlet collection. Mrs. Arocet gave me permission to check <u>Vertical File Service</u> and <u>Monthly Catalog of U. S. Government Publications</u> and then give the checked issues to her for her to decide whether or not the items should be ordered. I assumed that building a reference collection would be my responsibility, so I read reviews, checked lists, studied the curricula, and started a card file of titles which I recommended for purchase. Periodically I gave these cards to Mrs. Arocet because she said she wanted to make all final decisions in book selection. These recommendations just "sat" on her desk indefinitely and, as far as I could determine, few were ever ordered--at least they haven't arrived in the reference area.

As you know, I am an outgoing person and like people. I got along very well with both students and faculty members and they seemed so grateful for my help. This seemed to make Mrs. Arocet jealous and I was instructed not to contact faculty members but to give her secretary any bibliographies I compiled so they could be typed. I learned from the secretary that the bibliographies then were sent to the faculty member under Mrs. Arocet's name as though she had done the work.

No faculty members had rank; librarians were considered faculty and were expected to attend faculty meetings. I went to the faculty meetings until Mrs. Arocet forbade my going and said I could not be spared from the library that long.

The turnover in the positions of clerks, typists and student assistants was high. Oftentimes they were fired by Mrs. Arocet with only a few hours or a few days notice. During the six months I have been here, seven clerks or typists have been hired and fired. They are an unhappy, discontented group.

No procedures have been developed for any job. New persons are hired and told only very briefly what they are to do. For example, there is no procedure for checking in periodicals and the files are a "mess." Newspapers are not checked in at all--merely put on the shelves when they arrive. I asked Mrs. Arocet for permission to supervise the clerk who checks in periodicals and to work out procedures. She said that wouldn't be necessary as the clerk knew what she was supposed to do. In the six months I have been here, three different clerks have been assigned to checking in periodicals.

Student assistants spend most of their time when on duty just "goofing off" because they haven't been told what to do by Mrs. Arocet. When I am on duty evenings, I try to direct their work because there is so much to do. But most of them ignore my suggestions because they know I have no authority. I requested that some student assistants be assigned to reference and let me plan and supervise their work but Mrs. Arocet vetoed the idea saying she preferred to supervise all of them.

As you can see, I am not getting professional experience; in fact, what I did as a student assistant in Morgan University Library was more "professional" than what I am currently doing. Mrs. Arocet wants to control everybody, make every decision, and keep all authority.

Do you agree that I should change jobs? I doubt if Mrs. Arocet would write a recommendation for me, but I think the Dean of Faculty would as he realizes how domineering, autocratic, and unreasonable Mrs. Arocet is.

Sincerely,

Norma Swan

Case 94

DUE PROCESS AND TENURE

A disguised, rewritten account of the Bodger case would not have as much impact, drama, and force for librarians and prospective librarians as studying the actual events and problems which have been thoroughly documented in print.[1] This case illustrates several types of control--legal board control, indirect control and pressures, and how the press can pose as judge and jury in trying and condemning one librarian. This "landmark" case in librarianship involved intellectual freedom, tenure, the U. S. Bill of Rights, and due process as they apply to librarians. The published report of the ALA Office for Intellectual Freedom and the evaluation by David Berninghausen demonstrated the care, deliberation, cost, and persistent confrontation required for such an investigation to defend the basic rights of librarians as citizens and as reputable members of a profession.

---

[1] Berninghausen, David. "Defending the Defenders of Intellectual Freedom." American Libraries, 2:18-21, January, 1971.

"Proceedings and Findings Pertaining to a Request for Action Submitted by Mrs. Joan Bodger Under the Program of Action in Support of the Library Bill of Rights." American Libraries, 1:694-704, July-August, 1970.

SELECTED REFERENCES ON ROLE PLAYING

The titles listed here have been selected for their relevance for librarians and for library management education.

Because they did not consider role playing as it is defined in Chapter I, the following areas have not been included: psychological interviewing and counseling, social case work, psychiatry, psychotherapy, psychodramatic methods in group therapy; also excluded were titles which dealt with other aspects of roles: role theory, role conflict, role performance, role perception, role disparity, role expectation, occupational role, and minority role.

Titles available from the Education Resources Information Center (ERIC) and from the National Technical Information Service (NTIS) (formerly called Clearinghouse for Federal Scientific and Technical Information) are identified by the accession numbers assigned by those agencies.

Ablesser, Henry. "Role Reversal in a Group Psychotherapy Session." Group Psychotherapy, 15:321-325, 1962.

Adult Education Association of the United States. How to Use Role Playing and Other Tools for Learning. Chicago, 1955.

Agar, Michael. "Simulated Situation: A Methodological Note." Human Organization, 28:322-329, Winter, 1969.

Allan, Jan. "An Imaginary Community - Hotel." CITE Newsletter, 2:P16-17, January, 1969. (ED 034 755)

Allen, Richard G. "Training For Diversity; Extensive Development for Hospital Administrators." Training and Development Journal, 21:29-36, May, 1967.

Alvin, Robert. "Acting Course For Salesmen." Sales Management, 84:90+, pt. 2, January 15, 1960.

American Institute for Research. Situational Problems for Leadership Training. Final Contract Report, Washington, D. C.: Personnel and Training Branch, Psychological Sciences Division, Office of Naval Research, 1961.
  pt. 1 "Development and Evaluation of Situational Problems" by Theresa B. Trittipoe and Clifford P. Hahn. (AD 254 818)
  pt. 2 "Situational Problems for Role Playing and Case Study Use." (AD 254 819)
  pt. 3 "Review for Petty Officers of Leadership Research." (AD 254 820)
  pt. 4 "Categorized Bibliography of Leadership Research Literature." (AD 255 015)

Amidon, Edmund J., and others. A Fresh Look at Supervision. (ED 011 878)

Anderson, P. "Role Playing in the Library." Library Journal, 93:267, January 16, 1968.

Argyris, Chris. Role-Playing in Action. Ithaca, New York: Cornell University, 1951. (Bulletin No. 16, New York State School of Industrial and Labor Relations, May, 1951)

Arnholter, Ethelwyne. "Social Drama for Retarded Adolescents." Exceptional Children, 21:132-134, January, 1955.

Asmussen, Dennis G., and Cole, Richard A. "Land-Use Alternatives Model for Upper Elementary Environmental Education." Journal of Geography, 69:267-72, May, 1970.

Ault, Leslie H. A Situational Test of Training Effectiveness. New York: Xerox Corporation, 1968. (ED 019 625)

Barnes, Douglas, ed. Drama in the English Classroom. Champaign, Illinois: National Council of Teachers of English, 1968.

Barron, Margaret E. "Role Practice in Interview Training." Sociatry, 1:198-208, June, 1947.

Barry, Charles E. "Executive Responsibility Can be Taught in the Classroom." Personnel Journal, 38:172-174, October, 1959.

Bartolomew, Allen A., and Kelley, Margaret F. "The Personal Emergency Advisory Service." Mental Hygiene, 46:382-392, July, 1962.

Beaird, James H., and Standish, John T. Audio Simulation in Counselor Training. Monmouth: Oregon State System of Higher Education, 1964. (ED 003 221)

Beauchamp, Mary, and others. Building Brotherhood - What Can Elementary Schools Do. New York: National Conference of Christians and Jews, 1967. (ED 001 996)

Berg, Paul Conrad. Language Barriers of the Culturally Different. Paper Presented at the Twelfth Annual Meeting of the College Reading Association, Boston, March 13-15, 1969. (ED 029 767)

Berlin, Irving N. "From Confrontation to Collaboration." American Journal of Orthopsychiatry, 40:473-480, April, 1970.

Bever, Buz, and Kresse, Frederick H. Teacher's Guide to Paddle-To-The-Sea. Boston: Children's Museum, 1967. (ED 034 101)

Blansfield, Michael G. "Consider Value Analysis to Get the Most Out of Role Playing." Personnel Journal, 34:251-254, December, 1955.

--------. "Role Playing: A Suggested Method of Introduction to Training Groups." Journal of the American Society of Training Directors, 11:19-22, 45-46, January-February, 1957.

Bock, Barbara. "Role Playing Reality." Educators Guide to Media and Methods, 5:44-48, March, 1969.

Bogardus, Emory S. "The Use of Sociodrama in Teaching Sociology." Sociometry, 18:542-547, November, 1955.

Bogdanoff, Earl. An Epidemiological Game: Simulation in Public Health. Santa Monica, California: System Development Corporation, 1963.

Bolda, R. A., and Lawshe, C. H. "Evaluation of Role Playing." Personnel Administration, 25:40-42, March, 1962.

Borg, Walter E., and Silvester, J. Arthur. "Playing the Principal's Role." Elementary School Journal, 64:324-331, March, 1964.

Borgatta, E. F. "Analysis of Social Interaction: Actual, Roleplaying, and Projective." Journal of Abnormal and Social Psychology, 51:394-405, 1955.

Bott, Robert. "Role Playing in the Raw." Journal of the American Society of Training Directors, Part I, 13:38-40, December, 1959; Part II, 14:31-32, January, 1960.

Bowers, Patricia, and London, Perry. "Developmental Correlates of Role-Playing Ability." Child Development, 36:499-508, June, 1965.

Bowman, Claude C. "The Psychodramatic Method in Collegiate Instruction." Sociatry, 1:421-430, March, 1948.

Bowman, Garda, W., and Klopf, Gordon J. Training for New Careers and Roles in the American School. New York: Bank Street College of Education, 1969. (ED 028 146)

Boyd, Gertrude A. "Role Playing." Social Education, 21:267-269, October, 1957.

Bricker, A. June. "Pre-Natal Nutrition." Practical Home Economics, 3:63, 106, September, 1967.

Burns, Charles L. "Using Role Playing in Christian Education." International Journal of Religious Education, 32:13-15, 37, January, 1956.

California University, Los Angeles, School of Nursing and Continuing Education in Medicine and Health Sciences. Pilot Project - Mental Health Training for Public Health Nurses and School Nurses. (Final report. USPHS Mental Health Grant No. 8891, 1964-1967).

Los Angeles, California: The University, 1967.

Carter, Margaret I. "Youth Participation in a Community Mental Hygiene Program." Mental Hygiene, 35:581-588, October, 1951.

Carter, Mary Duncan, and Schryver, Louise. "Human Relations, Best Public Relations; Role Playing as a Technique." Library Journal, 83:129-132, January 15, 1958.

Casey, Joseph R. "Dramatize the Poets." English Journal, 41:373-4, September, 1952.

--------. "Learning by Acting: Sociodrama in a Psychology Class." Clearing House, 27:233-235, December, 1952.

Cecile, Robert E. "Proposal for the Teaching of American Foreign Policy in the Secondary School." Social Studies, 59:105-108, March, 1968.

Champagne, David W., and Hines, John F. Use of Simulation as a Teaching Strategy in a Course on Change in the Schools. Pittsburgh: School of Education. University of Pittsburgh, 1970. (ED 038 675)

Chapman, Elwood N. "Role Playing in Cooperative Retail Training Class." Occupations, 29:358-9, February, 1951.

Chesler, Mark A. Dissent and Disruption in Secondary Schools. Detroit: Metropolitan Detroit Bureau of School Studies, Wayne State University, 1969. (ED 033 462)

--------. Teacher Training Designs for Improving Instruction in Interracial Classrooms. Prepared for U.S. Commission on Civil Rights' Conference on Race and Education, Washington, D.C., November 16-18, 1967. Ann Arbor: University of Michigan, Center for Research on Utilization of Scientific Knowledge, 1967. (ED 022 730)

--------, and Fox, Robert. Role-Playing Methods in the Classroom. Chicago: Science Research Associates, 1966. (Teacher Resource Booklets on Classroom Social Relations and Learning).

Chicago Urban League. Jobs Now. Chicago: Young Men's Christian Association and Illinois State Employment Service, 1967. (ED 016 125)

The Cincinnati Police-Juvenile Attitude Project. Cincinnati: University of Cincinnati, 1968. (ED 029 351)

Coleman, James S. Simulation Games and Social Theory. Baltimore: Center for the Study of Social Organization of Schools, Johns Hopkins University, 1968. (ED 017 237)

Coleman, William. "Role-Playing as an Instructional Aid." Journal of Educational Psychology, 39:427-435, November, 1948.

Colton, Winifred J. Leaders Unlimited. New York: Young Men's Christian Association, 1969.

Cooper, Morton, and Southard, Curtis G. "The Mental Health Exchange: An Important Function of a Community Mental Health Center." Community Mental Health Journal, 2:343-346, Winter, 1966.

Corpus Christi University. A Plan for Improving the Education of Disadvantaged Children Through In-Service Training of Administrators, Trainers of Teachers, and of Classroom Teachers. Washington, D.C.: Office of Education, 1969. (ED 032 289)

Corsini, Raymond J. "Role-Playing, Its Use in Industry." Advanced Management, 25:20-23, February, 1960.

--------. Roleplaying in Psychotherapy; A Manual. With the assistance of Samuel Cardone. Chicago: Aldine Publishing Company, 1966. (Modern Applications in Psychology).

--------.; Shaw, Malcolm E.; and Blake, Robert R. Roleplaying in Business and Industry. New York: Free Press of Glencoe, 1961.

Crean, Robert. Some of My Best Friends. New York: National Conference of Christians and Jews, 1966. (ED 002 002)

Crystal, Josie. "Role-Playing in a Troubled Class." Elementary School Journal, 69:169-179, January, 1969.

"Cybernetic Make-Believe Helps Pupils Enjoy Economics Lessons." Nation's Schools, 83:88-89, March, 1969.

Dailey, Charles A. Project Gatekeeper. Washington, D. C.: American University, 1967. (ED 016 137)

Dale, Richard S. "Role Playing." Journal of Business Education, 32:114-116, December, 1956.

Darroch, Russell K., and Steiner, Ivan D. "Role-Playing: An Alternative to Laboratory Research?" Journal of Personality, 38:302-11, June, 1970.

Davison, W. Phillips. "Public Opinion Game." Public Opinion Quarterly, 25:210-220, Summer, 1961.

De Phillips, Frank A.; Berliner, William M.; and Cribbin, James J. "Role-playing Methods." In their Management of Training Programs. Homewood, Illinois: Richard D. Irwin, 1960. pp. 177-180.

Dies, Robert R. "Critical Incident Role Play." Training in Business and Industry, 7:31-33, January, 1970.

Dillman, Everett G. "Role-Playing as a Technique in Police Selection." Public Personnel Review, 24:116-118, April, 1963.

Ditz, Gerhard W. "Role-Playing; To Gain Insight Into Prospects." Printers' Ink, 291:31, September 10, 1965.

Dix, Dorothy M. "Role Playing in Nursing Education in the Psychiatric Field." Group Psychotherapy, 15:231-235, September, 1962.

Donelson, Kenneth, ed. "America's Culturally Different Children." Arizona English Bulletin, 12:5-10, October, 1969.

Dove, Charles James. "Intercultural Training for Foreign Assistance." Unpublished Ph. D. dissertation, University of Michigan, 1968. (University Microfilms, order number 69-12,087)

"Dramatization Devices Teach Ministers Their Work." Life, 44:83-86, May 19, 1958.

Dumas, Wayne. "Role Playing: Effective Technique in the Teaching of History." Clearing House, 44:468-470, April, 1970.

Dworkis, Martin B. "The Playback: A Technique of Management Training." Personnel Administration, 25:50-53, November-December, 1962.

Eachus, Herbert T., and King, Philip H. Acquisition and Retention of Cross-Cultural Interaction Skills Through Self-Confrontation. Akron: Aerospace Medical Research Laboratories, Wright-Patterson Air Force Base, 1966. (Available from NTIS)

Eastridge, Richard R. "A Game of Mice." Audiovisual Instruction, 15:94-95, March, 1970.

Eiger, Norman. Program to Train Trade Unionists and CAA Staff Workers as Community Action Trainers. New Brunswick, N.J.: New Jersey Community Action Training Institute, Rutgers Labor Education Center, 1967. (ED 012 859)

Elbing, Alvar O., Jr. "An Experimental Investigation of the Influence of Reference Group Identification on Role Playing as Applied to Business." Unpublished D.B.A. dissertation, University of Washington, 1962. (Abstracted in Dissertation Abstracts, 24:123-124, July, 1963.)

--------. "The Influence of Prior Attitudes on Role Playing Results." Personnel Psychology, 20:309-320, Autumn, 1967.

Elms, Alan C. "Role Playing, Incentive, and Dissonance." Psychological Bulletin, 68:132-148, August, 1967.

--------. Role Playing, Reward, and Attitude Change. New York: Van Nostrand Reinhold Co., 1969.

Engle, Shirley H. "Decision Making: The Heart of Social Studies Instruction." Social Education, 24:301-4, 306, November, 1960.

Fantine, Mario, and Weinstein, Gerald. Immediate Reinforcement and the Disadvantaged Learner. Syracuse, New York: Syracuse University Urban Teacher Preparation Program, 1963. (ED 001 659)

--------. One Lump - Inductively, the Relevance of the Inductive Approach to Disadvantaged Learning. New York: Ford Foundation and Syracuse, N.Y.: Syracuse University, 1964. (ED 002 276)

Faust, Helen F., and others. Room to Grow. Philadelphia: Division of Pupil Personnel and Counseling, School District of Philadelphia, 1968. (ED 035 003)

Feffer, Melvin. Role-Taking Behavior in the Mentally Retarded. New York: Yeshiva University, 1970. (ED 039 681)

Fessler, Donald R. Citizen Participation in Community Development. Blacksburg: Virginia Polytechnic Institute, 1967. (ED 014 042)

Foley, A. W. "Extemporaneous Role-Playing." Personnel Journal, 34:177-180, October, 1955.

Foster, Robert John, and Danielian, Jack. An Analysis of Human Relations Training and Its Implications for Overseas Performance. Alexandria, Virginia: Defense Documentation Center, 1966. (Hum RRO Div. no. 7, Technical Report 66-15. Contract DA44-188-ARO-2, Department of the Army).

Frank, H. "Role Playing and Tape Recording Add New Dimensions to Class Discussion." Marriage and Family Living, 22:181-183, May, 1960.

Franks, Ted, ed. Role Playing in Industry. New York: Beacon House, 1959. (Sociometry Monograph No. 36, pp. 123-192.)

Frazier, Clifford, and Meyer, Anthony. Discovery in Drama. Paramus, New Jersey: Paulist Press, 1969.

Fulmer, R. M. "Lectures Can Lead to 'Lethal Lethargy.'" Administrative Management, 31:76-78, April, 1970.

Gardner, James E. Safety Training for the Supervisor.

Reading, Massachusetts: Addison-Wesley Publishing Company, Inc., 1969.

Garrett, Pauline Gillette. Interdisciplinary Approach to Preparing Home Economics Leaders for Emerging Programs Serving Disadvantaged Youth and Adults. Columbia: University of Missouri, 1967. (ED 016 834)

Garvey, Dale M. Simulation, Role-Playing and Sociodrama in the Social Studies. Emporia, Kansas: Kansas State Teachers College, 1967. (Emporia State Research Studies, volume 16, no. 2) (ED 028 102)

Giammatteo, Michael C. Suggested Exercises for Training Inner City Teachers. Portland, Oregon: Northwest Regional Educational Laboratory, 1969. (ED 029 840)

Gillette, Thomas L. "Toward a Student-Centered Marriage Course." Marriage and Family Living, 21:155-159, May, 1959.

Glogau, Lillian, and Krause, Edmund. "Do Families Need Rules?" Grade Teacher, 86:62-66, May-June, 1969.

Gode, Winifred. "The Value of Role-Playing in Training Schemes." Industrial Welfare, 42:235-237, July-August, 1960.

Gold, Michael M., and Stedry, Andrew C. "The Effect of Role-Playing in a Problem-Solving Situation." Industrial Management Review, 6:81-95, Fall, 1965.

Goldberg, Gertrude, and others. New Careers: The Social Service Aide. Washington, D.C. New Careers Institute, University Research Corporation, 1968. (ED 025 466)

Goldfarb, Jean, and Riessman, Frank. Role-Playing and the Poor. New York: Mobilization for Youth, Inc., 1963. (ED 001 554)

--------. Role-Playing With Low-Income People. New York: Mobilization for Youth, 1962. (ED 001 073)

Goldfarb, Ronald L. "Rapping With Convicts; Conference in Annapolis, Maryland." New Republic, 161:21-23,

July 19, 1969.

Gordon, Jesse E., and others. Role Modeling and Role Playing in Employability Development Agencies. Ann Arbor: Manpower Science Services, Inc., 1969. (ED 035 030)

Gordon, Richard M. "Interesting Modifications on Role Playing." The Journal of the American Society of Training Directors, 10:25-29, 48-51, September-October, 1956.

Gorvine, Harold. "Teaching History Through Role Playing." History Teacher, 3:7-20, May, 1970.

Graham, Grace. "Sociodrama as a Teaching Technique." Education Digest, 26:44-46, March, 1961.

Graham, Robert G., and Gray, Clifford F. Business Games Handbook. New York: American Management Association, Inc. 1969.

Grambs, Jean Dresden. "Dynamics of Psychodrama in the Teaching Situation." Sociatry, 1:383-399, March, 1948.

--------. Intergroup Education Methods and Materials. Englewood Cliffs, N.J.: Prentice-Hall, 1968.

--------. "A Psychodramatic Approach to the Teaching of Personnel Relations in a Course on Supervision." Unpublished Ph.D. dissertation, Stanford University, 1948.

--------, and Kinney, Lucien B. "Sociodrama in High School Classes." Social Education, 12:341-343, December, 1948.

Greenwald, Anthony G. "The Open-Mindedness of the Counterattitudinal Role Player." Journal of Experimental Social Psychology, 5:375-388, October, 1969.

Greenwood, Louise, and others. Preschool Instructional Program for Non-English Speaking Children. Austin: Texas Education Agency, 1964. (ED 002 514)

Hagan, Margaret, and Kenworthy, Marion. "The Use of

Psychodrama as a Training Device for Professional Groups Working in the Field of Human Relations." Group Psychotherapy, 4:23-27, April-August, 1951.

Hagenau, E. L., and others. Participation Experiences. Olympia: Washington State Board for Vocational Education, 1967. (ED 018 655)

Haines, Donald B. Training for Culture-Contact and Interaction Skills. Ohio: Aeronautical Systems Division, Wright-Patterson Air Force Base, 1964. (AD 611 022)

--------, and Eachus, Herbert T. A Preliminary Study of Acquiring Cross-Cultural Interaction Skills Through Self-Confrontation. Ohio: Aeronautical Systems Division, Wright-Patterson Air Force Base, 1965. (AD 624 120)

Hallowitz, Emanuel, and Riessman, Frank. "The Role of the Indigenous Non-professional in a Community Mental Health Neighborhood Service Center Program." American Journal of Orthopsychiatry, 37:766-778, July, 1967.

Hamilton, John L. "The Psychodrama and Its Implications in Speech Adjustment." Quarterly Journal of Speech, 29:61-67, February, 1943.

Hammer, Richard. "Role Playing: A Judge is Con, a Con is a Judge; Workshop on Crime and Correction, Annapolis, Maryland." New York Times Magazine, p. 56-57+, September 14, 1969.

Hancock, Chester H., and others. Army Management Views. Fort Belvoir, Virginia: Army Management School, 1968. (AD 688 098)

Hannah, Arlene, and Riessman, Frank. Teachers of the Poor. New York: Mobilization for Youth, Inc., 1964. (ED 001 053)

Hart, Howard A. "Using Films for Attitudinal Change; An 'Evaluative' Role Play Technique." Training and Development Journal, 22:32-34, December, 1968.

Harvey, Oswald J. Cognitive Determinants of Role Playing. Alexandria, Virginia: Defense Documentation Center,

1963. (Technical Report, no. 3)

--------, and Kline, James A. Some Situational and Cognitive Determinants of Role Playing: A Replication and an Extension. Boulder, Colorado: University of Colorado, 1965. (Report no. TR-15, Contract NONR-1147). (AD 627 590)

Hendry, Charles E. "Role-Practice Brings the Community Into the Classroom." Sociometry, 7:196-204, May, 1944.

--------; Lippitt, Ronald; and Zander, Alvin. Reality Practice as Educational Method. New York: Beacon House, 1947. (Psychodrama Monograph 9)

Hesseling, P. "A Communication Exercise For Training Managers." Personnel Management, 47:93-98, June, 1965.

Hitchings, W. G., and Ryan, J. M. "Role Playing - An Aid Toward Understanding of Position Management." Personnel Information Bulletin (Veterans Administration) pp. 17, 30, November-December, 1966.

Hughes, Earl F. Role Playing as a Technique for Developing a Scientific Attitude in Elementary Teacher Trainees. Fort Lauderdale, Florida: Nova University, 1970. (ED 040 060)

Hunnicutt, C. W. Urban Education and Cultural Deprivation. Syracuse: University of Syracuse, 1964. (ED 001 435)

Ishiyama, Toaru; Batman, Robert; and Hewitt, Eileen. "Let's Be Patients." American Journal of Nursing, 67:569-571, March, 1967.

Jackson, Ronald E. A. Development of Dormitory Staff as Sub-Professional Counselors. Grand Forks: University of North Dakota, 1966. (ED 012 946)

Jansen, Mathilda J., and Stolurow, Lawrence M. "An Experimental Study of Role Playing." Psychological Monographs: General and Applied, 76:no. 31 whole no. 550, 1962.

Jennings, Helen Hall. "Sociodrama Teaches Democratic

Living." *Journal of Home Economics,* 44:260-262, April, 1952.

Johnson, Dale L., and others. "A Human Relations Training Program for Hospital Personnel." *Journal of Health and Human Behavior,* 7:number 3, Fall, 1966.

Johnson, Mead R., and Rau, Gilbert. "Sociodrama Applied on a Teacher-Training Campus." *Peabody Journal of Education,* 35:93-96, September, 1957.

Johnston, Marjorie C. "How Can Modern Language Teaching Promote International Understanding?" *Bulletin of the National Association of Secondary School Principals,* 40:P70-85, December, 1956.

Joseph, Myron L. "Role Playing in Teaching Economics." *American Economic Review,* 55:556-565, 572-578, May, 1965.

Kane, Peter E. "Role Playing for Educational Use." *Speech Teacher,* 13:320-323, November, 1964.

Kariel, Henry S. "Experiencing Politics." *Social Studies,* 57:287-293, December, 1966.

Kaull, John L. "Combining Role Playing, Case Study and Incident Method for Human Relations Training." *American Society of Training Directors Journal,* 8:16-19, 35, July-August, 1954.

Kautz, William D., and Wald, Max. "Closed-Circuit Television as an Inservice Aid." *Audiovisual Instruction,* 12:1048-1049, December, 1967.

Kay, Lillian W. "Role-Playing as a Teaching Aid." *Sociometry,* 8:263-274, August, 1946.

Kegan, Robert G. "The Seventh-Grader as Artist." *Independent School Bulletin,* 59:26-27, May, 1970.

Keitel, Helmut. *Development and Dissemination of Materials for the Teaching of World History in a Foreign Language (German).* Sussex, Wisconsin: Common School District, 1969. (ED 035 332)

Kellogg, Ernest E. "A Role Playing Case: How To Get The

Most Out of It." Personnel Journal, 33:179-183, October, 1954.

Keltner, John W. "The Task-Model as a Training Instrument." Training Directors Journal, 19:18-21, September, 1965.

Kerckhoff, Alan C. "Early Antecedents of Role-Taking and Role-Playing Ability." Merrill-Palmer Quarterly of Behavior and Development, 15:229-47, July, 1969.

Kessel, J. Bertram. "Role Playing Vitalizes Pre-Camp Training." Journal of Health, Physical Education, Recreation, 28:16, 59, January, 1957.

King, Philip H. A Summary of Research in Training for Advisory Roles in Other Cultures by the Behavioral Sciences Laboratory. Ohio: Wright-Patterson Air Force Base, 1966. (AD 648 517)

Kirk, Beverly Clem. "Preparing Office Clerical Workers Through Role Playing in the Secretarial Block Class." Business Education Forum, 21:8, February, 1967.

Klein, Alan F. How to use Role Playing Effectively. New York: Association Press, 1959.

--------. Role Playing in Leadership Training and Group Problem Solving. New York: Association Press, 1961.

Kuykendall, Pauline J. "Role-Playing Dramas Teach Nutrition." Practical Forecast for Home Economics, 11:F26, October, 1965.

Laird, Dugan, and Hayes, Joseph R. "Better Letters Through Role Playing." Training Directors Journal, 17:31-33, May, 1963.

Lamb, Howard. "Role Playing." Today's Education, 58:67-68, January, 1969.

Lauer, Rachel M. Communicating Sense and Nonsense. 1964. (ED 001 823)

Lawshe, C. H.; Bolda, Robert A.; and Brune, R. L. "Studies in Management Training Evaluation: II. The Effects of Exposures to Role Playing." Journal of Applied Psychology, 43:287-292, October, 1959.

----------.; Brune, R. L.; and Bolda, R. A. "What Supervisors Say About Role Playing." Journal of the American Society of Training Directors, 12:3-7, August, 1958.

Lazier, Gilbert N., and Sutton-Smith, Brian. Assessment of Role Induction and Role Involvement in Creative Drama. New York: Teachers College, Columbia University, 1970. (ED 039 254)

Leemans, Anne F. "Teaching Methods: A Survey." In Education in Public Administration. Edited by Donald C. Stone. Brussels: International Institute of Administrative Sciences, 1963. pp. 29-43.

Levin, Barry Livingston. "The Use of Role Playing as a Method for Producing Self-Perceived Personality Change." Unpublished Ph. D. dissertation, Columbia University, 1959. (Abstracted in Dissertation Abstracts, 20:779, 1959).

Levine, Harold G., and McGuire, Christine. "Role Playing as an Evaluative Technique in a Certifying Examination." Journal of Medical Education, 42:264-265, March, 1967.

Levit, Grace, and Jennings, Helen Hall. "Learning Through Role Playing." Adult Leadership, 2:9-16, October, 1953.

Lorber, Fred, and Schrank, Robert. The Bloomingdale Project. New York: Mobilization for Youth, Inc., 1964. (ED 012 290)

Lowe, Ross E. "Varying the Routine in Consumer Education Classes." Journal of Business Education, 45:Pt. I, 73-75, November, 1969, and Pt. II, 115-116, December, 1969.

Lowy, Louis. Training Manual for Human Service Technicians Working With Older People. Boston: Boston University Bookstores, 1968.

McCalib, Paul T. "Intensifying the Literary Experience

Through Role Playing." English Journal, 57:41-46, January, 1968.

McCoy, E. M. "Role-Playing in Comparing Communism to Democracy." Senior Scholastic, 83:15T, October 18, 1963.

McGehee, William. "Role Playing, Sensitivity Sessions, Where They Fit Into Training." Textile World, 115:60-63, December, 1965.

--------, and Thayer, Paul W. "Methods and Techniques in Industrial Training." In their Training in Business and Industry. New York: John Wiley, 1961. pp. 184-224.

Machaver, William V. "The Leader's Role in Role-Playing." Journal of Industrial Training, 7:6-16, 45-47, January-February, 1953.

McNamara, John Harold. "Role Learning for Police Recruits; Some Problems in the Process of Preparation for the Uncertainties of Police Work." Unpublished Ph. D. dissertation, University of California (Los Angeles), 1967. (University Microfilms, order no. 67-11, 263)

Magers, Joan. "Role-Playing Technique in Teaching a Novel; Great Expectations." English Journal, 57:990-991, October, 1968.

Maier, Norman R. F.; Solem, Allen R.; and Maier, Ayesha. Supervisory and Executive Development; A Manual for Role Playing. New York: John Wiley, 1957.

Malt, Lillian G. "Improving Performance: Role Playing in Management and Supervisory Training." Personnel Management, 47:45-49, March, 1965.

Mann, Carola H. "The Effect of Role Playing on Role Playing Ability and Interpersonal Adequacy." Unpublished Ph. D. dissertation, New York University, 1957.

Mann, John H. "Experimental Evaluations of Role Playing." Psychological Bulletin, 53:227-234, May, 1956.

--------, and Mann, Carola H. "Role Playing Experience

and Interpersonal Adjustment." Journal of Counseling Psychology, 6:148-152, Summer, 1959.

Mason, Ralph. "Education for Business Through Role Playing." Journal of Business Education, 35:338-339, May, 1960.

Mekeel, Susan J. "Ideabag: Characterization - Love It or Leave It." Media and Methods - Exploration in Education, 6:60, April, 1970.

Mescon, Michael H. "Sociodrama and Sociometry: Tools for a Modern Approach to Leadership." Journal of the Academy of Management, 2:21-28, April, 1959.

Meyer, Warren G., and Haines, Peter G. "Role-Playing: A Helpful Technique for Distributive Education Trainees." American Vocational Journal, 31:15-16, March, 1956.

Miller, Arthur, and others. Demonstration Program in Remedial Reading and Language Arts. Boston: Action for Boston Community Development, Inc., 1964. (ED 001 532)

Miller, Harry L. "Small Groups: In the Classroom." In his Teaching and Learning in Adult Education. New York: Macmillan, 1964. pp. 85-122.

Morasky, Robert L. "Case Method Approach to Teaching History." Social Studies, 57:199-204, October, 1966.

Moreno, J. L. "Psychodrama in Action." Group Psychotherapy, 18:87-117, 1965.

Muney, Barbara F., and Deutsch, Morton. "Effects of Role-Reversal During the Discussion of Opposing Viewpoints." Journal of Conflict Resolution, 12:345-356, September, 1968.

Munger, E. S., and others. The Caltech Political Military Exercise. Pasadena: California Institute of Technology, 1967. (ED 027 862)

National Association for Public School Adult Education. Adult Basic Education. Washington, D. C.: National Education Association, 1967.

National Commission on Resources for Youth, Inc. Supervisor's Manual: Youth Tutoring Youth. New York: The Commission, 1968. (ED 034 247)

--------. Youth Tutoring Youth: Supervisor's Manual. New York: The Commission, 1968. (ED 028 992)

National Conference of Christians and Jews. Human Relations and Audiovisual Materials. New York: The Conference, 1960. (ED 002 012)

National Education Association. Unfinished Stories for Use in the Classroom. Washington, D. C.: N. E. A. 1968.

Naylor, Naomi L. Curriculum Development Program for Preschool Teacher Aides. Edwardsville: Southern Illinois University, Center for the Study of Crime, Delinquency, and Correction, 1967. (ED 013 122)

Neil, Hugh. "Humanization: A Learning Experience." Journal of Creative Behavior, 4:77-84, Spring, 1970.

New Careers Development Center. A Design for Large Scale Training of Sub-professionals. New York: Training Laboratory, New Careers Development Center, 1967. (ED 025 465)

"New Dimensions Added to Role-Play." Sales Management, 101, pt. 2:173-175, September 15, 1968.

Newcomer, Donald S. Audio-Visual Techniques in Language Teaching. Burbank, California: Unified School District, 1959. (ED 001 835)

Nichols, Hildred, and Williams, Lois. Learning About Role-Playing for Children and Teachers. Washington, D. C.: Association for Childhood Education International, 1960. (Bulletin 66)

Noar, Gertrude. Prejudice and Discrimination. New York: Anti-Defamation League, B'Nai B'Rith, 1964. (ED 001 984)

Nylen, Donald, and others. Handbook of Staff Development and Human Relations Training, Materials Developed for Use in Africa. Washington, D. C.: National Training Laboratories, 1967.

O'Donnell, Walter G. "Role-Playing as a Practical Training Technique." Personnel, 29:275-289, November, 1952.

Ohlsen, Merle M. Counseling Children in Groups. Springfield: Illinois State Office of the Superintendent of Public Instruction, 1966. (ED 010 890)

Oregon State Department of Education. Teacher's Guide to Self Understanding Through Occupational Exploration. Salem: Division of Community Colleges and Vocational Education, Oregon State Department of Education, 1968. (ED 024 965)

Pagano, Jules. Education in the Peace Corps, Evolving Concepts of Volunteer Training. Brookline, Massachusetts: Center for the Study of Liberal Education for Adults, 1965.

Pantagua, Lita, and Jackson, Vivian C. Role Play in New Careers Training. New York: School of Education, New York University, 1968. (ED 025 820)

Pareek, Udai. "Simulating Reality: Role-Playing." In Lynton, Rolf P. and Pareek, Udai. Training for Development. Homewood, Illinois: Richard D. Irwin and The Dorsey Press, 1967. pp. 148-153.

Passow, A. Harry. Instructional Content for Depressed Urban Centers. (ED 002 531)

Paynter, W. J. "The Lipman Experiment." Personnel Magazine (London), 32:36-37, October, 1966.

Peskin, Dean B. "Role Playing and Role Conflict: A Case Study." Personnel Journal, 45:279-289, May, 1966.

Phelan, Joseph G. "The Principles of Role-Playing." Journal of the American Society of Training Directors, 12:3-13, December, 1958.

--------. "Reducing Worker Dissatisfaction Through Retraining First-Line Foremen, Using 'Intensive Industrial Role Playing'." Journal of the American Society of Training Directors, 16:42-44, 46-49, May, 1962.

Pines, Maya. "The Coming Upheaval in Psychiatry." Harper's Magazine, 23:54-60, October, 1965.

Plati, Thomas J. "Role Playing; An Exciting Way to Explore the Atom." Science Teacher, 37:81-82, February, 1970.

Pointer, Avis Y., and Fishman, Jacob R. New Careers Entry-Level Training For the Human Service Aide. Washington, D.C.: New Careers Institute, University Research Corporation, 1968.

Pollaczek, Penelope Pearl, and Homefield, Harold D. "The Use of Masks as an Adjunct to Role-Playing." Mental Hygiene, 38:299-304, April, 1954.

Porterfield, Austin L. "Some Uses of Literature in Teaching Sociology." Sociology and Social Research, 41:421-426, July, 1957.

Proctor, John H., and Thornton, William M. "Playing Roles." Journal of the American Society of Training Directors, 14:36-39, November, 1960.

Pulliam, C. "Boom Town!" School and Community, 56:30-31, March, 1970.

Ramey, James W. "Teaching Medical Students by Videotape Simulation." Journal of Medical Education, 43:55-59, January, 1968.

Ramirez, Judith Valla. Teacher Behavior in Role-Playing; A Study in Interaction Analysis. Stanford University, California: Stanford Center for Research and Development in Teaching, 1969. (Research and Development Memorandum no. 43). (ED 028 998)

Rayner, C. L. "Is Role-Playing Unrealistic?" The Manager, 29:691-693, September, 1961.

"Reform of Freshman English." School and Society, 96:332-333, October 12, 1968.

Reich, Binda, and Schanck, Susan. Teacher's Guide to Japanese Family. Boston, Massachusetts: Children's Museum, 1966. (ED 034 102)

Reinhart, Miriam Myrtle. "The Effectiveness of Role-Playing-Discussion in Teacher Training." Unpublished Ph.D. dissertation, New York University, 1953. (Abstracted in Dissertation Abstracts, 14:312-313, 1954.)

Riessman, Frank. It's Time For a Moon-Shot in Education. 1965. (ED 013 777)

--------. "The New Community-Based Non-Professional Mental Health Aide." Journal of the Fort Logan Mental Health Center, 3:87-100, Winter, 1965.

--------. "Role Playing and the Lower Socioeconomic Group." Group Psychotherapy, 17:36-48, March, 1964.

--------. The Significance of Socially Disadvantaged Status. 1963. (ED 013 258)

--------. Some Suggestions Concerning the "First Stage" in the Client-Caseworker Relationship. New York: Mobilization for Youth, Inc., 1964. (ED 001 070)

--------. The Strategy of Style. New York: Mobilization for Youth, Inc., 1964. (ED 001 074)

Ritvo, Miriam M. "Practicing Skills in Human Relations Training." Adult Leadership, 11:42-44, June, 1962.

"Role-Play, Short Wave, and Mathetics." Training in Business and Industry, 3:18-21, December, 1966.

"Role Playing." Journal of Industrial Training, 7:no. 1 (whole issue) 3-34, January-February, 1953.

Rosenblatt, Daniel. "Role Therapy in a Mental Hospital." Social Casework, 46:263-270, May, 1965.

Royal Air Force. Technical Training Command. Research Section. Training Methods: An Analysis of Research Findings. (Research Task no. 234). Brampton, England: Royal Air Force, June 1, 1966.

Rudolph, Sister Catherine. "Books and Role Playing." Elementary English, 47:46-48, January, 1970.

Salisbury, Lee H. Role Playing: Rehearsal for Language Change. 1970. (ED 038 634)

Savitzky, Charles, and others. Developing Work-Study Programs for Potential Dropouts. Albany: New York State Education Department, 1965. (ED 001 426)

Sayres, William O. "Role Participation in the Teaching of Anthropology." Journal of General Education, 10:108-113, April, 1957.

Schmidhauser, Harold B. "You, Too, Can Role-Play." Journal of the American Society of Training Directors, 12:2-11, March, 1958.

Schmidt, Wesley I. Group Guidance in the Elementary School. Springfield: Illinois State Office of the Superintendent of Public Instruction, 1966. (ED 010 891)

Schuman, Claire S., and Tarcov, Oscar. To Clarify Our Problems - A Guide to Role-Playing. New York: Anti-Defamation League, B'Nai B'Rith, 1964. (ED 001 976)

Schwarz, Fred R., and others. "Effects of Management Development on Manager Behavior and Subordinate Perception." Training and Development Journal, 22:numbers 4 and 5, April and May, 1968.

Shaftel, Fannie R. "Role Playing: An Approach to Meaningful Social Learning." Social Education, 34:556-559, May, 1970.

--------. Role-Playing For Social Values: Decision-Making in the Social Studies. Englewood Cliffs, New Jersey: Prentice-Hall, 1967.

--------, and Shaftel, George. Building Intelligent Concern for Others Through Role-Playing. New York: National Conference of Christians and Jews, 1967.

--------, and Shaftel, George. People in Action. New York: Holt, Rinehart, and Winston, 1970.

--------, and Shaftel, George. Role Playing the Problem Story. New York: National Conference of Christians and Jews, 1952. (ED 002 004)

--------, and Shaftel, George. Values in Action. New York: Holt, Rinehart, and Winston, 1970.

--------, and Shaftel, George. Words and Action. New York: Holt, Rinehart, and Winston, 1967.

Shapiro, Arthur Hill, and others. "Are You Game to Play Grievances? Special Simulation Kit for School Administrators." Nation's Schools, 83:50-60, June, 1969.

Shaw, Malcolm. "Bad Feedback in Role Play Halts Learning." Sales Management, 99:51, pt. 2, November 20, 1967.

--------. "Role Playing." In Training and Development Handbook (Sponsored by the American Society for Training and Development). Edited by Robert L. Craig and Lester R. Bittel. New York: McGraw-Hill, 1967. pp. 206-224.

--------. "Role Playing - A Procedural Approach." Journal of the American Society of Training Directors, 10:23-24, 54, March-April, 1956.

Sherwin, M. R. "Role Playing in Discussion Groups." Parents Magazine, 34:119-120, May, 1959.

Shipman, G. "Role Playing in the Classroom." Improving College and University Teaching, 12:21-23, Winter, 1964.

Smilansky, Sara. Effects of Sociodramatic Play on Disadvantaged Preschool Children. New York: Wiley, 1968.

Sobel, Morton J. Tip on Books - Resource Materials on Intergroup Relations Education. 1963. (ED 002 567)

Solem, Allen R. "An Experimental Test of Two Theories of Involvement in Role Playing." Journal of Psychology, 44:329-337, October, 1957.

--------. "Human Relations Training; Comparison of Case Study and Role Playing." Personnel Administration, 23:29-37, September, 1960.

Spector, Paul, and Preston, Harley O. Working Effectively Overseas. Washington, D. C.: Prepared for the Peace Corps by the Institute for International Services of the

American Institute for Research, 1961.

Speroff, B. J. "Substitution Method in Role-Playing Grievance Handling." Personnel Journal, 38:9-12, May, 1959.

Stanton, Erwin. "Role Playing in Training Supervisors in Human Relations." Office, 57:77-80, March, 1963.

Stanton, Howard; Kurt, W. Back; and Litwak, Eugene. "Role-Playing in Survey Research." American Journal of Sociology, 62:172-176, September, 1956.

Staton, Thomas F. "The Role-Playing Method." In his How to Instruct Successfully: Modern Teaching Methods in Adult Education. New York: McGraw-Hill, 1960, pp. 124-156.

Steed, Stanley M. Teaching Dictionary Skills Through a Slang Dictionary. 1968. (ED 023 557)

Stein, Calvert. "Psychodrama for Nurses in a General Hospital." Group Psychotherapy, 14:90-94, 1961.

Stewart, Edward C., and others. Simulating Intercultural Communication Through Role-Playing. Alexandria, Virginia: Human Resources Research Organization, 1969. (ED 041 226)

Stieglitz, Sarah Thorwald. "Review by the Court." English Journal, 39:452-454, October, 1950.

Strauss, Jack, and Dufour, Richard. "Discovering Who I Am: A Humanities Course for Sixth Grade Students." Elementary English, 47:85-120, January, 1970.

Stroh, Thomas Frederick. The Uses of Video Tape in Training and Development. New York: American Management Association, 1969.

--------. "Video Tape Feedback in the Development of Listening Skills by Industrial Salesmen." Unpublished Ed. D. dissertation, Columbia University, 1968. (University Microfilms Order no. 69-15,170)

Taylor, A. L. "A Sitting-Thing." CITE Newsletter, 2:P25-27, January, 1969. (ED 030 658)

Taylor, John F. "Role Playing With Borderline and Mildly Retarded Adolescents in an Institutional Setting." Exceptional Children, 36:206-208, November, 1969.

Terrace, N. "Acting Your Way to Better Health." Independent Woman, 32:360-362, 382, October, 1953.

Thomas, William C. "Preparing For Arbitration: A Do-It-Yourself Technique." Personnel, 44:47-50, November-December, 1967.

Trout, Lawana. "Teaching the Protest Movement." The Florida FL Reporter, 7:142-144, 166, Spring-Summer, 1969.

Truax, Charles B. "The Training of Nonprofessional Personnel in Therapeutic Interpersonal Relationships." American Journal of Public Health, 57:1778-1791, October, 1967.

Tupes, Ernest C.; Carp, A.; and Bert, Walter R. "Performance in Role-Playing Situations as Related to Leadership and Personality Measures." Sociometry, 21:165-179, September, 1958.

U. S. Civil Service Commission. Youth Opportunity Campaign - Summer 1966. Washington, D. C.: Civil Service Commission, 1967. (ED 013 961)

U. S. National Park Service. Teaching Methods Manual; rev. ed. Washington, D. C.: U. S. Department of Interior, 1967. (In-Service Training Series) "Role Playing," pp. 84-85.

Venditti, Frederick P. Teaching in Valleybrook Elementary School. Knoxville: University of Tennessee, College of Education, 1968. (ED 032 240)

Walters, R. G., and Lansner, L. A. "Participating in Sociodrama." Business Education Yearbook, 10:92-111, 1953.

Weinstein, Eugene A., and others. "Interpersonal Strategies Under Conditions of Gain or Loss." Journal of Personality, 36:616-634, December, 1968.

--------; Wiley, Mary Glenn; and DeVaughn, William. "Role

and Interpersonal Style as Components of Social Interaction." Social Forces, 45:210-216, December, 1966.

Westerville, Evelyn C. "Role Playing." Marriage and Family Living, 20:78-80, February, 1958.

Wieringa, C. F. "Role-Playing." Management International Review, 8:101-113, Issue no. 1, 1968.

Williamson, Sharon, and Green, Ruth. Teacher's Guide to Medieval People. Boston: Children's Museum, 1966. (ED 034 096)

Wilson, Laval S. "I Didn't Know it Felt That Way." PTA Magazine, 64:20-22, June, 1970.

Wohlking, Wallace. "Guide to Writing Role Playing Cases." Training and Development Journal, 20:2-6, November, 1966.

--------. "Teaching Effectiveness and Feedback Mechanism." Training and Development Journal, 21:2-10, June, 1967.

Wood, Mildred Weigley. "Use of Role Playing in Teaching Family Relationships." Practical Home Economics, 31:12-13, November, 1952.

Wright, William M. "Those Educational Methods . . . !" Association of American Colleges Bulletin, 42:562-567, December, 1956.

Yeoman, Marjorie A. A Study of the Introduction of Role Playing Into the Leadership Program of a Naval Shore Activity. Monterey, California: U. S. Naval Postgraduate School, 1965.

Zeleny, Leslie D., and Gross, Richard E. "Dyadic Role-Playing of Controversial Issues." Social Education, 24:354-358+, December, 1960.

Zimbardo, Philip G. "The Effect of Effort and Improvisation on Self-Persuasion Produced by Role-Playing." Journal of Experimental Social Psychology, 1:103-120, 1965.

Zinn, Howard. Education Without Schools in the South. 1965. (ED 002 081)

Title Index to Cases

Case	Case No.
Access To Legal Materials	86
The Ad Hoc Faculty Committee	75
The Anonymous Caller	84
Anxiety	25
Attempted Bribery	10
An Attempted Theft	87
"Bandaid" Work	42
A "Bargain"	53
Busy, Busy, Busy	62
Caught in the Middle	61
Chronic Insomnia	30
A Circulation Department	65
A Circulation Librarian	19
Clearance	54
The Clique	17
Community Control	81
Community Relations	74
A Company Union	60
Confrontation	88
Conversion to a Public Library District	76
Creation of a Supervisor	27
A Determined Agitator	90
The Dirty Long-Johns	6
Dress Policies	14
Due Process and Tenure	94
An Embarrassing Policy Decision	67
Faculty Reading Lists	59
Federally Subsidized Employees	63
A Fire	40
Gift Appraisals	55
Grant Funds	80
Harassment at Stonechat Branch	85
Hemlock High Resource Center	71
Homicide	47
I Am a Librarian Not a Psychiatrist	39
The Immature Reference Librarian	11

395

Individual Recognition	56
An Information Center	9
Insubordination and Arrest	35
Irrational Behavior	32
Job Interview: Alvin	2
Job Interview: Elizabeth	3
Job Interview: Floyd	4
Laissez Faire	70
A Leave of Absence	36
A Library Office Secretary	69
Marijuana	29
Maternity Leave	38
A Medical School Library	68
Mission of Research Libraries	57
Momentum	50
Moonlighting	45
Murder	34
Music	24
Nepotism: Fern	15
Nepotism: Frank	16
A New Junior College	41
A Newspaper Room Clerk	8
On Parole	43
Out to Lunch	51
Participative Management	72
Personality Disorder	37
A Pilferage Racket	83
Political Posters	28
Privileged Information	18
Promotion	20
Questionable Practices	82
A Receptionist	23
School District Unification	31
School Reorganization	52
Selection Policy	49
"The Shelf"	46
Sibilance	22
Slander and Lies	13
A Sordid Scheme	73
Staff Concern	44
Staffing Problems	93
Steam in the Stacks	64
Steve and the "Checklist"	48
Stinky	12
Student Periodicals	58
Teen Age Problems	91
A Ten-Point Veteran	78

Title Index

Termination	33
Transfer	21
The "Troubleshooter" in Serials	26
The Tupola Family	79
An Uncertified School Librarian	5
Unexpended Balances	92
The Unwanted Gift	77
Volunteers	66
Water, Water, Everywhere	89
Who Should Hire Librarians?	1
Winter University Personnel	7

Subject Index to Cases

	Case No.
Absenteeism	
Personality Disorder	37
Academic Freedom	
Privileged Information	18
Academic Status	
A Leave of Absence	36
A Medical School Library	68
Winter University Personnel	7
Access to Materials	
Access to Legal Materials	86
Mission of Research Libraries	57
Anxiety	
Anxiety	25
Appraisals	
Gift Appraisals	55
Arrest	
Marijuana	29
Attitudes	
Confrontation	88
A Newspaper Room Clerk	8
Termination	33
Authority Relationships	
Volunteers	66
Behavior	
Anxiety	25
Chronic Insomnia	30
The Dirty Long-Johns	6
I Am a Librarian Not a Psychiatrist	39
Insubordination and Arrest	35
Irrational Behavior	32
Job Interview: Elizabeth	3
Job Interview: Floyd	4
A Newspaper Room Clerk	8
Personality Disorder	37
A Receptionist	23
Sibilance	22
Termination	33

Subject Index

Board of Trustees
    A Determined Agitator   90
    Selection Policy   49
    A Sordid Scheme   73
Bribery
    Attempted Bribery   10
Budget
    The Ad Hoc Faculty Committee   75
    A Determined Agitator   90
Building Problems
    Creation of a Supervisor   27
    A Fire   40
    Hemlock High Resource Center   71
    Music   24
    Steam in the Stacks   64
    Water, Water, Everywhere   89
Building Program
    A New Junior College   41
Censorship
    Clearance   54
    A Determined Agitator   90
    Mission of Research Libraries   57
    Selection Policy   49
    "The Shelf"   46
Certification
    An Uncertified School Librarian   5
Chain of Command
    An Embarrassing Policy Decision   67
    Insubordination and Arrest   35
    Irrational Behavior   32
    A Library Office Secretary   69
    Participative Management   72
    Volunteers   66
Change
    The Ad Hoc Faculty Committee   75
    Community Relations   74
    A Company Union   60
    A Medical School Library   68
    Sibilance   22
    Staff Concern   44
    The "Troubleshooter" in Serials   26
Children's Services
    Confrontation   88
Civil Service
    A Newspaper Room Clerk   8
    A Ten-Point Veteran   78

Committees
    Staff Concern   44
Communication
    An Embarrassing Policy Decision   67
    A Leave of Absence   36
Community Action Program
    Federally Subsidized Employees   63
Conduct
    The Immature Reference Librarian   11
Conflict
    Music   24
Conflict of Interest
    Attempted Bribery   10
    Moonlighting   45
Control, External
    Federally Subsidized Employees   63
Control, Indirect
    Dress Policies   14
    The Unwanted Gift   77
    Who Should Hire Librarians?   1
Control, Legal
    A Company Union   60
    Conversion to a Public Library District   76
Controlling   73-94
Damage Suit
    Steam in the Stacks   64
Dealers
    A "Bargain"   53
Decision Making
    A Fire   40
Delegation
    Busy, Busy, Busy   62
    Creation of a Supervisor   27
    Participative Management   72
Disciplinary Action
    Chronic Insomnia   30
    The Immature Reference Librarian   11
    Insubordination and Arrest   35
    Irrational Behavior   32
    Marijuana   29
    Murder   34
    A Newspaper Room Clerk   8
    School District Unification   31
Discrimination
    Moonlighting   45
Dishonesty
    A Sordid Scheme   73

Subject Index

Disloyalty
    Slander and Lies — 13
Division of Work
    Caught in the Middle — 61
    Creation of a Supervisor — 27
    Laissez Faire — 70
Drugs
    Marijuana — 29
Due Process
    Due Process and Tenure — 94
Economic Opportunity Act
    Federally Subsidized Employees — 63
Employees - Rights
    Political Posters — 28
Employment Policy
    Promotion — 20
    Transfer — 21
    Winter University Personnel — 7
ESEA Project
    An Uncertified School Librarian — 5
Ethics, Professional
    Attempted Bribery — 10
    A Circulation Librarian — 19
    The Clique — 17
    Faculty Reading Lists — 59
    Gift Appraisals — 55
    The Immature Reference Librarian — 11
    Individual Recognition — 56
    A Leave of Absence — 36
    Out to Lunch — 51
    Privileged Information — 18
    Questionable Practices — 82
    Slander and Lies — 13
    A Sordid Scheme — 73
    Staffing Problems — 93
    Unexpended Balances — 92
Exchanges
    A "Bargain" — 53
Faculty Committee
    The Ad Hoc Faculty Committee — 75
Faculty Council
    "The Shelf" — 46
Faculty Intervention
    The Unwanted Gift — 77
Federal Funds
    An Uncertified School Librarian — 5

Fines
    Steve and the "Checklist"   48
Floor Plans
    Hemlock High Resource Center   71
Fourteenth Amendment
    Access to Legal Materials   86
Fraud
    A "Bargain"   53
Fund Accounting
    Questionable Practices   82
    Unexpended Balances   92
Funding
    Grant Funds   80
Gifts
    Attempted Bribery   10
    Gift Appraisals   55
    Out to Lunch   51
    The Unwanted Gift   77
Grapevine
    Caught in the Middle   61
Grooming
    Dress Policies   14
    Stinky   12
Health
    Chronic Insomnia   30
Incompetence
    Caught in the Middle   61
    A Circulation Librarian   19
    Nepotism: Fern   15
    Nepotism: Frank   16
Insecurity
    Anxiety   25
Insubordination
    Insubordination and Arrest   35
    School District Unification   31
    Sibilance   22
Intellectual Freedom
    A Determined Agitator   90
    Due Process and Tenure   94
Interviews
    The Dirty Long-Johns   6
    Job Interview: Alvin   2
    Job Interview: Elizabeth   3
    Job Interview: Floyd   4
    Promotion   20
    Termination   33
    Transfer   21

Subject Index

Invasion of Privacy
    Privileged Information   18
Job Description
    A Leave of Absence   36
    Who Should Hire Librarians?   1
Leadership
    Creation of a Supervisor   27
Leave of Absence
    A Leave of Absence   36
    Maternity Leave   38
Library Bill of Rights
    Due Process and Tenure   94
Line and Staff Relationships
    The Unwanted Gift   77
    Volunteers   66
LSCA
    Access to Legal Materials   86
Mental Illness
    The Dirty Long-Johns   6
    I Am a Librarian Not a Psychiatrist   39
    Murder   34
    Personality Disorder   37
    School District Unification   31
    A Ten-Point Veteran   78
Misrepresentation
    Slander and Lies   13
Mission
    Access to Legal Materials   86
    Mission of Research Libraries   57
Morale
    Chronic Insomnia   30
    The Clique   17
    Political Posters   28
    The "Troubleshooter" in Serials   26
Motivation
    Federally Subsidized Employees   63
    Momentum   50
    Music   24
Nepotism
    Nepotism: Fern   15
    Nepotism: Frank   16
    The Tupola Family   79
Organizational Structure
    Participative Management   72
Organizing   60-72
Orientation
    Creation of a Supervisor   27

Participative Management
- Participative Management ... 72
- Staff Concern ... 44

Patron Control
- Harassment at Stonechat Branch ... 85
- Steve and the "Checklist" ... 48
- Teen Age Problems ... 91

Performance
- Anxiety ... 25
- A Library Office Secretary ... 69
- Sibilance ... 22

Personal Appearance
- Dress Policies ... 14

Personal Hygiene
- Stinky ... 12

Personality
- A Library Office Secretary ... 69
- A Receptionist ... 23

Personnel Code
- Clearance ... 54
- Marijuana ... 29
- Maternity Leave ... 38
- Moonlighting ... 45
- Out to Lunch ... 51
- Political Posters ... 28

Personnel Policies
- The Immature Reference Librarian ... 11
- A Leave of Absence ... 36
- Nepotism: Fern ... 15
- Who Should Hire Librarians? ... 1
- Winter University Personnel ... 7

Personnel Problems ... 1-39
Planning ... 40-59
Policies
- A "Bargain" ... 53
- Clearance ... 54
- An Embarrassing Policy Decision ... 67
- Faculty Reading Lists ... 59
- Gift Appraisals ... 55
- Grant Funds ... 80
- Individual Recognition ... 56
- Mission of Research Libraries ... 57
- Moonlighting ... 45
- On Parole ... 43
- Out to Lunch ... 51
- Selection Policy ... 49
- Staff Concern ... 44

Subject Index

Policies (cont'd.)
    Winter University Personnel   7
Political Action
    An Embarrassing Policy Decision   67
    Political Posters   28
Political Interference
    The Tupola Family   79
Political Pressures
    Gift Appraisals   55
Position Classification
    Who Should Hire Librarians?   1
Pressure Groups
    Community Relations   74
"Privileged" Information
    Privileged Information   18
Probation
    Irrational Behavior   32
    A Ten-Point Veteran   78
Procedures
    A "Bargain"   53
    Faculty Reading Lists   59
    Homicide   47
    Laissez Faire   70
    Momentum   50
Promotion
    Irrational Behavior   32
    A Library Office Secretary   69
    Promotion   20
Promotion Policies
    The Dirty Long-Johns   6
Public Relations
    Community Relations   74
    Confrontation   88
    A Determined Agitator   90
    Water, Water, Everywhere   89
Public Service
    A Newspaper Room Clerk   8
Reassignment
    A Library Office Secretary   69
Recruiting
    The Dirty Long-Johns   6
    Job Interview: Floyd   4
Reorganization
    "Bandaid" Work   42
    Caught in the Middle   61
    A Company Union   60
    A Fire   40

Reorganization (cont'd.)
   Hemlock High Resource Center   71
   Laissez Faire   70
Reprint Publishers
   Questionable Practices   82
Resignation
   An Information Center   9
   A Leave of Absence   36
Rest Breaks
   The "Troubleshooter" in Serials   26
Rules and Regulations
   Access to Legal Materials   86
   Clearance   54
   Homicide   47
Salaries
   Creation of a Supervisor   27
Security
   The Anonymous Caller   84
   An Attempted Theft   87
   Water, Water, Everywhere   89
Selection of Employees
   The Clique   17
   The Dirty Long-Johns   6
   Job Interview: Alvin   2
   Job Interview: Elizabeth   3
   Job Interview: Floyd   4
   A Medical School Library   68
   On Parole   43
   The Tupola Family   79
   An Uncertified School Librarian   5
   Who Should Hire Librarians?   1
Selection of Materials
   "Bandaid" Work   42
   A New Junior College   41
   Selection Policy   49
   Student Periodicals   58
Service to Industry
   Faculty Reading Lists   59
Staff Associations
   A Company Union   60
Staff Harassment
   A Determined Agitator   90
   Harassment at Stonechat Branch   85
Staff Morale
   Individual Recognition   56
   Momentum   50
   Music   24

Subject Index

Staff Morale (cont'd.)
 Participative Management   72
 Staffing Problems   93
 A Ten-Point Veteran   78
 Winter University Personnel   7
Staff Orientation
 Homicide   47
 Teen Age Problems   91
Staffing
 I Am a Librarian Not a Psychiatrist   39
 Laissez Faire   70
 A New Junior College   41
 On Parole   43
 Promotion   20
 School Reorganization   52
 Transfer   21
Status
 An Information Center   9
Strategy
 "Bandaid" Work   42
 Grant Funds   80
Supervision
 Busy, Busy, Busy   62
 Caught in the Middle   61
 Creation of a Supervisor   27
 The Dirty Long-Johns   6
 Insubordination and Arrest   35
 Laissez Faire   70
 A Medical School Library   68
 School District Unification   31
 Staffing Problems   93
 The "Troubleshooter" in Serials   26
Tardiness
 Chronic Insomnia   30
 Personality Disorder   37
Tenure
 Due Process and Tenure   94
 Irrational Behavior   32
 A Medical School Library   68
Termination
 The Dirty Long-Johns   6
 Slander and Lies   13
 Termination   33
Thefts
 An Attempted Theft   87
 Harassment at Stonechat Branch   85
 A Pilferage Racket   83

Thefts (cont'd.)
    A Sordid Scheme   73
Training Programs
    Federally Subsidized Employees   63
Transfer
    Transfer   21
Turnover
    A Circulation Librarian   19
    Staffing Problems   93
Unions
    Steam in the Stacks   64
U. S. Bill of Rights
    Due Process and Tenure   94
Unity of Command
    Federally Subsidized Employees   63
Vandalism
    Water, Water, Everywhere   89
Veterans Preference Act of 1944
    A Ten-Point Veteran   78
Volunteers
    Volunteers   66
Work Groups
    The "Troubleshooter" in Serials   26

INDEX TO CHAPTER I

Accident prevention: training programs, 59
Acculturation for leadership, 22
Acting vs. role playing, 25
Action development, 26
Administrator's role, 22
Adult basic education: teaching methods, 54
Adult leadership, 77
Adult meetings, 77-79
African nations: leadership training, 64
Agency for International Development: training program, 67
Aging and youth problems, 77
Agricultural economy: teaching, 49
Alter-ego, 72
American foreign policy: teaching, 47
American values, 67
Anonymity, 97
Anthropology: teaching, 50
Arbitration hearing, 79
Arithmetic: role playing situations, 43
Art education: dramatic situations, 53
Attitude change techniques, 34, 36
Attitudes: Peace Corps, 67
Attitudes of administrators, 23
Attitudinal reaction to forced compliance, 35
Audiolingual methods, 67
Audiotape recordings: training methods, 72
Audiotape replay, 81

Bartering: role playing transactions, 44
Behavioral adjustments, 29
Behavioral indices of social adequacy, 36
Behavioral science: teaching in medical school, 54
Bibliographical citations, 21
Black Muslims, 42
Black power: teaching children, 42
Business courses, high school: teaching, 47
Buzz groups: and feedback, 90

Caltech Political Military Exercise, 51
Camp counselors: pre-camp training, 73
Capitalism: teaching, 49
Car theft: role reversal, 88
Career guidance program for children, 46
Career ladders, 73
Case content, 34
Case focus, 96
Case method, 32; in area training, 67
Case preparation, 91-98
Case research, 95-96
Case studies: simulated reality, 27; types, 32; training employers of disadvantaged, 72
Case studies and role playing: similarities, 32; differences, 33
Case writing, 91-98
Cases: format and structure, 92-95; as teaching instruments, 97
Character impersonation, 49
Characters in literature, 50
Charades, 86
Chemistry: teaching, 50
Chicago Urban League: job readiness program, 71
Child-rearing practices: in Israel, 41
Child study, 77
Children, non-English speaking: teaching, 43
Citizenship: teaching concepts to children, 38
Civil Rights: teaching children, 42
Civil Service Commission: training programs for non-college youth, 71
Civil service positions, 74
Clarity: in role playing problems, 85
Classroom control problems, 66
Classroom disturbances in high school, 66
Classroom instruction: examples of role playing, 37-55
Climate: for role playing, 82
Closed-circuit television, 54; teaching medical students, 59
Communication: research methodology, 81
Communication exercise, 61
Community action training programs, 75
Community development, 77
Community psychiatry: altered service patterns, 58
Compensatory education: for disadvantaged, 40
Conception of self, 35
Concepts of preschool children: in Israel, 41
Conflict: training for school administrators, 79; categories in cases, 97

Conflicts, 28
Confrontation: educators and, 64
Consumer economics: teaching, 47
Continuing education, 56
Cooperative retail training: teaching, 47
Correction system, 78
Counseling: for job interviews, 71
Counselors, 72-73
Counterattitudinal role player, 35
Creative role playing, 84, 91
Criminology: use of role playing, 77-78
Cross cultural skills, 68
Cross cultural studies, 67
Cultural anthropology: research methodology, 80
Cultural assumptions and values, 66
Cultural awareness: training for, 67
Cultural definition of illness, 54
Cultural differences and similarities, 89
Culturally deprived children: and role playing, 39-41; teaching English, 42

Decision making: as a learning method, 28
Decision-making process: and role playing, 25; experience in teaching, 45
Department of Labor Manpower Administration: job counseling, 70
Department store buyers: training, 64
Desegregated classrooms: teacher training, 65
Developmental problems, 37
Dilemmas, 37, 38, 43
Director's notes, 93
Disadvantaged adults, 68
Disadvantaged children: teaching of, 39-41, 65
Disadvantaged learner: and teacher preparation, 53
Disadvantaged persons: job counseling, 70; employment readiness program, 71; in human and public service, 73
Discrimination: teaching about, 46
Disguise, 97
Dissonance and attitude change, 36
Distributive education: teaching methods, 47, 50
Drug addiction, 80
Drug-related behavior, 80
Dyads, 89
Dying and death, 54

Economics: teaching methods, 51

Education: utilization of role playing in teaching, 53
Educators: training programs, 64-66
Elementary grades: utilization of role playing, 37-47
Emotions: teaching about, 58
Employability development agencies, 70
Employability of disadvantaged persons, 70
Employee screening procedures, 69
Employers: interaction training, 72
Employment agencies serving disadvantaged persons, 70
Enactments, 37, 49, 81, 86-89
English as a standard dialect, 42
English composition: teaching freshmen, 51
English literature: teaching methods, 49
Environmental education: teaching method, 44
Epidemic: hypothetical, 58
Episcopal Church: laboratories, 72
Eskimo children: language instruction, 42
Ethical behavior: teaching through role playing, 38
Ethnic relations: teaching, 50
Evaluation of personnel, 23
Executive development programs, 30, 56, 59, 85
Executive self-development, 94
Experience practice, 26

Failure in school: underprivileged children, 40
Fair Packaging Act: skit about, 47
Family life problems, 77
Family living situations: role playing, 44
Family relationships: teaching, 47
Federal Meat Inspection Act: skit about, 47
Feedback, 31, 34, 90-91
Fictitious names, 97
Filmstrips: value clarification, 38
Flanders' Interaction Analysis, 65
Focus: problem stories, 93
Foreign languages: teaching, 47; Peace Corps training methods, 67
Freedom schools: use of role playing, 40
French medieval manor: activity project, 44

Gaming, 27, 52
Geography: teaching, 49
Greater Boston project: work with older adults, 75
Grievance procedures, 78-79
Group-centered learning method, 29
Group conference technique: training supervisors, 64
Group cooperation: fostered through simulation, 28

Group counseling: classroom techniques, 45
Group dynamics, 52
Group guidance, 45
Group preparation and instruction, 85-86
Group responsibility: teaching concepts to children, 38

Harvestore unit: training salesmen, 57
Hawaiian children: language instruction, 42
Head Start: training, 75
Health science interviewing, 59
Health sciences: utilization of role playing, 58-59
Higher education: examples of role playing, 50-55
History: teaching through role playing, 48
Home economics: teaching, 50
Home economics leaders: training, 60
Honesty: teaching of, 43
Hospital administrators: training methods, 58
Hospital social workers: training of, 58
Human behavior, 23, 29
Human ecology: teaching, 54
Human interaction, 25, 45
Human relations learning, 28, 30
Human relations skills, 22, 31
Human relations teaching: in elementary grades, 37
Human relations training, 56, 64, 66, 94
Human service aides: training, 73
Human service technicians working with older adults, 75
Humanities course: and group behavior, 43

Impersonations of historical characters, 48
Improvisational drama, 36
In-basket exercises, 27, 32
In-service training, 56, 73
Indigenous nonprofessional aides, 58
Indigenous persons overseas, 68
Individual integrity: teaching concepts to children, 38
Initiative: development through simulation, 28
Inner city teachers, 65
Institutes, 56
Instructional strategies, 36
Insurance salesmen: training, 56
Integrity: teaching, 43
Interaction analysis, 36
Intercultural communication, 67
Intercultural interaction, 67
Intercultural training program, 67
Intergroup education, 46

Intergroup relations: problems for discussion, 72
Internalization, 54
International crises: teaching, 52
Internship programs, 22, 28
Interpersonal relations, 29, 39, 46
Interpersonal skills: essential for librarians, 21
Interpersonal stress, 89
Interpretative reading, 43
Interracial classrooms, 65
Interviewers: training of, 69
Interviews: conducting, 68; employment, 71
Invisible consultants, 72
Israeli preschoolers, 40

Japanese families: studied through role playing, 44
Japanese history: teaching, 44
Job counselors, 70
Job interviewing, 47, 68, 70, 72
Job skills, 74
Junior leader training programs: Young Men's Christian Association, 72

Labor-management disputes, 78-79
Labor relations counselors: training, 79
Laboratory methods, 26, 32
Land-use alternatives model, 44
Language arts: utilization of role playing, 41-43
Latin America: case study, 68
Law and law enforcement: teaching, 47
Leader: in role playing, 82, 84
Leadership literature, 60
Leadership rating, 91
Leadership research, 60
Leadership training, 60, 64
Learning methods, 28
Learning reinforcements, 29
Learning styles of low-income populations, 74
Learning-on-the-job, 23
Learning through doing, 26
Length of cases, 33
Letter-writing program: United Airlines, 63
Library school classes, 85
Library science: use of role playing, 50
Library use: and role playing, 40
Library workshops, 85
Listening skills, 81

Maladjusted children in schools: and group guidance, 45
Management education: value of role playing in, 21; and the decision process, 25; courses, 30
Management games, 61, 62
Manpower Administration Bureau of Work-Training Programs, 74
Marriage and the family: teaching, 51
Marriage education: enactment, 87
Masks, 43, 65, 88-89
Medical education: adaptations of role playing, 54, 55
Medical insurance firm: management development, 60
Medieval history: activity project, 44
Mental health education: training programs, 58
Mental health professionals, 64
Mental hospital aides, 59
Mental hospitals: patient social interaction, 58
Methodology: of role playing, 38
Mexican-American children: teaching, 65
Mime, 43, 86
Ministers: role playing, 72
Minority groups: language teaching, 42
Minority housing, 77
Mirror analysis, 54
Mirror image, 67
Mobilization for Youth: on-the-job-training program, 71
Models: construction, 62
Multiple group role playing, 63, 89, 93

National Commission on Resources for Youth: tutorial programs, 76
National Institute of Mental Health: study of drug addiction, 81
Neighborhood Youth Corps, 76
New Careers Development Center, 74
New careers training, 73, 74, 75
New York City Police Department: recruit training, 76
Nurses: training, 58
Nursing: teaching, 50
Nutrition: teaching, 47

Observation guides, 91
Observers: preparation, 86, 93
Occupational guidance: teaching, 50
On-the-job training, 73
Open-ended stories, 46
Opinion change, 34, 35
Oral expression: value of simulation, 28

Overseas assignments: training for, 66-68
Overseas problems, 67

Pair groups, 89
Paired interviews, 64
Pantomiming, 43, 86
Paraprofessional personnel: training for schools, 76
Parishioners: problems, 72
Participant involvement, 34
Participation: supervisory training sessions, 62
Participative leadership style, 29
Participative learning experiences, 51
Patient diagnostic interview, 55
Patient management conference, 55
Patient social interaction: in mental hospitals, 58
Patterned language drill, 42
Peace Corps: training, 67-68
People-type problem areas in libraries, 22
Percentage: teaching of, 43
Performance evaluation: secretarial course, 48
Personal interaction: as a learning method, 28
Personal values: teaching of, 43
Personality: teaching, 50
Persuasive communication, 36
Photo-problems, 38
Physical arrangements: for role playing, 83
Pitfalls: for leaders, 83
Play behavior, 41
Poetry: dramatization through role playing, 49
Police department: applicant screening, 69
Police-juvenile relations, 77
Police recruits: role learning, 76
Political science: teaching, 52
Position management, 62
Practice management, 26
Prejudice: teaching about, 43, 46, 72
Preschool child care, 75
Preservice methods courses in education, 66
Preventive medicine: training personnel, 59
Prisoner's careers, 78
Problem or tension-centered role playing, 72
Problem pictures, 37
Problem selection: role playing, 84
Problem situations, 38
Problem-solving: in simulation, 27
Problem stories, 37, 92
Professional attitudes: nurses and teachers, 24

Programmed instruction: as part of game format, 49
Project methods, 32
Projective role taking test, 36
Projective techniques vs. role playing, 69
Psychodrama, 26, 83
Psychodynamics of reacting to patient illnesses, 58
Psychological counseling, 26
Psychology: teaching, 50
Psychosomatic medicine: training programs, 58
Psychotherapy, 26
Public administration: teaching, 50
Public health nurses: training, 58
Public opinion: research methodology, 80
Public opinion game, 80
Puppets, 72, 89

Race relations: teaching children about, 42
Reality practice, 26, 30, 87
Reality role playing, 48
Reinforcement of learning, 31, 33, 51
Religious education: utilization of role playing, 72
Reluctant learners: teaching English, 42
Remedial reading: and role playing, 42
Research methodology: use of role playing, 79-81
Research studies: attitude and behavior change, 35
Residence hall counselors, 73
Resistance to change: training program, 62
Responsibility to group and self: teaching, 43
Retail store: training managers, 63
Retarded adolescents: utilization of role playing, 47
Revenge: teaching about, 43
Role flexibility, 25
Role identification, 88
Role induction, 36
Role involvement, 36
Role modeling, 70
Role player, 25; instructions, 86, 93
Role playing: definition, 24-36
Role relation of the doctor and patient, 54
Role reversals, 78, 87-88, 89
Role-taking bahavior, 36
Rutgers Labor Education Center: training for community action, 75

Safety education: training foremen and supervisors, 59
Sahara desert tribe: English language project, 43
St. John's College: Workshop on Crime and Correction, 77

Salesmen: training, 56
School administrators: grievance procedures, 79
Scotland: experiment in teaching English, 42
Screening device for new salesmen, 57
Screening job applicants, 68
Secretarial course: teaching, 47
Selection interview, 70
Self-acceptance: teaching of, 43
Self-concept, 45
Self-confrontation by videotape replay, 68
Self-insight, 29, 30
Self-persuasion, 36
Self-rating and attitude change, 35
Sensitivity training, 26, 72
Simulated reality experience, 27
Simulation, 27; as a means of developing skills, 31; drug addiction, 81
Simulation exercises, 67
Single group role playing, 87
Situational problems, 60
Situational role playing, 66
Situational tests, 26
Skill practice, 30
Skits, 42, 47, 93
Slow learners: and role playing, 41
Social interaction: with indigenous personnel, 66; analysis of, 69
Social service aides: training, 75
Social stratification: teaching, 50
Social studies: teaching, 44, 47
Sociodrama, 26, 40, 43
Sociodramatic play: disadvantaged preschool children, 41
Sociology: teaching, 50; research methodology, 79
Solo role playing, 72
Southern Illinois University: a training model for non-professional preschool aides, 75
Special education: for disadvantaged, 40
Speech blockage: and role playing, 43
Speech correction: and role playing, 43
Spontaneous role playing, 84, 91
Staff development, 64
Stimuli: and learner reaction, 31
Student confrontation, 64
Student-school conflict, 65
Stuttering: and role playing, 43
Styles of learning: in children, 39
Supervisors and executives: leadership training, 59-64

Symbolic model: in simulation, 27

T-groups, 66
Tape recorder: use in training, 61, 81, 90
Task-Model Procedure, 62
Teacher behavior: in role playing, 36
Teacher education programs: in-service, 65
Teacher-student interaction, 36
Teacher training: utilization of role playing, 53; methods, 54
Teacher training students: effects of role playing on attitudes, 31
Teaching behavior, 65
Techniques of role playing, 72, 81-91
Telephone: use in training, 61
Total Involvement Practice Selling (TIPS), 57
Training programs: which utilize role playing, 55-77
Tutorial program, 76

Underachievers, 76
Underprivileged children: teaching of, 39-41
Understudy: as a learning method, 28
Unemployed poor: job counseling, 70
Unfinished stories, 38, 40, 92
United Airlines: training programs, 63
United Nations Security Council: simulation, 48
U. S. Air Force: training of military advisors overseas, 68; candidate screening, 69
U. S. Office of Naval Research: leadership training, 60
University of Cincinnati: police-juvenile relations, 77
Urban education, 77
Urban teacher preparation program, 53

Values: teaching through role playing, 38
Veterans' Administration: leadership training, 62
Vicarious experience, 29, 33; interviewing, 69
Videotape recording, 36, 54, 59, 66, 68, 72, 81
Vocational counseling, 70
Vocational education: for disadvantaged, 40
Vocational guidance: teaching, 50

Warming up, 86
Waterways of northeastern North America: teaching, 44
Weiringa variation, 88
Work-study programs, 73
Workshops, 56

Young Men's Christian Association: junior leader training programs, 72
Youth Opportunity Campaign, 71
Youth tutoring youth, 76

Z
678
L65
v.4

JAN 20 1972